COMPARING IMPOSSIBILITIES

Hau
BOOKS

www.haubooks.com

COMPARING IMPOSSIBILITIES
SELECTED ESSAYS OF SALLY FALK MOORE

Sally Falk Moore

Foreword by John Borneman

Hau Books
Chicago

Cover and layout design: Sheehan Moore
Cover Photograph © Sally Falk Moore
Typesetting: Prepress Plus (www.prepressplus.in)

ISBN: 978-0-9861325-5-1
LCCN: 2016902725

Hᴀᴜ Books
Chicago Distribution Center
11030 S. Langley
Chicago, IL 60628
www.haubooks.com

Hᴀᴜ Books is marketed and distributed by The University of Chicago Press.
www.press.uchicago.edu

Printed in the United States of America on acid-free paper.

For my always lively daughters, Penelope and Nicola Moore, who, with lots of attention and cheerful skepticism have seen me through many many years.

Contents

Acknowledgments and Sources

I want to acknowledge my considerable early debt to two people, Sarah Robinson and Jane Bestor, both anthropologists—Robinson also a lawyer, Bestor also a historian. Many years ago, when I was house-bound for some months, they encouraged me to think about putting together a book of readings. They not only assembled many of the necessary materials with which I could proceed, but gave the project liveliness by being interested in similar theoretical questions themselves. Conversation with them was an indispensable start. I would also like thank the original publishers of this collection's chapters for extending their permission to reprint them. The sources, also attributed in the editor's notes at the beginning of each chapter, are as follows:

CHAPTER ONE

2005. "Part of the story: A memoir." *Ethnos* 70 (4): 538–566.

CHAPTER TWO

2005. "Comparisons: Possible and impossible." *Annual Review of Anthropology* 34: 1–11.

CHAPTER THREE

2009. "Encountering suspicion in Tanzania." In *Being there: The fieldwork encounter and the making of truth*, edited by John Borneman and Abdellah Hammoudi, 151–82. Berkeley: University of California Press.

CHAPTER FOUR

1991. "From giving and lending to selling: Property transactions reflecting historical changes on Kilimanjaro." In *Law in Colonial Africa*, edited by Kristin Mann and Richard Roberts, 108–30. Portsmouth, NH: Heinemann and James Currey Educational Books.

CHAPTER FIVE

1989. "History and the redefinition of custom on Kilimanjaro." In *History and power in the study of law: New directions in legal anthropology*, edited by June Starr and Jane F. Collier, 277–301. Ithaca and London: Cornell University Press.

CHAPTER SIX

1992. "Treating law as knowledge: Telling colonial officers what to say to Africans about running 'their own' native courts." *Law and Society Review* 26 (1): 11–46.

CHAPTER SEVEN

1977. "Individual interests and organizational structures: Dispute settlements as 'events of articulation.'" In *Social anthropology and law*, ASA Monograph No. 14, edited by Ian Hamnett, 159–88. London: Academic Press.

CHAPTER EIGHT

1987. "Explaining the present: Theoretical dilemmas in processual ethnography." *American Ethnologist* 14 (4): 727–36.

CHAPTER NINE

1964. "Descent and symbolic filiation." *American Anthropologist* 66: 1308–20. Reprinted in 1967. *Myth and cosmos*, edited by John Middleton, 63–76. New York: Natural History Press. Also reprinted in 1976. *Selected papers: 1946–70*, American Anthropological Association 75th anniversary commemorative volume, edited by Robert F. Murphy. Washington, D.C.: American Anthropological Association.

CHAPTER TEN

1976. "The secret of the men: A myth about Chagga initiation." *Africa* 46 (4): 357–70.

CHAPTER ELEVEN

1973. "Law and social change: The semi-autonomous social field as an appropriate subject of study." *Law and Society Review* 7: 719–46.

CHAPTER TWELVE

1977. "Political meetings and the simulation of unanimity: Kilimanjaro 1973." In *Secular ritual*, edited by Sally Moore and Barbara Myerhoff, 151–72. Amsterdam: Royal Van Gorcum.

CHAPTER THIRTEEN

1998. "Changing African land tenure: Reflexions on the incapacities of the state." *European Journal of Development Research*, Special Issue on Development and Rights, 10 (2): 33–49. Also published in 1999. Lund, Christian, ed. *Development and rights: Negotiating justice in changing societies*. London and Portland, OR: Frank Cass.

SALLY FALK MOORE
Cambridge, MA
August 2015

Recording Uncertainty and Disorder on the Ethnographic Scene

John Borneman

For nearly a half century, Sally Falk Moore has been giving us ways to explain the present. *Comparing Impossibilities* brings together some of Moore's key articles on law, anthropology, and Africa. Trained as a lawyer before pursuing a PhD in anthropology, at a time when few women were admitted into either profession, she brought classic concerns of anthropology, such as kinship, tradition, political organization, and the state, into conversation with the most heated contemporary debates about law. She was a pioneer in making the depiction and theorization of law an object of anthropological inquiry, influencing its study in ways that still remain underappreciated, and thereby changing the ways we think about law, process, and historical transformation today.

In dialogue with classic and contemporary social theory, yet avoiding tendentious discussion, two themes run across the body of Moore's work. First, the significance of temporality as "process" in the depiction and analysis of social phenomena. Second, the integration of the principles of uncertainty and unpredictability—and of unintended consequences—into our understanding of objects. Influenced by the ethnographic work on events by the British anthropologist Max Gluckman, Moore at an early date independently and rigorously developed a theory of "process" that has had an impact on anthropology and related fields far beyond the number of citations she receives for her concepts. She identifies "diagnostic events" as the key concept of a processual approach: "I wanted to suggest a time-oriented method that could take the transitional, the temporary, and the changing into account, and examine its larger social ramifications, its more enduring consequences" (p. 25, this volume). The analyst construes, in retrospect, some happening witnessed during fieldwork as a diagnostic event, occasions of significance in which one can see the unfolding of history in the present as predictive of the future.

Attention to such events, either everyday happenings or rituals, requires a departure from static notions of social structure and from a focus on social reproduction. Diagnostic events suggest how the non-normative and accidental might provide windows into change and the future as well as reproduction of the present. Although one of Moore's major innovations has been to create "secular rituals" as an object of study, the articles in this volume focus instead on the everyday, and analyze events such as automobile accidents, a court-directed auction of a piece of land, and unconventional ways of acquiring land.

While most of the articles are deeply and passionately about law and Africa, they address the great anthropological tradition of raising and anticipating—often by decades—topics of enduring significance in all of the social sciences and legal study: How is custom reframed by modernity? What part do states and other political actors play in the mobilization, disappearance, renewal, or creation of custom and tradition? What is secular ritual? Moore also raised crucial and lasting questions concerning gender and the body, incest, development, property transactions, events, knowledge, and politics. All of these articles have been previously published between 1973 and 2009. They are given much deeper significance by their collection in a single volume, and by the inclusion of two original chapters in which Moore reflects on the history of the discipline and its coherence in relation to her own childhood, education, lived experience, and career.

Sally Falk Moore entered the graduate program in anthropology at Columbia University in 1948. She had completed a degree in law (as one of the two women in her class, the other being the future women's rights activist and Congresswoman Bella Abzug) and had worked at a Wall Street firm for one year before taking a leave of absence to join the prosecution staff of the Allied Occupation in Germany for what has become known as the Nuremberg Trials. Moore identifies two sets of experiences around this time as formative in leading her to anthropology. The first was frustration in the Nuremberg experience, which was limited to six months, and the second was her encounter with poverty and love with poverty and love on a short trip to Haiti (where she met Cresap

Moore, her future husband) visiting an ethnographic fieldwork site the summer before entering graduate school. At Nuremberg, Moore recounts, she learned that even the best intended law is dependent on its execution; laws are embedded in a particular politics of the moment. Law in practice is not the same as written law, and the outcome of law's execution is unpredictable. The uncertain impact of laws contrasted greatly with the predictability of law taught in her law school training. In Haiti, her second formative experience, Moore learned of the importance of the serendipitous and coincidental in both tragedy and romance, in contrast to an orderly and secure childhood and youth in a prosperous New York City family of Hungarian and Russian Jewish immigrants.

In the middle of her PhD studies, while completing her dissertation on the relation of local law to state law in regulating property relations in the Inca Empire, Moore married and gave birth to two daughters, putting aside her academic career. She remained active in intellectual debates without holding an academic position while accompanying her daughters and husband, Cresap, a historian, in his research and employment. In the early 1960s, the family moved to Los Angeles, where a set of coincidences and fortuitous events presented her with the opportunity to found the anthropology department at the University of Southern California. It was in this milieu that she became friends with some prominent African anthropologists, became well versed in the Africanist literature, and learned Swahili. But she did not begin formal fieldwork in Africa until 1968. She was recruited to UCLA in 1977, before a final move to Harvard University in 1981, where she is currently Victor S. Thomas Professor of Anthropology, Emerita, and Affiliated Professor of International Legal Studies at Harvard Law School. Since retiring, Moore has remained active in publishing, reviewing, and lecturing, still committed to anthropology and Africa, and to the advising of numerous African students who come to study with her at the Harvard Law School.

Moore's influence on the profession as a mentor is also important to note.[1] I entered the graduate program at Harvard in 1983 intending to work with Sally— she asked that students call her Sally, the only senior faculty member at the time who made this request. I was switching disciplines (from political science to anthropology), careers (from an equestrian to an academic) and coasts (from Seattle

---

1. I am very grateful to Julia Elyachar and James Ferguson for reading a draft of this preface and giving me some extremely useful commentary and criticism. Both were, like me, former students who Sally mentored. Both would probably have framed these essays in other ways, a sign that there are other interpretive and historical yields to be discovered in this work.

to Cambridge). Most excited by her work on secular ritual and law, I wanted anthropology to teach me the skills to study politics through the ethnographic method, and I was already determined to do this in a divided Berlin. At Harvard, Sally was intellectually critical and unquestioningly supportive. She gave me—like all of her students—a wide berth in defining my object of study. She rarely mentioned or drew attention to her own work, which did not mean she would refrain from criticism of work of others that she found weak, self-aggrandizing, or pointless. Moore seemed reluctant to take on a maternal role with male students who were particularly needy, but also went out of her way to help students in need, including addressing directly female student concerns about balancing a career and a husband (some newly married ones considered dropping out), and took on the advising of advanced students when their major advisor withdrew support.

Sally taught a course on the anthropology of law through the Harvard Law School. This course introduced students of Law and of Anthropology to all of the major theoretical frames for the study of law in anthropology, and coupled theoretical readings with case studies and ethnographic films. In her other courses, Sally taught on subjects that were at the time novel objects of inquiry in anthropology, such as migration and confinement. She always assigned classic social theorists together with contemporary anthropologists. When I entered her office to discuss issues that came up short in seminars, I usually found a newly purchased book on her desk—I specifically remember seeing new books by the anthropologists Dan Sperber, Claude Meillassoux, and Jack Goody. Noticing my curiosity, Sally spontaneously offered them to me to read even before she herself found the opportunity. I eagerly read them within the week, and then returned for a discussion for which she was always ready, despite being exhausted from fulfilling her administrative responsibilities (she also served as Dean of the Graduate School at the time) and, quite frankly and in retrospect, from having to silently bear the self-importance of some professors at university meetings. At several such moments, she began the conversation ironically with, "I have been such a good girl."

Although one of my major tasks in graduate school was to read the literature on Europe, I realized only when it came to writing up my fieldwork that Sally's understated yet political approach to the study of a socialist country (Tanzania), and her work with African scholarship, provided me an invaluable comparative perspective, complemented by in-depth area knowledge imparted to me by her colleagues at the time with whom I also studied: Stanley Tambiah on India, Charles Lindholm on Pakistan, Nur Yalman on Sri Lanka, and David Maybury-Lewis on Amazonian societies.

This experience of being mentored gently and humbly, with intellectual rigor and honesty, strikes me today as psychologically wise. It was the mien of a profoundly generous and personally sovereign scholar who has learned the most from her experience outside the academy. What she learned is also reflected in the comedic style used in her writing that foregrounds the non-normative, unintentional, and serendipitous over the predictable, normative, and agentive. Her style contrasts with the tragic-realist style of most of her contemporaries, who often conflated the experience of the world with the weight of its tragic plots. Normative structures of dominance, exploitation, and organized cruelty may indeed shape "the weight of the world," to cite a title from Pierre Bourdieu (2000). And yet, the insistent transmission of this weight in a tragic mode forecloses appreciation of the range of its actual experience. Sally attempts to replicate the range of this experience for readers in her writing, stylistically unadorned, deflecting attention from herself at every turn, even-handed in her criticisms, alert to what was outside her frame of reference, and skeptical of final conclusions.

In what follows, I focus on the enduring contemporary relevance of Moore's *oeuvre*, emphasizing her work on processual anthropology, legal anthropology, and ethnographic method. Each chapter begins with a question, which is linked to what Moore (from here on, I will use the academic convention of referencing only her last name) calls an *ethnographic scene*. For Moore, a *scene* is a descriptive account of empirical reality, often a case study or research encounter. She then situates this ethnographic scene in what she calls a *process* that she subjects to concise theoretical and comparative analysis. Theory and scene impact on one another throughout. Moore sacrifices neither complexity nor parsimony to arrive at an explanation. In fact, one is left at the end of each analysis with a deeper sense of scales of entanglement *and* of comprehension, or at least partial comprehension, and an orientation for further thinking. This manuscript contains thirteen chapters, divided into four parts: 1) The Anthropologist and Anthropology; 2) Perspectives on Africa; 3) Excursions into Mythology; 4) Social Fields and their Politics.

PROCESSUAL ANTHROPOLOGY

The ethnographer, Moore writes, is "to witness the present as it is being produced" and to link that present to that which came before, and to the larger-scale structures and events not readily observable to the ethnographer. "What is the present producing?" she asks. "What part of the activity being observed will be durable, and what will disappear?" (p. 195). The present that one sees as fieldworker is usually not the grand events but, rather, "ordinary events . . . that might give unanticipated indications of what is going on" (p. 25). One observes ordinary scenes—e.g., harvesting crops, eating food, marrying, telling stories, selling plots of land, burying the dead, migrating to another country—that might index what is durable and what will disappear. That is, one is also observing indices of the future. Such an understanding of ethnography is "not to do away with the synchronic ethnographic frame, but to exploit fully the historical within it" (Marcus and Fisher 1986: 96). To this end, Moore suggests the ethnographer be attentive to "diagnostic events," ordinary happenings that are not produced by the ethnographer's presence.

The ethnographer's task, then, is to witness the production of the present as part of a process or of several processes. Some of the scenes witnessed will repeat themselves in the future, some will disappear, some will endure only in part or in changed form. Since much of significance occurs outside the ethnographer's watch, so to speak, happening both before and after his or her arrival and period of fieldwork, the synchronic frame must be supplemented with other sources—e.g., archives, news, historical accounts. The study of temporality as process, which can be revealed in diagnostic events, is, for Moore, the central object of anthropology.

Through the 1980s, Moore developed and elaborated a notion of process as "history of the present." This differs from other approaches to temporality within anthropology and history, notably from Foucault's genealogical perspective that was attracting a large following at the time. Especially in her emphasis on the future, process is more like a permanent pregnancy, an unfolding in which birth and death are neither negative nor positive events but indicative of an uncertain outcome, something not yet there. Process is not the same as chronological time, not the clock, the day, the month, the decade, nor the year. It is not the same as the history of the past, as a Rankean "how things really were"—meaning the facts of history and the essences behind them. It is not the same as the *longue durée* pioneered by the French Annales School of Marc Bloch, Lucien Febvre, and Fernand Braudel; those historians worked with the dichotomy of event and structure, and associated the *longue durée* with structure, with attitudes, and with actions that resisted the event, and that endured despite intervening events. Although respectful of such visions of writing history, Moore is interested less in a rapprochement with the past than with finding the historical emergent in the present and the meaning of history for fieldwork-based ethnography.

Process is punctuated by events. It does not, as in the Annales School, resist events. Nor does it oppose event to structure, as did Claude Lévi-Strauss in his search for universal cognitive categories. Moore's approach to fieldwork and history can be seen in her research on Tanzanian socialism after colonialism. It was deeply informed by archival research, but differed from this practice among most postcolonial theorists in that she did not seek to ethnographize colonial history, nor to foreground the use of ethnographic methods within colonial rule, nor to replicate the historian's craft by making anthropology into a textual or archival discipline. This does not mean she opposed historical writing. Her very first work, *Power and property in Inca Peru* (published in 1958), and her signature ethnography, *Social facts and fabrications: "Customary" law on Kilimanjaro, 1880–1980* (published in 1986), were both straightforward historical accounts using primarily archival material, though the latter work's interpretations were heavily dependent on her fieldwork. In method, however, Moore remained committed to the notion of ethnography, obtained by means of the lived experience of fieldwork, itself a process marked by events. While she was resolute in insisting that the present could not be understood except through what came before it—history—she also insisted on the singularity of the experience of fieldwork, and of the contribution such experience could make to the reading of historical artifacts.

One reason for this commitment to fieldwork presence, a vision closely aligned with Malinowskian ethnographic fieldwork, was undoubtedly Moore's own delayed experience of fieldwork. For the first two decades of her research in anthropology, she worked with archival sources and with archaeological evidence. She did not begin fieldwork in Africa until she was in her forties, meaning that she was an anthropologist long before she did fieldwork. By the time of her African fieldwork, other experiences, along with three years of psychoanalysis, had led her to be skeptical of appearances, to look critically at normative frames, and to take nothing for granted. The history of the present that she experienced and witnessed in her research was pregnant with both colonial and postcolonial/socialist experience, as well as with the Cold War that accompanied and often framed socialism. Naïve notions of agency and social control that circulated widely in American anthropology of the 1970s and 1980s were nowhere to be found in her writings. Moore also did not find support for the idea that anthropology in Africa had ever been a handmaiden of colonial authorities, an idea argued by many other anthropologists and postcolonial scholars alike that also made her own ethnographic research in Africa suspicious to postcolonial authorities.

It is helpful to contrast Moore's notion of historical process with her better-known contemporary in historical anthropology—Marshall Sahlins. For Sahlins in the 1980s, structure persists and finds its expression in events. Taking his cue from the linguistics of Saussure, structure is to event as langue is to parole. Events tend to reproduce culture, which can be depicted as a set of structures and categories within an already constituted order. Indigenous cultural orders of meaning tend to shape events of all magnitudes—though Sahlins focused on radical events, cross-cultural encounters marked by radical differences. Cultural orders tend, in his work of this period, to survive such radical events, even if in modified fashion, through the integration of new elements.

Moore, by way of contrast, focuses on the temporality of process. She does not begin by analogizing the distinction between langue and parole. Events are never, she writes, "the expression of history," or part of "totalizing coherent systems of the kind anthropology has so often described" (p. 200). In her view, "Events are to processes what categories are to structures" (p. 209). As she makes clear in many of the articles in this collection, change can never be understood by looking at category systems alone. Categories present themselves to us as normative orders. A change in categories does not always index change but may in fact be intended to enable and mask continuity. Renaming the old creates the semblance of change, but new self-representations do not necessarily reflect a new reality. For Moore, people, groups, and institutions (including the state) struggle to control category systems and, from within that location, to assert their moral authority. What categories exactly refer to is a question for empirical research on historical processes.

The insights that Moore gained from her life and work outside the academy and through fieldwork help us understand contemporary news and political events as well. Moore rarely took up such events in the West, but they would occasionally appear in her writing as analogies for readers (and most readers were from or lived in the West), suggesting that that Euro-American worlds could be understood in the same frame as African worlds. "Irangate," she writes, referring to the illegal trade in arms for hostages with the Islamic Republic of Iran carried out by the United States, "is better seen as part of a sequential process of uncertain outcome than as exemplifying a fixed and known grammar of politics" (p. 199). She writes this sentence in the context of an argument with Sahlins about event and structure in the Sandwich Islands. She does not explicate Irangate, but uses the reference to illustrate the relationship of event to process instead of event to structure. The scandal is difficult to understand as scripted to follow a political grammar. It involved many actors, organizations, and states hostile to each other yet cooperating through many opaque layers of deception—"a sequential process of uncertain outcome."

The assumption of the existence of a stable cultural and social order prior to a historic event was only one site of resistance to Moore's notion of process. Another was the assumption that social systems tended toward equilibrium. Accordingly, change was thought of as a disturbance, largely attributable to external forces such as colonization or exchange with foreign units. Especially in the structural-functionalism of British social anthropology, the study of social change was considered a special field of inquiry. For Moore, "continuity and change" were part and parcel of the same process, not to be studied in isolation of each other. Maintaining continuity was not a natural process of (re)establishing equilibrium. Processual analysis could reveal as false some of the apparent continuities generated by more structural forms of analysis. Or conversely, what often appeared as change might mask continuity. Moore (1978a) proposed looking not only at replication of structural forms but at their processual diversification, how, for example, through sequential organizational "pyramiding," creating units adjacent to one another rather than in formal hierarchies, established interests could disguise sometimes profound political change. Old or lower-level units were left intact while the pyramiding of organizations made for substantive changes in their functions and coercive capacities.

Throughout the 1970s and 80s, most social theorists repeated assumptions of replication of social structures, even though they sought to depart from the more static Parsonian theory of social roles, conformity to norms, and a tendency toward equilibrium in social systems. From a processual perspective, Pierre Bourdieu's theory of relations between habitus, dispositions, and practices, or Anthony Giddens' theory of individual agency and social structuration, to name two dominant theorists of the time, were insufficiently dynamic and not particularly helpful orientations for fieldwork. One is witnessing instead, Moore argues, a "complex mix of order, anti-order, and non-order." (p. 201).

The ethnographer in the field would be better served by thinking of *process* and its relation to events than of *practices* associated with a particular grammar. The fieldworker's task, seen from this perspective, is about "recording uncertainty and disorder on the ethnographic scene" (p. 201). We witness "what seem to be and indeed may be contingencies of form. . . . [O]bservations and interpretations are less neat than those of the structuralisms, but there is a concomitant gain in the detailed depiction of the specific and explosive mixture of the contestable and the unquestioned in current local affairs. There is therefore a tentativeness about processual interpretations of fieldwork that is absent in the structuralisms" (ibid.). Acknowledging the contingency of the observed and the known, one nonetheless finds that through witnessing the ordinary scenes of life one can analytically identify "diagnostic events" that address both the large-scale and the future. "Those struggles to construct orders and the actions that undo them may be the principal subject matter of ethnography as current history" (p. 209).

LEGAL ANTHROPOLOGY

Moore's processual approach revises significantly the study of law and society, specifically the understanding of law among anthropologists. She disrupted extant analytical frames by rejecting evolutionary and typological schema, situating juridical-political processes in "semi-autonomous fields," and historicizing legal change by locating history in the present instead of in the past. I remember this sense of radical revision clearly from my early studies at Harvard. I recall expressing to Moore my boredom with case law (which lawyers explicate by referring to other cases rather than to other contexts or specific fields) and discomfort with the prospect of many hours in courts during fieldwork. Moore told me not to worry: "What goes on outside the courtroom is more significant than what goes on within it." She encouraged me, in other words, to pay close attention to law's execution and consequences, its perlocutionary effects, and to be skeptical of its doctrinal or propositional claims.

Rather than confining the law to written texts, lawyers, judges, prosecutors, and the frames of legal scholars, Moore views law as a significant window from which to observe the objects it thinks it is regulating. Law is one particular relationship to these objects, a powerful one, as it is officially sanctioned by the state and its coercive apparatus. The objects—e.g., traffic accidents, land claims, lineage disputes—have, of course, their own logics of rules and practices. And these logics govern action in what Moore calls semi-autonomous social fields, discrete analytical domains, each dynamic with a life of its own but crisscrossing another. She opposed abstracting law from "the social context in which it exists," acting as if "it were an entity capable of controlling that context" (p. 252). Instead of studying "law" and "society" as organic wholes, we should focus on semi-autonomous fields where its component parts—the actors, norms, rules, institutes and structures—are never fully subordinate to law and its ideology. The state itself should be seen as many competing projects in a semi-autonomous social field, influenced in unexpected ways by the effects of legal attempts at social engineering. Because such fields are diverse, proliferating, and interacting with each other, they pose obstacles to the regulatory aims of central governments, thereby producing unintended effects that circle back to influence the function of law and structure of states.

One example of such circling back that she offers is of what today would be framed as corruption but she calls "fictive friendship." Analyzing the dress industry in New York City, she notes how in order to "stay in the game" there must often be "a flow of prestations, attention, and favors in the direction of persons who have it in their power to allocate labor, capital, or business deals" (p. 259). In this way, an "obligatory, public, strongly instrumental relationship takes on the forms and symbols of friendship" (ibid.). That is, instrumental relationships are converted into forms of friendship to get things done, while maintaining an ideology of legal business transactions in a social field that functions (or should function) autonomously, divorced from the criteria of descent and marriage that characterize the field of kinship.

An analysis of the present examines the ongoing interaction within a field and between different fields. Legal anthropology casts a specific, illuminating light on some social fields, but Moore did not think this light was the only one, or should necessarily be prioritized over others. All knowledge is contingent, and its production is part of ongoing historical processes in which law and the state are integrally involved.

Perhaps the most radical and immediate shift in legal study occasioned by her work was her insistence on looking at the history *within* the present rather than as a matter of past action and contexts. It is now, in fact, widely accepted that we cannot look into the past except though the present, that the observer's perspective is always part of the scene depicted. Acknowledging the contingency of all action and thought, Moore asked what this might mean for the relation of tradition or custom, or what is thought of as "customary law" to state law. She had already researched the relationship between local law and state law in the Inca Empire. Subsequently she posed the question for Africa in the colonial and postcolonial periods. Why do we assume, she asked, that tradition is prior and opposed to a present modernity? Moore rejected not only the evolutionary frame—that customary law is an earlier and more primitive form of state lawbut also the liberal pluralist frame—that custom is a (pure) indigenous expression opposed to (imposed) state law in a plural legal system. Rather, she observed from her empirical study of property and land claims in Tanzania that customary law first appears as a category at the very moment state law enters the scene.

Before customary law, there was "reglementation," taboo, and other forms of prohibition, sanction, and prescription, some vague, some concrete. But when colonial authorities introduced state law, the analytic need arose to give "that which came before" a name and a place, a form with which state law could articulate on its own terms. Scholars and administrators dubbed this prior "customary law," even though it was systematized and formalized only with the advent of state law. For a long time, both postcolonial authorities and many anthropologists expected that state law would eventually replace custom as a prior normative system. Moore found no evidence for the disappearance of custom, however, but instead only for its transformation. She writes, "What might be called 'the colonial legacy' includes the ongoing tension between a centralized national system of courts with a standardized set of principles and rules, and the locally anchored, anti-centralized system of the rural communities" (p. 130). With this tension in mind, Moore suggests treating "dispute settlement as ceremonies of situational transformation" that articulate with different scales (p. 168).

In many of the chapters here Moore examines this tension between state law and "custom" (usually in quotation marks) with respect to her research on the Chagga in Tanzania. She uses the empirical material on the Chagga to interrogate theory rather than theory to interrogate the Chagga. In several of these chapters, she takes up land claims and asks how those claims invoke custom when it serves specific purposes in a conflict between parties. Moore makes clear how all parties to a conflict at times adapt their understandings to changing contexts. She details how belief in the ability to cause supernatural harm could in some cases be persuasive in making claims, and how neither the truth nor falsity of claims (nor what the law actually stated) but the testimony of key witnesses was often the most significant factor in the outcome of a case, situated in the sociopolitical contexts in which witnesses are asked to testify. She also asks how mobilizing administrative officials in the socialist state could be an effective means to achieve a desired outcome. To retain in our purview such complexity of scale and context, "competing and contrary ideas" and "contradictory consequences," Moore writes in a way that is both descriptively ambitious and theoretically modest.

ETHNOGRAPHIC METHOD

The study of process through diagnostic events requires major adjustments in ethnographic method that differ significantly from other attempts to innovate the methodological apparatus of anthropological study. Above all, observations over time take on more importance than observations at a single time. Such an insight troubles projects of current graduate students, whose fieldwork time is increasingly shortened so that even the one-time study in one place is sometimes reduced to nine months in several places. Today, graduate students are often presenting research results at conferences, and even defending dissertations, before sufficient time has passed for them to observe the unfolding and elaboration of a diagnostic event.

Moore was writing some of her early articles at a time when the anthropological study of ritual, and its theorization, was at its apogee. The two perhaps most dominant approaches—e.g. the exegetical/structural approach of Victor Turner and the key symbols and meanings approach of Clifford Geertz—were focused on social and cultural production and reproduction. Moore was centrally concerned not with explaining social reproduction but with process—ongoing change—and more specifically, with the role of planning in shaping the future. For her work in Tanzania, she theorized socialism itself, the planned economy and the planned society, as an attempt to shape the future. In this, she anticipated and influenced work of students and colleagues in what is now referred to as "development studies."

Secular ritual was one of the first objects Moore elaborated in which the stakes were the future. This type of ritual had not before received attention precisely because the anthropological focus in ritual was on tradition and social reproduction. Before Moore, anthropologists saw secular ritual as a corrupted form or they conflated it with modernity, thus undoing its specificity. At the same time, the popular "secularization thesis," held in some quarters of anthropology, assumed that a decline of religious faith would mean a decline in ritual in general. Secular rituals, Moore argued, drew much from religious ritual, especially the appeal to an unquestioned order, but their distinctiveness lie elsewhere: precisely in their intent to transform the social. Secular rituals were a kind of intervention to change the social, and state law was one of the primary means to direct such change. Moore identified this as the "paradox of directing change and preserving 'custom'" (p. 134). Secular ritual would not eliminate custom, but, on the contrary, often preserve it to enable the orchestration of change. Yet things never go as directed; state law has many unintended consequences. After elaborating the significance of secular ritual, Moore then expanded her insights to social fields outside ritual to include study of everyday occurrences, such as those mentioned above. In research on the everyday, she began to give theoretical significance to the unexpected and accidental, not as sources of resistance or compliance, but as integral parts of processes in various semi-autonomous social fields that themselves must be interpreted within wider sociopolitical contexts than those observed during fieldwork.

Moore's mode of fieldwork in Africa was not the usual long single-period abroad of graduate study but consisted of visiting and revisiting several sites in intervals of months or even years. She became a wife and a mother during her early years of graduate study, and thus had no recourse to the classic model of a single man freed to do research and absented from social obligations because others could assume his responsibilities at home. Resembling the structure of hide and seek, in that she kept returning, disappearing and reappearing, this way of doing fieldwork assured her interlocutors of her commitment to them over time. Over the long term this changed the nature of her relationships, creating the trust and confidences that she writes about in the first several chapters of this volume. The sense of enduring and reciprocal (though not symmetrical) relationships that she built also changed the kinds of knowledge people shared with her. Moore's processual approach grew out of this empirical experience, and understandably made more sense of this changing data over time than a static approach. What she was observing, then, was no longer the "tribal, homogeneous, bounded unit," but certain general processes specific to place and people.

This change in mode of fieldwork participation also led Moore to revise the comparative project central to anthropology as a discipline. Rather than compare traits or cultures, or abandon comparison altogether (as many anthropologists of my generation have done), she sought to compare processes, transformations that could be witnessed at various stages during fieldwork. The ongoing smaller-scale sequences observed in fieldwork were subsequently, in analysis, to be linked to large-scale processes.

Finally, it is worth asking what Moore's processual approach to law means methodologically for the study of the state, which has since become an important object for anthropological analysis. She did not follow the regnant methodological approaches that take as their objects doctrine, ideology, legal categories and discourse, or "judicial, legislative, and administrative rules." Although well aware that the state has an ideology, often masks its interests, and exploits and dominates people, Moore refused to reduce the state to those negative and co-ercive functions. In fact, there are a variety of ways in which states intervene to change their subjects. She called her approach to the state "multi-sited." By that she does not mean that one works in several different places during the course of a research project. Instead, she hopes to "provide a view of the state, not as a totality, but as an organizer of particular projects" constituting different sites. "In every instance a struggle exists about the organization and management of the program" (p. 41). In contrast with many of the current anthropological conceptions of the state, for Moore the state is not an abstract entity, but one that intervenes with projects in many sites in the worlds that people create. The state is not necessarily opposed to the people, nor to society, nor is it something people always resist.

Law appears, for her, as one logical and perhaps special nexus between state and society, and so is policy, which is often bound by law, or at least by rules. The state indeed has its own rules, laws, and moral claims, but, despite its relative power, it is not in control of its agenda any more than an anthropologist is in control of the fieldwork setting. Those rules and laws are contingent on their ex-ecution and reception. Thus central to the study of the state is "the observed ir-regularity of fit between recent official and unofficial ideas and activities" (p. 78). The growing field of policy studies within anthropology may benefit greatly from such an approach, where one grants no privilege to the propositional con-tent of laws and rules, but studies their place in the context of execution, ad-ministration, and reception, as well as of competing projects. The ethnographer can make an original contribution to policy studies if policy is understood as analogous to magic, an instrumental attempt to order the future, which will always have delayed and unintended consequences.

Though I have concentrated largely on Moore's contributions to the study of process and law, there are in this volume many more social fields explored, more objects re-conceptualized. In Chapter 9, for example, she explores the contem-porary relation between kinship systems with stringent incest prohibitions that nonetheless tell creation myths that imagine the originary unit as incestuous. She argues against the Frazerian approach that interprets mythological incest as an indication or account of a prior period. "It is far more likely," she writes, "that these stories are a fictional validation of the present than an embroidered remnant of the past" (p. 222). In many ways, she anticipates in her query of the "mystical powers over fertility" the focus on alternative ways of imagining

"procreative capacities" that new kinship studies in anthropology have documented empirically, ranging from single mothers who make no reference to
male lineage claims, to lesbian mothers, two mothers, gay male parents without
a mother, to transsexual parentage. In Chapter 10, Moore explores a nineteenth
century Chagga ritual myth about the stitching up of the anuses of boys after
circumcision as the social function of illusion—"pretending that something they
knew to be false was in fact true" (p. 214). This is the social glue of what have
more recently been dubbed public secrets. She seeks to understand the contemporary relevance of this myth. It is, she argues, tied to contemporary male needs
to hide defecation ("male anal closure"), to prohibitions on homosexuality, and
to the openness of the female body, specifically symbolized in menstruation. In
this analysis, she anticipates the contemporary focus on gender as performative
embodiment. In short, this volume speaks as much to the future seen in the past
as to process itself as future.

An Oblique Introduction

A fieldwork research project may seem definable in advance. Can the ongoing activity of the inquiring anthropologist be defined in advance? Given multiple interlocutors and shifting situations, radically different interpretations may attach themselves to the project and its proponent as it proceeds.

There is an academic field that grandly claims to study humankind in any and all of its ways. That field is anthropology. It is ready to give attention to all the doings, ideas, and inventions of any people. The anthropologist can explore any goings-on in a given society, either in the past or in the present. Ideas that people have had, relationships that they have made, art works that they have produced, violence that they have committed, all are within the compass of the discipline. And contrary to the popular conception of it, anthropology is by no means just about traditional folk customs. In recent years, an anthropologist has written about the Truth and Reconciliation process in South Africa (Wilson 2001). Another has written about the post-socialist world of Eastern Europe (Hann 2005). And still others have addressed human rights (Goodale 2009). The list of contemporary topics goes on and on and is endless in its variety.

What, then, does one have to know, or to learn, or to write, to become an anthropologist? The answer to that question has changed over the years. Long before the twentieth century there were many amateur observers, missionaries, travelers, traders, and colonial officers who had an interest in non-Western peoples. Some of them carefully recorded what they saw and what they thought about it. There were also museum collections of the objects that these voyagers found in different parts of the world.

The material was tantalizing and attracted intellectual interest. But this habit of observation and collection did not immediately generate an academic profession that would systematically classify and interpret the unfamiliar in non-Western material and train a younger generation to explore other societies. That professionalization did not begin until the second half of the nineteenth century. In fact, the first professorship in anthropology was awarded to Edward Tylor in 1896 at Oxford University.

The interest in collecting information about non-European societies continued, and in the twentieth century there were many opportunities for research in areas under colonial rule. Eventually, the methods used to mount studies of so-called "other" peoples were turned to studies of the West and its institutions. Now it is clear that all societies, or the study of parts of them, can be approached through socio-anthropological methods.

Today, much of social anthropological knowledge is based on fieldwork—on direct contact with people in a chosen milieu. The preoccupation is with ongoing life, and with the way the people think and talk about what they are doing. Fieldwork is an invaluable technique. It provides insights not available in any other way. But for a single anthropologist to learn about a whole society in its breadth and depth, fieldwork must be combined with other sources of information.

Clifford Geertz put it succinctly, in his autobiographical account about working in Morocco and Indonesia: "[I]t is, of course, quite definitely not the case . . . that an adequate account of the working of culture in such world-historical places as these [Morocco and Indonesia] can be constructed on the basis of personal interactions and immediate observations—listening, looking, visiting and attending. Both countries, and both towns within those countries, are ingredient [sic] in forms of life geographically very much wider and historically very much deeper than those they themselves directly display. . . . Without such ground, there is no figure. . . . Understanding a form of life . . . involves more than the assembly of telling particulars or the imposition of general narratives. It involves bringing figure and ground, the passing occasion and the long story, into coincident view" (Geertz 1995: 49, 50, 51).

This means that not only the fieldwork, but also gathering the supplementary information one needs to make large scale sense of the local is a complicated but necessary business. And the situation that surrounds the immediate first-hand research may involve unforeseen obstacles.

When the anthropologist enters a foreign society, he/she may quite easily become the object of suspicion. What are the anthropologist's motives in inquiring so deeply into the affairs of people they hardly know? What is he/she really interested in? What is this person going to take away? Is he/she perhaps a political agent from another country? Will contact with such a person get one into trouble?

I was lucky enough to revisit the site of my field study in Africa every few years over a many year period. It was a postcolonial era during which anthropology had a bad name in Africa. Anthropologists were reputed to have been agents of colonialism. I was granted a research permit partly because I was also a lawyer and wanted to study the legal ideas and practices of the people on Kilimanjaro, in Tanzania. It was known that I was an anthropologist, but the focus of my project was a legal one.

Because of my revisits, the extent and trust of my close contacts solidified. My African acquaintances came to understand what I was up to. My frequent interlocutors spoke to me cheerfully and volubly, and they vouched for me with others. Even outside this warm circle, many people who did not know me were helpful. But some remained wary. Suspicion easily attaches to an outsider. And upheavals in the world, though far away, can leak fear into the local scene.

I offer, as illustration, the following tale of an unwelcome adventure that occurred on my way to and from my field site on Kilimanjaro. It will serve as an example of the manner in which political events in the world beyond Tanzania were an undercurrent in my life as an anthropologist. This particular incident did not directly affect my work, but it will show dramatically how, in an alien milieu, one's identity is not necessarily in one's own control.

THE ELEMENT OF CHANCE

Many experiences, though initially carefully planned, are shaped by chance. So it was when living in England at the time, I bought a bargain ticket on Egypt Air to take me to Nairobi, on my way to Kilimanjaro. It was at a time in the 1970s when many Indian families had been ousted from Kenya. Also at the time, strong messages were also being given to Indian residents in Tanzania that they were outsiders, and not welcome. Many went to England to start again. In order to maintain family contact with those who had not left, when they could, Indian relatives in England went back to East Africa to visit. They took the cheapest airfares going. One had only to glance at the English newspapers to see that for trips to East Africa, Egypt Air was a low bidder.

These ads for airfares were unusual. They did not specify a date of departure, only something approximate—a flight between the dates of x and y. Egypt Air explained that they did this because when they started out they did not have a plane-load, but rather were in the process of assembling one. When they had sufficient passengers signed up, they would specify a date and locate an empty plane. This looseness of closure was just fine for me, and it meant that Egypt Air's fare was substantially lower than others. I had a fellowship to do fieldwork in East Africa, but there was no harm in saving a little on the cost of travel since I was not tied to a particular date of arrival. I bought a round trip ticket, London-Nairobi-London.

On the departure date that was eventually set, I went to the airport with my suitcases. Everything seemed quite routine, as it might on any international voyage. The surprises were ahead. First we put down unexpectedly in Cairo, not in Nairobi, and we were told that we would have to leave the plane. Before we did, the air attendants confiscated our passports, assuring us they would be returned when we took flight again. I was very uneasy about this and wanted to telephone our embassy. No dice. We were not permitted any communication with the outside world. There was no arguing with them. They told us we would be put up in a local airport hotel, and then that in the morning, like it or not, we would be taken on a tour of Cairo, to perfume shops. There was no option to refuse.

Fortunately for me there was a young man in the crowd who had experienced this all before. He assured me the passports would be returned as promised, and that I had nothing to worry about. He made it all sound very plausible by telling us that what was wanted from us was some hard currency, which it was hoped we would expend on our shopping tour, and that we would be let go afterwards. So a very tired and largely unwashed group set out in a bus early the next morning to see the perfume shops.

We did not leave during the next day. Nor the next evening. Sometime between three and four in the morning we were marched out on to the airfield. Our luggage was all in a pile near the entrance to the plane. We were told we could mount the stairs if we identified our bags and they were then marked to be loaded in with us. This was a security precaution.

I saw at once that my bags were not in the pile. The uniformed men around the plane refused to let me go back to the airport building see if I could find them. Eventually I simply took matters in my own hands and strode back to the terminal. I did find my bags and one more crisis was averted. Our passports were returned on the plane.

All did not go altogether smoothly thereafter. The plane went to Dar es Salaam instead of Nairobi, but we were not allowed to dismount. Then they took us, at last, back to Nairobi. Why the detour? Why were we trapped? No explanation.

I proceeded peacefully from Nairobi to Kilimanjaro. There I had a quiet period of rural fieldwork, talking with people, making maps, taking genealogies, hearing disputes in the courts, and the like. I did not give Egypt Air another thought until a few months later when I returned to Dar es Salaam for the return journey. And that was when the plot thickened.

I went to the offices of Egypt Air to confirm my already paid-for return ticket. Not only did the men at the counter refuse to confirm, but they told me I must pay a substantial additional sum for the ticket, and pay it in cash. They had an explanation. Oil prices had gone up precipitously and they had to make up the difference in cost. I agreed to pay provided they would give me a letter explaining the price rise. They agreed to do so. I then went to a bank, and came back to their offices a half an hour later full of good cheer and with a pocket full of cash. But suddenly gloom had descended on the staff. The man who had agreed to produce the letter was not there, and his promise had vanished with him. I decided to play it tough. "I will sit here and wait for my letter until he returns from his lunch. I will pay you then. I am a lawyer. An agreement is an agreement. I will have my letter."

Then they conferred hastily and told me that the person from whom I could obtain the letter was the treasurer, that his office was upstairs and that I should go to him. I did. The treasurer was a trim forty to fifty year old. His office was small, but compact. In Swahili I ordered two cokes from the office attendant who entered for a moment and asked if we wanted anything to drink.

Why did I know some Swahili? Conversation with the treasurer proceeded in an informal and friendly fashion. I explained my mission in Tanzania, and asked him if he had been in Dar es Salaam for a long time. We exchanged more such travelers' trivia. No mention was made of the letter I was waiting for. When I asked about it, the treasurer assured me that there were no secretaries around and that not until after lunch would there be anyone available to type my letter.

Then I was appalled to see that the treasurer started busying himself with sealing off the room. He started by pulling down the shades. That did not seem strange. The sun is often too strong in that part of the world. But a real scare did not seize me until he pulled down a shade on the door and locked the door. He explained, "At this time of day there are so few people around. We are safer by ourselves. There are things to steal in this office."

Then he proceeded to interrogate me rather fiercely. Where had I bought my skirt? Where did I get my bracelet? What souvenirs had I bought? I explained that I had been to Tanzania many times and did not buy souvenirs since I was not a tourist. Then he started to quiz me about American movies. Which ones did I like best. I did not know many of the movies he mentioned. They were adventure films. Not my kind of thing. The questioning went on and on and had a serious turn to it. I was beginning to be very uneasy. Time was passing. There did not seem to be an end to the questions.

I began to think about how I could get out of there. The relentless interrogation continued. I had a friend who had advised me years before, "If you get into trouble with an official, there is a way out: become a marshmallow, all sweetness and softness. Play the feminine card." So, I decided to do just that. I started to say stumblingly that the letter did not matter, that it was the money, that I had hoped to spend the money in London buying a particular dress, and now that I had to make the extra payment, I could not afford it. I would go downstairs and make the payment and make no further demands about a letter.

After a while, and more questioning, the "treasurer" let me out. I was greatly relieved to be a free being again. The interview had seemed quite threatening. Why was he so much interested in my affairs, my clothes, my doings in general? I left, but I felt more and more nervous as the afternoon progressed. I decided to do something I had never done before. I decided to go to the American Embassy.

Like many anthropologists working in Africa, I was very aware that the official relationship between Tanzania and the US was not the friendliest, and that the less contact with the official side, the better. I had never connected with the embassy before. I did not want to take the risk of being thought an American agent, but my fright caused by the Egypt Air treasurer moved me to consult them.

I made a collection of my academic credentials and my passport to take with me. Then I went to the building in town where I knew the Embassy was situated. To my horror, the Embassy office was closed. I could hear that there were people inside. I shouted through the door that I was an American citizen in trouble and I needed advice. After a while they opened the door and let me in.

I thought surely they would think my fears exaggerated. I began feeling like a fool. Was I anxious about something of no importance? In fact, they listened to my story attentively and when I was finished to my astonishment they said, "We think we know what happened. The Egyptians have been running an illegal operation as far as the airline goes. They are unlicensed. They are convinced that there is an Israeli spy somewhere waiting to show them up. They think you are the person because of your asking for the letter. We will have to fix this."

We talked for a few minutes. They told me to go back to my hotel and to count on leaving in two days, on the day scheduled by Egypt Air. They added, no doubt thinking to reassure me, "If you don't turn up in London in three days, we will just put out a search for you."

The next day I telephoned the Embassy to say that if matters were as uncertain as they sounded, I would simply buy another ticket and go home on British Air. Never mind the expense. The question of not turning up in three days had made me more anxious than I had been. What did they think? They got back to me in a few minutes saying they had another idea. They would "create an incident" and I need worry no longer. But I must go back on Egypt Air as arranged.

When I got to the airport on the appointed day I realized what the Embassy staff meant by "creating an incident." They had formally accused Egypt Air of harassing a US citizen. Not only were the American Embassy people at the airport to see me off, but so was every imaginable Egypt Air official and a handful of Egyptian diplomats. They were all at the airport in office dress to apologize and wish me a good flight.

A mountain had cleverly been created out of a molehill. I was still a bit scared, but that fear was dissolving as we spoke. Indeed the flight was entirely smooth and without incident. We did not stop in Cairo. No one's passport was confiscated. Everything proceeded as it normally would and I met my smiling husband in London as expected.

However, I had become very conscious of the many meanings that connected in the Egypt Air experience. After my little adventures in Cairo and in Dar es Salaam I certainly realized that in Africa, whatever I said about myself, there would be people who would attribute to me whatever identity suited their idea of my person. It was not in my control. I had had to appeal to the Embassy for help and I was very grateful both for their recognition of my identity as an American, as a research person, and most of all, for their intervention.

I was very much aware of the critical political attitude that the U.S. had toward the Tanzanian socialist experiment. I was also very aware of the officially negative view Tanzania had toward the capitalist USA. Could I escape that set of explicit mutual rejections and just get on with my work? Among other things,

I wanted to study the way in which socialism at the national level had worked its way into local affairs on Kilimanjaro, among the Chagga people. I wanted to do this by examining the changes and continuities in local law over the century. I was certainly going to come back, probably many times. For my project to succeed, the sources had to be accessible, my Chagga friends had to continue to be generous, and I had to be tactful. And also, given the implications of the Dar es Salaam adventure, I had to be lucky.

STUDYING LIVES IN MOTION: THE IMPERATIVE OF PROCESS

I hasten to add that a preoccupation with law does not imply a commitment to studying a fixed order. Just the contrary: there is nothing more indicative of what may be happening in a society than to look at its declared norms to see who uses them, who enforces them, who ignores them, who gets around them and how. This conception of the research task has a history.

When I started graduate study in anthropology in 1948 at Columbia I soon found that there was nothing in the curriculum directly touching on law. By way of social anthropology, there were a number of "area" courses offered. The content of these was a large set of thumbnail ethnographies. Thus we might take a course on the Peoples of South America or the Peoples of Africa. What the lectures and readings contained was a summary of the prevalent customs of each of a number of peoples. These were presented in terms of a list of their institutions enumerated as: social organization, kinship, the economy, and religion.

It was the post-Second World War era of area studies. The comparative information that anthropology had to offer was tailored to large geographical categories. And within them what we had to learn was the content of a survey of ethnographic types. From my perspective, it was too much of an overview and not enough of an inside view.

All this was interesting but it did not tell one much about how people in such societies lived, competed and strategized, and dealt with governments to which in many places they were at least technically subject. We did not address the colonial situation. Nor did we consider what the peoples did with the inflow of information to them about the larger world. What did they know about the possibility of labor migration?

Some eminent professors, like Alfred Kroeber, broke the static quality of the typological model in their own way. But Kroeber's was as grand a vision as the idea of area studies itself. He was interested in history, in "diffusion," how certain ideas and skills and artifacts found their way from one people to the next. This was a counter-weight to the nineteenth century classification of all cultural types in an order of simple to complex. In the nineteenth century, the simple to complex classification was thought of as a schematic representation of a possible way that social evolution had taken place. Karl Marx and Friedrich Engels, Lewis Henry Morgan, and many others bought into this idea.

By the time I was studying, the evolutionary model was on the way out for all but a few Marxists. However, the simple to complex classification lived on. It served as a way of making order out of the enormous amount of ethnographic data that had been assembled about a huge variety of societies all over the world. The powerful intellectual byproduct of this bird's eye view was to conceive of societies as examples of cultural types. What was lacking was an internal perspective, one that would describe what social life was like inside one of these traditional systems.

Fieldwork, with attention to the strategic actions of individuals, might have been a way to produce that working knowledge. And more consequently, it could have produced a dynamic picture of people in action, making their lives, taking a chance, losing a try, guessing right, outdoing a neighbor, and the like. But that was not on the departmental agenda, preoccupied as it was with anthropology as cultural typology. Typologizing could not produce the action perspective. Yet it later became the preeminent technique of the next generation of American anthropologists. I have called this redefined focus the study of process. It treats anthropological fieldwork as the study of an active present, as contemporary history. This processual turn did not only occur in the United States. It was also emerging in British social anthropology, and was to be found in much theoretical sociological work from Bourdieu to Habermas.

Process puts the focus on what is happening: what social results are evident and what links there are to other events, shaping matters both on the small scale and the large scale. It is a moving picture. This obviously does not eliminate the importance of tradition, of customary ways of doing things, but it puts tradition in its place as one shaping factor, one resource for people moving along in their lives and justifying their actions to themselves and to each other. Process is oriented to movement in a time and over time. It encompasses social change as well as social continuity. It is the research orientation of much social anthropology today.

Many of the essays in this book demonstrate this perspective as applied to fieldwork. A few others are autobiographical, sketching how I got here. And the remaining ones are reflections on some odd and interesting materials in the written record.

SALLY FALK MOORE

PART ONE

The Anthropologist and Anthropology

*Anthropology is obsessed with causality, but can only address it indirectly. What causes the form of society to be as it is? Why do people do what they do? Why do they think what they think? And what is the history of these manifestations. The first section of this book presents two essays which approach such questions obliquely. How did I become the kind of anthropologist that I am. Life-history and education? Historical moment? The second paper considers the way the discipline of anthropology itself has moved from making comparisons of **form** to comparisons of societies in **historical process**? The third paper gives clues to what goes on in the life of the anthropologist while she is doing fieldwork. It tells stories off the center of research that give the flavor of the experience in the round. Thus, the three articles in this section are offered to introduce the reader to some of the characteristics of the fieldworker, and the fieldworker's investigations.*

The paper on comparisons deserves an extra note. An earlier version of that article began by reviewing the general history of comparisons in anthropology (not published because it was too long). That history showed what the academic discipline of anthropology has at various times thought important, dwelling on the supposedly fixed cultural characteristics that were once thought to be the key differences between societies. The abreviated paper offered here is about the impossibility of comparing modern development projects for two reasons, because (1) they were studied over a period of time, hence "in history," and (2) given their location in different, moving societies.

This approach is distinguished from earlier comparisons that compared social "types." This emphasis on ongoing historical processes permeates all the papers in this book.

Eventually, in the third paper, I emphasize that there are many aspects of the field work situation over which the anthropologist has no control. Some of those can be quite alarming. And even on the benign side, the factor of chance plays a big role in fieldwork. What was the year of contact? What were the surrounding circumstances. Who else was there when the fieldworker landed in the new place? What was happening? We now want to know how things were moving in general. What was in process. What was in motion? What was the observed world becoming? And what was it doing to the anthropologist?

*A **processual** approach to anthropological fieldwork uses witnessed events, and narratives of events, as important data. In the classical days of social anthropology, seventy five years ago, or more, the central focus of ethnography was on identifying the customary practices and normative rules of a society. Descriptions of events, when they occurred, usually figured as illustrations of custom. But now events are inspected as much more, as a window on historical processes, and on the dynamics of social relations. The rules and customs material still matters, but knowing how it all works matters more.*

CHAPTER ONE

Part of the Story
A Memoir

In this memoir I have tried to give some account of the private life as well as the professional life; how I got from being an intense young lawyer to being a cheerful old anthropologist. Two themes are threaded through the story from beginning to end: the gender factor and the many enormous political upheavals of the twentieth century.

The gender issue came up repeatedly. It sometimes determined employment opportunities. An example: before I became an anthropologist I had studied law. I received my LLB in 1945 at the age of twenty-one. On graduating, I joined the Wall Street law firm Spence, Parker, and Duryea, which had just made a woman a junior partner something which was almost unheard of at the time. She was Soia Mentchikoff, who was later to become Karl Llewellyn's wife. I knew Llewellyn as a law student. He was a distinguished and eccentric professor at Columbia Law School and had sponsored me for the Wall Street job. Later he collaborated with anthropologist E. Adamson Hoebel, an anthropologist, on what became a well-known book on Cheyenne law (Llewellyn & Hoebel 1953; for a criticism of their work, see Moore 1999). The law firm was very unusual in being willing to hire women lawyers at all. There were three of us

---

Editor's note: This chapter is a reprint of Moore, Sally Falk. 2005. "Part of the story: A memoir." *Ethnos* 70 (4): 538–566.

in a firm of more than forty men. The other firms which interviewed me seemed less likely to hire, and even less likely to promote.

Later, after I became an anthropologist and began to publish, I could not for some years be hired in the universities where my husband had a position, since there were "nepotism" rules everywhere. It all turned out well in the end, but there were many unpleasantnesses along the way. A small current example: as a member of the American Academy of Arts and Sciences I recently attended a large reception before the meeting. When I was introduced to a distinguished physicist he attempted to place me by asking, "What department is your husband in?"

Apart from the gender question, the political background of the mid-century and my own human rights sympathies shaped my major professional choices in anthropology. The end of the colonial era and its sequel had much to do with spurring my interest in the socialist years in Tanzania. That was where I did my major fieldwork, visiting intermittently over many years from 1968 onwards. But even in accomplishing that project, there were limitations. What I could investigate and write about the realities of Tanzanian socialism was constrained by the fact that I wanted to continue to be welcome to work there. The Tanzanian government was very anti-American for much of the time that I was there, very anti-anthropological (anthropology was seen as the handmaiden of colonialism), and very sensitive to any criticism. I was exceptionally lucky to be able to work in Tanzania at all. I was acceptable as a lawyer, not as an anthropologist. My initial research sponsorship came from the University of Dar es Salaam Law School. A local study of law on Kilimanjaro provided a means of satisfying some of my political interests without irritating the authorities, at least some of the time. Among other reasons, I chose to work in a predominantly Christian area because I thought that being a woman in that setting would be less of a barrier to making contact with men than it might have been in a Muslim part of Tanzania. That turned out to be so. I had the access I needed to do the fieldwork.

This memoir is a story of walking between the walls of exclusion, exploring political themes whenever it was possible, and advancing the cause of one female without getting into major trouble.

BEGINNINGS

In 1946, after a year in a Wall Street law firm, I took a leave of absence and went to work at the Nuremberg trials. I was the youngest and least important lawyer on the prosecution staff. I left Nuremberg six months later, principally to get a divorce. I was eager to close that personal chapter in my life. I left on a troop ship on which there were many hundred soldiers and six women. It was December and the seas were rough. Everyone was seasick. Through some sort of misguided attempt to entertain us, we were treated to very loud music all day long. It was a horrible trip. If one went up to the deck to get some cold air, one had to walk past hundreds of soldiers lying on the deck and ready to hoot at any woman in sight. It was an unpleasant experience.

I landed in New York, and soon went out to Reno to settle the marriage business. When I returned from that adventure, divorce papers in hand, the next question for me was what to do professionally. I could have gone to work in the Washington office of the Nuremberg people (Telford Taylor invited me to do so) or I could have returned to the Wall Street firm (they had invited me to return). I did not want to do either. I spent some months trying to reach a decision. I decided that what I wanted most was a job at the United Nations, which was then just starting up. I found its preoccupation with human rights very appealing.

Getting such a job was going to take considerable time. There was a national quota system at the United Nations. In order that it be a truly international organization, even though located in New York, the number of Americans employed there was severely limited, and openings for Americans would appear only rarely. I applied in the normal way, and was in fact, interviewed, but greater hope of landing a job came another way. My sponsor for the Bar and old patron, Max Lowenthal, a lawyer and Washington lobbyist, said he thought a friend of his in the State Department would be able to help me. I was doing some research for Lowenthal on a book he was writing on the Federal Bureau of Investigation (Lowenthal 1950). I declined to be mentioned in the acknowledgements, lest the FBI become interested in me. Lowenthal hoped that his book would help President Truman fire J. Edgar Hoover. Truman read the galleys and scribbled approving comments in the margins before sending them back to Lowenthal, whom he knew. However, when the New York Times asked Truman what he thought of the book, he replied that he had never heard of it.

As for my potential job at the UN, Lowenthal explained that the contact who was to help me was involved in various legal controversies. Until these blew over, he might not be able to assist us. Alas, his friend was Alger Hiss, accused of being a communist and ultimately imprisoned. His troubles with Richard Nixon had just begun. Max thought they would blow over, but in the meanwhile I would have to wait, perhaps for another year.

With a year to spend, I decided to go back to Columbia University and try to find out what was known in the social sciences about how to allocate responsibility for the actions of a society. It was clear to me that the leaders being tried at Nuremberg were only at the surface of a much wider and deeper phenomenon. I considered various social sciences at Columbia at the time, particularly sociology and political science. I spoke to members of the anthropology faculty about my interests and they were very encouraging. It was clear that they would accept me. They were especially pleased because the only person in anthropology and law at that time was E. Adamson Hoebel who had worked on the aforementioned Cheyenne book with Karl Llewellyn. So, because I could not get a job at the UN immediately, I went into anthropology for what I thought would only be an academic year.

At the time, I felt somewhat unsettled emotionally. I did not want to make another mistake in marriage. I was floating around professionally. Since my parents were willing to pay for it, in the spring of 1948 I began what turned into three years of psychoanalysis. My brother was in psychoanalytic training and we had many friends who were involved in the profession or in therapy, so going into therapy was not an unusual event in our social circles.

Meanwhile a coincidence determined the course of my summer, introduced me to my next husband, and fed my appetite for anthropology. A college friend, Edith Efron Bogat, who lived in Haiti and with whom I corresponded, invited me to come down and see her new baby. I had learned from Charles Wagley at Columbia that Alfred Metraux and his group were doing fieldwork in the Marbial Valley and, through Wagley, Metraux invited me to visit and do a workshop on law for his team.

I thought it would be perfect to see Edith and to visit Metraux. Edith had married a Haitian in his fifties. She was his fifth wife. The house was full of his children of varying ages, and well-appointed with servants. Messieurs Bogat, Edith's new husband, was one of the General Motors representatives in Port au Prince. He was an impressive figure, and usually carried a gun. I went to stay for a few days in the Bogat household before going to Metraux's camp. While I was there, a friend of Edith's, Cresap Moore, came to say goodbye to her. He was returning to the States to finish college and get on with his life. He had spent a year in Haiti, living in a hut on the beach, working on a novel (never finished), learning how to play the drums from some Haitian masters, and consorting with the people involved in the Haitian art renaissance. This lively and mixed group of people included Haitian models and artists, such as Gourgue and Hector Hyppolite, as well as Americans, including Selden Rodman, the editor and art critic, and Jason Seeley, the sculptor. Meeting Cresap was a fine introduction to Haiti since he spoke Creole and had many Haitian friends. They called him "Gros Blanc." He was six foot six and had flaming red hair and a gold earring. Needless to say he was quite a presence.

The first evening we went out together, he took me to a ceremony for the recently deceased painter and voodoo priest, Hector Hyppolite. Thinking in terms of New York dates, I appeared in a silk dress. Cresap rejected this costume and told me to change at once into something more suitable for sitting on a dirt floor. I had no idea what to expect. The ritual for Hyppolite was in a dark hut, illuminated by a fire in the center. There was drumming and singing. Chickens were sacrificed—their necks were wrung. Women stood up and sang and danced, were possessed, and fainted. The culminating event of the evening was the burning of a pair of long white pants that had belonged to Hyppolite. A message from the mourners that went with them would surely reach him.

A few days later, after Cresap had flown back to the States, I travelled to Metraux's camp on horseback with a Haitian guide walking ahead. I duly gave a workshop on law, tramped around with Metraux in the hills, meeting his informants, and seeing starvation up close—a baby so sick that flies walked across its eyes and it did not blink. Metraux was not deterred from his project of the moment. What he was interested in was measuring what the mother had eaten that day. She cooked in a discarded can on an open fire. We could see what she had. The deprivation she endured was horrifying.

There were tarantulas in our camp. They were reputed to frequent the outhouse. Metraux never visited the outhouse without a huge machete, or *panga*, for protection. We laughed every time he absented himself. The rest of us took our chances. The local people brought him a child with a high fever asking him to cure her. He accepted her in his camp. I thought he was crazy because she might have died, and he hadn't the slightest idea what was the matter with her. In fact, he was lucky. She improved after a few days.

After some weeks in Haiti, I returned to New York to study anthropology. The idea I had was that at the end of the year I would go on to a law job, ideally at the UN. The year of anthropology started, but the position at the UN did not materialize.

In anthropology, though I sampled what the faculty recommended, I also made my own explorations. I discovered Claude Lévi-Strauss' *Les structures élémentaires de la parenté* (1949) which had just come out. Dazzled as I was by the issues in the book, and full of questions, I found that there was no one with whom to discuss it. No one on the faculty had read it. I resolved to continue to read and study it on my own, and to make my way into the discipline on a route of my own choosing. Questions about law and society in the modern world were not going to be answered in the curriculum that was offered, nor indeed in the popular understanding of anthropology. I wanted to enlarge my knowledge of political dynamics, but at the time, anthropology was occupied with other matters.

In the popular press the fashion for culture and personality studies was everywhere. Margaret Mead and Ruth Benedict were the household names. Of course, I had read the classic Mead and Benedict books before I read much other anthropological material. While I sympathized with their political agenda, among other things their plea for more freedom, behavioral and sexual, I had my doubts about many aspects of their approach. No doubt this arose partly from ideas about human complexity and variability culled from my own psychoanalysis.

My experience of psychoanalysis was personally illuminating and intellectually fascinating. I saw the Mead and Benedict writings as poetic, always interesting, but wildly conjectural and unsupported. The jump from ideas in individual psychology to social typology seemed too easy. I knew that if I were to have worked with Mead, I would have been in trouble because I would have to disagree with her. My interest in the connection between psychology and cultural issues would have to find other outlets (see Moore 1964, 1976).

Benedict died in 1948, just before I entered the Department. As for Mead, she was not a member of the Department of Anthropology at all, but as hidden away as possible (not very) in the independent Museum of Natural History. The gossip was that the Department was afraid to appoint her lest she take it over. She was a dynamo, there was no doubt of that. Some graduate students chose to work with Mead nevertheless, and I regularly heard tales about the goings-on in her shop. Once, for example, a fellow student told me that when Mead was about to go off on a trip for some months, she offered to lend to any of her assistants a small, not very attractive, and very worn little fur cape. She explained that she had originally acquired it because an analyst had told her, "It would strengthen Gregory's [Bateson's] reality perception." Of course, I have no idea whether this story was true, but it fitted with her solicitous and remarkably personal exchanges with her assistants. In return for this closeness, there was a kind of orthodoxy among her student followers, a uniformity of view. They were acolytes. It seemed clear to me that a serious critical analysis of her writings, or of the issues they raised, would not be welcome. These considerations, and the fact that association with Mead did not meet with favor with the rest of the faculty, discouraged me from making any connection with her.

There was a story which floated around among the students about a confrontation between Steward and Margaret Mead, between whom there was little love. Mead had apparently cited Steward in print a number of times. She always spelled his name as "Stewart." He was said to have threatened to retaliate by spelling her name as Margaret Meat.

The interests of the faculty were in the distribution of cultures in the world, the archeological record of developments from simple to complex socio-technical forms, and the effects of contact and diffusion. The historical preoccupation was evident. For them, the structural-functional approach of British social anthropology was ahistorical and conjectural. It was more than rejected, it was scarcely mentioned. All of British social anthropology was anathema. The strong link between American cultural anthropology and archeology, along with the interest in history and social change, pushed the synchronic British structural-functional preoccupations off the screen. Except for Kroeber's interest in the high civilizations of the Old World, from India to China and Japan, from Egypt to Mesopotamia, the focus on the Americas predominated.

The people on the Columbia Faculty at the time and with whom I had much contact included Alfred Kroeber, Julian Steward, Charles Wagley, Paul Kirchoff, Joseph Greenberg, the linguist, and Duncan Strong, the archeologist. This was very much the time in anthropology when what one was taught was the "Peoples of Africa" or "Peoples of South America"-type of course. Because this was still the four-fields period in anthropological training, one also learned a little biological anthropology (a little Mendel, a few fruit flies, and Shapiro's study of Pitcairn Island), a little languages of the world material (Greenberg's revised maps of the languages of Africa), and a little archaeology on paper (Strong's finds in Peru). There was a great emphasis on material culture. For the graduate students, the objective was to know the profiles of the cultures of as many peoples of the world as one could hold in one's head. Culture was something that people "had," and they did what the culture prescribed.

Kroeber was the broadest mind of our faculty. His lectures were always interesting because he placed whatever he had to say against a vast background of learning, and he was less interested in artifacts than in artistic facts and in the ésprit of civilizations. Kroeber taught the Big Picture. He may have done his fieldwork among the Yurok, but we never heard about his California work. He fascinated us with his interest in high civilizations. He gave a course on India. He told us about the diffusion of chess and playing cards, how the figure of the Madonna moved from East to West. He regaled us with his perspective on the "superorganic" nature of culture. And, probably because of his earlier interest in Freud, he taught what seemed to be the most avant-garde course in the department: "Culture and Personality." But apart from Kroeber, there was no interest in that approach in the Department.

While I was an advanced student, Kroeber was asked to contribute a history of the Anthropology Department to a Bicentennial History of Columbia. Since he was the first Ph.D. produced by Franz Boas, there could not have been a more fitting request. However, he did not want to be bothered to write the history, so he asked me to do the piece and offered me his notes. I was delighted. That became my first publication (Moore 1955). Contact with Kroeber about this article emboldened me. When he told me excitedly that he had just received a very interesting book on adat law (Indonesia), I asked him if I might borrow it since the library would not yet have received it. He suddenly became unusually austere, "I never lend books to graduate students," he said.

Julian Steward, armed with his theories of cultural ecology, taught a course on the peoples of South America. At the time Steward was occupied with the start of the project of putting together the existing data on all of the peoples of South America. Many authors contributed. This gigantic work was published in multiple volumes by the Smithsonian Institution (Steward 1946–50).

Steward presented his ideas about the primacy of environmental and economic factors in the formation of a "cultural core." Other cultural features, not closely connected with subsistence activities and economic arrangements, were treated as secondary. The secondary features were often the ones that interested us, but they did not figure in his grand explanatory scheme.

The theoretical issues—nineteenth-century ideas about social evolution, Marx, Leslie White's interpretations—were never presented to us as such. For Steward, the cultural core was a "fact." Curiously enough he also did not speak to his classes about the lively Puerto Rico fieldwork project he was then supervising (1948–49), which involved Eric Wolf, Sidney Mintz, and a number of others. We did not hear much about it until they began to return.

The department person who did talk about his fieldwork was Charles Wagley. He was the only faculty member who made the ethnographic adventure vivid. But, true to cultural anthropology, all the experiences he reported were treated as *facts* about cultural practices. If there was a larger framework to which these data were connected, it was to questions of cultural borrowings from other peoples. Fieldwork, in the eyes of the department, was for the purpose of gathering new examples of the huge variety of human experience, what Leach later called "butterfly collecting" (Leach 1961).

It was therefore evident to me that I would have to navigate an independent course through the discipline. Law did not figure prominently in the writings by anthropologists, and questions about law in the modern world raised issues that the cultural anthropologists rarely touched upon. Worse still, for me, at the time, fieldwork was out of the question. I was briefly tempted to go with a Wagley project in Brazil in which a whole team of students were to be dispersed in a number of sites, each with a Brazilian partner. They were to meet periodically to compare notes and then go back into the field. However, Cresap's response when I had proposed to go to Brazil had been, "O.K. Go. But I may not be here waiting for you when you return." I did not want to take the risk of losing him, so I decided to do my dissertation comparing the legal systems of the two great precolonial empires of the Americas, the Inca and the Aztec. As it turned out, I became convinced that the material on the Aztecs was so complex and so voluminous, that I had better limit myself to the Inca where the literature was finite, and much of it had been reprinted. Duncan Strong became my dissertation supervisor because of his interest in Peru. However, he left me pretty much on my own, since my topic was not one that touched on his work.

Though not completed for some years, my library dissertation, *Power and property in Inca Peru*, won the Ansley Award at Columbia, a publication prize for the best dissertation in the Faculty of Political Science (which included all the social science departments) (Moore 1958). The delay in finishing it was due to the fact that Cresap Moore and I married in 1951 and began what were to be many years of moving and child rearing.

Cresap was an historian of nineteenth-century Britain, with a particular interest in electoral politics. He discovered a new resource for analysis, the many poll books which made a public record of all the votes cast, as well as the addresses and occupations of the voters. No one had used these before. In very detailed work in many constituencies, he used the poll books to show the structure of English electoral politics, the way people voted in blocs and how these blocs were led. When we lived in Cambridge, the kitchen was hung with drying photocopies of poll books alongside of drying diapers. We went to England periodically for his research, and also moved from one academic institution to another as his career required. Our first child was born in 1952, our second in 1955.

I continued to work on my dissertation in Cambridge, still in England, and in London when I could find baby sitters. I wrote in the evenings. I read anthropology continually. Beyond the Inca material, I began to formulate questions about comparative kinship matters that could be addressed in the library, and about which I would later publish. The first puzzle I wrote about was a technical one about Crow-Omaha kinship terminology. Among other observations, I noted the fact that women did not use the same terms for kin as men, nor were their terms mirror images of the male system. Yet all the anthropological literature was based on the terms used by the men. I was surprised by this omission in the construction of typological models, but I should not have been. There were heavy intellectual investments in the classifications built on male terminology and the material on women would have complicated the picture enormously. As far as I could tell, my discovery went unnoticed though it was published in *American Anthropologist* (Moore 1963).

The second puzzle I addressed was one that was related to my interest in the Freudian material. I asked myself a question about mythological first families (Moore 1964). One of the problems such myths have to cope with is *whom do the children of the first couple marry?* Do they marry each other? If not, do potential spouses appear, and from where? And finally, is there any correlation between the marriage of the children of the first family and the type of kinship system of the society, and if so what is it? This branched out into questions about the mythological relationship siblings had to each other's fertility. At this time I was writing and publishing, I did not go to meetings. The children and the household needed my attention, and no relatives or substitutes were available, I did not have an opportunity to talk with people interested in the same issues, or who had read my work. That soon changed.

THE FIRST TEACHING JOB

In the early 1960s, while we were in England, Cresap received an offer from the University of California, Los Angeles. He accepted and a few months later we moved to California. While looking for a house, we stayed in a posh hotel suite on Sunset Boulevard. It had its own shock value. In the bureau drawer in the suite I found a leather shoulder holster for a gun, the kind that fits well concealed under one arm with a strap that goes across to the other shoulder, under a jacket, of course. Who had stayed in those rooms before we did? I thought of keeping it, but worried about the implications. Then we went to a supermarket to get some supplies, and in the station wagon next to us there were two monkeys in diapers. "Holy Moly," I remember telling myself, "This place, California, is unbelievable."

We bought a house that was relatively inexpensive. The valley, in which it was situated, had recently been devastated by a bush fire. It was the kind of fire that burns one house and then skips to three houses down the street and destroys another. Our house was one of the ones that survived. Something we did not know at first was that the family of an anthropologist lived next door. It was the family of Joseph Weckler, a Professor at the University of Southern California. He and his wife were separated, so he did not live next to us, but the family was very friendly and I came to know him through them. He was in a state of distress. He had a serious drinking problem, but that was only one of his troubles.

The University of Southern California, where he taught, had just abolished the anthropology department as a separate entity, and incorporated it into the sociology department. There had been two staff members in the department, Weckler and an archaeologist. However, once the archaeologist heard about the merger with sociology, he thought he would have no future and had better move to another California institution. He did so at the last minute before term began. Weckler thought it was possible to convince the administration that a social/cultural anthropologist could be substituted for the archeologist and asked me if I would be willing to take the job. I had, of course, never had a teaching position, though I had a book out and several articles in print.

I had previously tried to get a job at UCLA but had been told they did not need me. One of the people who interviewed and rejected me said by way of explanation, "We already have a woman." Given that UCLA was out of the question, the USC job sounded like a fortunate happening. In 1963, I accepted Weckler's offer with alacrity. All was well for a few weeks. However, five weeks into the term, Weckler committed suicide and I became the only anthropologist at USC isolated in a sociology department.

I used the vacancy caused by Weckler's death to convince the administration to split his salary and make it into two junior positions. I hired some advanced graduate students from UCLA (recommended by Hilda Kuper) to fill the courses Weckler had left vacant. One was Barbara Myerhoff, and the other was Jay Abarbanel. Later I was also able to hire a young sociologist, Roy Bryce, a student of Leo Kuper's. I felt hugely encouraged by the fact that I was no longer the lone anthropologist, and I had some people with whom to talk. USC had permitted Weckler and his archeology associate to give graduate degrees. I ended the graduate program since the staff was (and had been) inadequate to support such a program. We would concentrate on the undergraduate offerings.

The effect of my contact with Abarbanel was unexpected. Jay was trained in British social anthropology. He had done fieldwork in a *moshav* in Israel, in a project supervised by Max Gluckman. I learned much about Gluckman and the Manchester School through him. I had, of course, read Gluckman's *The judicial process among the Barotse* and much of the literature on law in the British tradition (Gluckman 1955), but I had yet to read much beyond the legal. I read on. I found the sociological thrust of structural-functionalism an intellectual relief.

The emphasis on the organization of groups appealed to me, as did the search for the social significance of customary practices. The link with law and politics was much more evident than it had been in the cultural tradition of American anthropology. I was almost seduced. However, as I went along, I found the way the idea of *function*, as used by Radcliffe-Brown and his acolytes, was not always illuminating. He interpreted all customs as contributions to social cohesion. But how much did each contribute? Which were more important than others? There was something abstract and almost mystical about the idea of the cohesive totality to which a contribution was being made.

My interest in the British literature of social anthropology was further stimulated by my friendship with UCLA professors Michael Smith and Hilda and Leo Kuper. Mike Smith had been born in Jamaica, and worked in the Caribbean as well as in West Africa. In the course of the Caribbean work, he came to know David Lowenthal, an old schoolmate of mine, who later became a geographer, and a professor at University College, London. David was the son of the Max Lowenthal who had sponsored me for the Bar and who had tried to contact Alger Hiss for me. David Lowenthal told Mike Smith about my book on the Inca. Mike read it and got in touch with me as soon as he arrived at UCLA.

Contact with Smith and the Kupers was frequent and talk was wonderful and always lively. We saw one another frequently, both in and outside the university. They were opinionated, kept up with what was being published in anthropology, and argued about everything from politics to food. Hilda was the hostess for all foreign visitors, and gave wonderful parties. She had a very naughty dog named Senini. When a carefully prepared buffet was unavailable to him, because the table was too high, he simply pulled on the tablecloth until all the food came down to the floor. When Hilda went back to Swaziland for a year, Cresap and I took care of Senini, and tried to teach him better manners.

I soon began teaching an undergraduate course at USC in the history of theory—one of the undergraduates I taught was Craig Calhoun, now President of the Social Science Research Council. I also organized a seminar (with my junior colleagues) for advanced majors doing small field projects in Los Angeles. The question we explored was whether the theoretical approaches then current could apply to the field materials brought in by the students. It was Weber and Durkheim on Sunset Boulevard. Later on, as a byproduct of the interest in communal living prevalent among the students at that time, was a panel I organized for the American Anthropological Association. It eventually resulted in the volume *Symbol and politics in communal ideology* (Moore & Myerhoff 1975).

THE FIRST WENNER-GREN CONFERENCE: I MEET THE LAW AND ANTHROPOLOGY CROWD

In the summer of 1966 my career reached a more public turning point. Laura Nader, who had read my book on the Inca and liked it, invited me to a conference on law in culture and society. The meeting took place at Burg Wartenstein, a castle outside of Vienna which the Wenner-Gren Foundation had bought just after the war as a summer conference center. The castle, unheated, was too cold to use during the winter, but it was a magnificent setting for an intellectual gathering. All the major figures in the anthropology of law were present: Isaac Schapera, Paul Bohannan, Max Gluckman and his junior colleague Richard Werbner, Leo Pospisil, E. Adamson Hoebel, Frank Cancian, James Gibbs, Laura Nader, and Philip Gulliver. In addition, there were two sociologists, Vilhelm Aubert and Gresham Sykes, and three legal scholars, Herma Kay, Geert van den Steenhoven, and Raymond Verdier. There were also three student rapporteurs: Klaus Koch, John Rothenberger, and Carl McCarthy.

The Burg Wartenstein Conference took place on two levels: there were the formal sessions when the conferees sat around a green baize table presenting papers and discussing them, and there were the evenings when we sat at smallish tables for dinner. We drank large quantities of very nice wine, and had good food. We danced. There was singing and other frivolities. The odd thing about the table arrangements was that in addition to the conference people, there were young ladies in Tyrolean dress who sat with us. The Wenner-Gren administrator had apparently thought that since most of the people at the meeting were men, it would lighten things up if local Tyrolean geishas were provided. In fact, of course, they were a big nuisance since though they spoke English, they knew nothing about anthropology. We felt obliged out of politeness to talk to them. But after a few words, they settled for smiling, and we continued to develop our evolving friendships. Memorable moments arose when Gluckman danced the Charleston, and when Pospisil did the *kazatzski*. Pospisil also sang with a wonderful deep baritone voice. This jollity softened the arguments that took place during the daytime.

A major, quite fierce debate took place between Gluckman and Bohannan. Bohannan argued that Gluckman misrepresented Lozi law by using Western legal concepts to describe African ideas. Bohannan argued instead that only native terms should be used, for only the local language could be counted on to represent native legal ideas. Since Bohannan was attacking Gluckman's work directly, and Gluckman's magisterial person indirectly, Gluckman did not take kindly to this criticism. The dispute was serious, rather personal, and created some tension in the conference. There was a lot of "taking sides."

The tense outcome was not surprising. Gluckman's was the first book on an African court. Bohannan's followed soon after. Gluckman knew a good deal about Western law before he did his fieldwork, and was looking at Lozi reasoning for analogies and universals. Bohannan had approached Tiv law without any such intellectual baggage. For him, it was easier to describe the Tiv as unique, special, in the faux-naïve way that anthropologists often use when confronted with exotic material. He had no comparisons in mind. Laura Nader asked me to introduce both views in the book of papers that ultimately was produced from the conference, so the details of their disagreement became a matter of serious intellectual concern for me (Moore 1969a, 1969b). At the time of the conference, I had not yet done any fieldwork and relied on the monographs of others to do my papers. For this conference, my paper re-analyzed the question of whether descent rules should be thought of as absolutely determinative of the rights and obligations of persons in any kin-based society. Was descent the same as law in African unilineal systems? Did it involve "jural rules" as some thought? Or was descent an ideal principle of organization, which was not always adhered to? I argued that a new look at the variability of practice that might surround descent rules was in order, and that the variability was not random, but part of the system itself. Using a classic African ethnography of the patrilineal Lango, I showed that while among them there were many rules associated with descent that were stated in mandatory terms there also were numerous techniques by which the effect of the rules could be adjusted or indeed circumvented (Moore 1969a, 1969b). This was a stealth attack on the over-systematization of kinship models, as opposed to practices, that prevailed at the time. Obliquely, this paper raised theoretical issues about the custom-bound conceptualization of non-Western societies often used by Western anthropologists.

PREPARATIONS FOR FIELDWORK IN AFRICA

The next major shift in my professional life would land me in Africa. But the path to that point was circuitous. At USC, my tiny anthropology section was doing very well. I had even succeeded in getting publicity for it by giving a taped course on television. It consisted of sixty half hours for CBS. I did the tapings in the evenings, while carrying my full teaching load during the day. At that time, I succeeded in convincing the administration to add to our numbers by giving us a chair in social anthropology. I even found a suitable candidate to fill the post for a year or two, Kalervo Oberg. Since he was retired and did not want a long commitment this would give me time to find a young and distinguished candidate to succeed him. Alas for my scheme, when his final retirement was imminent, the position was withdrawn from anthropology and given to the sociology department. I was furious. So much work had gone into building an anthropology department from scratch. I wanted to leave USC and I began to think about changing direction and going to Africa to do fieldwork. The long-term implications of such a commitment had to be worked out with Cresap. But he gave me his blessing, and, indeed, wanted to come to Africa with me in the beginning.

I spoke with my friends at UCLA in the African Studies Center and asked them if I could spend a year there preparing myself. The 1967–68 year at UCLA was so arranged. I was launched. I started studying Swahili. I applied to the Social Science Research Council and received a fellowship. And in the summer of 1968, and the summer of 1969, with husband and two daughters, I made two trips to Kilimanjaro. The same year, my review of the literature on law was published in the *Biennial Review* (Moore 1969c).

On Kilimanjaro, one of the first people who helped me with my work was Hawkins Ndesanjo Mremi, a local coffee-grower and a small-holder who had

had some experience in the courts. He had been recommended by the then
Magistrate of Marangu. Over the years Hawkins was only one of many people
who helped me along the way, but I became especially close to him and his family. One of his sons, Emmanuel, was a very good student. Many years later, in
the 1990s, Emmanuel wanted to be trained as a pharmacist. Fortunately, I was
able to finance his five-year course at the University of Kharkov, thus expressing
my affection for and deep indebtedness to his family. Emmanuel is now back
in Tanzania working in his profession. Thus do fieldwork connections indirectly
change the course of some lives.

When I returned from Kilimanjaro in 1970 USC began to make amends,
and wooed me back by obtaining a full professorship for me, which I received
in 1970. In 1973–74, I again made two field visits to Kilimanjaro, spending
the winter in London. I was collecting material that would enable me to trace
the history of legal change from precolonial origins through the colonial and
socialist periods on Kilimanjaro. From 1970–75, I also taught at the USC Law
School. Harold Solomon, a professor there, was keen on developing a social science dimension in the law curriculum, and, for a time, I was it.

Pivotal to my fieldwork work was my interest in the dynamics of social systems, their organization and trajectory. In 1973, I published a paper on "semi-
autonomous social fields" (Moore 1973). I had been struck by the degree to
which the Chagga ran their own affairs, though they were legally subordinate to
the political system of Tanzania. In the same paper, I offered an American example to show that under the shadow of US and NY legal norms, there were other
customary, but obligatory, practices surrounding behavior in the "better dress"
business in New York, with the information on the garment industry being supplied by my good friend, the psychoanalyst, Manuel Furer, whose father was in
the business. As a sociological phenomenon, there was nothing unusual about
the quasi-independence of these social fields, and nothing strange about the obligatory nature of nonlegal rules. Such double conditions, found intertwined together, legal and nonlegal, are commonplace. But the relationship of the official
with the unofficial activity is variable and the degree to which the one does or
does not control the affairs of the other has considerable theoretical and practical
interest. In many situations, the relationship is directly pertinent to the workings
of law. By giving this situation a name, and by characterizing the unofficial by its
semi-autonomy, I hoped to define an object for comparative research.

In another vein, my interest continued in the connection between mythology and social practice. I wrote a paper that was critical of some of the neatly

organized oppositional symmetries of symbols by Lévi-Strauss and Robert Hertz. The paper took as its data a Chagga initiation myth. It was originally entitled "The well-stitched anus" since that was what the myth concerned. However, over an elegant and delicious lunch in London, John Middleton told me that while the editor of *Africa* liked the paper, he thought the title was a piece of "academic pornography" that could not be countenanced. I duly changed the title to "The secret of the men." The content was published in *Africa* as originally written (Moore 1976). Somewhere along the way a correspondence had begun with Rodney Needham (who had translated both Hertz and Lévi-Strauss) and my interest in many questions was very much enlivened by his opinionated letters.

SECULAR RITUAL AND SOME WORK ON CONFLICT

A burst of professional activity followed. I published the first of many articles on material that I had gathered among the Chagga on Kilimanjaro (Moore 1970, 1972, 1974) and I began to organize a series of conferences. I recruited Max Gluckman and Victor Turner to help me mount a conference at Burg Wartenstein in August 1974, and it resulted in a book on *Secular ritual* in 1977 (Moore & Myerhoff 1977). My own papers in that volume addressed some of the ideas of Émile Durkheim, and the general thesis put forward in other works that ritual, secular or religious, was a direct expression of feeling, thought, and social arrangements. My observations of political meetings in Tanzania showed that ritual could as easily be a mask, a series of acts whose routine and standard character could hide wide differences of opinion and emotion. Obliquely, this was a criticism of some of Victor Turner's interpretations. However, I was not about to differ with him publicly, being shy of confrontations, especially with my friends.

It was an exciting time because in addition to my junior colleagues at USC, I could talk regularly with Hilda Kuper and Mike Smith who lived not far away. I participated in the interdisciplinary seminars for faculty and graduate students they ran for the African Studies Center at UCLA. Visitors to those seminars included many distinguished Africanists from abroad. Ford Foundation money paid for their travel. Among the regular visitors was Max Gluckman, as he was a close friend of Hilda and Mike. My friendship with all three deepened. There were also a number of African students some of whom expected to return to the political scene in the home country. They had strong views about whether

postcolonial Africa should be analyzed in terms of the ethnic/religious or politi-
cal/class fault lines where potential conflicts would arise or whether economic
development and the engagement with the new African leadership should be
the focus. They had much more than an academic stake in the discussions which
changed their character from cool academic conversation to heated political
debate. *Pluralism in Africa* describes some of the controversial themes discussed
(Kuper & Smith 1969). This was obviously far from a conventional ethnographic
approach with its emphasis on cultural differences and political divisions.

This was an interpretation that did not necessarily posit harmony and coherence in African society. As I began to see more and more of life on Kilimanjaro,
I, too, was put off by the attitude one often found in the literature that everything was far fairer, more moral, and more supportive in the preindustrial village
than in contemporary society. This was really a grumble about the modern world
read backwards. To present a more realistic view, I wrote a paper on old age on
Kilimanjaro (Moore 1978b). What preoccupied me was the meaning of spending all of one's days in a "life term social arena" with the same neighbors, in the
midst of the same village, always carrying an unforgettable personal history. As
I saw it, the social costs were as consequent as the social advantages.

Back to legal questions: in the mid-1970s a meeting of the Association of
Social Anthropologists focused on the outcome of dispute settlements. When
could the outcome be attributed to the superior political position or power of
one of the parties or when was the result determined by legal norms? It was a
discussion that pitted the views of Philip Gulliver (Professor of Anthropology
at UCL) about the politics of dispute against the more normative interpretation that had been expressed by Gluckman. The well-known book, *Rules and
processes*, by John Comaroff and Simon Roberts, addressed many of the issues
raised at this meeting (Comaroff & Roberts 1981).

My own paper dealt with a land dispute between two Chagga men, members of the same lineage, in which the wealthier, more educated individual tri-
umphed over his peasant cousin (Moore 1977a). The outcome was decided by a
local party official, a neighbor of the two men. I defined this particular dispute
settlement process as an "event of articulation," meaning that the local dispute
was linked through its mode of settlement with the larger party apparatus. I was
interested in the way Tanzanian socialism was reaching down to constituents.
What I hoped to do on a theoretical level was to encourage the classification of
various types of events in terms of their wider social effects. This was a modest
beginning of an answer to structural-functionalism. It concentrated on practical

social effects, rather than on vaguely defined contributions to social cohesion, and relied for its data on events rather than customary norms.

A YEAR AT YALE AND SOME NEW CONTACTS

In 1975–76, I was offered a professorship at Yale. My younger daughter was a student there, which made the offer doubly attractive. I agreed to come for a year hoping that a similar offer would materialize for Cresap. It did not, and we went back to California. But, by chance, that year was to provide me with two very important contacts, one was with a Mchagga who was getting his Ph.D. in the political science department, and the other was with a student in the anthropology department who had just returned from Mali.

The Chagga student was Justin Maeda, an astonishing young man who had already made an immense commitment to his education. He was the son of a man who had once been the mayor of Arusha, but the father was dead and there was no way that Justin could pay for a Western education. An opportunity arose when a Lutheran mission helped him to apply to a college in Sweden for a fellowship. He went to Sweden, learned the language, managed to get a college degree and came back to Tanzania. Then he taught in the propaganda college set up to retrain school principals and teachers in the right way to think about and teach socialism. After some years, he got a fellowship to study for his Ph.D. at Yale, where I met him. Before he visited me, he had never been invited into an American house. He was struggling to write an acceptable dissertation. I was able to help him. Later, when he became the Director of Development Studies at the University of Dar es Salaam and I was in Africa, I learned some unpublishable stuff about Tanzanian politics from him. We had limited contact, but his existence was a reassuring thing. Knowing him gave me some confidence about working in Tanzania during a very anti-American period in its history.

I felt some of the repercussions of this national policy on one of my visits to Kilimanjaro. I was there alone. I was followed on the mountain by a government security person. I was locked out of the court record room which had always been open to me previously. I was asked to report to the security officer in Moshi. I was also told that I must write out all the questions that I wanted to ask anyone during my fieldwork and submit these to the security person for approval. Life became quite difficult and the atmosphere was threatening. I stayed for a while, but not as long as I had intended. But as long as I did stay, I thought that if matters became difficult, if I were arrested, for example, I would try to get in touch with Justin. He knew how unpleasant things could become and indeed had told me before I left Dar es Salaam that if anything went wrong, I should flee to the home of his brother who lived near Arusha. At the time I could not imagine what he meant. But once I was on the mountain, being followed, I came to know what he was talking about. After some weeks of harassment, I decided to leave before anything serious happened. I was frightened. Some years later, the next time I went to Tanzania, the political climate had changed. The problems with the security people had evaporated and I was able to work undisturbed. I remained friends with Justin and met him and his wife in Nairobi while he was working for UNICEF which he continued to do for a number of years, serving in Harare and elsewhere.

The second person important to my future whom I met during that 1975–76 year at Yale, was John Van Dusen Lewis, the Yale graduate student who had just returned from Mali. As I will explain later, in 1991 he reappeared in my life and hired me as a consultant to work for the Club du Sahel in West Africa. I did so intermittently until 1997. In short, the year at Yale, while it was disappointing at the time because of the absence of a job for Cresap, had some very substantial benefits. We saw a lot of my daughter, Nicola. And, in addition to meeting Justin Maeda and John Lewis, I also came to know and like David Pilbeam and K.C. Chang who were professors in the Yale anthropology department. Both of them moved to Harvard soon after my 1975–76 year in New Haven.

UCLA AND HARVARD

In the meantime, back at UCLA, there was a move to recruit me from USC I suppose I became more desirable because I had been at Yale. In 1977, I moved from USC to UCLA. Some of those who opposed my UCLA appointment argued that there was no point to it because in the long run I would not stay. Their unease was prescient. In 1978, I went to Harvard as a visiting professor for the fall semester, half in the Law School and half in the Anthropology Department. In 1979 and 1980, I returned to Kilimanjaro to do more research. I returned to UCLA for the obligatory year after a leave, but accepted an appointment to a professorship in Harvard's anthropology department in 1981.

Cresap's mother passed away around the time we were considering the move. She left him some trust income. As a result, he realized that he could leave his professorship at UCLA without becoming financially dependent on me. He was eager for a change. Both of our daughters and much of the rest of our family lived on the East Coast, and we had a much loved summer cottage on Cape Cod, so there were more than scholarly motives for moving to Harvard.

In 1978, I gathered together a collection of my published papers, which was put out by Routledge as *Law as process* (Moore 1978a). A new essay served as an introduction. My interest was in the tension between an anthropology that emphasized the norms and symbols of culture as a fixed and determinate body of knowledge, and what I saw as an essential inconsistency with that view, i.e. the emerging anthropological work on agency in action and creativity and social imagination. That work emphasized that people had situational choices, could make up rules, and could create symbols and assign meanings to them. Established norms and symbols might prevail in some affairs, but there were many matters simultaneously in the cultural domain in which there was a certain normative indeterminacy. There were substantial implications here for the study of law in society.

By the time I moved to Harvard, I had for some time been hard at work on a book about a century of law on Kilimanjaro. It was not conventional at the time to combine ethnography with a historical account. I felt that an ethnography based only on the period of my own fieldwork would not tell enough of the story, for 1880 to 1980 had been a period of major economic and political transformation on the mountain. In precolonial times, Kilimanjaro had been a major site for caravans to rest and restock as they traveled from the coast to the interior and back. German colonial rule followed with intense activity by Lutheran and Catholic missionaries. There were also the beginnings of the introduction of coffee cultivation. Coffee growing continued apace in the British colonial period, and in the 1920s a Chagga coffee cooperative was formed to market the coffee. Independence in 1961 meant that socialism would rule under the government of Julius Nyerere. The landholding arrangements of the Chagga were heavily interlocked with their kinship practices, so that in land matters they had one foot in the cash economy and the other in traditional practices. The history was complex, and any account of their contemporary situation had to describe a mix of very modern preoccupations and traditional practices. I delivered the manuscript of *Social facts and fabrications: "Customary" law on Kilimanjaro, 1889–1980* to the Cambridge University Press in 1983, which was eventually published in 1986 (Moore 1986a).

From 1985 to 1989, Cresap and I were Masters of Dunster House, one of the residential houses in which Harvard undergraduates reside. But that was not the end of Harvard's administrative use of me. From 1986 to 1989, I was also

Dean of the Graduate School, with oversight of all of the University's doctoral programs. I continued to teach during all of this administrative work. It was not easy. The administration suggested I stop teaching, but I feared that this was the thin edge of a wedge to make me permanently into an administrator, something I did not want to become. Cresap managed much of Dunster House affairs with the administration's enthusiastic approval. I asked to be released from the Deanship, and was ultimately allowed to do so in 1989.

In 1990, I was shocked to see in the newspaper that Gibson Kamau Kuria had taken refuge in the American Embassy in Nairobi. He was a Kenyan human rights lawyer and had been a professor at the University. I had met him years before as I passed through Nairobi on my way to Tanzania. Originally I wanted nothing more than to discuss land rights and customary law in Kenya with him. He was teaching material related to that topic at the time. I knew nothing of his political activities. Later he was dismissed from the University and eventually was jailed by the Moi regime in 1987 because he filed a suit on behalf of two political detainees. In 1990, he was clearly in danger again. I decided to try to help him. I telephoned the Africa desk at the State Department, and explained that I would try to find him a place in the Human Rights Program at Harvard. They were keen to get him out of the Embassy and indicated that he would likely be allowed to leave. Henry Steiner, head of the Human Rights Program at the Law School, indicated that I would have to raise funds to support him, but provided me with the names of companies that might be willing to contribute. It all worked out, and he came to Harvard for a year or two, then returned to Nairobi to continue the fight for civil liberties. I have seen him since in Nairobi, and, of course, now that Moi is out of office Gibson's crowd of human rights lawyers has won prominence in the new government.

At Harvard, as House Master and Dean, I had very little time for my anthropological ambitions, but they were not modest. I wanted to change the perspective of ethnography, to find ways to make the sense of time more palpable. I used the events my Chagga interlocutors told me about, or that I witnessed as we went along, to construct a new methodological approach.

PROCESS AS AN ANTHROPOLOGICAL OBJECT

Having looked at a century of the history of Kilimanjaro and the recent introduction of socialism, I realized that my immediate ethnographic work was an attempt to witness the present as it was being produced, as a process. And I linked that process to what preceded it. To take ethnographic advantage of the specificity of time requires recognizing the importance of momentary local events, to judge their possible larger scale or longer term significance. I am not talking about events in the way that historians have often used the term, to refer to happenings that changed the course of history. I am talking about more ordinary events as opportunities for insight, events that might give unanticipated indications of what is going on. Ethnographers have long selected particular events, often collective events, usually as illustrations of points they want to make about the normative structure and customary practices of a society, viz. Clifford Geertz' (1972) famous cockfight paper. These are events used ethnographically as replicas of structures already known.

I was proposing something different, to install the collection of event-data as a regular fieldwork technique to *discover* what is going on, to give clues. The clues may lead to an alertness to trends on the small scale or a large scale. Of course, fighting, riots, house burnings, and the like are such events. But there are other, more mundane events. For example: is impatience with the government revealed in conversations about prices in the market? Do disputes over land suggest growing land shortage? When a young person dies, is the death attributed to AIDS or to supernatural malevolence or both? What does this indicate about the sources of knowledge for local people?

Event-data should supplement the fieldwork techniques that we already have available. These are happenings outside the anthropologist's control, unlike the answers to framed questions. Making sense of events is not only full of requirements for the ethnographer, but rewards her/him with unsought and unexpected meanings. Even stories about events that are not witnessed are rich in clues: "Let me tell you about how my uncle cheated his stepson." Wishing to promote such an addition to existing field methods, as president of the American Ethnological Society in 1987, I had my opportunity. I gave a paper that described what I called a processual approach to ethnography. I gave a name to the specific innovation I proposed, "diagnostic events," as the centerpiece of the approach (Moore 1987). I wanted to suggest a time-oriented method that could take the transitional, the temporary, the changing, into account, and examine its larger social ramifications, its more enduring consequences. I saw the need for a method that would include the possibility of capturing a moment as a moment in a stream of time, I also wanted to emphasize the element of selection by the ethnographer of the happenings that he thought particularly revealing—i.e., diagnostic, in relation to whatever particular question he wished to address—whose trajectory he wished to follow.

There can be false leads, of course, and unique events. But false leads will reveal themselves when one looks for further clues, for repeated indications of the direction in which things are going. The analysis of diagnostic events was to be an adjunct to the fieldwork study of process, the observation of segments of cumulative trends.

I continued to publish papers and to edit collections on various aspects of process and on the ethnography of the present. Some examples were, on the process of negotiation in disputes (Moore 1985, 1995), on the legitimation of Government and Party in Tanzania (Moore 1988), on the production of cultural pluralism (1987), on the reflection of historical change in property transactions (Moore 1989, 1991a), on the process by which a Chagga relative could be turned into a stranger in order to be disinherited (Moore 1991b), on the production of legal knowledge for and by colonial officers in Africa (Moore 1992), on a redefinition of culture (Moore 1993b), on moralizing states, meaning both political units and states of mind (Moore 1993a), on postsocialist micropolitics on Kilimanjaro in 1993 (Moore 1996), on how some human rights lawyers in Kenya prepared the way for future accountability in cases they knew they would lose (Moore 1998), and on the international production of authoritative knowledge for development policy (Moore 2001b, 2002). This writing has not been purely descriptive. Many of these papers used fieldwork material to give a picture of some part of the ethnographic present. But the material was always used to make methodological and theoretical points that lay beyond the description itself.

Looking at process means examining sequences. One of the most recent subjects on which I have reflected has been a set of development projects. Looking at such projects while they are under way amounts to redefining the ethnographic object. No longer is one looking at an ethnic group and its practices. Instead, one is looking at a planned intervention in an existing society. The focus becomes the story of the unfolding of the intended project, deformed by the milieu in which it is taking place.

This year (2005) the editors of *The Annual Review* asked me to write a general introductory essay for the current volume (Moore 2005). I chose to write about comparisons in anthropology. I wanted to show why comparisons seemed so simple to manage to writers in the nineteenth century and to anthropologists in the mid-twentieth but are so much more difficult to mount today. The explanation is in the difference in what is being compared. It is very difficult to compare the process by which half a dozen development projects move forward in completely different social settings. There are too many variables when one is dealing with an entity that is changing and takes context into account. For reasons of length, I had to cut all the historical background of this article, but the part of the article that concerns certain modern development projects remains.

I have long had an appetite for learning about directed change. That appetite was fed by many aspects of the study of law, and was related, of course, to my experience with Tanzanian socialism. There were further developments of this interest. From 1991 to 1997, my African involvement expanded beyond East Africa. I became a consultant on various francophone West African affairs. When I taught at Yale in 1975–76, I was the only Africanist in the anthropology department. At that time, by default and good fortune, I supervised the initial dissertation writing of John Van Dusen Lewis when he returned from fieldwork in Mali. We got along very well so that much later on, in 1991, to be exact, he recruited me for consulting work for the Club du Sahel in which he was an administrator and a major force. The fact that I spoke French was a great advantage. In connection with the Club, there were many organizational meetings, most of them in Paris, but we also met in Berlin and Montreal. I learned a great deal about the rhetoric of development from these meetings and some things about the practical problems that arose in the field. The Club was composed of a group of Sahelian countries, but it was financed by the US Department of State and the OECD.

As a consultant, I was sent several times to Burkina Faso, also to Mali, and to Senegal and the Cape Verde Islands. I worked with the Club on and off until 1997. On all of these consulting trips, which were short visits of two weeks or so at a time, I was given an assignment. I was asked to inquire into something in particular, and wrote a report when I returned. How is the decentralization policy working? How was the supervision of land tenure and land management going in the hands of a new administrative agency? The reports were all confidential and could not be published. But the great pleasure of working for John was that I could write whatever I wanted. I was not restricted in any way which meant that I could be critical of policy and could dictate my own conditions. There were a few such conditions. I said I would not take the job unless they were met. I asked that I not be confined to interviewing government officials. I would see these officials with politesse and pleasure, but I also wanted to visit some villages. Further, when going into the countryside, I wanted to be accompanied by someone who spoke the local language so that I could have some dialogue with the villagers. All of these demands were met. It was an ideal circumstance in which to have a quick look at conditions in West Africa.

My husband went with me on some of these assignments and identified himself to the Africans as my photographer. He also told them that he came along to make sure I would come back, which always made people laugh and put them at ease. Some of my writing in the 1990s refers to my experience in West Africa, both on the policy side and on the African side. In 1994, I published a small general book on the encounter between *Anthropology and Africa* (Moore 1994).

Apart from my fieldwork-derived writing, one of the things I have also done more than once is to try to summarize the state of the field of law and anthropology for colleagues and students. This, then, is another theme that recurs during my career. In 1969, I wrote the first article on law and anthropology to appear in what was then the Biennial Review of Anthropology (Moore 1969c). In 1986, I contributed an article to a book on *Law and the social sciences* on the classifications, typological interpretations and bibliographical resources having to do with the legal systems of the world (Moore 1986b). In 2000, I accepted the invitation of the Royal Anthropological Institute to give the Huxley Memorial Lecture, a retrospective look at a half a century of law and anthropology (Moore 2001a). And most recently, in 2004, Blackwells published a reader I edited and to which I contributed segments of instructive prose as well as the Huxley Lecture. Not surprisingly it is called *Law and anthropology* (Moore 2004).

My husband, Cresap, died in 2001, after fifty years of marriage, leaving a big hole in my heart and my life. I am close to my two daughters and to two charming grandchildren, Ben, sixteen years old and Sam, twelve. Most recently, I have also enjoyed many conversations in the frequent company of the sociologist Daniel Bell, and regularly derive much wisdom and warmth from the enduring friendship of the psychoanalyst Sanford Gifford. I have a whole host of other friends in the Cambridge community on whom I rely. Harvard generously allows me to keep an office in the Department so I stay in touch with sundry graduate students. I keep on writing. My past is very much with me. The Law School is mounting a conference on the Nuremberg trials this fall which I shall attend, and I managed to get to Africa for a holiday six months ago. I will therefore conclude that possibly, in a little while, there may well be a postscript to this memoir.

If I had to summarize in a few sentences the knowledge-products of this long career, I would choose those that are ongoing, since these ideas and variants of them seem to be very much in use. The first is surely the idea that to be comprehensible law must be thought of in anthropological terms, its remarkably ritualized procedures as well as the ambitions and conceptions of reality imbedded in its substance and expressed in its institutions. The second is the recognition that obligatory norms are created and enforced in ordinary social life, outside of legal institutions, but often have as much force as law for those people inside the semi-autonomous social fields that generate these norms. The third is the methodological strategy of seeking to identify diagnostic events in fieldwork. The fourth is the conception of fieldwork observation as the witnessing of process. And the fifth is the struggle to compare instances. Surely these ideas are all relevant to contemporary work. Who knows what will come of them?

CHAPTER TWO

Comparisons
Possible and Impossible

INTRODUCTION

In a provocative opener to a chapter on comparisons, Fredrik Barth wrote,

> Though anthropology is almost invariably characterized in textbooks as a comparative discipline, it is striking how unsympathetic social and cultural anthropologists of different theoretical persuasions are to each other's formal comparative operations, and how little agreement there has been on what might constitute "The comparative method in anthropology." (Bowen & Petersen 1999: 78; see also Burton & White 1987 and Herzfeld 2001)

In fact, the flourishing and fading of ethnographic comparison offer a rich illustration of changes in the methods and objectives of anthropology.[1] During

---

Editor's note: This chapter is a reprint of Moore, Sally Falk. 2005. "Comparisons: Possible and impossible." *Annual Review of Anthropology* 34: 1–11.

1. I thank Julia Elyachar, Cathy Hoshour, Michael Likosky, Bret Gustafson, and Sarah Robinson for patiently explaining the details of their ethnographic projects to this eager learner. I regret that the *Annual Review* did not have space to publish an earlier version of this article that reviewed the historical background of comparisons in anthropology. Such a history would have made even clearer the extent to which the work of these five people has been an innovative contribution to the discipline.

the nineteenth century, societies were compared in the hope of discovering the sequence of social evolution. By the mid-twentieth century, evolution was abandoned by all but a few anthropologists, and most comparisons were undertaken to describe the details of variation and difference in the ways of life of non-Western peoples. If the objective was to understand the whole range of the human experience, order had to be made out of this jumbled knowledge. For the purposes of comparison, the characteristics of each society were treated as stable, and typologies were generated. Overwhelmingly, the approach was synchronic.

But, if one fast-forwards to the present, new approaches to ethnography emerge. Many of these are concerned with processes over time. Transformations in the fieldwork scene are often observed or expected. What is in being is often compared with what existed before, even with what the situation might become. What matters to the anthropological observer is to follow the shifting form and the trajectory of the moving, interacting, social parts and the ideas that accompany them. The dynamic that sets things in motion is a major concern, for example, the growing interest in the reaction to political or economic shocks. These may be changes of regime such as the end of apartheid or the dismemberment of the former Soviet Union. These may be disruptions that create refugee streams or such economic transformations as the current expansion of Chinese industry. But mundane processes are also of interest. Although the specifics of time, place, and population are scrupulously reported, one ubiquitous puzzle is to discern the connections between local practices and larger-scale systems.

These new themes are easily identifiable in today's comparative literature. Thus, Chris Hann has assembled a group of papers on decollectivization in the postsocialist era and has concluded that, despite the radical changes, the process has resulted in the retention of significant values, "people actively strive to hold onto the valued elements of the older moral economy . . ." (Hann 2003: 37). However, there is more to it than that. "For many postsocialist citizens, markets have collapsed, and becoming the private owner of land is increasingly perceived to be a poor substitute for lost entitlements" (ibid.: 38). The papers in Hann's book show the process by which social variation was produced despite legal standardization.

In *Settling accounts*, John Borneman (1997: 144–45) compares postsocialist countries that had procedures for dealing with injustices committed in the socialist period with those countries that did not have such procedures. He proposes four criteria to explain different post-socialist outcomes:

(1) that accountability is central to the definition of democratic states . . . (2) that accountability is established in part through retributive justice: a reckoning with the past . . . (3) that retributive justice necessarily links prosecution of wrongdoing to the fate of the victims, whose dignity is reestablished through social and jural processes, and whose trust in the legal system is a key index of state legitimacy, and (4) that the failure to engage in retributive justice leads to cycles of retributive violence directed either against an internal scapegoat or an externally identified enemy

He uses comparative materials on East Germany and Eastern Europe to make the case that violence resulted in the countries in which procedures for addressing the injustices of the past did not exist.

Richard A. Wilson's *Human rights, culture and context* (1997) assembles a number of papers, some on the theoretical questions involved and some giving ethnographic descriptions with reference to entirely different parts of the world, such as Guatemala, Mauritius, and Hawaii. What does he make of these disparate examples? He says, "Human rights are not founded in the eternal moral categories of social philosophy, but are the result of concrete social struggles" (ibid.: 23). "The universality of human rights (or otherwise) becomes a question of context, necessitating a situational analysis . . . human rights doctrine does get reworked and transformed in different contexts" (ibid.: 12, 23).

Comparisons of the kind found in Hann, Borneman, and Wilson involve before and after accounts, providing a time-conscious ethnography. All three scholars set the theme of their inquiries in terms of what are or appear to be features common to all the instances they adduce. But their analyses focus mainly on the major differences of context and consequence observed. They are struck by the varied reworking of relationships and ideas, even where there is a common initial political, legal, or doctrinal concept that sets the trajectory in motion. The many variables involved make comparison problematic.

THE COMPARATIVE STUDY OF PROCESSES

These differences of context and consequence provide two opportunities for further comparative theoretical development. First is the detailed examination of attempts to shape the future; the second is the chance to wrestle further with the comparative study of process and the vexed questions of causality. Many actions observed in fieldwork have a future orientation; but actors' ideas about the future have not had as much ethnographic attention as they deserve. This may be changing, however. The growing interest in policy studies is one indication of anthropological concern with the formation of the future as a topic for serious ethnographic inquiry (see Shore & Wright 1997; Wedel & Feldman 2005).

Individual or collective acts, such as a country adopting a constitution, an individual writing a will, or someone being appointed to head a government department are attempts to shape the future. These acts involve conceptions of the future. But there are also many things that happen without this kind of definite advance conception, without the same degree of intentionality. The deforming of the planned and the formation of the unintended are outcomes familiar to everyone.

When processes are named, they are often identified by an end point—for example, the process of industrialization. Or they may be named for an ongoing condition such as the process of competition. Identifying processes in this way implies that they can be distinguished from other simultaneous happenings and separated for analysis. To what extent is this separation possible? What can anthropology make of this moving track? And what can it make of the ongoing unfolding and processing of ordinary life, of the mundane functioning of institutions? In some parts of the world politicians and scholars alike put a positive gloss on ongoing shifts by identifying them as "modernization."

Clifford Geertz (1995: 137) states that achieving modernity "is a process, a sequence of occurrences that transforms a traditional way of life, stable and self-contained, into a venturous one, adaptive and continuously changing, and it is as such, as *modernization* that it has appeared in the social sciences." The road to modernity was

> less simple, the road less smooth and unidirectional . . . a surprise only to enthusiasts—theorists of national liberation, peasant revolution, or economic take-off into endless growth. . . . Modernity turned out to be less a fixed destination than a vast and inconstant field of warring possibilities, possibilities neither simultaneously reachable nor systematically connected, neither well defined nor unequivocally attractive. "Becoming modern" was not just closing gaps or negotiating stages, mimicking the West or growing rational. It was laying oneself open to the imaginings of the age and then struggling to realize them. Finding a course, not following one. (ibid.: 138)

> The way we live now is a stage in a vast historical proceeding with an intrinsic dynamic, a settled direction, and a determinate form. (ibid.: 137)

Geertz is clear about the fact that the classics of social science, those of Adam Smith, Marx, Weber, and Durkheim, "did not altogether agree as to what the dynamic, direction and form were" and that those who followed were also divided on this matter. Then, however, he turns to the way the postcolonial world saw modernization as an idea, rather than the social scientist's view of it as a historical process. He considers the wide appeal of such an idea. "The modernization idea seemed especially well made, convenient at once to ex-masters and ex-subjects anxious to state their inequalities in a hopeful idiom" (ibid.: 137, 139).

Behind the observations of ethnographers today there is an awareness of such ideas and their attraction, an awareness of the effective presence of national and transnational politics, of world religions, population movements, international trade, ecological disaster, and much more. Linking such large-scale processes to ongoing smaller-scale sequences may, however, demand more understanding of causality than anthropology can muster, and yet the question must be asked.

The challenge to ethnography presented by the scale and impact of global situations, planned and unplanned, is attracting much attention and academic puzzlement (Burawoy 2000; Moore 2001b). As Akhil Gupta & James Ferguson have observed, to transcend the specificity of local observations, anthropologists today must situate themselves in the midst of an enormous variety of knowledge forms (1997: 38). Tapping such resources is essential. Information about the translocal circumstances apprehended only at a distance is necessary to consider a broad causal context. In fact, for some decades, many anthropologists have regularly practiced this enlarged "shifting locations" approach to fieldwork hailed by Gupta & Ferguson (ibid.: 38).

FORMING THE FUTURE: PROCESS IN FIVE CASES

To illuminate some of the comparative problems of a processual approach, I sketch below the outlines of five relatively new fieldwork reports of particular merit. Each of the five reports came from an anthropologist observing in midstream a planned project for social change. Obviously, such projects, because they are inserted into ongoing societies, are bound to be affected, if not radically reshaped, by the milieu. Also, because an explicit change is the objective, the before-and-after comparison is critical to the definition of the enterprise. Many such projects involve the implementation of public policy, national or international. To the extent that they are national, they reflect aspects of the character of the state, particularly if the state is perceived not only as a durable structure of organization in the Weberian sense, but also as "part of a discourse of contested political claims" (Hobart 1987: 33).

Different in origin and purpose, each project describes an explicitly declared objective, a vision of how to form the future in a particular sector. These anthropologists focused their attention on the side developments that emerged on the way to the designated objective. These side developments constitute the theme that links these five otherwise disparate projects. The ancillary activities were taken together with the thrust of the plans as part of the ongoing process. The importance of these unplanned add-ons, and the way they were inserted and attached themselves and infiltrated and transformed the intended project in each case, is central to each story.

Scholars and laymen alike know that planned social interventions generally produce some unexpected results. That is not the point being made here. The anthropologists involved in these studies were exploring the methodological implications of defining an ongoing social project as the ethnographic field of observation. They were examining a domain of activity and following the process as it moved along. They were tracking the modifications and emendations of what might be called "the cultures of control" that were being used to form the future (in this connection see Cooper & Packard 1997 on development).

What kinds of projects do the cases below address? To compress the description for the purposes of this review, I follow a theme close to the question of control as it crosses all the cases: the theme of accountability. This theme brings out some of the political contrasts between the instances because accounting is one of the means through which claims and struggles about control, and discourses about meanings, are expressed (see Maurer 2002). Accounting is therefore a broadly useful way of resorting the data to present a glimpse of the issues. Allowing for very different understandings of accountability to emerge, it becomes apparent that demanding an accounting not only serves official purposes, but also can serve as a protest tactic against official action.

An Egyptian instance

Julia Elyachar (2002, 2003, 2005) describes a situation in Cairo involving two very different demands for an accounting, one small-scale and one large-scale. The small-scale demand is put forward by the master of a car-repair workshop who wants to assert what he conceives as his rights to a piece of land. He wants the Governorate to show its map of the distribution of land. He goes to a government office to further his cause and demands to see a proper map so that he can make his claims. The functionary he approaches "cannot find the map" though the office in which he works is the official place where such records are supposed to be kept.

The other demand for an accounting is on a different scale—not from bottom up but top down. It emanates from the World Bank, which is pouring money into the so-called informal economy of Egypt and wants to know how many microenterprises there are (such as the one headed by the master of the car workshop). The Bank, quite understandably, wants to know how its money is or is not reshaping the Egyptian economy. In other words it wants to map the economy into a set of categories it has defined. But for reasons of inefficiency and disorganization (if not corruption) and fictive categorization, neither the territorial map nor the economic map can be found. No full accountings can be made.

The Indonesian transmigration program

Cathy Ann Hoshour's description of part of a vast Indonesian resettlement program shows in detail why an accounting of land distribution at the new sites could be neither demanded nor obtained (Hoshour 2000). She describes the ways in which "informal" practices of local officials that do not conform to the rules and policies of the central administration have become normalized. In Indonesia's transmigration program the plan was to move large segments of the population from the "inner" islands to "outer" islands to relieve population pressure and to improve their economic situation. The lands to which these segments of the population were to move were officially characterized as largely unoccupied, though in fact they were occupied.

Two categories of migrants seeking land were moved to the "outer" island of Sumatra: a set of Sumatrans and a set of nonlocal transmigrants. Fixed percentages of the two populations were prescribed by law as eligible for land. Those rules were not obeyed by the allocating bureaucrats. Non-local migrants were favored in the allocation of land, a circumstance that led to much bitter resentment. In the midst of much dispute about who was to receive which lands, a lively market grew in the sale of land entitlement documents, called "packets." These were photocopied, and copies were sold as if they were originals, so the same piece of land was frequently allocated more than once. When Hoshour left there were fewer than 200 unallocated land packets left in the projects, but there were more than 2000 persons who had documentary confirmation that they were entitled to one of these pieces of land.

Obviously, adherence to the official rules and plans of the transmigration program for distribution, and indeed for eligibility, eluded practice. New rules and transformed practices had become normal. Local officials developed their own version of criteria for land distribution and redefined eligible migrants' rights as they saw fit. As implementers whose dominated subjects had no recourse, their official position and the cumulative effects of their practices caused their invented forms of regulation to become normal. The people in the social field they controlled had no means of demanding an accounting, and the central government looked the other way for its own reasons.

Malaysia's ambitions

Michael Likosky (2005) describes a set of Malaysian government strategies designed to capture the approval of an international audience of business men and investors. Elaborate arrangements surround the plan to change Malaysia into a high-technology center. Likosky shows that the plan incorporates two very different attitudes toward accountability, one responsive to international standards and the other disregarding them. The particular project he examines is the Malaysian multimedia super corridor, designed to attract industry.

Here the accountability question can be asked in two contexts: in a human rights context and in a commercial context. Likosky points out that by Western standards, Malaysia has a blatant disregard for human rights and the rights of workers. But he also traces the extensive measures taken to attract investment and reassure investors that they are investing in a responsible regime and that their money will be safe. One of the measures taken is to establish an International Advisory Board. The notion is that the membership of the International Advisory Board is so commercially respectable that its reputation will rub off on the Malaysian government project. From the official Malaysian point of view, the existence of the advisory board would curtail foreign criticism. It would show the world that even though Westerners believe that the Malaysian government treads on the rights of some of its citizens, such ideas are the result of Western prejudice.

The advisory board is there, among other things, not only to drum up business and investment, and to put Malaysia in direct touch with international business networks, but to objectify Malaysian accountability and reliability in commercial matters. This they offer to counter suppositions that might grow out of its bad reputation on civil rights and unease about its financial viability.

Bolivia: Incorporating minorities

Bret Gustafson's study addresses a Bolivian educational program. The program was designed to integrate its non-Latino population into the national stream through bilingual education (2001, 2002). The state's bilingual education program was a demonstrable rejection of a past in which minority ethnic groups with their own languages were politically peripheralized and the Latinos dominated everything.

Bolivia wishes to be seen by the world as a responsible democracy, caring for all its people. It wants the broad constitutional reforms it has enacted to show that minority ethnic groups will be able to participate in its affairs. It also wants this reform to be recognized by the international community. By these means, Bolivia is imposing democracy from the top down. The program has not been passively received. Rather, democratization has been seized by minority groups as an opportunity to make claims on the government.

Gustafson considers the ways in which the political careers of persons in the educational bureaucracy found new expression in the bilingual education project. And he addresses the political opportunities linguistic facility presented for the ethnic Guarani. He notes the proliferation of indigenous organizations that have sprung up to make Guarani claims heard, claims for more ethnic recognition, for land and territory, and in the background, possibly for oil and gas rights. The democratization and bilingual education projects have indirectly stimulated the construction of many modalities through which the Guarani can make their demands known. They claim that the Bolivian government should be accountable to them. Yet was this what the enthusiasts for bilingual education anticipated?

Regulating fishing in the US Northeast

In the final case to be discussed here, Robinson addresses the regulation of the fishing industry in New England and the enormous efforts by the US government to obtain the consent of the fishing population affected by the changes (Robinson 2000). The purpose of the current regulatory measures was to limit

fishing so as to give the devastated fish population a chance to breed and rees-
tablish itself. What is astonishing after a review of the struggles that surround
instances of nonaccountability from outside Western Europe and the US is to
see how many institutionalized avenues of accountability are, in fact, officially
involved in this federal government project.

First of all, many nonofficial persons were drawn into the process of generating regulations. There are regional councils, which have official and nonofficial
members. There are other interested councils, such as the Environmental Defense Council, which are alert to local and long-term interests. Every effort is
made to produce transparency and to generate consensus on the part of local
people to the regulations that will affect their livelihood. There are innumerable
public meetings and public hearings, and if the results of this democratic collaboration do not reach satisfactory agreements, and objections to the regulations
or the procedures remain, there are institutionalized settings where objections
can be voiced. Congress can be lobbied. Lawsuits can be filed in the courts.

Here, accountability for regulation and its effects is built into the regulatory process itself. The citizenry enthusiastically asserts itself as do the many
administrative agencies concerned. Social and administrative careers are made
and unmade. There are what seem to be permanent issues, permanent public
conversations. The debate goes on.

COMPARING CULTURES OF CONTROL IN ACTION

These five cases, taken together, are accounts of very different plans and practices mobilized to form the future. The cultures of control they illustrate differ
locally, and they differ in their chains of connection with global affairs.

> Radicals and skeptics alike write history by postulating changes or continuities
> at the global level that are presumed to imprint themselves on the local level.
> We have found no such isomorphism between local and global. At both levels
> movement is manifold and multiple, combined and reversible, uneven and un-
> predictable. We therefore work in the opposite way, ascending from the local to
> the global by stitching together our ethnographies. (Burawoy 2000: 343)

What can be said about these five case histories as a collection? First, they are
offered together to show that the extended context of each project, its total

immediate surrounding and beyond, with all of its peculiarities included, must be taken into account if the nature of the ultimate organizational forms, and of the composite aggregate, is to be understood.

Second, in all the fieldwork instances cited here, the unit of study is not a project to be, but the process of its implementation and the accumulating additions to the initial intention. The project is observed at a particular point in time, one that was under way before the research started and one that will continue when the research grants run out. Emphasis is given to the diversions of plan and purpose that emerge as matters proceed. The deepening and solidifying of special interests and strategies develop apace, and what began as something unusual and "on the side" may intensify and become part of a set of normal expectations, a part of the scheme of things. In each case, the cumulative, combined direction in which the process is moving is an outstanding feature of each analysis. The possible, or even likely, trajectory of the future is only suggested. At what point in the sequence can one make such judgments? The cases seem to ask whether they can be made at all.

Third, the cases make clear that the stylized representations of what is going on are often as important as the operations themselves. The representations are in fact not just packaging. In this kind of regulatory setting the packaging is part of the product, and legitimation is an inherent part of the discourse. It is a part of the " . . . production of truth in our current regime of power" (Rabinow 1984: 241, paraphrasing Foucault). These are studies of the "cultures of control" in settings in which the practical consequences are dramatically visible.

As one might expect, the "cultures of control" of governments have a considerable legal dimension. For legal studies in anthropology this amounts to a major shift of focus, out of the courtroom and into the world. The ongoing process implicates forms of control other than governmental. This is not the study of disputes, although disputes figure in all these settings. This is not the study of judicial, legislative, and administrative rules, although many rules are involved. The multi-sited approach here provides a view of the state, not as a totality, but as an organizer of particular projects. In every instance a struggle exists about the organization and management of the program. The data are specific, grounded, and extended.

The cases briefly presented here address the issue of state control. The turbulent diversions that accompany the unfolding of the projects and the imbedded struggles for control that manifest themselves at the heart of things are as much a part of the projects as the directed social formulations envisioned at the start. The combination is a sociological commentary on the possibilities of and limitations on intentional social direction.

These five projects are not comparable in any sense in which earlier forms of anthropological comparison were undertaken. The projects all attempt to accelerate modernization in some domain and to give it a particular stamp. They are created to change matters. They are not instances of ethnic "custom" to be compared in the Radcliffe-Brown manner. Just the opposite, they are creating new relationships. As the projects become embedded over time, new structures are formed, some in the original plan and some not. In every case, a supplement to the designed form has been created out of it, on top of it and on its side. This supplement is parasitical in the original project. It may divert some resources, and it may alter to some extent the direction in which the project was proceeding. All the supplementary structures disturb the original purposes. They are diversions as well as accretions.

Bringing literacy to the Guarani has also brought them into transnational contact with the political activism of other ethnic minorities. Their political claims are not what the literacy program foresaw. In Malaysia, the supplementary structure of organizational legitimizers has come to have a life of its own, and among other things, "demands for democratization were reframed as public relations challenges" (Likosky 2005: 180). Regulating fishing in Massachusetts has produced innumerable organizations to express community and environmental reactions in a democratic manner. The distribution of land in Sumatra has generated a market for printed "titles" and a set of corrupt practices by local officials. By losing files and documents Egyptian bureaucracies have found innocent-appearing ways to thwart land claims and the programs that depend on them.

These cases emphasize the unplanned activities that attached themselves to the ongoing proceedings. By inserting themselves deeply, such activities become part of the whole trajectory—the situational dimension of processual combinations. Are the responses and diversions as much a part of the process of reaching for modernity as the projects themselves? The reactions noted here are not, on the whole, forms of resistance to the original projects, nor are they attempts to stop them. They are outgrowths of them, responses to them, and accretions on them.

Taken together, these cases illustrate two major tendencies in contemporary anthropology: the tendency to treat ongoing activities in an observable social field as an object of fieldwork and the tendency to incorporate, as part of the interpretation, a wide sociopolitical context that is not necessarily observed. The case studies inspect the state not as a whole, which is impossible, nor simply as imagined, but through specific, operative projects of the state to insert certain reforms. The modern state is seen neither only in Weberian terms as an overarching form of the organization of domination, nor only as a sovereign keeper of public order and collector of taxes, but as an instigator and implementer of multiple projects. But this way of seeing the state quickly reveals the incapacities of the state as well as its powers, the competitions for control in the same fields of action, the surrounding fallout from its moves as well as its direct impact. A few years ago, looking at states and their misconceptions, James Scott (1998) focused on "How certain schemes to improve the human condition have failed." The case studies here are not concerned with success or failure, but with what attaches to these schemes, what grows at the heart of the project activity. Although these case studies are not used to practice some sort of metonymic sociology in which the part is taken for the whole, the projects, by merely existing, qualify any description of the state that launched them. Here, the state is treated as a composite, and the projects are treated as significant components of the composite. These case studies of processes at the local level provide insight into the quality of organization on the large scale.

Although the cases take as the point of departure a governmentally defined societal "problem" and the official programmatic "solution," they also address the accompanying circumstances in which the State is operating. The context looms larger than the projects. The cases involved are studies of process, broadly understood, local, national, and global. The cluster of persons and activities surrounding the programs is looked at along with the larger milieu. The surrounding situation includes those who define and implement the program and those who are affected by it, but the situational description extends to those in the larger scene who are doing other kinds of business and may use the project for their own schemes. The intertwining of these mixed motivations and mixed intentions characterizes the process.

If we are comparing processes, we are entering a domain of comparison radically different from those of past ethnographers. The processes described here were imbedded both in projects and in the wider context in which they were undertaken. The processual approach redefines the object of study, addresses the passage of time, and often makes comparison problematic. "The use of comparison in contemporary anthropology is more akin to the unselfconscious, commonsensical comparison of everyday judgment, than to the formal cross-cultural comparison of analytically defined variables. This being so, it also shares with everyday judgment its lack of rigour . . ." (Holy 1987: 16). It could be worse.

CHAPTER THREE

Encountering Suspicion in Tanzania

My fieldwork in Tanzania extended over many years, from 1968 to 1993. It was intermittent, a few months at a time, and then an interval of months, or a year or two, and then another visit. The reflexive remarks that follow are retrospective and selective. There are too many stories to tell.

The first summer I was accompanied by my husband and two teenaged daughters; they refused to be left behind. The advantage: I could "show" my family to my Chagga acquaintances and demonstrate that I was an ordinary human being in an extraordinary situation. They understood that in my "real life" I was a teacher. On later trips when I went to Kilimanjaro, it was sometimes with my husband, sometimes alone.

We lived in a very shabby old hotel on Kilimanjaro, in Marangu, just at the end of the only paved road from the town of Moshi, twenty-five miles away. I had breakfast and dinner there. The hotel kitchen packed me a hardboiled egg and some fruit and bread to take with me for lunch. I would eat it wherever I happened to be and share it with whomever. It was a basic form of Chagga politeness to share. Even very small children are taught this fundamental

Editor's note: This chapter is a reprint of Moore, Sally Falk. 2009. "Encountering suspicion in Tanzania." In *Being there: The fieldwork encounter and the making of truth*, edited by John Borneman and Abdellah Hammoudi, 151–82. Berkeley: University of California Press.

principle. From them I accepted mushy half-chewed bits of banana as their mothers watched. After a time, the kitchen began to produce more than one egg and more than one slice of bread for my lunch packet. During this period of fieldwork, I had no worries.

But my mood was not consistent. Over the years, I went from completely comfortable and confident, to uneasy, to frightened, and back. What is clear is that the objective information I collected about the Chagga and published about that period in Tanzanian history stands (Moore 1986a). I disdained reflexivity in writing, because I considered it my job to observe and report on Chagga affairs, not to document my own experience. I wanted what I had to say to be something others could confirm. The ingredients of a more personal narrative were greatly restricted at the time by the political implications of publishing such materials.

For one thing, I wanted to be able to return to Tanzania, and I did not want my comments to include material that might lead to being refused research permission. For another, I did not want anything I had to say to be used to harm anyone. I met my quota of dunderheads in the bureaucracy who claimed moral superiority as they spouted the clichés of the new socialism, and I met plenty of property owners ready to cheat their closest relatives, but I was not going to write about any of them in ways that would make them identifiable.

I thought the fact that I was a white American, hence politically suspect, meant that anything not directly relevant to an impersonal objectivist account should be deleted. The uneasiness about whatever might imperil my research permission was a continuous concern. I thought that to keep one's head down and make oneself as inconspicuous as possible was the way to go, though there is no way that a white person can be inconspicuous in an African country. Enough time has passed so that I can now write about my experience without the worries I had in the past.

There is something inherently weird about many a fieldwork situation. Intruding on the lives and affairs of communities of strangers, even when they are cheerfully willing to have one do so, is not a normal way of making friends. The Chagga understood very well that I was collecting information about their way of life for scholarly purposes. They also understood that this had a professional rationale, that it would somehow further my career. They were not shy about asking me who was paying for me to be there.

What I did not anticipate was the extent to which I became privy to activities that were illegal, or disapproved, by the new socialist regime of Julius Nyerere and his government. Most of these activities were entirely commonplace in the communities with which I had contact. Even the local members of officialdom were unperturbed by them. I was much more shocked than they were.

For example there was the matter of *masiro*. The newly introduced philosophy of landholding prohibited the local custom of lending a plot of land with the expectation of having it returned one day. *Masiro* was a ritual gift presented annually to anyone from whom one had borrowed a plot of land. This was a way of recognizing that the original owner had title—i.e., had continuing rights in the land. Indeed the original owner could reclaim the plot if he had the means to compensate the occupier for any improvements that had been made. The government had abolished all title, saying that all land belonged to "all the people." It followed that the payment of *masiro* was illegal because it acknowledged the existence of ownership as distinct from the use of a plot.

Of course people went on paying *masiro* secretly and thus memorialized a whole web of contingent rights in land that the state not only did not recognize, but prohibited. Any *masiro* paying constituted a political insult to the land law project of the new regime. I did not tell anyone about the instances of which I knew. That would have turned these matters into public issues. I was more than discreet, if anything, self-effacing. And I was pleased with the result of my silent complicity. I felt that I was trusted. That was my conception of my local place until the political wind changed in the middle and late 1970s.

I should add that in the eyes of some of the African scholars I met at the University of Dar es Salaam, I was suspect from the beginning for very different reasons. Not only was I an American but I was identified with the Chagga and their reputation for insufficient enthusiasm for the regime. The Chagga had their reasons. For one thing they had been dealt a terrible blow by the national educational policy. The Chagga had long been very keen on getting an education for their children. In the colonial days when school had to be paid for, they made considerable sacrifices to put at least one child into the system. After President Nyerere and socialism came in, elementary school became universal and free. That made the Chagga very happy. But the bad news was that higher education was virtually cut off for them. The proportion of educated Chagga in schools and in public positions was considered too large. To rectify this imbalance for the next generation, places in upper schools were reserved for children from ethnic groups that were not sufficiently represented in the national scene. Excluding the Chagga from eligibility for higher education was a form of ethnic affirmative action. Understandably, the Chagga resented this. They tried to start some independent schools and were refused permission.

At the University of Dar es Salaam, the excitement about Nyerere and his program was so great among the persons committed to African Socialism that even this understandable resentment was not forgiven. After all, the policy was for the good of the state. And when I reported some goings-on on Kilimanjaro that did not conform to their conception of the situation, they responded by saying, "Oh well, that is just the Chagga; what else can you expect?"

My research was sponsored by successive deans of the Law School at the University of Dar Es Salaam. I was known to be an anthropologist, but my law degree trumped the rest. Anthropology was thought to have been the handmaiden of colonialism and was anathema. I was fortunate to obtain official permission to study the social context and history of law on Kilimanjaro. There were very few Americans admitted. Even the Peace Corps was expelled.

The Chagga of Kilimanjaro were well known, and their adaptation to the new laws that came with socialism was patently worth exploring. Much earlier in the century, in the 1920s, to be exact, they had organized one of the first African-run cooperative societies in the continent. For decades they sold their crop of coffee into the world market through this cooperative, and gradually moved further into a partially monetized economy. I was impressed with the co-op's success and the fact that it was not run by outsiders, but by Africans themselves.

Before I started my fieldwork I assumed that the existence of the cooperative would make the Chagga especially welcoming of a socialist at head of state. I was wrong. "They do not need to teach us *ujamaa*. We already have *ujamaa*," they said. "*Ujamaa*" was the term used for socialism. They meant that the *ukoo*, the patrilineal lineage (often localized), and the neighborhood—i.e., the sub-village—were the foci of cooperation, and they felt they did not need the Party to reorganize them into cooperative communities

To prepare myself for fieldwork I had read what was available in the library about the Chagga, and I wondered why there was not a full monograph about them by an anthropologist. Two anthropologists had done studies on Kilimanjaro. One was Michael Von Clemm, whose dissertation at Oxford was closed to all readers because he feared it contained material that might be damaging to some Chagga individuals. The second was a man named I. Kaplan who published very little on his experiences. He had apparently promised the Chagga chief Marealle to send him a copy of his dissertation when it was finished.

Marealle sighed when he told me about Kaplan, "Now it has been seventeen years, and I have heard nothing."

What there was in the way of information available to me was a very large tome on the subject of Chagga law by a remarkable German missionary. It described material from the precolonial nineteenth century to 1916 (Gutmann 1926). There were also the writings of travelers: a book by the British colonial officer, Sir Charles Dundas (1924), and a very useful history of the rivalries between various Chagga chiefdoms by Kathleen Stahl (1964). Reading Gutmann in California in preparation for my first trip, I thought that the descriptions of Chagga traditions he gave were of a world that had surely passed completely. I was expecting that the Chagga would have discarded the whole of their exotic past and opted for a socialist philosophy, literacy in Swahili, a cash economy and Christianity. I was wrong.

Chagga modernity was selective. Since the principal way in which the Chagga obtained the plots of land on which they depended for a living was through kinship, through inheritance, many of the traditional customs attached to kinship remained. And in spite of being nominally Christian, substantial dimensions of otherworldly belief were not abandoned. The ancestral dead could easily affect the lives of the living.

Why did this people not get the attention of anthropologists? Was it that they were not primitive enough to be of interest? In the 1960s it was still the fashion in some quarters of anthropology to seek out the least modernized people for study. After all, they would represent the *real* Africa, the original state of being, not some transformed product of exposure to colonial ways. When I told Meyer Fortes about my plan to go to Kilimanjaro he said, with evident disdain for my choice, "I bet they all wear pants." I took seriously the "modern," prosperous vision of them that was imparted by the Yale anthropologist, George Murdock. Murdock had visited Tanzania. He described in glowing terms the modern building in Moshi town that housed the cooperative headquarters. He was impressed. But the building spoke to the prosperity of the cooperative. It did not tell much about the residents of the mountain.

I was determined to learn about their situation. But before I get on with describing my fieldwork labors, I want to introduce the reader to some unsettling stories. These represent the general atmosphere in which I lived and worked. What went on around me, particularly in the 1970s was quite disturbing. These anecdotes intimate that underneath the peaceful life in the countryside there was an underlying disorder that might seep, perhaps even burst, into my life.

The ideals of African socialism generated immense enthusiasm in Tanzania and overseas. But in the end, despite the continuous reiteration of the ideology, the policies and practices of the government did not deliver what was promised.

ANECDOTE #1

One day, in the seventies, when I was in Dar es Salaam, I went out to the University to see the young man who had recently been appointed Director of Development Studies. We were old friends. I had known Justin Maeda in the U.S. when he was a Ph.D. student at Yale in the department of political science. He was a Mchagga (Mchagga, singular for Chagga person, Wachagga, plural for Chagga people, Chagga, the term without prefixes used in English to designate the people). He was a very serious, hard-working fellow who had, through a Lutheran connection, gone to Sweden, learned Swedish, and obtained an undergraduate degree from a Swedish university. (How's learning Swedish to show a zest for education!) Then, for a time, he became a teacher in a Dar es Salaam political education college. It was an educational unit organized by the government for the instruction of those who needed a short course in the values of African socialism, for example, for the principals of the schools and others in responsible positions. Getting that job was a real show of political favor.

In 1975–76, when we met, I was teaching at Yale, and I had already been to Kilimanjaro a number of times. The Political Science Department asked me if I would help him with his thesis. I agreed to do it; to read each chapter as he produced it and to give him general advice. He was writing up case studies of villages he had visited. They were villages that had been reorganized to fit the *ujamaa* model, the socialist model of what a village should be. One village had succeeded economically, others had not. When he wrote his first draft, his purpose was plainly to please the government, to tell them that the *ujamaa* model was a glorious experiment. His prose read like a political brochure. It was an appalling replication of government speeches and texts, no doubt rather like what he had been teaching at the government political college. Yale's political scientists were not pleased.

However, in the footnotes, and in the tables of numbers, what was plain was that the successful village had been successful before it became an *ujamaa* village, and that the others, having no such luck, were, in various degrees, failures. I persuaded him that he should be more candid, should put the data that was in the footnotes in the text, and should eliminate some of the propaganda. I told him that he was young and that political change would probably come in his time, and that the propaganda in his thesis might not have a long shelf life. Be that as it may, I told him he should write about what he actually saw, not the political commentary, that he had good data and that that should be the focus. He should believe in his thesis.

He revised it accordingly and got his degree. Needless to say, with a Ph.D. from Yale in a country that had very few people with graduate degrees, his career in Tanzania was assured. He soon found himself the Director of Development Studies at the University of Dar. I had, by that time, begun to understand something of the Tanzanian strategy about Development. In the governmental reform that came with socialism, development agencies were created to match every existing department of government. Rather than dismantling existing ministries and incurring the hostility of everyone who worked for them, the ministries were left more or less intact, but a parallel "government" was more generously funded in the form of development programs. The task of the Institute of Development Studies was to survey the country's development projects, compare them, and report on them to the Government, to see whether they were carrying out the directives of the state, and with what success. It was a substantial enlargement of my friend's Ph.D. project.

When I saw him in his office, he was very welcoming, and I was very glad to see him. We exchanged family news. I told him what I was up to on the mountain. And he told me about his department. But toward the end of our conversation he had something surprising to say. He told me that if I ran into trouble, I should flee and take refuge with his brother who lived in a rural area near Arusha, not far from Kilimanjaro. He gave me details about how to get in touch with the brother whom I had never met. I was astonished by the implicit warning. There had been no intimations of such trouble on previous visits. But I was glad to know he and his family would be ready to help, should it become necessary. I left the campus and went back to town. I was suddenly worried. What threatening possibilities did he have in mind? What could happen?

ANECDOTE #2

Unfortunately I cannot remember the exact date at which I saw soldiers accosting young girls in Moshi town. I know that it was in the 1970s. The soldiers appeared to be tearing at the girls' clothes, ripping the hems of their skirts. I could not imagine what they were doing. Later I found out what was going on when one of the soldiers approached me. He said I should be arrested because my skirt was too short. He told me that there was a campaign on to make women dress more modestly. Short sleeves, a *décolletage*, all these were considered immoral. I had heard that this campaign had originated with the Muslims on the coast, but now it seemed to be official policy. My offense was that my skirt did not cover my knees.

Up in the countryside where I lived and worked, the soldiers were never seen, so I never took the reports of a campaign seriously. Nor did anyone else. I had never been approached before. But in the town the soldiers got on with the work of making women conform. Apart from accosting young girls, the real fun for the soldiers was to capture a tourist, anyone who was white. I took refuge in a shop where I could buy a newspaper, but the soldiers followed me. Fortunately, by chance, I was leaving Tanzania a few days later and I was only in Moshi to make some last minute arrangements. I told them I was not staying and would they please leave me in peace. They did.

When I got back to the hotel by bus to finish packing, I was told about some people who had not been so lucky. A white couple who were driving in their car were stopped and pulled out by some of the soldiers on the morality campaign. Their hemlines were inspected and the tightness of trousers assessed. Their clothes were deemed immoral. They were both arrested, and their car was impounded. They were told to leave the country.

Of course, a few years later, the next time I returned to Tanzania, there was no short skirt campaign. That any of this had happened was barely remembered. I went on about my ethnographic business (in a longer skirt) without any trouble.

ANECDOTE #3

From the start, I was living high in the banana belt in a seedy old hotel at the end of the macadam road that comes up the mountain from Moshi town, about twenty-five miles away. The hotel was surrounded by the homesteads and gardens of the Chagga. It was not possible to rent one of these small houses in the villages because Nyerere denounced landlordism as a wicked capitalist way to make a living. So rather than offend, I settled for the inelegant hotel which was often empty.

As part of the final decolonization effort, it was Tanzania's policy to African-ize all organizations. Thus the old German lady who owned and ran the hotel on Kilimanjaro was told to look for an African whom she could make the manager of her hotel. There had been various attempts to get her into trouble so that the hotel could be confiscated and taken over by envious others with Party connec-tions. She was a Tanzanian citizen so her possession of it was entirely legal at the time, and those who tried to wrest it from her control were not successful, though they certainly tried to get hold of it.

Among the tourists who arrived one day was another old German lady. Few German tourists ever came so the company was particularly welcome. The owner and the guest chattered away and seemed to like one another. The visi-tor had come to the mountain because she wanted to affix a plaque on a rock somewhere on the mountain in memory of her father, Hans Meyer. He was said to be the first European to have climbed Mount Kilimanjaro. He had done his explorations in the 1880s and 1890s. He established that the ice fields of Kibo, one of the peaks, were already decreasing rapidly

Global warming has done the rest. I am told that now much of the snow and ice have vanished.

Meyer's daughter had an African driver who had brought her to the hotel and had previously taken her touring in the country. She liked the driver and she proposed him as the Perfect Candidate for the job of hotel manager. He had been to secondary school. He spoke English. He was courteous and entirely presentable. He was not a Mchagga, but she said that did not matter. The hotel owner was pleased to have her manager problem solved.

The young man was hired and given one of the small cottages that were at-tached to the hotel as a place to stay. All the other hotel help were Wachagga and did not live on the premises, but stayed with their families. An elderly, somewhat dilapidated fellow known as the *askari*, "the soldier," sat (and slept sitting up) at the entrance door at night, but otherwise the hotel was without help between dinner and breakfast. In short order, the Perfect Candidate was made the nominal manager of the hotel. The German visitor had her plaque screwed into a rock somewhere and left.

Well, the Perfect Candidate soon gave the old German owner reason to get rid of him. He began pimping. He installed girls in his room. All day men came and went. I was asked if I had seen anything. I had not. But others had. There was no doubt about what was going on. For the old lady there was much delicacy about making accusations against an African. The people who wanted to get her into trouble so they could take over the hotel were always watching so she had to be careful. She met this setback rather the way she had met all previous misfortunes that I knew about. She would come into the main reception room, arms akimbo, waving her hands and saying, "Cinema, cinema!" (pronounced *seenay-ma*). She alleged that there was so much drama in her life that she did not need any artificial entertainment, television or film. She could not have had those bourgeois luxuries anyway. At that time there was electricity at the hotel only for a few hours in the evening, provided by a generator. There was just enough dim light to play solitaire (Now there is electricity all the time.)

I do not know how she pulled it off, because it happened while I was away, but the German owner did manage to get rid of her delinquent manager. The next time I visited there was a different manager, the first of a series. Some years later, the owner threw up her hands, gave the hotel to the Catholic church, and left to retire in Germany.

These vignettes will not tell you anything worth knowing about the Chagga, except that they are like other people, but it does tell you something about the general atmosphere. There was much that was unexpected that went on and some of it was threatening enough to make one nervous. There were many more incidents worthy of the cry, "Cinema, cinema!"

SOME DIMENSIONS OF "THE FIELD"

In 1967 the Chagga numbered nearly half a million. For the most part, the mountain was populated by owners of small gardens who grew coffee and bananas, and sheltered the occasional cow, goat, or chicken. Scattered among these small-scale farmers were a number of educated professionals who did not depend on the coffee for a living, but had off-farm jobs of one kind or another. I arrived on the mountain humbled by the scope and degree of scatteredness of so large a field project, but pleased by the fact that it was not the tribal, homogeneous, bounded unit that was the classic object of anthropological interest.

Kilimanjaro was not a conventional milieu for anthropological research, and law was not a conventional theme. I had chosen to work there for a number of reasons. One was that thanks to the missionaries, it had long been a Christian area. I thought that for a woman there would be fewer impediments for gaining access to courts and people, male and female, than would be the case in one of the Muslim communities on the coast where a woman might have difficulties. I also thought, because of the longstanding existence of their coffee cooperative, that the Chagga might be especially receptive to the socialist message. I was right about access, but wrong about the receptivity to socialism.

The Chagga had started the cooperative in the 1920s with the enthusiastic support of a British colonial officer, Sir Charles Dundas, who believed in the cooperative movement and introduced the idea. He was said to have ridden his horse all over the mountain, distributing coffee seedlings wherever he went. The co-op was run by Chagga and later they fought hard to keep it that way when the British administration tried to take it over. There were some ups and downs in the history of the KNCU (the Kilimanjaro Native Cooperative Union), but by the time of independence it was functioning quite efficiently, selling Kilimanjaro coffee into the world market. The government of Nyerere reorganized the cooperatives of Tanzania several times, but for the locals, the ordinary business of selling the coffee from their gardens continued.

Contrary to what I had supposed, there was no link for the Chagga between the cooperative movement and the socialism of the Tanzanian nation. In fact in the period running up to independence, the Chagga and their leaders had been very slow to join the Party, TANU (the Tanzanian African National Union). Their comments to me about socialism were wry, to say the least. "Nyerere says we should get *ujamaa* (African socialism) but we already have *ujamaa*. We cooperate." "The government tries to help us. We used to get coffee insecticide from the Indian merchants. They were thieves and they charged a lot. Now the government has fixed a low price on coffee insecticide. That is good. (Pause . . .) But now there is no insecticide!" (Laughter . . .) It had found its way into the black market. So, they told me there was a black market and I knew that it was, by definition, illegal. This was the first of many mundane illegalities of which I became aware.

What was the attitude toward the new government? I had other glimpses of that. For example, I saw how the villagers received official visits. One day the District Commissioner visited the area. Schoolchildren were waving green leafy branches all along the route taken by his limousine. He waved regally in return. Should one attribute significance to the fact that, except for teachers, there were no celebrating adults participating in the greeting? Was this non-appearance a passive protest? After independence membership in the Party was a nominal requirement but no one outside of the leadership felt terribly moved to do more than was required. Membership cards were given to everyone. Membership was universal and obligatory. As for the hotels' part in the visits of dignitaries, it was obliged to give every major visitor and his entourage, a feast awash in beer. The hotel was obliged to foot the expense, and to make it known that it was an honor to serve such important people. The resentment was confided to me afterwards.

The official attitude toward the United States was negative. The foreign country that was idealized was China. This official stance however did not determine the behavior of most individuals toward me, far out in the countryside. There were odd exceptions. Here is one: when I decided to try to find out whether most men married "the girl next door," whether affinal networks were localized, I had a surprise. I went to a Lutheran church, met the Pastor, and asked him gently what I was trying to find out: if he had any marriage records that would tell me which sub-village the spouses came from. At first he said I could not see the records. Then he asked me whether I was from the CIA.

Obviously more conversation was needed to persuade him that I was not a spy. What he thought the CIA would do with the marriage records of this little village, I have no idea. And how he knew of the CIA was a mystery. Anyway, I told him more about my life, that I was a teacher and that my studies had nothing to do with the American government. And after a while he melted and was willing to show me his marriage records, and was ready to tell me at length about the "cases" of offenses against the teachings of the church that came before him. Principally these seem to have been about adultery.

In the town of Moshi, and in Dar es Salaam, I expected that my research permission would give me official access to institutions and to written records. My study was sponsored by the Law School at the University of Dar es Salaam, and after showing my credentials to innumerable bureaucrats, the files were usually opened. But a small organization like a local church was another matter. The Pastor had no way to check my credentials, and no criteria for judging the authenticity of the letters I showed him. If he gave me the access I wanted he was risking a reprimand from the local Party officials for overstepping the rules. Such access was a question of my own ability to approach people tactfully and generate friendships, and of course, to make it known that I would pay people for their time if I needed their help regularly. In the early years, all of that seemed unproblematic.

Thus it was startling in the mid-1970s to begin to experience expressions of hostility. That began after several trips had established me as an acceptable person in many households, and as a close friend of my regular assistants. Strangers were something else. One of the first signs was a trivial event that occurred as I walked down toward the river at the bottom of the hill on which I lived. There was a Teacher's College on the way. In accordance with local custom, I greeted all the people I met on my path with *"Jambo"* and usually the greeting was reciprocated. They were often students on a break from their classes. But one day, the reply from a young man was *"Jambo shetani,"* or "Hello, devil." I just walked on, but I was a little unsettled.

Another day some children stopped me on the road and wanted to touch my skin and hair. That was ok. Others had done this before. But then they followed me on my way and started to chant insults, that I might be a witch, that I might have witchcraft materials in my bag and the like. I was surprised. Eventually they tired of that game and we went our separate ways. When I told my favorite assistant, Hawkins, about this, he said that there had been a lot of propaganda on the radio about strangers, that the Chagga were instructed to tell the authorities if they ever saw a stranger in their villages, that these people were dangerous, they might be spies, or witches, and that their presence should be reported at once. Clearly there was nothing personal about this, but that did not make it pleasant, and I began to feel that I could not charm all strangers, that something had happened to the friendly ambience of Kilimanjaro.

On the smallest scale I did everything I could to avoid giving offense. Having been warned that I might be robbed on the roads where I often walked alone, I did not wish to appear wealthy. I did not wear a watch, though I sometimes concealed one in my bag. I did not wear any jewelry, save a plastic bracelet of the kind that could be bought in any Chagga market. When asked for money by local people I met as I walked, I could honestly reply that I had none with me. In conversation, I would avoid comparisons between the American way of life and the African way. I would answer what I was asked as openly and honestly as I could, and I looked for opportunities to show that I wanted to learn from my African friends. I caused much merriment when I said I wanted to learn how to carry things on my head as Chagga women did. They found my clumsiness hilarious. All my ignorance about how to plant and how to grow things delighted them, to say nothing of my errors in Swahili, and my tendency to get lost on the winding paths between the banana gardens. They would laugh at me with evident pleasure. I found the laughter good-natured and was pleased by the benign attention. But surely they knew as well as I did that I had come by plane, that the cost of getting there was more than the annual income of most farm families. And perhaps more irritating, I was free to come and go. They had to stay on Kilimanjaro. I had more choice. I was a worldling, and they were stuck.

When I went to local political meetings to see how the socialist project was going in the village, I was welcomed. I remember one such outdoor meeting during a period of drought. The rains were overdue and people were worried. During the meeting the rain began, first a drizzle, then some really heavy rainfall. People jumped for joy, hugged me, and very nicely said, "Mama, you have brought the rain. Thank you, Mama." Not that they really believed that, but their behavior certainly was a counterfoil for the occasional nastiness of others.

The minutes of Party meetings were kept quite regularly. They were embedded in Party mythology as thick as peanut butter. For one thing, the agenda of such meetings was supposed to be produced by The People *quite spontaneously*. If needed, the People were to accept Party help in translating their wants into bureaucratic form, but the ideas were supposed to emerge from local discussion. I obtained minutes of meetings from a variety of villages, and as I suppose I should have expected, the major topics taken up were identical, whatever the village. The Party leaders inserted their official conception of things into the expressed opinions of The People. Did the higher ups believe in all of this unanimity? How aware were they that they were deceiving themselves? This was obviously not a topic I could discuss with Party officials, and I withheld comment. What was obvious to me was that this was part of the tendency of the Party to make records that would confirm its view of the "peasantry" and its needs.

The Chagga in general seemed to accept such Party action as "the way things are." And, of course, the local Party men were themselves all Chagga. Some prestige seemed to attach to their office, and they may have been able to obtain special favors from time to time as a result. In former times, the relation of the ordinary farmers to persons in authority involved connections with the chiefs and their many deputies. One of the first acts of the independent government, to which one would have expected some reaction, was to abolish chiefship. It sounded as if the socialist ideal of political equality could be realized instantly. The Chagga people with whom I discussed this seemed to think that their former chiefs were free loaders, and that it was not a bad idea to unseat them. The truth is, the old duffers were still addressed as "*ex-chiefu*," and shown respect.

Some of the old chiefs lived in the largest and most modern houses. I suppose there was some worry among the residents of the chiefdom that they might somehow come back into office. Anyway, some were rich by local standards and their networks were extensive and still sometimes powerful. They might do one a favor.

I stayed away from the chiefs until many years into the field project, lest being identified with them would impair my attempt to manifest political neutrality. Toward the end of my visits I came to know Petro Itosi Marealle, who had for a short while been one of the most important chiefs among the Chagga. Rather than leave so powerful a man on the mountain to ruminate about the new government, or perhaps to organize opposition, Nyerere gave Marealle a series of important administrative appointments that required his presence in Dar es Salaam. There he could be watched and kept busy.

The old chief was a very sophisticated man, had written a book about Chagga culture (Marealle 1947), and had met Nyerere in London when Nyerere was doing an M.A. at the University of Edinburgh. When Nyerere came to Moshi in 1956, Marealle invited him to visit at home. Marealle had visited Oxford in 1961.

Marealle eventually retired from his independence period government jobs in Dar es Salaam and during one of my later field visits came to live in his house on the mountain. He often came to the Kibo hotel in the late afternoon to have a beer and to buy a few bottled beers to take home for his three wives. By that time I was no longer worried about how people would feel if I were seen talking with him. At his invitation, I went to see him at his house and he showed me old photos and files of correspondence, which included some notes from Malinowski.

Petro Itosi Marealle was always very happy to boast of ways he had gotten around the rules of the government. He had a Japanese car on which he did not have to pay any duty because his son had sent it to him from Japan in the proverbial diplomatic "pouch." The son was an ex-military officer of high rank. He was sent to China for a time, and then to Japan, and then to London, in a state of temporary exile because Nyerere thought he had been part of a coup plot by a group of military officers. It sounded like a very benign alternative to jail. The son who had been in exile returned to Kilimanjaro at about the time that Tanzania decided to have multiparty elections. He was thinking of putting his hat in the political ring, so confident was he that he was politically forgiven.

In addition to the house in Marangu on Kilimanjaro, foxy old Petro Itosi also had a house in Dar es Salaam. Having more than one house was strictly forbidden. This second house was occupied by a diplomat, and what was a rental was concealed under the form of a sale, the price being paid in installments. He discussed this with me with a twinkle in his eye. He had pulled off another fast one.

Petro Itosi's daughter-in-law was not as secure as he was. Another one of the Party rules was that no one could possess more than one piece of land, and he/she could not have more than he worked himself. While the chief's family could obviously afford to hire a person to work in the gardens that surrounded their house, I often saw his daughter-in-law laboring in the garden. She was afraid that one of the locals might complain to the Party about their land holding and their land might be at risk. So, she quite ostentatiously worked the land and made sure that I saw her doing so. I suppose that was to make sure that she had an influential witness.

Everyone knew what the rules were about land holding because the Party gave the abolition of title a great deal of publicity. All title was taken by the State, and in theory the title to all land belonged to The People. So what did real people have after that was enacted? They had possession. And the right to possession could be bought and sold. A special land court was established and the confusions that might have arisen from these new laws were supposed to be dealt with there. However, most Chagga villages simply made do with their own customary understandings about these matters, and carried on as before. For most people, the issue of multiple plots did not come up, or if there were more than one plot, they managed to assign the extra plot to a female relative without male issue, with the secret understanding that the plot was still the donor's, and would eventually revert to him.

As for ordinary people, coping with institutions, I was puzzled about how people figured out what the rules were. I learned that there were unofficial "bush lawyers" who helped people in their dealings with officials and with the courts. I wanted to meet one. My assistant, Hawkins, duly produced a very lively, middle-aged bush lawyer who told me about some of the cases in which he had been involved. The most interesting thing I learned about him was that he was illiterate, yet knew what documents people needed in the courts. For example if a woman wanted to collect damages for a beating she had received from her husband, the bush lawyer would tell her she needed a note from the hospital detailing her injuries. He was known as a person who knew what documents were required and what to do with them. He coped with his illiteracy by having a young assistant who could read. After some time had passed in our conversation, seamlessly, almost parenthetically, he started to tell me about a lengthy controversy in which he himself was involved. He hoped that I could help him. I inferred that he had wanted to meet me, not only for the little gift I would give him at the end of our interview, but because being a lawyer myself, I might be able to help him re-open his case. The account went on for a long time, and was full of detail. I could not help him, and I had to listen as he expanded on his dilemma.

Listening to what people wanted me to know, rather than what I was trying to find out, was a large part of the fieldwork encounter. From discussions of the family troubles of my many contacts, to hearing about the Pastor's congregation, to learning the details of the bush lawyer's own "case" I listened interminably. The bush lawyer hoped that if I thought over his case, I might change my mind. He talked on. I wished him well. In the end, he gave up, and made the gesture that I learned was conventional. He tapped his lower lip again and again, meaning "feed me." That was the request for pay.

MAP-MAKING, LAND TENURE, AND CHAGGA CRUELTIES TO KIN

In the beginning of my fieldwork, as I launched myself into work, I started by inquiring where the nearest court was. Just as I had hoped, it was only a short walk from the somewhat seedy climber's lodge where I was staying. I asked permission to observe a session of the court and it was cheerfully granted. I sat on one of the benches in the back and listened. When it was over I approached the Magistrate to ask him whether he knew anyone who could sit with me and explain what I did not understand. He said he had just the man, one who lived in his village about six miles away. He introduced me to him the very next day. After a week or so, it became clear to me that Hawkins Ndesanjo, as he was called, would be an excellent research assistant. We settled on a modest salary (after I found out what a white collar job paid) and he fitted himself into my schedule, and into my project. Sometimes he accompanied me to one court or another, sometimes he was sent on his own to copy some documents or make some inquiries.

Finding people to help me to learn what I needed to know was not difficult. Shortly after, in another village, I found a schoolteacher who had some free time, and she too, became involved in my work. I later consulted a Catholic priest at the mission station in Kilema, and he referred me to an elderly gentleman named Stanislaus Mosha who had lots of time and lots of information and, like everyone else, lots of relatives. I particularly wanted my assistants to be persons who did not know each other, and who came from a variety of villages, to insure that the information I obtained would be a set of independent views. I wanted to test what one asserted against the statements of another. For most of them, their willingness to work for me continued over the years.

People were friendly, not shy, and ready to smile. Since cash was not easy to come by, they were more than willing to help. In fact they wanted to tell me much more than I asked about. They soon told me many stories about their kin and neighbors. One story led to another. I collected genealogies and tried to get my new friends to make approximate maps of the areas nearest where they lived.

The map making and the genealogies that accompanied it turned out to be the greatest methodological find of my entire time on Kilimanjaro. Making maps was a technique that threaded itself through my many visits over the years. My interest in the social context of land law was central to my project, and was a major issue in the lives of the Chagga. Early in the process I asked Hawkins Ndesanjo to draw me the location of his house, his neighbor's house, and that neighbor's house, and so on in an extending circle of houses. That way I found out that if they possibly could, if there were any plots of land they could claim, kinsmen lived next to each other. The question in my head was one that Jack Goody had asked me when I gave a pre-fieldwork paper at Cambridge, "Are these Chagga living in localized kinship groups?" I did not know the answer at the time, but I did know for certain once I had the maps.

In the end we produced a master map of about three hundred adjacent families, representing a number of patrilineages in a sub-village of Mwika. Of two hundred and forty one plots of land in that particular sub-village, the largest lineage had thirty-three member households. It was the lineage of a former chief. Twelve lineages had on average fifteen member households, and a dozen had five or fewer. These relatively small clusters had members in other localities. No one was completely isolated. Everyone had kin clusters which if not adjacent, were nearby.

I saw at once that some of the former chiefly lineage lived on the more desirable sites near the main road, but scattered their relatives throughout the chiefdom. Others lived in kinship clusters when they could, but leapt at any empty plot that came to be available. Even more interesting, I was able to show that some relatives looking further afield formed residential clusters in other areas, up-mountain, or down mountain. The up-mountain areas were restricted because there were laws designed to preserve the forest belt. But down-mountain was much more open to settlement.

At the same time as the map-making I began a systematic census of the residents in each household, not just their number but the answers to a lot of questions about each resident: age, education, relationship to the owner, person from whom he had acquired the land, lineage of the spouse, whether they had ever been involved in any legal disputes, whether there were absent members of the family, and we asked other nosy things. The lay of the land was public information, and no one was hesitant about giving it to Hawkins or to me. I am less sure about whether the dispute question was answered honestly, but some people used it as the occasion to talk about how they had been wronged.

The census was an eye-opener, since decades of history was embedded in that geography. Almost all the land was inherited so mapping was a way of coming to know the antecedents of the residents. And more, it was a way to understand that the land was thought of as being held in trust for descendants, as being entailed.

The entailment was a customary moral imperative. And more, it turned out that this simple device, mapping, would tell me obliquely that there were far too many descendants, that subdividing would not work for the next generation, and that it meant that more land disputes were surely in the offing. If further subdivided, the plots would be too small to feed a family.

There was no unoccupied land into which to expand. Coffee bushes and bananas were permanent crops. They required a certain climate, and the land for this was already crowded. The banana belt required a particular altitude. Higher on the mountain it was too cold, and down at the base of the mountain, on the flat lands, an entirely different set of crops was cultivated, annual crops of maize, beans and millet, with a different history and a different set of customs attached. Some people cultivated both kinds of land. But in recent decades irrigation projects made it possible to build and live in the lower areas. Some people did move there permanently. Others cultivated the lower area seasonally (some even with tractors) but lived on the higher slopes.

The cultivation of this lower area land had a very different history from the permanent tree-crop gardens higher up. Long ago, it was controlled by the chiefs who allocated plots annually. Thus from the point of view of the law, there was not a single system of traditional Chagga land tenure, but at least two systems. I did not try to explore the lower area plots except indirectly, through information culled from owners of upper area plots.

The solution for many young people facing the shortage in the banana belt was to move away from the mountain, to go to the cities. But it took me some years to establish the details about this out-migration. It did not at first occur to me to ask much about the absent members of the households. Originally I thought leaving was just an occasional thing, something that individuals did. But later my mapping and census taking showed the trend was wide-spread.

I was standing in the midst of was a demographic change of some magnitude. This must have affected the way people felt about their situation and must have made some of them feel very insecure. There was a clear change. One lineage whose affairs I followed in detail will serve as an example. The contrast between 1968 and 1993 was marked. The lineage had thirty household heads in 1968. Over time they sired eighty sons. By 1993, fifteen of the original 30 had died and they were succeeded by sons. Many of the still living fifteen shared their land with sons. But in 1993 it is notable that of the fifty-three adult members of the younger generation, twenty-seven had gone to live in the cities. The land shortage was affecting family life in a radical way. And the population increase was given no quarter. Everyone had many, many children, in some cases from several marriages.

The plots of land people lived on could be occupied permanently. The rainfall on the mountain and the general practice of manuring made continuous replanting of the same gardens possible. Unlike many African communities, which moved their area of cultivation when the land was exhausted, the Chagga did not have to do so. This, I surmised even before I had seen the mountain, meant that there must be a good deal of land law surrounding rights to the up-mountain gardens. And so there was.

The collection of quantitative material about the location of households continued as a steady background underlying other aspects of the fieldwork. One of the advantages of the mapping and census was that a lot of the work could be administered primarily by my assistants. In general, the research assistants were not keen on my developing new contacts, lest they lose their jobs to another person. Consequently I kept them separated, and only sketchily informed about my study of villages other than the one in which they were working. I could check at leisure, but they could do the bulk of the surveying. It was work that could be done in my absence, on days when I had something else to do, or even when I went back to England and the US. At the same time I collected other documentary records, case records from the courts, yearly records from the co-operative, and other materials. But the more personal side of things went on as well. Intense personal contact with some informants over many months, and in the case of Hawkins and his kin, over years, told me about the emotional strains that lay embedded in the land-facts.

This was evident in dramatic ways. For example, there was a man in Hawkins' lineage who went into debt, deeply into debt. He drank. He bought things. He spent money he did not have. He was reputed to be irresponsible. His brothers came forward and paid what he owed. I thought this was a piece of fraternal generosity, of lineage solidarity, so often spoken of in the work of other anthropologists working in Africa. I thought this was an example of what Goran Hyden (1980) had called, "the economy of affection." In fact, Hyden attributed the failure of socialism in Tanzania to the primacy of "the economy of affection." According to him socialism could not catch on with the "peasants" because of their commitment to family ties.

It turned out that I was wrong in thinking that the brothers paid the debtors' obligations out of affection. What the more prosperous brothers wanted was that the debtor sink more deeply into trouble so that they could then lay claim to his land. They wanted to take it over cheaply, as if the land itself were surety for the debt that was owed. Because of the strong sense of lineage entailment, brothers were supposed to be offered first refusal whenever there was a land sale. In this case, the brothers competed with each other and approached the debtor separately and secretly. There was a great deal of pressure not to sell to an outsider, a non-kinsman, complete with moralizing admonitions. This debtor became enraged at his brothers and found their contempt for him unbearable. The result was that for spite he did sell his land to an outsider, and settled the debts to his brothers out of the price he got. I asked one of his kinsmen whether he got a better price from the outsider than he would have from his brothers, and I was told that the choice of an outside buyer was not for that reason. It was his anger that forced the choice.

Like most of the interesting accounts of kin-cruelties, I could not verify his motives in detail. However, the behavior of the brothers was not unusual. The frequency of such slaps in the face particularly dealt by the more fortunate to poor relatives made it clear to me that Chagga lineages were often very punitive to their kin.

I felt sorry for the poor fellow but I could not show it. I had to behave indifferently the way Hawkins did. I wondered whether the issue was simply the willingness to sell to an outsider, or whether the kinsmen had disliked him for years. Were there other, older issues? I could not find out. I was told that he was a bad sort, had always been, and that was the end of the conversation. I tried to discover where he would go, what he would do. No answer was forthcoming.

There were ongoing ways in which kinsmen showed that they despised one of their number. They might, for example, exclude a member from all family rituals and celebrations as a punishment for some violation of their standards of fraternal performance. A particular instance comes to mind. In a Mwika lineage that I knew well, one poor fellow begged for a goat from his cousin, saying he was going to use it in a ritual slaughter to hire a *mganga* (customary healer) to make his sick son well. But once he obtained the goat, he sold it in the market and kept the proceeds. All hell broke loose. His kinsmen deemed him a liar and an immoral, cheating person, and he was not invited to share in his brother's slaughterings or in kinship beer parties for years thereafter. Exclusion and internal forms of avoidance were considered absolutely justified. I held my tongue, but I was shocked by the durability of these rejections.

How did the new socialist government affect this land-short, kin-based scene? The Kilimanjaro branch of the national Party (TANU, the Tanzanian African National Union), was, on independence, reorganized to include everyone. Membership cards were given to all. Local ten-house cells comprised the base of the Party, and multiples of these cells formed higher units, the ward, the division, the district. The head of each ten-house cell was called "the *balozi*" to whom reports of any events of interest in the cell were to be reported. He was to keep records, and to note births and deaths, anti-government activity, meetings, lawbreaking, land transfers and the like. On paper it sounded revolutionary, but in practice, it was not a radical change. The membership of these ten-house cells consisted of the same close clusters of neighbors and relatives who, staying in place and living for years in the same houses on the same plots of land, were very involved with each other. As I was to find out, not too much about the location of lineages had changed on the ground, save the population pressure which would not abate. And, for the most part, the Party leaders were the people who had been prominent in the area before independence.

In short, on Kilimanjaro, at the lowest level, the new socialist administrative changes gave new names to much of what had been there in the first place. At higher levels the new government defined a flow of information upward, and sent orders downward, through a Party administrative structure that had not existed earlier. Government functions and innovations were carried out by a hierarchy of "development committees" and development officials which worked closely with the TANU organization.

The Chagga learned much about formal organization from the bureaucracies of the socialist period. Some of these models were transferred to lineage organization. For example: in the late 1980s the leader of one lineage, a senior elder, died after a long illness. He had made many sacrifices to his ancestors, but succumbed nonetheless. His successor was chosen in 1990. Using the vocabulary of Party organization, the new head called himself the "lineage chairman."

He was a dynamic fellow and had a bright idea about how to aggrandize his position. He wanted to fuse his lineage branch with another, geographically close branch that had long been autonomous. This consolidation would increase the number of households he led from about thirty-five to about seventy, making him more powerful and locally more important.

From Independence on, formal organizations other than the Party were discouraged, indeed prohibited. Even big meetings of kinsmen were forbidden unless permission had been obtained in advance. The government was always worried that anti-government plots would be cooked up by any group. But by the 1980s, the socialist orthodoxy had faded and freedom of assembly began to be possible again. The lineage chairman succeeded in persuading both branches to agree to the consolidation. He was very businesslike. He made a list of all the household heads in a notebook and then proposed that every member household contribute a small sum of money for a collective fund. He had learned this lesson from the socialist reorganizations. That was his model and it worked well. He opened a bank account (the first he had ever had), deposited the money and designated it to be spent on vocational apprenticeships for those young people in the lineage who had not passed the exams for secondary school. These young school leavers could become bricklayers, or carpenters, or tailors, or find some other way to be trained to make a living in the cities.

The membership agreed and the plan was under way. However there was one dissenter, a man who had been the head of the second branch of the lineage who lost all authority to the chairman when the amalgamation of the two branches took place. He wanted to maintain two branches, so that he would continue to be head of something. He boycotted all the chairman's meetings, and refused to contribute to the common fund. The chairman sent him a stiff letter saying that he was banished from all the beer drinks, rituals, or celebrations that might be held in either branch. He replied that the ancestors would have approved of the consolidation and that the rival was violating the fraternal bonds of the ancestors.

The rival bore up for a year in his state of exclusion, but eventually wanted to be reinstated in the amalgamated lineage. The chairman imposed certain conditions. The rebellious kinsman should prepare a beer party for the whole lineage, admit his guilt and apologize. Then he could be reinstated. He did as he was told and bygones became bygones. However the contradictory nature of the structural events should be noted. The chairman was enlarging and strengthening the ties between the lineage branches, but through his use of their career-training funds, encouraging out-migration of the young.

The central government made manifest some of its views of the land shortage problem in ways that were a mix of inviting and mildly threatening. In 1967, a year before I arrived, a directive was issued and speeches were made by the District Commissioner about population pressure. I obtained copies. Kilimanjaro residents were urged to move to other parts of Tanzania because of land shortage. The government organized a program to send volunteers to Mwese in southern Tanzania. People who volunteered would be helped to found new communities. They would be transported by bus, given several acres of land, and various start-up necessities. They were to be given some acreage to be held individually, but the major effort was to have them cultivate a large communal plot as well. They were to be pioneers. They were not only going to help themselves, but they would help build the nation through development. They were exhorted to start planting and start building when they arrived.

The pressure to volunteer for this program went on for some time. When I started to work on the mountain my informants knew people who had gone in the first wave of excitement, but some had come back, with bad stories about how the conditions of life in the wilderness were not as idyllic as had been promised.

Rumors abounded. I wanted to explore this more closely, but I did not want to go directly to the persons who had decided to return to Kilimanjaro. I thought that contacting them might be provocative. The disappointed volunteers would be fearful because the government was surely displeased with them, would want to be reimbursed for the start-up goods with which they had been furnished, etc.

I was aware that the government wanted approval of its projects and I did not want to make myself conspicuous in a negative way. What I did instead was to ask the people I knew what they could tell me about the families of the people who had volunteered, and the status of the volunteer in the family. Those volunteers (and there were only a few) about whom I was able to collect information had all been in one or another kind of difficulty with their extended families. Either there had been fights, or lost competitions for land with a favored relative, or other troubles. For me, it was evident that volunteering to be a pioneer was not entirely due to a dedication to socialism and development. The Party people chose to see it that way, but it seemed not to be so. It was a personal decision connected with their guesses about their future at the heart of the family. Of course there also were many others who were not in good situations and did not volunteer. But there was whispered anti-government talk associated with the pioneering program.

Family life went on rather as before. In the central belt, each little small-holding of land continued to grow its coffee and its bananas. Most people lived in mud and wattle houses with thatched roofs, the wealthier in mud brick houses with tin roofs. In general, no one, except the buildings of the Lutheran and Catholic missions, the local dispensary, and the few dwellings of those who illegally tapped the pipes, had running water. (I knew specific instances of this tapping-into-water-pipes illegality.) Normally, women would fetch water at the local pump, fill their huge cans, and carry it back on their heads. The women all bought and sold vegetables at the same local markets. In general there was no household electricity.

Allied with China, and deeply suspicious of anything American, the Tanzanian state often declared its determination to be self-reliant, and exhorted the citizens to be self-reliant as well. Certainly Tanzania wanted to shake loose from old British ties, and feared that international development loans would have political, not just economic, costs. But Tanzania could not always be self-reliant. When, early in the years after Independence, there was a threatened coup, I was told that it was the British navy sitting in the harbor of Dar es Salaam that saved the government.

Vigorously Africanist in its orientation, the government made Swahili, not English, the national language. Local tribal languages would continue as the domestic language of many households, but Swahili was the language of public action, and the language of the schools. On Kilimanjaro the domestic language was Kichagga, the language in schools Swahili. Yet English remained in use in key institutions, such as the University of Dar es Salaam. You could take English out of the discourse of the police, but you could not take it out of the books that were in the libraries.

A number of institutions that were supposed to continue, or change for the better, simply deteriorated. One might take the gardens of the President's house in Dar as a metaphor for more serious matters, as well as the deterioration of the University buildings. President Nyerere, unlike many other African heads of state, made a point of living modestly, not enriching himself from the fruits of his office, not availing himself of the pomp and circumstance that other political leaders in Africa enjoyed. He resided in Dar es Salaam in a large building near Oyster Bay that must once have been a colonial residential showplace. There was, however, a visible objectification of the modesty of the new regime. Around Nyerere's house, instead of a well-tended garden representing his high office, there was a patchy, neglected lawn. On it, as remnants of past colonial luxury, there were scrawny peacocks pecking through the litter, like dissatisfied chickens.

In 1969, the University, situated outside of Dar es Salaam, was a model of European design. The buildings of white stucco were tastefully dispersed around the campus. The buildings were lovely and remarkably, were cool. Their louvered windows let in breezes that one hardly knew existed. It was a marvel, a treasure. However, a few years later, the inefficiencies that were characteristic of the regime were evident. The louvers on the windows were broken. The toilets did not function and their smell made itself known. When I asked to Xerox something, people told me proudly that they had a Xerox machine, but that it was "temporarily" out of order, that I should go to the library. I went to the library, and they had a Xerox machine, but they said "unfortunately we have no paper." The records of local cases from the law courts around the country were collected and were said to be officially archived at the University. But when I went to the room at the University where they were housed, I saw that the records were scattered on the floor, only a few on the shelves. After picking up some of this mess myself, I spoke to various people about it from faculty members to custodians. Their universal response was, "Picking things up is not my job." Zeal for the institution was not to be expected. Faculty at the University were paid so little that they all had to have other sources of income to survive. I knew someone who had managed to buy a pick-up truck. She hired a driver, and he ferried goods from one part of Tanzania to another. It was her "side business." A faculty member had to cancel his appointment with me because he had to go home to explore a deal about electric light bulbs. The normal activities of a university were only part of the life of faculty members.

THE BIGGEST SHOCK

One day when I came back from a busy day of seeing people, I was given a message at the hotel that a certain person in Moshi, a Mrs. M., wanted to see me at once. I asked if anyone knew who she was and they told me that she was a security person, and that I had better go. I went to Moshi the next day and she said in an accusatory tone, "I have heard about you. We have been watching you. Yesterday you went to the market and you stayed there a long time. You watched everything." She went on, "I am asked, 'Why is this stranger here among us. What is she doing?'" Yes, I answered, I was there. "I am trying to understand how the market works, how the women arrive at a price for each item being sold."

She was plainly not satisfied. She told me that my work must be supervised. For a start, I would have to submit a written list of all the questions I intended to ask of anyone, and to indicate who would be asked. Then if the list were approved, I could go on with my research. I was very uneasy. She continued, "You should be glad about this. It shows they [who?] are being politically responsible. You are in trouble. But this is not a racial matter. Tanzanians do not care what race you are. It is not hostility. They are taking political responsibility. Please be careful."

Dismayed, I got on the bus, went back to my room and started to compose a list of ambiguous questions. I thought if my inquiries were general enough and innocuous enough, she could hardly object. And probably this security officer was essentially justifying her position. On the optimistic side, I thought that if I complied with the request to write a list she would be happy and let me go. I was wrong. I also thought, more pessimistically, that I was being trapped into getting into trouble. I hand copied the list, since there was no copying machine to be had anywhere near. I duly went to Moshi the next day and handed in my questions. The security lady would not see me that day and I left the list with her secretary. Things sounded bad. Eventually she returned a list of questions, but they were not mine and they had been so altered that I did not know how to proceed.

The next day, I tried to feel normal and less afraid, and I went to one of the places where I worked regularly. I decided not to ask anybody any questions but to go to the court that was near where I lived, the one where the Magistrate had been friendly and had found me a research assistant. I would look at the files of case records as I often did. When I got there, I found that the courtroom was empty. The little room where the case records were kept was locked. And nearby there stood a young man I did not know. He said, "Perhaps you should do something with development, not with us. I must inform my superiors about what you have been doing. You are not to go in there [the room with the records] anymore."

I was dumbfounded. I asked him by what authority he was keeping me out. He replied that the orders came from a high official. I told him I would have to contact my friends in Dar es Salaam to clear up this "mistake." He said it was useless.

I went back to my room and resolved to go to Moshi the next day to arrange to get an air reservation to leave. I was able to make the arrangements. I did not go back to the court. And I knew that to go to Dar to see people who might reverse these orders would take considerable time and maybe produce nothing. Who knew what was going on inside the Party, and what risks were involved. I remembered what my friend the Director of Development Studies had said about the possibility of trouble. I left a month earlier than I had intended, in November, 1979.

What is clear is that the Party regulars, at least at relatively low levels, conceived of socialism as a total system. It was, for them, rather like Durkheim's idea of mechanical solidarity. Anyone who came from a place that by definition was structured by other principles was a threat. As an American, I did not have to do anything, just my presence and existence was dangerous to the total system. I had labored hard to win the trust of the Chagga, the people whose lives I tried to understand, and person-to-person, I had succeeded. But there was no way I could win the trust of the small-time bureaucrats in the Party offices. I would wait them out.

When I returned in 1993, everything about the tightened Party discipline of the late 1970s was virtually erased from official memory. The Tanzanian economy had been in a shambles. Nyerere had stepped down from the Presidency in 1985. He was succeeded by Mwinyi, a man from Zanzibar and a Muslim. The World Bank and the IMF, pressured the government to change to an open market economy, and Mwinyi implemented the change. Nyerere, speaking a few years after his retirement in a talk at the London School of Economics, said about Tanzania's socialism, "We failed."

As for me, in the 1980s, I did research in West Africa. In 1993, I went back to Tanzania. My research application was processed and approved by the University in Dar es Salaam without a murmur of disapproval. The Law School was welcoming. In Moshi the Party bureaucracy signed everything without incident. The security lady had disappeared. I went up-mountain and met with my old assistants. Apart from the absence of the old German lady, the death of Petro Itosi Marealle, and the fact that the Catholic Church had somehow transferred the hotel to a Marealle relative, it was as if nothing had changed.

CODA: UNCERTAINTY IN THE FIELDWORK SITUATION, INDETERMINACY IN THE CULTURE

I started fieldwork in my forties. I had begun my professional life much earlier as a lawyer. I was an associate attorney in a Wall Street law firm for a year, and then for six months, participated in the preparation of one of the prosecution cases at the Nuremberg trials. Subsequently switching professional focus, I studied anthropology. At the same time I went into three years of psychoanalysis. (How's that for reflexivity?) Afterwards I married and had children and began my teaching career. All this experience preceded my fieldwork in Africa. Going to Africa was not to be an adventure to discover myself. I wanted to learn about the effect on the countryside of the Tanzanian socialist experiment (installed at independence from British colonial rule) and to meet and talk with many individual Chagga about their lives and concerns.

In the course of my work in Africa, many things happened to me and around me, but many of these happenings did not have to do directly with the Chagga. I resisted writing a personal narrative, keeping self-reflexion quite separate from my fieldwork reports. The content of such an account might have had local political implications, which was worrying. And whose business was it that I felt this or that. I did not want to expose my own doubts and dilemmas to the profession, let alone to the political watchers. I did not want to make myself the center of my ethnographic descriptions. I did not want to dilute my account of the Chagga with stuff that was mostly about Sally Moore. I had read ethnographies in which one learned more about the anthropologist than about the people being studied. I did not want to write what John Borneman has called "auto-ethnography."

And I wanted to be as sure as I could be that what I was reporting about the Chagga was true. I was wary of typifying from limited evidence. The many return journeys I made to work in different so-called "villages" (a village was an administratively designated territory which might have as many as 20,000 inhabitants) were in part to make certain that I could distinguish the unique happenstance from the general state of affairs (the land shortage, for example). The people were diverse: educationally, religiously, economically, occupationally, and more. This was no uniform culture in the colonial sense of the imagined homogeneous "tribe."

I spoke Swahili, though not as fluently as I would have liked, but I did not speak Kichagga. On occasion where there were groups of Chagga, they often switched back and forth. Some Chagga spoke English which helped me very much. There were cultural commonalities among the people I came to know, practices and ideas which were very different from my own, but even in this there was much variation. Some people were more "traditional" in their ways and some were more "modern." As one of my assistants said to me as we passed a man working on his garden plot, "See that man. See what he is doing. In the old days he would not be doing that work. It would be *aibu*, shameful for a man to do woman's work." What is an anthropologist to do with such a piece of information? Was this just my assistant's idea? Was it a generally held view of the relations between the sexes? How recently had men begun to do this work?

On the part of the Chagga, there were many degrees of commitment to ethnic custom, of literacy, of devotion to the teachings of the Church (Catholic or Lutheran), of attention to African socialism, of worry about witchcraft. All of these institutions had tenets, and rules, and exactions for conformity. And all of them were circumvented at one time or another. In the beginning of fieldwork, to make sociological or cultural sense of all this diversity and multiplicity of practice and thought was difficult, to say the least.

On top of this, in writing about what I saw and heard and read I had to be mindful of the political implications of what I might say. Needless to say, and as will be obvious from this paper, I no longer feel as constrained, but at the time, I had to watch my step.

Long term fieldwork is never long enough to capture everything. It is not as if the field is a finite, bounded entity about which one learns more and more toward some goal of completion. There is no such thing as completion. First of all, the "whole" is never visible or measurable. Perhaps (*pace* Heisenberg) there ought to be a fundamental uncertainty principle attached to fieldwork. Second of all, things are changing all the time. One can only interact with a part of a society at a time. And while one domain is in view, events emerge elsewhere, often out of sight, that may affect what one is looking at. One is never finished. One simply stops. In the beginning the sense of incompleteness emerges like a self-accusation, but that attenuates when revisits have filled the file drawers with solid and not so solid data.

Like all cultures, Chagga culture is capacious. In its system of values it accommodates the traditional healer, as well as the hospital. It presumes that the inheritance of a banana garden is the best path to economic well-being. Yet for some enterprising individuals, the culture is also open to innovative investment and technical work as an alternative way to make a living. Cultures not only have regularities and norms, but also open zones of indeterminacy. People make choices. They use the zones of indeterminacy creatively. This greatly complicates fieldwork (see Moore 1975a: 210–35 for a theoretical discussion of indeterminacy).

Meanwhile change takes many forms, and long-term research makes one very much aware of the shifts. Adult children go off to the city to find work. The structure of the family changes. A man cannot count on being surrounded by his children as he ages. More women become converted to family planning. The price of coffee changes. The government changes. And so it goes, as Vonnegut would say.

It all spells uncertainty for any anthropologist trying to find a durable fix on the ethnographic scene. Association with particular informants over the long term may approximate friendship. I felt very warmly toward these people. And they were clearly glad to have me back every time. But with some others there were money problems, or unreliability was the difficulty. These can turn dealing with assistants into unpleasant transactions.

And the number of less significant disappointments is legion. I cannot begin to count the occasions when I made an arrangement to meet someone who did not show up. I walked many miles each day to make contact. The villages in which I did most of my work were four to six miles distant from my hotel, in Kilema and in Mwika. In a milieu without telephones there is no expectation that anyone will announce a change of plan. There is no way to do it. And afterwards, one has to smile and pretend it did not matter. It always mattered to me. If excuses were made, I could never tell whether they were lies. And perhaps worst of all, I felt I could never show anger. I hated this, but making a nice face was the price of getting on with the work. And in the long run, and the run was long, I think it paid off.

To the extent that reflexivity means being preoccupied with oneself, brooding over the disappointments and insults, celebrating oneself when the going is good, it is usually not worth writing about. But to the extent that reflexivity means self-awareness in the curious situation called "fieldwork," such self-consciousness is absolutely necessary. It is a complement to observing and talking with the very people one has traveled such a great psychological and physical distance to meet.

PART TWO

Perspectives on Africa

The group of papers in this section fall into two categories. One set of them gives a radically revisionist view of "native" African law. The other set proposes theoretical and methodological changes in anthropological ethnography: it deals with legal activities as a link between local and central organization, with "events" as central forms of data, and with significant social reorganization masked by apparent continuity in kinship relations.

As for the set on law: they underline the fact that "customary law," contrary to colonial theory, was, in part, a changing body of oral norms, ideas and practices, loose and vague in some matters, quite specific and rigid in others. Colonial governments thought of indigenous law as a fixed body of rules that could be stated as such. They contemplated obtaining and codifying a list of them. They imagined that African courts, guided by colonial supervisors, could then apply the acceptable written rules systematically. This codification never happened, nor could it have. The "rules" were not as the colonials imagined them. The reality was much too complex. Individual Africans invoked custom when it served their purposes but also adapted their conventionalized understanding of prevailing norms to changing external conditions as the situation and self-interest required.

Among the Chagga, for example, the pressure of land shortage made people use whatever argument they could muster, true or false, to make claims. The durability of land disputes, their continuation from one generation to the next, is evident in many of the cases described here. In the background is the general belief that one person can do supernatural harm to another. A competing land claim may be interpreted as a gesture of hostility, a potentially threatening act, a portent of worse.

Lest the anxiety about supernatural harm not persuade ones rival to abandon his claims, it was often possible to mobilize administrative officials in one's cause, to let authority do what threats might otherwise accomplish. Or a complicit relative or friend could be mobilized to tell a contrary justifying story, one that was not necessarily true. This demonstrates the interweaving of causes, the multiplicity of courses of action, the open renegotiability that surrounded the rules of the game, the so-called "customary law."

Over the twentieth century, to say nothing of the nineteenth, the people of Kilimanjaro experienced many directed structural changes in government organization, in economic relationships and in religious training. These imposed orders were subject to the same kinds and degrees of manipulation and reinterpretation by the Chagga as the supposed system of traditional legal rules. However, the Chagga had an official monopoly on what constituted "custom" and were not about to relinquish that label since it gave them authority. On the other hand when it suited them, they made contrary arguments about the need for "modernity." Case histories explore both.

Much of the ethnographic material in these essays is postcolonial and reveals the observed irregularity of fit between recent official and unofficial ideas and activities. Anthropology is well situated to observe and analyze the set of processes in which this tension operates and to ask when it is transforming or when maintaining the order of things. These papers demonstrate the application of a "processual" approach to ethnography.

CHAPTER FOUR

From Giving and Lending to Selling

Property Transactions Reflecting Historical Changes in Kilimanjaro

METHODOLOGICAL PROLEGOMENON

Reconstructing history from the statements of the living has its perils. "On Kilimanjaro land is the most important thing. Land goes from fathers to sons. That is the way it is here. That is our custom from long ago," a senior Chagga man instructs the anthropologist in 1974. They sit in front of his rectangular, tin-roofed, mud-walled house. "And did you inherit this very *kihamba* (banana garden) from your father? And did he receive it from his father?" Old Selemani answers as if the localized Chagga patrilineages now in place had always been there, located precisely where they are as he speaks. It is as if every son had always acquired his land from his father.

Such indigenous narratives about the permanent norms of "traditional" culture are problematic for a time-conscious anthropology. They are equally troublesome

---

Editor's note: This chapter is a reprint of Moore, Sally Falk. 1991. "From giving and lending to selling: Property transactions reflecting historical changes on Kilimanjaro." In *Law in Colonial Africa*, edited by Kristin Mann and Richard Roberts, 108–30. Portsmouth, NH: Heinemann and James Currey Educational Books.

for an anthropologically aware history. Past changes are well known to hide inside the framework of "traditional" institutions. History can be inconveniently
masked where the invocation of "custom" is a form of present legitimation.

Hard evidence of the realities of land acquisition among the Chagga of Kilimanjaro exists. It can be found in the records of law cases, the reports of the provincial commissioners and other government officials, and in the oral history of
particular plots of land. And those realities are (and have been) much more complex and varied than old Selemani's words suggest. He was right that sons often
inherit from their fathers. There is agnatic inheritance that tends to be lineal. But
there are also (and were in the past) other ways to acquire plots both from within
and from outside of the lineage. In 1900 there was plenty of unoccupied bush land
for the taking. Any man could pioneer and "develop" a new plot. By 1950 there
was no bush land available, though for the well-off there were still some plots to
be had for cash. Thus changing forms of external acquisition (i.e., from *outside*
the patriline) exist and have existed alongside of the chains of inheritance from
fathers to sons. And even the agnatic arrangement varied. Land might be had
from a grandfather or an uncle, or from another agnatic kinsman who happened
to die without sons. Circumstances differed because of the variable configuration
of families and their fortunes. The size of holdings varied, as did the accidents of
fate: who died first, how many sons there were in any lineage branch, and the like.
Even inside the lineage there often was much more to the story than might be
suggested by Selemani's statement about a simple succession from father to son.

Other misconceptions could result from projecting into an earlier time Selemani's emphasis on the centrality of land. To be sure, the Chagga have been
cultivators as far back as anything is known of them, and in the sense that land
has provided basic sustenance, it has always been deeply important. But a century ago there was an abundance of land and there was no cash cropping. If there
was a shortage of anything, it was of other resources, of which two were particularly marked a shortage of persons (both as labor and as political and economic
clients) and a shortage of cattle (for consumption and for various forms of exchange). Today on Kilimanjaro, cash cropping, land scarcity, and overpopulation
have given a new twist to the priorities. Current urgencies have also reshaped the
way the past is remembered. A corrective insight into the circumstances of the
colonial period in the words of those who were living through it can be found in
the records of thousands of law cases heard in the local courts on Kilimanjaro.

I have recently published a book on a century of Kilimanjaro's history
through the analysis of its so-called "customary law" (Moore 1986a). At its most

general, the thesis of that work was that what passed for "customary law" in the colonial period was a profoundly transformed version of earlier arrangements, in many respects an artifact of the colonial period. Local practices continued to change, as they do to this day, while being steadfastly certified as "customary" both by local people and by central governments. This paper should be read as a first postscript on the methods and conclusions of that larger work. But the intention of this paper is to do more than to place a few more unpublished cases on the record. The legal disputes I have chosen to describe here give some new glimpses of the consequences for the Chagga of the major economic and political changes that occurred in the region during the colonial period: the end of inter-chiefdom wars, the advent of cash cropping, the enormous increase in population, the progressive worsening of the land shortage, and the step-by-step transformation of the role of chiefs. The cases show that there were basic shifts in the interchangeability of different resources as the colonial period progressed, and concomitant shifts of practice. But perhaps even more interesting to the historical project from a theoretical point of view, the cases chosen also demonstrate the results of a methodological experiment. In selecting which of several thousand cases might illustrate certain economic changes most clearly, I employed an unusual criterion: I looked for cases which showed transactions between persons who were not agnatic kin, cases which also concerned the alienation to "outsiders" of patrimonial interests in persons and property.

The rationale was this: if, among the Chagga cases, one were to confine one's attention to controversies over agnatic inheritance, these would be bound to give rich testimony to the way patrilineages reproduced themselves locally from generation to generation. Like Selemani's statements, correct in themselves, but incomplete, this would leave an overwhelming sense of the persistence of cultural form. But if transactions are at issue in which the transfer is of patrimonial property to non-agnates, those being "non-routine" are far more likely to expose time-specific motives and conditions for allowing that patrimonial property to leave the patriline.

This method has been productive for the reconstruction of Chagga history. It could easily be applied to other settings in Africa and elsewhere. Attention to non-agnatic transactions serves to modulate the bias toward continuity and "reproduction" that would otherwise be built into a kin-focused approach. The logic of inheritance from father to son does not necessarily demand explications of the contemporaneous context. But the time-specific reasons why patrimonial property found its way to persons outside the patrilineage or from the public domain into private hands does require attention to the changing political and economic milieu. Imbedded in the strategies of what Habermas calls the "life world" are refractions of larger-scale circumstances (Habermas 1987: 118, 151).

The legal transactions and contestations between non-agnates selected for presentation here concern material interests in persons, in cattle, in land, and in cash. The ways in which (and the times at which) persons, cattle, land, and cash were or become interchangeable are obvious indicators of transformations in the political economy of the region. But because the legal cases and transactions urgently concern individuals, they also give insight into the human and cultural meanings of these systemic changes.

THE HISTORICAL BACKGROUND, A BRIEF SKETCH

For the Chagga the colonial period could be said to have begun in 1886 when Kilimanjaro was incorporated into German East Africa (Stahl 1964: 177). Thirty years later, in 1916, the British defeated the Germans and thus began their administration of the area. British rule continued until independence was achieved in 1961. The formal political sequence gives no indication of the fundamental changes in African life that colonial rule effected.

In the precolonial century the peoples of Kilimanjaro had been involved in the slave and ivory trades. They also had had a significant role in the provisioning of caravans. Hundreds of men plied their way from the coast to the interior and back again each year. They needed *places* to rest and to restock their supplies. Chagga chiefdoms welcomed this provisioning trade. In the same period, the several dozen politically autonomous chiefdoms on Kilimanjaro were chronically at war with one another. The inter-chiefdom fighting was probably closely related to competition over trade routes. Periodically one chiefdom would dominate others for a time, sometimes by forming a set of alliances. Eventually the leading alliance would collapse, the dominant chiefdom would be defeated and another would be ascendant for a time. A several-century history of these rivalries, rises and falls is known in outline (Stahl 1964).

There is no doubt of the openness of Chagga chiefdoms to contacts with the coast and the interior in the nineteenth century. By 1848 there were Swahili speakers permanently lodged in the entourage of the chiefs. They may have been there much earlier. By the 1880s the Chagga chiefdoms in the long-distance trade had acquired more than imported cloth and trade beads. They had rifles.

There is even evidence that the cash economy had begun to penetrate. When Sir Harry Johnston spent some months on the mountain in the early 1880s, he rented a plot of land for himself and his servants and paid the chief in rupees (Johnston 1886: 191–93). Johnston offered Mandara twelve rupees a month. Mandara demanded 100 and said he would not allow explorer Johnston to collect any more specimens of plants and butterflies until he paid the higher rent. As an insulting joke, Mandara sent Sir Harry a basket of vegetable refuse to "add to your collection" and demanded to be paid a few ells of cloth in return for the garbage. The Chagga still controlled their beloved Kilimanjaro and were not intimidated by Europeans. They were soon to lose their political autonomy, but in the meanwhile they continued to bargain for whatever they could extract from their European visitors.

The German colonial peace put a stop to the fighting, hanged some chiefs, deposed others, and made the installed chiefs answerable to their colonial rulers. The old long-distance and provisioning trades ended. Over time the political arena was completely reorganized. What had been dozens of chiefdoms were consolidated into fewer and fewer, first by the Germans, later by the British. This conveniently reduced the number of entities with which the colonial governments had to deal. The basis of chiefly power was transformed, as was the role itself.

In both the German and the British periods, each chiefdom had a law court presided over by the chief. Since there was no separation between executive and judicial powers until nearly the end of the colonial period, the judicial role was an extension of chiefly administrative authority. It served as an arm of the colonial government in matters such as prosecuting the failure to pay taxes. And, as we shall see, it sometimes served the personal interests of the chiefs. The courts were much more than instruments for the perpetuation of "customary" law.

From the violent upheavals of the beginning of the colonial era, through the more peaceful decades that followed, and until the present, most Chagga have lived in localized clusters of patrilineally related households. Each household is situated in the midst of its own separate garden compound, the boundary of which is clearly marked by a living fence of dracaena. The gardens produce subsistence crops of bananas, millet, and vegetables, and the Chagga also keep a few cows, sheep and goats. Those were the very foods supplied to the caravans in the old days. Today they are largely cultivated and kept for domestic consumption. And today there is one more important cultivar growing in the gardens: coffee bushes. Just as the nineteenth century traffic in the long-distance trade ended, a substitute form of commerce emerged. The Europeans introduced coffee-growing in the 1890s and the practice gradually spread over the whole mountain. Coffee became a major source of cash as each household added coffee seedlings to its gardens. For a while Arabica coffee made the Chagga relatively prosperous.

Fortunate in the climate and soil of their mountain, fortunate in the continuous availability of water, fortunate in having had a remarkably benign district officer assigned to them at the beginning of the British period who helped them reorganize their coffee production and fought for their interests, the Chagga adapted to their changing circumstances with a will. Most of them became Christians. Many were educated at mission schools, some at government schools (Shann 1956). As a people, they became addicts of education and came to share many of the ideas of progress held by their colonial rulers.

However population growth eventually denied them the continuing prosperity associated with their once-burgeoning coffee economy. Today the household gardens are too small to satisfy ever-increasing cash needs. The only families which remain prosperous are those with members who have salaried jobs or paying businesses in addition to coffee gardens. The Chagga are suffering from a severe land shortage. From a population estimated at 100,000 in 1900, the Chagga multiplied to 600,000 by 1978 (1978 Population Census). Land shortage was already perceptible in the late 1920s. At that time there was anxiety on the part of chiefs that the buying and selling of land for cash was about to begin. Up to that point the customary payment for transferred land had been "a cow and a goat." The chiefs wanted to forbid entirely the commerce in buying and selling of land for cash (Griffiths 1930: 63, 88). They had no success in making such a rule law, no doubt because their colonial masters thought a market in land would be a sign of evolutionary progress. Moreover, the provincial commissioners must have been entirely aware that in their regulation of land matters the chiefs were not disinterested parties.

During the colonial period chiefs used their administrative powers gradually to appropriate increasing control over the allocation of unused land. For the service of assigning a plot of land to a new holder, they received valuable "gifts of thanks" from beneficiaries. It is no wonder then that in their judicial and administrative capacities, chiefs who had once confined themselves to approving the allocation of uncultivated wilderness became more and more involved in the business of certifying the legitimacy of *all* land transfers and land claims. As a consequence they were increasingly able to use their positions to enlarge their own landholdings and those of their kinsmen and other fa-vorites. Probably in the late 1920s when they were arguing against land sales for cash, their fear was that a cash market in land would render chiefly inter-ventions less profitable, perhaps ever superfluous. This is one of the many bits of evidence that converge to suggest that early in the century competition for control over persons and cattle was the dominant focus of transactions, while by 1930, control over land and the pursuit of cash were beginning to become central. Almost from the inception of the colonial period transactions in all four—persons, coffee, land and cash—existed contemporaneously, so the pe-riodization of the pre-1930 and the post-1930 economies is to be understood as a matter of emphasis, not as a contrast between absolutely different circum-stances. What was involved was a long-term cumulative shift, a directional transformation, in demography, in production and exchange, and in cultural and political ideas.

THE CASES

The three sets of cases that follow have in common the transfer of agnatic prop-erty to a non-agnate. They differ from one another in almost every other respect. *The first set of cases* shows an economic preoccupation with property in cattle in the first half of the colonial period. These cases also expose Chagga attitudes toward controlled human beings and differentiate sharply between male and female. In the first case a biological daughter is treated as a "pawn," and offered as a pledge for a cattle debt. In the second, an unrelated, captured male child comes to be treated legally as a son and is preferred as an heir to a biological daughter. The dispute between them is over the inheritance of cattle. *The second set of cases* concerns the attempts of men to give land to their sons-in-law and the historical change in attitude toward such transfers. Such gifts become less acceptable as land shortage becomes more acute. The assertion of patrilineal interest becomes stronger, not weaker over time. This is one of many indica-tions that the characteristics of "the patrilineage" are historically specific and not necessarily "the same" from one period to another, even though the entity called "the patrilineage" persists. *The third set of cases* concerns three types of situation affected by increasing land shortage: the attempts by land lenders to reclaim their land and terminate tenancies at will, the attempts to classify un-occupied land as "abandoned" in order to install new holders, and instances in which loans of cash are secured by land used as collateral. The last type of case shows how the use of land as collateral created a new mode through which land became vulnerable to transfer out of patrimonial control. Together the three sets of cases clearly reflect the implications of an ever-deepening commitment to cash cropping and a money economy. Incidentally they also bring to light the shifting role of chiefship, as chiefs strategized to serve their own interests in a changing economic milieu.

Transactions such as are reported in these three sets of cases, many of them involving loans and collateral, have a special use for the historian. Such transactions expose changing Chagga ideas of economic equivalence at particular moments in their past. A time series of relevant law cases can demonstrate the changing connections between different categories of exchangeable resources. The cases chosen for discussion here show substantial shifts in the kinds of debts that Chagga men could incur and in the kind of collateral they could offer when borrowing. Indirectly the cases illuminate the strategies that individuals could use to advance their own interests, the kinds of choices that were available. At the beginning of this century human beings could be offered as collateral in cattle transactions. Many later cases show that subsequently animals were regularly traded for land. After several more decades land itself could be offered as collateral for large loans of cash.

Radical changes also took place in the modes of official intervention. In the early cases the chief appears on stage rapaciously using every occasion to acquire personal rights over persons and cattle. However, at that time a chief's consent was not necessary to transfer land (see Gutmann 1926: 305; HRAF: 273, on the German period when the chiefs consent was not needed). Later chiefs were more constrained in matters of persons and beasts and instead concentrated on increasing their income through patronage and land acquisition. At that point they actively interposed themselves in all land allocations and transactions (Hailey 1938: 848 cites a Chagga Native Authority regulation legitimating the transfer of land only if *made with the authority of the chief*). Thus in the middle colonial period the chiefs' "traditional" dual capacities as allocators of unoccupied fields and as presiders over litigated controversies expanded and came to have entirely new significance. For everyone, the shift to coffee cultivation and the increase in population produced a reinterpretation of the value of land as against cattle and cash and concomitantly the revision of many land-related practices. Throughout, the chiefs and other dispute hearers were presumed to be invoking and applying "customary law" rules. That was what their colonial governors both expected and required. To the extent that the Chagga did actually use the "traditional" rules, this apparent reiteration of the past was done in rapidly altering circumstances. The significance changed. The cases give clear evidence of this historical sequence.

Case Set I

A.   PLEDGING A CHILD IN EXCHANGE FOR A COW: A HUMAN BEING AS COLLATERAL IN THE EARLY 1900S

A case in which a child was used as collateral for a cattle loan arose in the first decade or two of this century. The controversy was heard before Salema, the chief of Moshi, who ruled from 1900 to 1917. We owe the description of the situation to the missionary, Bruno Gutmann, who was on Kilimanjaro when the case was litigated (Gutmann 1926: 128–29; HRAF: 111–12; cited and discussed in Moore 1986a: 106–107). The case involved one of Chief Salema's subjects who had borrowed a cow to pay a cattle debt and who had failed to repay the beast.

Some years before the hearing, the borrower, Mavin Ovenja, had obtained an animal from his wife's sister's husband to satisfy a cattle creditor who was pressing him. The wife's sister's husband lived some distance away in another chiefdom. By way of collateral, Mavin gave one of his daughters to the lender. The idea was that when that daughter was old enough to marry, if the debt had not been paid, the lender could either betroth the girl to his own son without paying bridewealth or could let her marry someone else and collect the bridewealth from the marriage. (In the meanwhile he had the use of her labor.) In time the borrower's daughter was duly betrothed to the lender's son. All would have been well except that the young woman refused to marry the son and ran away, back to her parent's house.

The chief resolved the case by paying his subject's cattle debt himself. This was not simply an act of generosity. By doing so the chief acquired the right to the debtor's daughter's bridewealth. He stood in the place of the original creditor. The chief, acting as judge, both settled the debt and inserted himself as successor to the legal rights of one of the parties before him. The case neatly demonstrates the way the chief could use his role in the early colonial period as lender of capital, as a person directly involved in the transactions of his people when he chose to be, and possibly also as a strategizing patron who had his own material interests at heart when he moved to intervene. [It is not clear from the case whether the chief took the girl into his own household. The frequent use of female child labor by the chiefs in their households at the time was deplored by Gutmann who called it a form of slavery (1926: 388–89; HRAF: 348–49).]

Thus a daughter and/or her future bridewealth appears to have been one of the best forms of security a man without beasts could offer against a "borrowed" animal. Animals that were borrowed to be disposed of (as opposed to animals borrowed for "keeping") were used to pay bridewealth, *were* slaughtered in ritual, or were used to pay debts. Lending a cow to be thus consumed or given away involved a high risk. The lender was taking a considerable chance if, as was frequently the case, the borrower had uncertain prospects of acquiring a beast with which he might later make a repayment. The creditor who pressed for repayment had recourse to the other major scarce resource: labor. A defaulting cattle-debtor either had to supply a child as a debt-slave, or had to work off the debt through his own labor (Gutmann 1926: 231–32, 472, 477–79; HRAF: 204–05, 424, 429–30). Bananas and other produce form the debtor's garden were sometimes due to the creditor for a time, but there is no talk of the creditor acquiring a right to the land itself (Gutmann 1926: 231–32, 474–86; HRAF: 204–05, 426–37).

There was another, entirely different form of cattle "borrowing" in which the borrowed cow was not to be disposed of, but rather placed for "keeping" to be fed and bred. The borrower got the milk and manure and had certain rights to meat at slaughter time. Such a cow could be demanded back at will by the lender. That kind of cattle placement was often (usually?) made with non-kinsmen to conceal assets from relatives who might demand that a beast be "loaned" to them (see Moore 1986a: 67–70). Since the return of the cow so placed could always be demanded by the owner, and the possessor had no right of alienation or disposal, there was less need for any form of collateral. However, taking children as security may have reduced the likelihood that the possessor of the animal would pretend the beast had died while in fact transferring it to someone else. Thus the practice of child placement as collateral may not have been unusual just before the turn of the century when it appears to have been commonplace for the inhabitants of Moshi and Marangu to place their cattle with men in Rombo. In return, and by way of security, the Rombo cattle keepers gave their children as collateral/hostages to the cattle lenders. Early in the colonial period the Germans ended this practice and the debt-pledge children were returned (Gutmann 1926: 479; HRAF: 430).

Despite the colonial prohibition, the use of female children as collateral seems to have continued long after German times in some places on the mountain. Case number 7 Mwika 1930 (in volume labelled Kitabu cha Shauri 1927) mentions another female child given in lieu of the debt of a cow. When she reached adulthood the young woman ran away and returned to her father. The man who had supplied the cow sued the father of the girl in 1929, and the girl's father was then ordered by the court to pay three cows. The father then fell ill and died. The subsequent 1930 case was brought by the court against the man to whom the cows were to have been paid because he had appropriated one of the cows of the son of his debtor by force instead of bringing the matter to the chief. For using self-help rather than coming to the chief, the man was fined 20 shillings. in this case there was no question of the chief taking on the debt of his subject. Instead there was a strong assertion of the power of the court and its monopoly on enforcement.

There is always much less certainty about founding an argument on the absence of evidence than on its presence, but as far as one can tell, early in the century the Chagga never offered land as collateral against the borrowing of cattle.[1] It seems entirely logical, economically and socially, that land would not have been a desirable form of collateral at that time. First of all, land was not a particularly scarce resource. Bush land was plentiful. The colonial imposition of peace, and the mandatory end of the interchiefdom wars took the danger out of living at the outskirts of existing settlements. Bush land was thus not only available but had stopped being undesirable. Since every man had had enough land to fill the subsistence needs of his household, and could get more by cultivating bush, even had it been possible, the opportunity to acquire an extra kihamba plot from a debtor probably would not have been particularly attractive. Moreover, landholding in the banana belt was closely associated with membership in a lineage and local community. For creditors to appropriate a piece of land in the heart of the debtor's kinship area would not have had much attraction. The creditor or his kinsman would likely have been unwelcome outsiders. Thus any garden plot, even if it was economically equivalent to another, was not socially interchangeable with other pieces of land of the same size and productivity. Hence the availability of land and the social correlates of landholding made land an unsuitable form of collateral for cattle debts.

That was the situation in the early years of this century when the practice of coffee cultivation was at its inception. At that time most arable land was

---

1.   See tables showing the changing subject-matter of cases in various chiefdoms during the British colonial period in Moore 1986: 174–79.

still used exclusively for food crops, most of which were consumed locally. In that pre-1916 period there was no cash market in land. There was a kind of individual property in particular plots for married adult males, with associated, but conditional, rights of disposition. Coffee was first introduced in the Kilema mission in 1895 (Shann 1956: 29–30). The subsequent German imposition of taxes probably provided a spur to coffee cultivation and certainly hastened the generalization of the cash economy. Taxes were first imposed in 1897, but it was possible to work off the obligation by doing labor on public projects. By 1905 free labor in lieu of taxes was abolished and paid work was substituted (Iliffe 1979: 160). But for the Chagga coffee provided a way of obtaining cash without working for the colonial government or for the settlers.

For those early years of the century there seems good reason why I can find no mention of land offered as security for a cattle debt, or any other debt. The cases confirm what other indications suggest. In that period the highest value seems to have been put on human labor and on cattle.

B.   AN "ADOPTED" WAR CAPTIVE AND HIS RIGHT TO INHERIT CATTLE: HUMAN
BEINGS AS PRIZES OF BATTLE IN 1930

In some of the late nineteenth-century accounts of Kilimanjaro, there is sub-stantial mention of the slave trade (Johnston 1886: 97, 180, 184). Slaves were certainly part of the caravan traffic to the coast that passed through the Kili-manjaro area. There is no convincing evidence that the Chagga themselves kept slaves as such, though they incorporated women and children who were war captives into their households (Johnston 1886: 165 and case in this section). There is good reason to believe that adult male Chagga war captives were sold into the trade. Sir Harry Johnston said that when he reproached the Chagga chief, Mandara, for slaving, Mandara replied to the following effect, "What am I to do? To kill captives would be wrong. To return them to my enemies would mean that they would just attack me later. If I keep them in my own land, my people would say, 'if strangers are to occupy the soil, where is the room for our children to cultivate?' Then what can I do but sell them to the Arabs" (para-phrase of Johnston 1886: 181). Mandara's allusion to the slaves as enemy war-riors implies that his reference was to male captives.

The legal status of "adopted" young captives was raised in 1930 in litigation over an estate. A man who had been a captive child, one Kilegho of Kirueni vil-lage, sued his stepsister, Rebeka, of Mrimbo village, for eight cows *and* six goats, which he alleged was his proper share of his stepfather's estate (21 Mwika 1930 in Kitabu cha Shauri Mwika 1927). Rebeka was the biological child of Kilegho's stepfather. It is of interest that there was no controversy over the land of his stepfather to which he seems to have succeeded. His undisputed succession to the land implies that his stepfather's agnates had sufficient land not to contest his right. It also speaks to the legal incapacity of women to share in agnatically transmitted lands, though they could in some circumstances inherit cattle.

Kilegho's testimony says,

> Many years ago my father brought me as a captive from the war. I was very young—I had only four teeth, two on the upper jaw and two on the lower. When I arrived Rebeka was suckling and I shared the same mother with her. My status in the family was like that of any other child. My father had no other son. Then father died and left me with mother Matemu. I stayed with her until she died and I inherited the property of my father.

> By this time Rebeka had married in Keni Mriti [in Rombo where she lived with her husband]. Before father died he gave Rebeka one cow. He also gave Kinangaro and Kiloka, the sons of his younger brother, one cow each. Some weeks after the death of my father the relatives of my mother came to claim *mahari* [bridewealth]. I gave Sifueli [sister of mother] one cow, the remaining part of the bridewealth which my father had not paid.

Among the Chagga bridewealth obligations were usually not paid in full at the time of marriage but paid gradually over time. There often were payments still due when the woman died. The argument being made in the court was that an adoptive son who undertook to honor the bridewealth obligations of his deceased stepfather was behaving like a real son to his cost, hence should be deemed by the court to be a son.

> Later Sifueli came to *me* and told me that Rebeka and Kinangaro wanted to steal my cows. She then advised me to give her my cows to keep for me because she did not want me to be robbed. I agreed and she went away. The next day she came with Daniel. I took them and showed them two cows, one of which was being looked after by Kikwani and the other by Katore. Daniel wrote down the signs of the cows. I also told them about other people who had my cows and I asked them to go there and take them or put down their signs.

After all of this, Sifueli went to see Rebeka and they plotted to appropriate my cows. I would not have realized what the situation was had it not been for the subsequent action they took. They slaughtered one of my cows without informing me. When I got the news I asked Sifueli why they slaughtered my cow without my consent. She told me to bring the case before the Chief. I did. The case was heard and Sifueli said that she had possession of my cows on orders from Rebeka. Then I decided to bring a case against Rebeka before the court.

Rebeka the defendant said,

My mother Matemu died and left the cows to me. Now in the court I have been asked whether I gave Sifueli permission to hold Kilegho's cows. The cows do not belong to Kilegho. In the previous case the elders sentenced me and ordered me to pay Kilegho five cows. The three remaining cows were to be left for me. I disagreed with the decision. Kilegho and I have been in conflict for a very long time. However, I was forced to pay him the five cows and the court promised that it would reconcile me with Kilegho. I refused to be reconciled with Kilegho but agreed to pay him five cows. Of the six goats he is claiming, five of them have died and the last one will die soon since it is very ill.

Judgment:

Rebeka has no right to the inheritance although the property belonged to her mother. According to custom, such inheritance is only for males, for sons. Although Kilegho was not born of Rebeka's mother nor was he the son of her father, the parents had accepted the captive boy as their son because they had no other son. Thus the court judges that Kilegho is entitled to five cows and Rebeka to three cows. The reason is that though Rebeka is the real child of the parents, she is a female. With regard to the goats, Kilegho is to investigate whether they are alive or dead and must inform the court.

The court also said, "There are many people who have inherited as Kilegho has done, and it is not a new thing in the village." Rebeka lost her fee of 12 shillings 50. Those present were Chief Solomoni II and nine elders.

This case is not only evidence of the adoption of male captives in the upheavals of the late nineteenth century, but also shows clearly that such adopted male captives had greater rights of inheritance than female biological children.

The case gives some sense of the considerable number of animals a household might have had at the time, and that the practice of placing them in the households of others continued. Here, given the circumstances, the court found reason to treat a non-agnate as if he were an agnate.

Case Set II

TWO ATTEMPTS TO TRANSFER INHERITED LAND TO A SON-IN-LAW, ONE SUCCESSFUL, ONE UNSUCCESSFUL

The two instances that I shall describe here occurred over what must roughly have been a fifty-year period. Both involved the question of the consent of kinsmen to the alienation of land to an outsider, a man who was not a member of the lineage. In both cases a father of daughters sought to bestow land on a son-in-law. In Chagga law the father needed the agreement (tacit or explicit) of his agnates to make such a transfer of patrimonial property (Gutmann [1926]: 306; HRAF: 275). What is interesting is that in the earlier transfer (which occurred between 1910 and 1920) there proved to be no problem about allocating land to sons-in-law. In the later case (1959) the donor was thwarted by his kinsmen who withheld their consent. These cases show that the use of the agnatic consent rule was intensified as the colonial period progressed and land became scarce, even though other patrilineal ties were gradually attenuated. Thus the public political place of patrilineages weakened over the course of the century, and the existence of the missions and the spread of formal education diminished the hold of patrilineages over ritual matters. Nevertheless, patrilineal kinship became ever more important as an avenue to land, and patrilineal ties remain of major significance to this day.

The earlier of the two cases of land transfer to sons-in-law concerns Kinyala, a member of the M— lineage. Kinyala saw his three daughters married between 1910 and 1920. Having no sons, he gave each son-in-law a plot of land close to his own within the territory controlled by the M— lineage, but along its outside border (data from mapping and genealogical inquiry during fieldwork).

The oral report that Kinyala's kinsmen agreed to the transfer at the time seems entirely reliable. He was in the grandparental generation of senior men whom I knew. Not only did his descendants report that such consent was given, but they acted accordingly. When the original grantees died, no members of the M— lineage tried to reclaim the land on any ground, least of all that consent had been withheld, and the present generation would surely have made such claims had there been a shred of evidence to go on. When asked about this in the 1970s, one of the men in the lineage asserted that he and his kinsmen were barred from reclaiming the land because of the promises made by their ancestors. Today, the descendants of Kinyala's sons-in-law hold those plots with undisputed authority (see Moore 1986a: 228, situating Kinyala in the genealogical chart of his patrilineage). Their lands have simply dropped out of the M— 's lineage territory and form part of the heritable land of families from other lineages. This is an instance in which there is every reason to believe that the legal rules about alienation with consent described by Gutmann were in fact observed (Gutmann [1926]: 302–9; HRAF: 270–6).

A contrasting instance of an attempt to transfer land to a son-in-law occurred in 1959 (field material collected in the 1970s). Siara, a respected senior man, tried to give his son-in-law a plot of land from his own patrimony, but his kinsmen refused to agree to this. Subsequently Siara appealed to the chief to overrule their decision, but the chief upheld the kinsmen. Siara's was an odd case. Siara did have two sons, but one was a Catholic priest, hence would never marry and have children, and the other had been disinherited because of a quarrel between father and son. The disinherited son no longer lived on Kilimanjaro. What is more, that son's only surviving offspring were female. Siara argued that he had the right to alienate to a son-in-law since he "had no sons" in any social sense. His biological sons would never establish a line of descendants for him.

The chief decreed that Siara could not give away the land of his lineage in that way. Siara was, however, allowed to *sell* his land, take the proceeds, and give the money to his son-in-law to buy another plot. Thus the chief was not conserving the land for Siara's sons. I assume (but unfortunately did not ask) that Siara sold the land to one of his agnates, since by that time (1959) the consent rule had turned into a rule of first refusal. (A man who wished to sell was said to be obliged to offer his plot to his agnates before selling to any outsider.) What distinguishes this case is that Siara had not wanted to sell, but rather to *give* the land to his son-in-law. He wanted his daughter and grandchildren to live nearby. The same rule applied. The rule of first refusal was used as if a gift to a non-agnate were equivalent to an offer to sell.

The two "son-in-law transactions" suggest a certain historical continuity. Each involves the same stated legal norm: that the alienation of patrimonial land to a non-kinsman requires the consent of agnates. One might be tempted to say, then, that the legal rule was the same from 1910 into the 1950s. But to say no more would be a distortion, an overemphasis of form over content, since it omits crucial changes in the context. Over the century, coffee cultivation, population increase, and land shortage had made men more jealous of their agnates' land, and ever less likely to agree to its alienation especially if they could afford to buy it themselves. The rule of "first refusal" constituted a substantial transformation of the agnatic consent rule. In its practice, the localized patrilineage of the 1950s was was an artifact of the conditions of the 1950s. The patrilineage was not simply an atemporal entity perpetuating a "tradition." The new historical circumstances in which an old legal rule was used had become part of the new meaning of that rule.

Case Set III

A. LOANED LAND, COFFEE PLANTING, AND THE PAYMENT OF ANIMALS FOR LAND IN THE 1920S AND 1930S

Unlike loaned beasts, loaned land cannot be consumed by a borrower or made to disappear. Thus lending land was less risky than lending cattle and was often done. Among the Chagga loaned land could always be retaken by the donor, provided that it was possible to prove that all rights had not been transferred to the borrower, and that compensation was paid for improvements. A 1929 case shows the mounting tensions that arose over loaned land once coffee growing became an issue (26 Mwika 1929). The lawsuit was brought by a commoner named Joshua, of Kondeny village, against Naomi, the daughter of the then chief of Mwika, Mangi Solomoni of the Orio lineage. Joshua was unrelated to the Orios. The chief did not preside at the hearing since it involved a member of his immediate family (his daughter), but it seems likely that the village headmen and elders who heard the case were not uninfluenced by the chief's interest in the outcome. This formal judicial standing-back from a case because the judge is an interested party contrasts strikingly with the earlier case of the pledge child, in which the chief involved himself directly in the affairs of the disputants before him, and so-to-speak made himself a party to their transactions by interposing himself personally and financially in the resolution of their dispute. This change was probably of colonial provenance.

In 1921 (date not mentioned directly but inferred from internal evidence in the case text) one Joshua had asked Ngapanyi Orio (a relative of Chief Solomoni) for a piece of land on which to live. Ngapanyi provided him with an undeveloped piece of land and Joshua built a house on it and planted a banana grove. Three years later (probably in 1924) the case says that the government ordered everyone to plant coffee.[2] Joshua told Ngapanyi Orio that he wanted to plant coffee on the plot. Ngapanyi refused him permission to do so, asserting his right as an owner to refuse such an improvement. Had Ngapanyi allowed Joshua to plant the coffee, and had he later wanted to reclaim the land (as loaned land), he would have been obliged to pay compensation for the coffee bushes. That would have been expensive.

According to Joshua's testimony, Ngapanyi not only refused Joshua permission to plant coffee, but also forced him to transfer the land, house, and banana grove to Naomi, Chief Solomoni's daughter. It was understood that she would have to compensate Joshua for his improvements on the land, namely the house and the banana grove. Naomi was originally to pay two goats for the house. Naomi did not pay the two goats but instead gave Joshua a young heifer for the house and promised to pay him an additional goat later on for the banana grove.

Five years passed. Then in 1929 Ngapanyi Orio claimed his kihamba from Joshua, I suppose on the theory that Joshua was still the basic loanee, though Naomi was the resident occupant of the land. (Since the full "redemption price" had not been paid to Joshua, Ngapanyi could not yet claim the land as his own.) This reclaim demand was discussed by the elders (i.e., it did not go formally to the court) and Ngapanyi was ordered to pay Joshua two goats for the banana grove which Joshua had planted. Joshua then told Naomi to leave the kihamba which belonged to Ngapanyi Orio. She refused because she had bought the house and had paid a heifer for it and wanted to be compensated for giving it up. Joshua then took Naomi to court in the present case.

Naomi testified that she had returned to Mwika chiefdom from Mamba when her husband died. At that time she had gone to her father, Chief Solomoni, to ask him to help her to find a place to live. Joshua then agreed (under duress?) to "sell" her the house and the banana grove (not the land, but the improvements) for three goats. She did not manage to get the three goats, but paid a heifer (the equivalent of two goats) instead. Five years elapsed, and then

---

2.   That may well have been the way the matter was understood and communicated in Mwika. Major (later Sir) Charles Dundas, who was the officer in charge of the district from 1919 to 1924, relentlessly pressed coffee cultivation on the Chagga, thinking that would emancipate them in many different ways. One of his methods was to lend money to the chiefs to buy coffee seedlings for planting in their chiefdoms (Rogers 1972: 236–39).

Joshua brought her to court in this case to get the kihamba back so that he could return it to Ngapanyi Orio. Naomi said, "If Joshua wants me to move, let him bring my cow, the same cow and not another, whether it is alive or dead."

The decision in the case was as follows: Joshua was to return Naomi's cow as it was alive and now fully grown. Naomi was to turn over the kihamba to Ngapanyi Orio. Ngapanyi Orio was to pay Joshua two goats for the banana grove.

Joshua seems to have ended up with very little, and was also out of pocket for the two shilling court fee. What is apparent from the case is that little value was set on the kihamba until coffee growing was quite general and local land shortages were beginning to be felt. Land loans were treated as tenancies-at-will (as they had been even in German times and continued to be until legislatively abolished after independence). A reclaiming lender had always had to pay compensation for improvements in order to repossess his land, but that was the only constraint on ousting the loanee at any time. However, until land became the vehicle for a cash crop and became scarce and valuable, there was seldom reason to reclaim it. Land loans were heritable. The position of lender and borrower were inherited by the sons or other successors of the original parties and the relationship might go on forever, marked by the annual giving of ritual gifts to reassert the loan before witnesses.

This case, though jumbled in the record, is interesting on many scores. First, it shows that a widowed daughter of a chief could come home to her father and expect to be given a piece of land to live on in the patrilineal domain. Second, it suggests that the chief regarded it appropriate to require his kinsman to oust the unrelated holder of loaned land for such a purpose. There is a sense here of the power of the chief to impose his will on his agnates. Third, despite her highborn connections, the daughter seems not to have been able to muster the full payment of three goats. Was that a matter of poverty or disdain for the debt shown by a chief's daughter? It must have been clear from the beginning that all that was being transferred to Naomi was the right to occupy since no woman could acquire a disposable right in land. Thus the basic legal issue in the case was whether Joshua, the original loanee, still had an interest in the land as against his own lender, Ngapanyi Orio, because full compensation had neither been paid by Naomi, nor by Ngapanyi. Fourth, it shows that at that time and place lineage land was easily transferrable to non-kin provided it was merely loaned. Fifth, the case also suggests the standard of value equivalence: three goats for a house and banana grove, or a heifer and a goat. Improvements were what determined the price of reclaim, not some other notion of the value of the land itself. The emphasis on land loaning and redemption and the use of beasts in exchange, suggest a very different economy from that which prevailed later on.

How early in the century did cash transactions for land take place? As mentioned, earlier in 1927 the chiefs vehemently opposed the buying and selling of land and said it should be prohibited (Griffiths 1930: 63, 88). Yet by the 1930s the case records give indications of some full transfers of land for debts. In one instance a man appropriated land his debtor had temporarily abandoned. (The nature of the debt is unspecified.) The court allowed the creditor to keep the land because (1) the debtor had not made a timely objection, and (2) had also obtained a substitute plot from the chief, i.e. had abandoned the land his creditor had appropriated (10 Mamba 1930). Another Mamba case shows that a debt of animals was directly applied to the purchase price of a piece of land (32 Mamba 1931). In that case the defendant had sold the plaintiff a plot of land for three goats and a cow. The defendant had owed the plaintiff three goats, a debt which his father had incurred and he had inherited. In payment for the land, the debt was to be written off, and the plaintiff-buyer-creditor was also to pay one cow in addition, as well as to pay cash compensation for an improvement—i.e., for some coffee trees that had been planted on the land.[3]

The reason the defendant-debtor-seller gave in court for urgently wanting to transfer ownership to the plaintiff was not only to erase the debt of the goats and to acquire a cow and some cash, but because he feared that since he had moved to another chiefdom and the land was not occupied, he would lose all rights to it. He states in the case record that he had heard that there was a move on by the *mchilis* (headmen) and the *mangi* (chief) to appropriate all unoccupied land. His fears were well founded (see Griffiths Land Tenure Report 1930: 63, 88). To salvage what he could, he decided to dispose of the abandoned kihamba

---

3. There were complicating circumstances. The defendant's own right to the land was not unencumbered. The kihamba in question was one that the defendant had allowed a third party to use for a time—i.e., the land was "loaned." The third party had planted the coffee bushes on the land, but there was no question that he was only a borrower and not an owner. The plaintiff, the new owner, had agreed to pay compensation for the coffee trees. Normally that would have been the obligation of the defendant, the original owner and lender of the land. As indicated earlier, under Chagga law, a land lender who wants to reclaim his land must pay the land borrower compensation *for* any improvements before he can reappropriate it. However, in this case, the compensation for the coffee trees was *never* paid by either the defendant or the plaintiff, since the borrower abandoned the land, moved to Mwika (another chiefdom), and died there without having been compensated.

and sell it to the plaintiff for the cow, the erasure of the debt and the payment of coffeebush-compensation.

In another case (26 Mamba 1932) two men claimed the same kihamba that had earlier been an object of controversy between their fathers. The defendant was in occupancy. The plaintiff wanted the kihamba back. At one point in their various quarrels, the defendant offered to pay the plaintiff a cow for the kihamba in which he was a resident. The court held that the offer to buy the land for a cow was tantamount to an admission by the defendant that he did not own the land. The court thus ruled that the plaintiff was the rightful owner of the plot, and could recover it, but should permit the defendant to use the bananas growing on it for a period of two years to give the defendant time to obtain and develop another kihamba. These cases all speak of sales, but the land is being "sold" largely for beasts, rather than for cash (see also 25 Mamba 1932).

These cases are not only of interest because they suggest the form of transaction in which land was obtained from the chiefs or purchased from others in the early 1930s but also because of what they indicate about geographical mobility and the continued existence of some vacant plots. In the first (10 Mamba 1930) both the plaintiff and the defendant had moved from Mamba to Marangu (two neighboring chiefdoms) and had obtained land from the *mangi* (chief) of Marangu. This suggests that there was still no absolute land shortage everywhere at the time, since plots in some areas could still be had on request. The second case (32 Mamba 1931), involved a man (the occupier) who moved to Mwika from Mamba, as well as one who moved from Marangu to Mamba. Other Mamba cases in the same period also mention persons who moved. The many instances in which the original owner had for one reason or another ceased to occupy his land and then wanted to sell it or reoccupy it seemed to be particularly problematic and particularly indicative of historical change. In the days of land plenty an absentee could always expect to obtain land on his return and in theory, at least, had a preferential right to his original plot. In precolonial days, when the rule had its origins, the absence of a man was most often either to fight in distant wars or to be involved in the long-distance trade. What seems to have crept into the law during the colonial period as land shortage made itself felt was that land was deemed to be permanently abandoned the moment the holder settled elsewhere. Land shortage and the chief's potential reversionary right probably lies in the background of what seems to have been an increasingly precipitous assertion of abandonment (Gutmann 1926: 62, 302–09; HRAF: 50, 270–76).

It was always in the chief's interest to appropriate or reallocate abandoned plots. He received a "gift of thanks" and a grateful subject every time he allocated any land (see for example 46 Mamba 1933). In Mamba the chief's interest seems to have become enlarged over time to the point where the Native Authority (i.e., the chief) claimed that it had a continuing interest in land even after it was allocated. In 56 Mamba 1940 a man was prosecuted for selling a kihamba without the consent of the Native Authority. The kihamba was one of two that had been allocated to the defendant's father and which he, the defendant, had duly and properly inherited. Nevertheless, he was fined ten shillings for selling a kihamba which "belonged to the Native Authority." He was ordered to pay within ten days or be imprisoned for twenty. Chiefs were increasingly in competition with their subjects for the control of land and control over transactions in land. The cases from the 1930s give clear evidence that this tension existed even at a time before the money economy had created a cash market in land.

B. LAND AS COLLATERAL FOR A LOAN OF CASH IN 1957

Twenty years later, the picture was quite different. In Mwika in 1957 a case was brought that illustrates the profound change in the economy and in relative values that had taken place since the 1930s (44 Mwika 1957). In 1954 plaintiff and defendant made an agreement that plaintiff would lend defendant 1320 shillings. Defendant was to repay the money within two years plus a "profit" of 5 percent. If the defendant failed to repay the cash, the plaintiff had the right to appropriate the defendant's kihamba on payment of an additional 1880 shillings—in other words, the defendant's kihamba was the collateral for the original loan. Plaintiff and defendant were not kinsmen. The court ruled that the plaintiff could pay the additional 1880 shillings and take the kihamba.

Here land and cash are fully interchangeable. The relative value of beasts has gone down. In 1954 a standard official value was put on a cow of 200 shillings. All other animals *were* declared to be worth 50 shillings. A notice to this effect was sent to all the courts by the paramount chief (Keni Mriti Mengwe File in courthouse, labelled Kazi za Baraza 1951– , Document 38, Notice to All Primary Courts). The contrast with the price of a piece of land is dramatic. Even though one does not know the size or quality of the kihamba sold for 3200 shillings, the magnitude of the difference in price is so great that the time was clearly over when the old conventional "price" for a kihamba, a cow and a goat, had been acceptable.

CONCLUSION

To review a small group of legal transactions and disputes that occurred over a fifty-year period in one small corner of Africa is not to establish the basis for sweeping historical generalization. But the cases suggest lines of analysis that could be mined further. The present inquiry deepens the level of detail in the history of one locality and simultaneously illustrates some general methodological strategies.

The conceptual innovation introduced here was to approach economic and social change obliquely. The rationale is that change in social systems that are (or were) strongly kin-oriented can be profitably explored through a sequence of property transactions between persons who are not kin. Among the Chagga legal disputes that involve patrimonial property (or rights) acquired by non-agnates have proved to be very revealing. The rationale is that transfers of property that do not directly reproduce the kinship structure are likely to be the repositories of important clues about changes in the operation of the total system of allocation and exchange. The pattern of transfers within the lineage through inheritance and conventional allocation is by definition culturally conceived as reiterative. But the parallel existence of property transfers in which, from the point of view of the acquirer, the property is of extra-lineal provenance puts lineage affairs in a larger context. The Chagga transfers noted here concerned persons, cattle, land and cash.[4]

It is clear that among the Chagga a non-agnatic transactional world existed alongside the descent-based one long before the cash economy worked its major transformations. Some patrimonial property leaked into those transactions. Some historical changes are more visible in that non-agnatic domain than in the kin-based nexus, which had to legitimate itself in the courts during the colonial period by claiming to be traditional, customary, and ruled by norms. The nonagnatic transactions appear very much more directly as contract-like arrangements, or, in the case of appropriations and allocations, as discretionary acts. This is not to say that contract-like arrangements do not exist *within* lineages, or that lineage members do not exercise discretion in their allocations. On the contrary the negotiation and renegotiation of agnatic relationships is one of the basic facts of Chagga lineage life. But the rhetoric that surrounds lineage

---

4.   Transactions between non-kin in non-patrimonial goods and services constitute an
     important but quite different topic which has not been addressed here.

affairs often redefines the negotiated and discretionary as pragmatic exceptions made within the general practice of normative kinship "custom." The choice made here to concentrate on certain transfers of property to (or from) non-agnates tries to escape from the ideology of descent to inspect occasions for other rationales of action.

The cases described illustrate a series of transformations in human relationships, in political roles, and in economic values. These change the content of law. Thus what was once a generalized right to reclaim land that one had once occupied after a period of absence was subtly changed by a broadened concept of "abandonment." Greed for land in time of shortage led to a preference for interpreting the legal status of unoccupied plots as "abandoned," in order to install new holders. Also, as land came to be bought and sold the requirement that agnates consent to the transfer of patrimonial land to make such a transfer valid gradually became translated into a right to first refusal in case of sale. There are substantial contrasts between the cases in the pre-1916 period, those around 1930, and those in the 1950s. Some of these are an exercise in changing equivalences, for example, the case series that proceeds from a time when children were offered as collateral for cattle debts, through a period when beasts were exchanged for land, to a later point where land was offered as collateral for borrowed cash. The cases also give clues about changes in the chiefly role from a time when chiefs might interpose themselves personally in the affairs of those who brought their cases to him, through a time when the chief withdrew from a case in which he had an interest, to a point where chiefs intruded in every sale or assignment of land by requiring that their consent be obtained for a valid transfer to exist. Some of these changes seem to have taken place because of the intentional and direct intervention of the colonial government (such as the attempt to terminate the use of pledge-children, the pressure on chiefs not to be judges in their own causes, and the order to plant coffee). Other changes seem much more the product of non-legislated transformations in the economy. The shift from a preoccupation with the value of beasts to a preoccupation with the value of land and the increasing use of cash surely reflect the deep economic consequences of cash cropping, demographic increase, and land shortage.

Some of these cases clarify the particular manner in which at various times the patrimonial property of one man could find its way out of his patrimonial stream into the heritable hoard of another man who was not agnatically related. Others show some of the ways that property could be acquired from a chief, or by a chief, and suggest how important the acquisition of land and its allocation must have been to the formation of the chiefly role during the colonial period.

The instances reviewed here are few. There are many more cases to similar effect in the files. Even the ones noted here suffice to show that law cases can be used to extract telling details about a sequence of changing local circumstances over a historical period. Local law cases reflect the local history of African peoples rather than the history of the Europeans who ruled them. Methodologically, if certain types of property transfer are treated as "diagnostic events," that treatment not only sharpens the focus of analysis, and provides a basis for case selection, but the cases become a running commentary on the changing economy and surrounding relationships (Moore 1987). In a society in which ideas about kinship inform the legal frameworks that surround many claims to major items of property, there is no more telling confirmation of deep changes inside the kin-based property system than to examine shifts at its periphery.

CHAPTER FIVE

History and the Redefinition of Custom on Kilimanjaro

Local customary law "systems" within present African states are referred to from time to time in legislation and in the courts. These references read as if preserved parts of previous traditions actually existed intact. In Tanzania the Primary Courts are specifically given jurisdiction over cases arising under customary law (*sheria ya mila*) (Maelezo 1964). Yet it is obvious that in practice the congeries of custom that do survive enjoy their continued life in profoundly altered political and economic environments and have themselves changed in a variety of ways. The "customary rules" that do remain in use are not necessarily Tylorian "survivals," anachronistic fragments of the past that are neither part of nor appropriate to a contemporary world (Tylor 1958: 70). Instead, they must be seen at this moment as integral elements in an ongoing political order. In Africa the invocation of tradition can be as much a way of resisting the government as a means of cheating one's brother.

Present-day clusters of local legal "traditions" therefore require interpretation in at least two apparently contradictory dimensions—the dimension of

Editor's note: This chapter is a reprint of Moore, Sally Falk. 1989. "History and the redefinition of custom on Kilimanjaro." In *History and power in the study of law: New directions in legal anthropology*, edited by June Starr and Jane F. Collier, 277–301. Ithaca and London: Cornell University Press.

formal continuity over time and the dimension of sequential transformation. Emphasis on the sameness of form over time has often been important both in the strategies of individuals and in the policies of governments. The very concept of "customary law" has legitimating implications.

However, "custom" also means current local practice that may or may not be tied to the deep past. As a legal scholar of the Middle Ages named Azo (d. 1230) said a long time ago, "A custom can be called *long* if it was introduced within ten or twenty years, *very long* if it dates from thirty years, and *ancient* if it dates from forty years" (Plucknett 1956: 308). Tradition as it was and practice as it is are not necessarily the same. Context, content, and meaning shift, even as familiar forms are repeated for new reasons.

This chapter is an attempt to communicate a sense of the practical facts and theoretical significance of a historical instance of such metamorphoses—the past one hundred years of legal change among the Chagga of Mount Kilimanjaro.[1] If law in such a setting is analyzed over time, situated in the life of a particular community, then it follows that the changing circumstances of that community are part of the content of its legal system. To abstract legal ideas from the operating community in which they are "used" generates the kind of categorical and semantic analysis recently produced by Geertz (1983: 167). That kind of approach may tell us about ideological forms, but such "linguistic" or "literary" analyses of the conceptual elements in a legal order do not take one very far in understanding what people actually do on the ground or why they do it at particular times and places. I agree with Geertz that it is essential to know in what terms people think about basic moral and legal issues. Yet, however elegantly such ideas may be described, presenting the "traditional" categories of legal discussion without the context of discourse offers statements without speakers, ideas without their occasions, concepts outside history.

Instead, the two case histories of land disputes below, both chosen from the 1969 period, provide time-grounded instances of the use of "customary law" on Kilimanjaro in Tanzania. These stories make it clear that certain basic ideas with their source in the culture of a century ago are still current on the mountain and that they inform practice. But there is no way to read these microhistories without also noting that a cash crop is grown on the land that is often piously

---

1.   For a much more detailed historical account of the transformation of "customary law" on Kilimanjaro, see Moore 1986, which had not been published at the time the paper that is the basis of this chapter is presented.

talked about in terms of the buried bones of the ancestors, that interests in the same land were recently being bought and sold, that some of the players in the local drama are salaried teachers as well as landholders, while others are solely farmers, and that down the road there are courts and officials who are local agents of the central state. What is visible in the case histories is the surface of the complex intertwining of "old" and "new," of "customary law" and the coffee connection, of present relationships and old cultural forms.

That this product of history cannot be satisfactorily accounted for solely through a description of its interwoven present is evident. Anthropological field-work necessarily relies heavily on exploring what people understand their situation to be at the time they are observed. Yet close synchronic description, for all its irreplaceable value, necessarily limits analysis through enlarging the importance of the observed moment. Fieldwork being what it is, anthropologists are almost methodologically committed to overvalorizing what they observe and are told. That is the way the experience of others becomes part of their own. Yet where a longer historical background is known, awareness of that deeper past can change the way the observed present is analyzed. The present can be reconceived as the product of a sequence and as the moment before the future, as a scene in motion. Inquiries can be made into the conditions that have formed, transformed, and propelled these elements of which the present is constructed through given trajec-tories into their current combinations. Thus, after sketching the facts of the local case histories from the 1969 period below, I shall turn to the larger-scale historical background. Some conclusions about the concept of customary law itself follow.

ANTICIPATED INHERITANCES: TWO CASE HISTORIES FROM THE LATE 1960s

The Locale

On Kilimanjaro, in one of the Catholic districts past magnificent waterfalls bounded by steep ferny cliffs, lies the little subparish (*mtaa*) of R—. It is a maze of gardens interplanted with bananas and coffee bushes and vegetables. One neatly hedged garden is immediately next to another. Between them, a living fence of dracaena marks the boundary. Looking through the plants, from the paths that wind in and out of the homestead plots, one can glimpse the outlines of dwellings. There, in the middle of the plantings, lives a Chagga household, and sometimes more than one. Contiguous gardens often belong to agnatically related men, so a subparish is composed largely of localized patrilineal clusters, with some scattered individual households interspersed among them.

This green, leafy haven with gently flowing irrigation canals looks like a rural paradise. But it is not a paradise. An acute shortage of land disturbs all relationships, and a more difficult future hangs over the present. Men with enough cash are always looking for ways to buy a little more land for themselves. They want it for their own purposes now, but later for their sons. However, most men do not have enough cash to buy land. Only those who have salaried employment or small businesses or other access to money besides coffee find it possible to buy land. Most men acquire their land from kinsmen in the normal course of allocation and inheritance and have no means of acquiring more through purchase.

The "customary law" rule is that a father should provide his eldest son with a banana grove of his own on marriage, and that the youngest son should live in his mother's (or parent's) compound for life and bring his wife there and raise his children there and eventually inherit the parental house and land. Middle sons are supposed to look after themselves and go cultivate new plots in the bush. But that last rule cannot be obeyed. On Kilimanjaro there is no bush to cultivate, so when there are middle sons there is a serious problem of providing for them. In fact, even when there are only two sons, the paternal *kihamba* (banana) garden often is not large enough to divide for the support of two, let alone three, households.

For as long as anyone has known anything detailed about Chagga horticulture, the Chagga have relied primarily on their permanent, well-manured, and often irrigated banana gardens high on the mountain. Annual crops of maize, beans, and millet have also been cultivated on auxiliary plots in the lower areas to enlarge the food supply. In the old days, and in some places today, those maize lands toward the foot of the mountain were not held permanently and were farmed in a form of shifting cultivation, reallocated annually by the chiefs. These annual-crop lands were soon exhausted and had to lie fallow. At that point, a new area would be designated for cultivation and divided by the chief or his deputy. As population increase has forced the Chagga to spread down-mountain, and as further irrigation and fertilizers have made some lower areas more habitable than they once were, some of these lower area *shambas* have come to be permanently occupied.

In families with severely inadequate amounts of land, married sons without plots of their own sometimes build dwellings in the compound of their father and seek work as occasional laborers in the gardens of others. Life is difficult and impoverished for them. Only the households of shopkeepers and salaried persons are securely well-off. For every such prosperous household in a localized lineage, there are many others that are poor. Many live exclusively on the products of the small plots of land they have inherited.

This is the general setting in which the following case histories were collected. Both involve allusions to "customary law" rules as used in and out of the courts. The stories of the specific fortunes and misfortunes of these particular families demonstrate clearly enough the general persistence of a nexus of rule-statements and practices that historical evidence connects with the deep cultural past of the Chagga. They also sharply attest to the modernity of these uses of the "traditional."

Case 1: Bounded lands and limitless hatred

In the parish of R— there was a father with two sons. As they reached adulthood and married, the father divided his banana/coffee garden into two parts and gave each son half. He did not stay to live out his years in the half of the younger son, as custom dictated. He had the resources to make other arrangements for himself and went to live permanently in a *shamba* he had in the lower area.

The two sons were very different, and the course of their lives differed almost from the beginning. The firstborn son was a good student and eventually became a teacher. His respected, salaried job and his education made him one of the well-to-do men in the parish of R—. He married and had children, and for a long time all was well with him and his household. The younger brother did not fare as well. He never got past "standard four" in school and was functionally illiterate. He had no job to supplement the meager subsistence he and his wife scratched out of their land. Worse still, his wife bore him no children. This barrenness went on for so many years that it became plain there never would be any children from that household.

In such situations among the Chagga, suspicion inevitably develops between the wives of the brothers. The wife with children is likely to be suspected of having caused the barrenness of the wife without children. In this family there was no doubt that, in the absence of male issue in the younger brother's line, the elder brother and his line would eventually inherit all the land. Whether the wife of the elder brother had used witchcraft materials or was a witch, or whether she had simply cursed her sister-in-law, invoking the power of the Christian God, was not clear. But that she had used some such illicit means to achieve her ends was the talk of the neighborhood.

Now it happened that the teacher was posted to a school in another place and came home to the village of R— only during the holidays. Gossip in the village had it that on one occasion, just before leaving, he told his wife that she should pull up the boundary plants that marked the border between their plot and that of his younger, childless brother. He was said to have told her to "make herself at home" there and to plant vegetables. She did so in an area that was roughly ten paces by five in what had been the banana garden of her husband's brother. She also planted a new boundary at the edge of the area she had cultivated. The brother whose land had been encroached on was enraged and complained to their father.

The father returned to R— to try to make peace between the households of his two sons. With his own hands he pulled up the dracaena that had been placed at the new boundary, and he restored the old boundary and marked it with new plantings of dracaena. This he did before witnesses. The wife of the teacher was very angry about this and took her revenge. She went to the courthouse and complained to the magistrate that her father-in-law had violated Chagga "customary law" by entering her compound in the absence of her husband, his son. There is indeed a rule of customary law that a father-in-law should not approach his daughter-in-law, or enter his married son's compound, unless the son is present. The magistrate decided that the case was one that would more suitably be heard by lineage elders than by the court. Not long afterward, the elders convened and heard the dispute. The wife of the teacher not only lost her case, but was fined one *pipa* and eight *debe* of beer for violating the dignity of her father-in-law, to whom she owed respect. He was said to have been grievously and unforgivably insulted by being taken to court in this manner and on this charge.

The wife of the teacher did not brew the beer that she was fined and never paid it. Instead, she once again pulled up the boundary plants and placed them where she had put them before, and once again began planting in the area she had staked out. Her father-in-law again assembled witnesses and pulled up the dracaena. The daughter-in-law returned to court and this time was more successful. The father-in-law was put in the lockup for three days for having broken the peace and trespassed on his daughter-in-law. When he emerged from the cell, the father-in-law prayed to God to curse the disputed land and the woman who had created such disorder.

Not too long after, the wife of the teacher fell ill and went to the hospital. She returned home, but she never recovered from her illness. After a time she died. After her death, the father-in-law went to the banana garden of his son the teacher and said that it was now finished, that what he wanted had happened. Then he told his son the teacher that if he took the land of his brother without paternal permission all his children would die. The teacher was obdurate and told his father he would not return the piece of land taken from his younger brother unless and until the father brought back to life the wife he had caused to die.

Neither the father nor the younger brother would speak to the teacher thereafter, and the father provided the younger brother with another place to live near him in the lower area. The teacher was left in possession of the cursed piece of land in addition to his own plot, but it was said in the neighborhood that he did not dare eat any food that had been planted in that land for fear he would die. Nor could he go to his father to ask his pardon because of a conditional curse he himself had brought forth. During his wife's illness, when the teacher accused his father of bringing sickness to his wife, he also had sworn a mighty oath that should he ever ask his father's pardon the father should quickly follow the deceased wife into the hereafter. No doubt he had hoped thereby to frighten his father and save his wife. But his efforts were to no avail, and he was left a widower who could not beg his father's pardon. All the same, it seemed clear that he and his sons would inherit the cursed banana garden after all.

Case 2: The "kidnapped" heir

Under "customary law," a man who wanted to alienate a piece of land and give it to a nonkinsman could do so legitimately only after obtaining the consent of his agnates. That rule was of urgent interest to a well-to-do man named Antoni of the lineage of N—, who wanted to buy a small banana garden next to his own that was about an acre in size. Antoni had a salaried job at the mission, and his wife was a teacher, so he was a comparatively rich man. The plot he coveted was encumbered in a complex way. It had been the property of old man Salewi of the K— lineage, who had died a few years earlier. One of Salewi's wives had lived there with her two sons, Paul and Jacob, as they grew up.

In terms of Chagga customary law of yesteryear, her banana garden might have been expected ultimately to become the property of their youngest son, Jacob. But land shortage has produced revisions of practice. Now it is just as much a matter of practical custom for a father to divide the plot of his wife between her two sons as to leave it all to the younger in the traditional manner. The legal question at issue in this case history has to do with whether Paul, the elder son, had a right to a share of his mother's land. In 1969, only Jacob, the younger son, and his household lived in his mother's plot and used the proceeds from its produce. Both Paul and Jacob were entirely dependent on farming for their living. Neither had any additional source of income.

The elder son, Paul, did not live in the parish of R— at all. His father, Salewi, had given him a bigger piece of land in one of the lower areas, near Himo, a market center on the main road. Paul worked the land his father had given him and lived in the lower area with his wife and son. At first they occupied a rented house, but in 1969 Paul decided to build his own house in his own lower-area plot and started to do so, but to complete the house he needed more cash. At that point Paul decided he wanted to sell what he claimed was his rightful share of his mother's plot in the parish of R—. He was in need of money, and this seemed the only way to raise enough cash. He went to the sub-village head to tell him about his plan to sell the land to Antoni, as required by law. (The sub-village head happened to be a lineage relative of Antoni.) Paul told his own agnates about his plan and gave his kinsmen an opportunity to buy. This right to first refusal was the modernized version of the consent of agnates required by Chagga customary law. None of the lineage kinsmen came forward with an offer, so after a few weeks Paul posted the necessary formal notice in the local court announcing his intention to sell. At that time the notice had to be posted thirty days before the sale to give anyone who might have claims an opportunity to come forward. At first, no one made any objections known.

Antoni (the unrelated neighbor) went ahead and paid Paul 1,500 shillings toward the purchase price. However, in Chagga law the right to land does not pass until the full purchase price has been paid. The deal was by no means complete. This, of course, was known to several of Paul's kinsmen. They did not tangle directly with Paul, but went to his house near Himo and persuaded his sixteen-year-old son, Donasia, to come with them to R— to claim that the land was not his father's but his own. The implication of such a claim was that Paul was trying to alienate property that did not belong to him, and hence that he had nothing to transfer. Toward making this case, Paul's kinsmen brought young Donasia to R— and placed him in the protective care of the senior elder of their lineage, the lineage of the K—s.

The senior elder is the ceremonial head of the localized lineage. His authority rests on his position as the ritual intermediary between living agnates and the lineage ancestors. To offend him carries significant risks, this-worldly and other-worldly. Paul was enraged, but there was not much Paul could do because young Donasia had been persuaded that his father was doing him out of his rightful property. The K—s also whispered in Donasia's ear that if he ever showed his face in Paul's house again Paul would kill him. Donasia became the instrument of his relatives' intentions.

The claim of the K—s was that Salewi had left what might have been his eldest son's share of land directly to his *grandson* Donasia. There is in Chagga "customary law" a rule that a grandfather may skip a generation in his allocations to leave land to the firstborn son of his firstborn son if the son is already well provided for. That the firstborn son had land was clearly the case in this instance. What was not so clear was whether Salewi had in fact made such a generation-skipping allocation.

Meanwhile, Paul's younger brother Jacob was living on and using the very land that Paul and Donasia each claimed. In June 1969, Jacob took Antoni, the prospective buyer of the disputed plot, to court and alleged that Antoni had uprooted nine coffee trees in Jacob's property. The disputed plot was contiguous to Antoni's and had a common boundary with his. Jacob alleged furthermore that Antoni had thrown stones at Jacob when Jacob passed on the path in front of Antoni's compound. Antoni managed to get the case dismissed. He contended that Jacob and Paul had themselves uprooted the trees to frame him and to prevent him from completing the purchase of the land.

After winning that victory, Antoni lost the next round. The K—s appealed to the village executive officer and managed to persuade him to stop the sale. The executive officer was taken to the garden in question and shown the place where the bones of the K— ancestors were buried. This was proof that this was patrimonial property and according to Chagga tradition should not be sold without the consent of all. But the village executive officer also told Donasia that if he wanted to keep the land, he would have to find a way to pay back the 1,500 shillings Antoni had already invested. Donasia had no idea where he could get the money. He feared his father too much to approach him, and evidently with good reason.

Donasia's father, Paul, was known to be a very excitable and violent man. I was told that his sibling, Jacob, took the precaution of putting a spell on him to try to keep him calm through this period of altercation. It seemed very desirable to do so, as suddenly there was another bidder who offered to pay even more than Antoni for Paul's share (or Donasia's, as the case may have been). The person who came forward with the more tempting alternative offer was none other than the teacher in Case 1, a neighbor of all these contenders. There would be no end to the story.

INTERPRETING THE TWO CASE HISTORIES

This account of the two disputations has mentioned certain large-scale circumstances that lie behind the pressure on the land: population increase and the cash-cropping of coffee. The logical link between land shortage and bitterly disputed claims is not too difficult to find. Without land there is neither enough produced food nor enough coffee cash to buy food. Unless a landless man manages to get a wage-paying job (and those are few) or already had an income-producing business (and those are still fewer), landlessness can bring the poor perilously near to death. It can be physical death from hunger, or social death from the need to leave the community in search of a better situation elsewhere. The other form of social death is to be without offspring—at the end of the line. If you have male children, you need land for them; if you have no male children, it must mean that your agnates covet your land.

Belief in the potentially lethal repercussions that follow from oaths and curses are part of Chagga cultural cosmology. These misfortune-causing consequences of human words and occult acts are as consistent with present versions of Christianity as they are with precolonial Chagga ideas about the power of the dead over the living and the nature of "witchcraft" and "magic." The cases present word-caused homicide as a fact. Whether what is said is so or not is generally regarded as contingent, as possible. There are often differences of opinion. This is the way it comes up in conversation. Land shortage is death-dangerous in more than one sense.

Submerged in these two stories as well is the march of an unrelenting process, the process by which the better-off Chagga men try to do their poorer relatives and neighbors out of their land. In both these cases, we see that it is the salaried men (the salaried teacher in the first case, and the salaried mission-employee, Antoni, in the second) who are energetically on the road to acquiring more land. In both stories these acquisitive men or their wives are accused of offenses, and their antagonists use other legal maneuvers to try to foil their plans. The ultimate outcome of these particular struggles had not emerged at the time this material was collected. Indeed, in a sense, such struggles are unending. Nor is the outcome fully predictable in any particular instance. There are many possible reversals of fortune that even a relatively prosperous man may suffer. But in the long run it seems clear that the better-off, the more literate, the more able to get along in the modern sector will be able to outdo their less fortunate agnates and neighbors in the competition for resources. Even so, their accumulations will soon be subdivided among many offspring. Demography keeps wealth in check.

Thus, the case accounts only hint at economic differentiation and asymmetry of power, because these are not matters open to verbal disputation; they are incontestable circumstances. Instead, the discourse in and surrounding the cases goes to some lengths to present the normative rationales the claimants made for their arguments. That is where "customary law" enters the picture. Presumably some of the factual claims were fabricated. What is not individually constructed is the culturally embedded legal rationale. That commonality can be verified from other case histories by the dozen. (See Moore [1986a] for an extended description of the content of "customary law.")

The two land case histories are classical instances of recent situations that the Chagga themselves characterize as "customary law" cases, instances involving the mila, the customs of the Wachagga. Both involve practices and ideas that refer to the past but that are closely woven into the present fabric of rural Chagga life. It goes without saying that the Chagga know as well as anyone else that there are occasions when it is convenient to invoke tradition to obtain property. For other purposes, the very same people are likely to say that times have changed and new ways of doing things are more appropriate. The choice of the "modern" perspective or the "traditional" is often clearly a matter of strategy.

But the availability and the plausibility of the particular traditional arguments is not to be explained solely by the way they figure in the strategies of individuals. To take the actor's perspective in that narrow sense ignores the larger-scale conditions that determine the limits of individual choice. The parties to such legal disputes are not fully free to constitute their own reality. To a great extent they operate constrained by general circumstances that they do not control, and they are often subject to quite specific limitations set by more powerful others. These kinds of contextual constraints and asymmetries of power are the preoccupation of much current social theory (Lukes 1986). The problem is to keep a balance between the task of uncovering determinants and the task of identifying possibilities. What Bourdieu has proposed, both with his concept of the *habitus* and in his books on education and on taste, and what Willis has argued even more forcefully in *Learning to labor*, is that even what is experienced by the actors as purely strategic, innovative, or rebellious choice-making ultimately has, on the large scale, the effect of "reproducing the system" (see Bourdieu 1977, 1984; Bourdieu and Passerson 1977; Willis 1981). No one would argue that there are no continuities in categorical hierarchies and the various asymmetrical relationships they spawn, but the "reproduction" model is rigidly static as a total framework of analysis and it leaves a huge question unaddressed—How then do systems change? Neither Bourdieu's model nor Willis' interpretations fully address that question. How is an anthropologist working at the micro-social scale, nose-to-nose with the protagonists, to distinguish the process of change from the process of reproduction if both present themselves as change?

The solution is difficult and not always practical. Whenever possible, the local, small-scale, actor-centered materials of fieldwork must be reinserted into the long story of historical transformation. It is only because he knows what happened *afterward* that Sahlins can make what he does of the misadventures of Captain Cook (Sahlins 1981, 1985). Only because I know what happened *before* can I see Chagga "customary law" of the 1960s and 1970s as something very different from the late nineteenth-century body of practices to which "customary law" implicitly refers both for legitimation and for some of its specific cultural content. There is an impoverishment of understanding when an ethnographic situation is stripped of its deeper temporality. For the Chagga the question why certain traditional legal claims, arguments, and ideas have remained viable while others vanished is in large part answerable, but to answer it properly requires attention to history. Part of that story can be told succinctly.

REORGANIZING THE CHAGGA AS A PROJECT OF GOVERNMENTS

For a century governments have been telling the Chagga what they may and may not do and what parts of their system of "customary law" were acceptable and enforceable by the state and what parts were not. Colonial governments, first German (1886–1916), then British (1916–61), had a variety of plans to reorganize, control, and reshape Chagga life. (The missionaries and settlers who arrived with them had their own agendas too.) Since 1961 the postcolonial government, with its program of African socialism, has undertaken new reforms under very different ideological banners, but independence from colonial rule for the nation has not meant independence from central government directives for Tanzania's peoples. Dictation of change from above continues.

Given such a past and such a present, developments in the local system of "customary law" over the century can be seen as taking place in what is officially regarded as a residual category. At first, "customary law" was that part of an ear-lier way of life with which colonial government institutions either deliberately chose not to interfere, which they could not easily alter, or which were left in existence because they fell outside the locus of administrative attention. The distinction between "customary law" and government-made law was originally a product of the colonial encounter, but that encounter did more than create two parallel legal categories, one new and one old. It determined what part of the old would be preserved—or rather, it determined that part of the old would not be preserved. The rest—the residual category that did not offend against colo-nial definitions of morality and that was not inconsistent with colonial law and policy—was permitted to continue. Over time, substantial changes appeared in the content of that "customary law" sector. That is not surprising. The most important formal change in the place of traditional Chagga "customary law" which also affected its content is the fact that from the beginning of the colonial period to the present it has been harnessed to political and economic structures that are entirely different from those existing in the late nineteenth century.[2]

Direct state interventions in Chagga affairs, and their legal consequences, could be illustrated in a number of different ways, but none is more telling than the history of Chagga formal organization. A knowledge of the drastic reorganizations worked by governments puts in proportion the other half of the story: the fact that the localized patrilineages of precolonial times sought to preserve a degree of autonomy and succeeded in remaining significant entities in the allocation of property.

Much of what was transformed on Kilimanjaro in this century was changed through the agency of three major organizations of European provenance in-troduced on Kilimanjaro during the colonial period. All three are still there, and still very important, though they are now present in mutated forms. One

---

2. And the late nineteenth century undoubtedly was very different from the early nineteenth century. See Stahl 1964 and Iliffe 1979.

was the Christian church, in Lutheran and Catholic versions, together with their mission schools and hospitals. The second was the national, provincial, and district administrative structure now run through the national party (first called TANU, now CCM). The third was the coffee cooperative through which all Chagga have sold their coffee since the 1920s. In one sense, because the indigenous system of localized patrilineages has persisted, these other organizations of European origin might appear to be merely additions to, rather than replacements of, the most basic indigenous arrangements. But the powerful presence of these ubiquitous organizations worked deep alterations on every imaginable aspect of Chagga life and thought. They were inside the rural Chagga neighborhoods, not outside. Virtually every Chagga household belonged to all the organizations and was directly affected. As universal membership organizations to which virtually every household "belonged," they transformed economy, politics, religion, and knowledge.

The nineteenth-century Chagga chiefdom, as it had been, has utterly vanished. The precolonial chiefdom had a closed constitutional framework that permitted only certain kinds of groups to be formed. Chagga chiefdoms were a variant on a familiar East African pattern, with entities defined by *kinship* (exogamous segmented patrilineages and their member households, chiefship descending in one of the lineages), political entities defined by *community, geography*, and *authority* (subdistricts, districts, and chiefdoms), and crosscutting structures of mobilization defined by *age* (formal male age-sets and age-grades, and a less frequently activated and more generalized classification of women by age category). Military service and corvee labor were exacted through the male age-sets. In addition, there were *irrigation canal users groups* (groups of men whose household gardens shared the same man-made watercourse). The "canal users group" was sometimes coincident with the subparish, sometimes not. New groups were constantly being formed, but they were constituted within the framework outlined. There were new groups, but not new *kinds* of groups.

This system of chiefdoms, districts and subdistricts, lineages, age-grades, and water-sharing groups constituted the total formal corporate organizational structure of the Kilimanjaro area in the late nineteenth century (see Gutmann 1926; Moore 1986a; Stahl 1964). People could be mobilized for collective action through each of these entities. Each kind of group had not only an important productive role in the economy, but also substantial powers of control over its members. For males, they - were what I have called "universal membership organizations" Moore 1986a: 310–17)—all men belonged to all of them. The achievement o self-acquired social position took place largely within these milieus, as did transmission of property and position from one generation to the next. Each level and type of organization had its own internal means of enforcing its control over members and of hearing and closing episodes of dispute that arose among them.

There was, in practice, a degree of fluidity in the alignments and numbers of the collectivities that made up a chiefdom, and a degree of flexibility in the choice of leadership. Chiefs routinely stepped down in middle life in favor of their sons. The succession could be accelerated or decelerated as the political situation required. Chiefs could also be deposed and replaced. Households could move from one chiefdom to another. The chronic raiding and fighting both among the Kilimanjaro chiefdoms and with "outsider" chiefdoms, which characterized late nineteenth-century life, provided many opportunities to rearrange Chagga political affairs (and even to do away with incumbents in office) or forcibly to persuade chiefdoms to change their alliances or to become tribute-payers and clients of those who threatened them most. The control over regional and long-distance trade must have been a major factor in all this turmoil. The monopoly of chiefs over the most important items in the trade, especially over ivory, captured cattle, and other trade goods, gave chiefs a strong hold over the key people in the chiefdom. The chief, through redistribution, could offer incentives as well as deploy threats in relation to subordinates.

Once the colonial period began, all the balances in this political arena changed, even though some of the basic constitutive elements of its *form* continued in being. Warfare ended, the military aspects of the age-grade system were abolished, and the long-distance trade completely changed its character. Chiefs lost their acquisitive and redistributive monopolies, and Europeans took over the marketing of significant commodities. What had been independent chiefdoms became subordinate administrative units in a colonial state. The cash-cropping of coffee was introduced, and eventually coffee was planted by virtually every household in its own land. The Chagga continued to grow subsistence crops as well. Most families were converted to Christianity. Schools and shops sprang up. The population doubled and doubled again, going from 100,000 in 1900 to almost 500,000 in 1978.

All the while, in form, many of the major local organizational units of pre-colonial times were maintained. Chiefdoms, districts, lineages, and the water-sharing groups persisted. Some became larger, some smaller, some new ones were founded, some old ones abolished. But each type of entity continued, many just where they had been before. In 1961 chiefship was abolished once and for all, and a new formal division of administrative units was brought into being. But they were for the most part composed of the same old basic subdistricts and other low-level organizational entities that existed before. These continue in metamorphosed versions to this day. However, though locally conceived in terms of their continuity, the content and milieu of these organizational frameworks has continuously shifted and changed.

From the 1890s to 1961, each chief became more and more an agent of the administrative apparatus of the colonial state, collecting taxes, enforcing regulations, and presiding over a court—the jurisdiction of which was carefully limited by the government. With warfare gone and the long-distance trade in other hands, political rivalries shifted their focus. The colonial administrations, both German and British, gradually reduced the number of chiefdoms by half. Thus some chiefdoms became subordinate to others and lost their chiefly office. The manipulation of choice in this matter was not without input from the Chagga chiefs themselves. Politics became focused on position in relation to the colonial authorities.

Continuing a process of consolidation begun earlier, the British completely reorganized the structure of local government, creating new levels of administration and a type of centralization that had no foundation in the Chagga past. They united all the Chagga chiefdoms. By 1929, all the chiefs were grouped together in a single council, and that council not only became a legislative body through which many colonial ordinances were promulgated, but also was constituted as a court of appeal. The power of the chiefs in their local chiefdoms was gradually diminished. In place of the earlier almost complete judicial separateness of each chiefdom, the chiefdom courts over which they presided had become the lowest judicial bodies in a local hierarchy. By the late 1920s the chiefs had been put on salaries paid out of tax funds, and their tribute-demanding powers were curtailed. After independence, in 1961, though chiefship was abolished, most of the local courts the chiefs or their delegates had presided over for most of the century were continued in the same sites. Their place in the national hierarchy of courts was changed (Moore 1986a: 159–60). They were renamed Primary Courts and presided over by an appointed "magistrate." It was to such a court that our protagonists in the land cases went with their various tales of woe.

A process of economic reorganization parallel to the administrative consolidations of the chiefdoms and to the creation of the judicial hierarchy was undertaken. In the 1920s, at the instigation of a colonial officer in the district, the coffee cooperative was begun in order to centralize coffee sales and regulate production. The parallel between administrative centralization and the concentration of economic control is striking, as was the use of the law to effectuate this coordinated development. The cooperative came to be extremely successful, but that was a matter neither of accident nor of local popularity. A law was passed that in effect made it illegal for the. Chagga to sell their coffee to anyone other than the cooperative. There was to be no competition. Consequently, regulation and taxation of the coffee crop became much easier for the administration. Thus, supralocal centralized organizations to oversee the political and economic goings-on in the chiefdoms were in place more than fifty years ago.

Meanwhile, on the ground the localized patrilineages continued to control most transfers of land between kin, but it was not for want of trying to bring all land matters under central administrative control that the colonial government failed to do so. In 1930, to this end, the government proposed that a system of land registration would be beneficial. This was met with strong demonstrations of protest from the Chagga. Any intimation that the existing system of land tenure might be interfered with in any way was unacceptable. Although in 1930 land was beginning to be bought and sold, the colonial government could not take the political risks involved in tampering with the "traditional" system of land tenure. The reaction had been too strong. The Chagga were extremely wary on this point. It remains to be seen whether now, more than fifty years later, the independent government will fare any better if it undertakes fundamental interventions.

This cursory review of governmental, economic, and judicial reorganizations on Kilimanjaro, while lamentably limited as historical narrative, illustrates certain unstated but implicit definitional boundaries of the residual category "customary law." As perpetuated by colonial and post-colonial governments, the category obviously excluded most of those aspects of traditional law that had to do with political organization. Even where political offices were nominally continued, their attributes were carefully redefined by administrative fiat and legislation. Virtually all supralocal organization, political and economic, has been firmly under the control of regional and central authorities from the start of the colonial period to the present. By these means, political challenges to the state have been contained and certain local affairs have been directed from above. "Customary law," if understood as allowing local people to do their own cultural "thing," should also be understood to have been a carefully restricted fragment of "tradition."

As it turned out, the control of political affairs and of the coffee crop did not preclude leaving the allocation of individual rights in local land to the patrilineages. Thus the principal productive resource, the land, has remained in the domain of "customary law" to this day. As might be expected, however, the new product, the coffee, is governed by a new set of "customs."

CHANGES IN THE CONTENT OF CUSTOMARY LAW

Many *stated norms* of kinship tradition remain as they were, however the milieu has changed. With new kinds of property and a new environment, many new norms have also been generated to keep company with the old ones. Some examples of these changes follow.

Land rights conveyed from fathers to sons

The two case histories at the beginning of this chapter show plainly that, these days, the "customary law" rule that the youngest son should inherit his father's homestead and garden is often honored in the breach. In conditions of land shortage, other considerations prevail. The Chagga make the moral assumption that some land should be available to any decent married man. Where there is no one else to provide it, since there is no virgin land to pioneer, a father should try to provide some of his own land for each of his sons. If a father has several plots in scattered parts of the mountain, he may divide his holdings, sending one son away from the lineage cluster and keeping the other, or he may move himself. As indicated earlier, where the only solution available is to divide his own garden, a father may well do that, or if the father does not divide the land before his death, his kinfolk may do so after he dies. But a father may choose not to divide his land, and a son may find himself obliged to enter the migrant labor force or volunteer to be a pioneer in one of the new cooperative villages.

Whatever the pragmatic outcome in any particular instance, the "customary law" rules continue to be restated, and from time to time they actually do guide behavior. What are we to make of this? Is the "customary law" of succession and inheritance in existence or not? And is such a rule a law if, though a son may make claims on his father and may legitimize his claims by invoking customary rules, the son still cannot force his father to provide for him in the customary way? Could he ever do so? Today if the son makes his claims before a group of lineage elders, he may or may not succeed in getting them to decide in his favor. And even if they do side with him, the father may or may not heed their directives. Fathers had the right to disinherit sons in the customary system, and there is every evidence that they still claim this right and sometimes exercise it. When land questions get to the courts, the outcome may depend not on who is right but on who controls the key witnesses.

It is probably fruitless to speculate on whether the practice of dividing land represents a dynamic direction that might eventually end in an explicit change in the customary rules. It is clear that "customary law" statements can coexist as cultural artifacts contemporaneously with contradictory practices and contradictory norms. The Chagga emphasis on the existence of customs that only they are competent to administer is part of their use of tradition in their present political situation. Under these circumstances, there may be value for them in refraining from explicitly acknowledging change in the system to the extent of describing new practices as new rules. The definition of "customary law" that was a product of the colonial period has had substantial effects on the Chagga conception of the scope and nature of custom, and the scope and nature of their domains of autonomy.

Recently announced plans for projected changes in rural land law will, if implemented literally, generate profound new disruptions. Yet the plans may be adapted to local conditions. The government notes in its announcement of the new village plan that local custom should be respected as much as possible (Agriculture Policy 1983). Chagga peasants in the rural areas may know nothing of the plans as announced, but they have almost a century of experience in using "customary law" arguments to minimize official intervention in the sphere of their control. They are likely to continue.

Coffee rights and cash rights: The relative position of women and men

The general adoption of coffee as a cash crop on Kilimanjaro generated many rules and practices concerning the new kinds of property. These are now explained as analogies to customary rules or extensions of them to new items. So, for example, coffee bushes, being attached to the land and grown by the Chagga in their individually held banana gardens, have always been considered the property of the male household head, just as the bananas had been and still are. Most of the annual vegetable crops grown in the same gardens by the women of the household were regarded traditionally as female property and remain so today. Women also have rights in the crops of the *shamba* lands they cultivate on the plain.

It is the duty of the woman of the house to feed the family, so she cannot sell very much of her crop in the women's markets that dot the map of Kilimanjaro, but she may sell some of it. Sometimes she sells bananas, but does so legitimately only after obtaining her husband's permission because the bananas, like the cultivated land, belong to him. A widow may acquire the temporary use of the banana rights until she dies, provided she continues to reside in the plot she occupied during her husband's lifetime. The coffee rights are usually given to a male relative of her deceased husband. These he holds as a sort of trustee and guardian of the widow and her children. He should spend the monies for their benefit to the extent that the husband would have done, but these successor-guardians often keep most of the proceeds themselves. If the widow has an adult married son residing in her compound, he often has this role. When the widow dies, all rights in the land, the bananas, and the coffee revert to the male line.

The amount of cash a woman can obtain from her market sales is minute, compared with the cash a man is paid for the coffee he sells to the cooperative for processing and sale. The labor of women—indeed of men, women, and children—is mobilized in season to pick the coffee and to do preliminary processing. However, the women have no *right* to any share of that income. It is considered a male obligation to provide a wife and children with clothing, but that duty does not mean he has any obligation to supply her with cash as such. He may give her some cash specifically to buy a piece of cloth or a piece of meat, but he does not give her cash to spend as she likes. Thus, the rule that the coffee bushes and the coffee cash belong to men has meant that women have had much more limited access to the cash economy than their husbands have had.

A seemingly contradictory rule is that the coffee rights can be separated from the rights to bananas and land. Should the male landholder choose, he can allocate land and banana rights and keep the coffee rights. Many men do this. Thus a father who has only one plot of land may have his youngest son and the son's family residing with him in his compound. The father may be quite willing to give the son a corner of the compound in which to build his house, and he may designate a small area in which the son's wife may plant her crops. He may even give his son the full rights to the bananas in some part of the garden. Yet the father can retain the coffee rights to bushes growing on the same land for himself. If the son dares pick the coffee in these circumstances, he is guilty of a theft.

The legal idea of divisible and concurrent interests in the same property existed among the Chagga long before there was coffee on the mountain. Such interests existed with regard to land, crops, and cattle. The complex of rights in coffee and cash may be built on these old ideas, but the change in the economy has been so fundamental that these traditional analogies mask real innovations: the changed basis of the relative economic position of men and women, and the changed basis of the economic differentiation between households.

The buying and selling of land

Rights in land on Kilimanjaro probably began to be available for cash around 1930. This inference is based on the fact that in 1927 the chiefs expressed strong disapproval and petitioned the governor to forbid the buying and selling of land (Griffiths 1930: 60, 88). Before that, "traditionally," land is said to have been transferred for a conventionalized payment of a cow and a goat. Land-plot histories suggest that many "traditional" transfers took place long before cash payment was a common possibility. The time at which cash became an issue was also the time at which a serious land shortage was beginning to be felt in some localities.

One suspects that the reason the chiefs opposed sales for cash is that it threatened to reduce their prerogatives. In the customary system, all unused land in theory reverted to chiefly control. There was no land shortage in the nineteenth century. Political control over people and their labor was undoubtedly more important than control over land. Land had no value without labor to work it. The land was there for the asking. In the British colonial period, as before, the native authorities, the chiefs, and their appointees, and the district heads controlled the allocation of undeveloped land, or lands that had been "abandoned." (The latter differed from the land of people who were temporarily absent, who retained the right to reclaim previously held land when they returned.) In this period, the chiefs and their subordinates received substantial "gifts of thanks" for assigning these empty plots to others; they also often gave them to their own relatives. During the colonial period, chiefly consent came to be required for all land transfers. This was an expansion of administrative power. The chiefs disapproved of the buying and selling of land because they did not want to give up their reversionary claims or their controls.

The chiefs did not succeed in their plan. The buying and selling of land was not forbidden, and if anything it was encouraged. Ultimately even the buying and selling of land worked in favor of the chiefs. Because they were relatively rich men they were able to afford to buy land, which most Chagga could not do. This meant that they accumulated more lands than most others and enjoyed a continuing enhanced income from their scattered plots.

There was another category of people who had enough cash to buy land—the salaried men, and those with small businesses—a category that has grown enormously since 1950. Such men stood ready to buy land from anyone who was in debt or who because he had too small a plot to make a living was ready to leave and settle elsewhere. This does not mean that such buyers have become great landholders. On the contrary, the rise in population has been such that allocations to their many sons and grandsons has redivided the land again and again.

The purchase and sale of land has been conceived locally as an analogue of the former transfer in exchange for a cow and a goat. Indeed, when Chagga speak of past times when such transfers did take place, they often refer to them as sales, laughing at the "low price." Today, as a matter of law, the state holds all title to land in Tanzania, and rural people hold only the usufruct. A variety of national party guidelines about egalitarianism make multiple plot-holding more difficult than it used to be. Present party policy is that land should go to the tiller, but the buying and selling of the right to possession, and the right to beneficial use, continues on Kilimanjaro. Furthermore, the ingenious Chagga find many ways to place surrogates who are clients, or other dependent people, in their auxiliary plots so that the appearance of things will conform to party policies. Besides, the government policy that land belongs to those who work it says nothing about what happens when the tiller dies. On Kilimanjaro, "customary law" still reigns in such matters. Inheritance is a question of kinship. The rules, as I have shown, are subject to a great deal of situational amendment and negotiation, and probably always have been. Manipulation of this kind makes adjustments in conventional rules that are consonant with changing conditions. In name and in a certain sense in practice, much land law is still conceived of as "customary." But land law as it was no longer exists.

CONCLUSIONS

The two case histories from 1968 and the highly condensed description of a century in the life of the Chagga show that what is now considered "customary law" on Kilimanjaro has undergone many metamorphoses. Radical changes in local and larger-scale asymmetries of power and in the economic milieu have made that inevitable. The apparent continuities of customary law have changed in semantic content. The relationships and resources to which "customary law" refers are not as they were. Rights in land in 1880 and rights in land in 1980, however similarly stated normatively, are not rights in the same kind of entity, nor are the claimants in the same situations.

The answer to the question of what the category "customary law" means in these circumstances depends on who is using the concept and when it is being used. The courts have their own way of dealing with the issue. Both in the colonial period and now, local courts were and are specifically granted jurisdiction over questions of customary law. Because "customary law" is a residual category, and because it may be different in each locality, there is no specific legislation on the point of substantive content. On Kilimanjaro, "customary law" rules are to be determined case by case in the Primary Courts (as they were in the predecessor chiefly courts during the British colonial period). Two senior local laymen, the assessors, sit with each magistrate and are to be consulted on all points of customary law. The venerable assessors are assumed to have special knowledge of local norms and practices by reason of their standing in the community.

Within this law-finding structure, at least three possible meanings are conflated. One is that custom is a set of traditional rules handed down from generation to generation. A second is that custom is a matter of present general practice. A third is a more formal judicial meaning—that custom is the residual category of local norms claiming tradition as legitimation that pertain to matters on which there has been no legislation or binding judicial rulings by the central state, yet which the state is willing to acknowledge and enforce. The actual content of such rules and practices are different from one place to another and change from one period to another.

The very idea of "customary law" implies that there is a different kind of law with which it can be contrasted; so the concept itself is the ongoing product of encounters between subordinate local political entities and dominant overarching ones. Those encounters and the *legal* distinction between law and custom have a long history in the West. In Tanzania the colonial state (and now the postcolonial state) has had reason to allow certain kinds of limited local autonomy to be perpetuated. What is left of locally specific legal custom is the result of that political decision. A variety of governments and several generations of rural people have, for very different reasons, collaborated to encode the division between the central state and its subordinate peoples in this legal duality. All anthropological studies of African law must be read in this light, and not simply as accounts of traditional thought.

Today, "customary law" on Kilimanjaro is as much a creature of the present state and the present economy as it is a link with a past cultural heritage. The theoretical implication is plain: the unit of analysis in the study of such interdigitations must encompass both local and supralocal entities, and it must do so within a historically conceived framework. Contextualization has always been the principal method of social anthropology. But there is disagreement about the nature of the context. I argue that the analytic context is not only a legal cultural system in the Geertzian (1983) sense. The shifting political and economic milieus in which the cultural elements are used are an integral part of the anthropologic of such cultural forms.

CHAPTER SIX

Treating Law as Knowledge
Telling Colonial Officers: What to Say to Africans about Running "Their Own" Native Courts

When governments explain what they are doing "for the record," the regnant cultural logic of control is available for inspection. Nowhere does this logic seem more confidently expressed than in colonial settings. During earlier decades of this century, as British colonial officers in Tanganyika organized a system of African local courts, certain officials wrote detailed explanations of their plans and purposes for their subordinates. Their view was that they were conveying their superior knowledge of law and morality to the often benighted Africans. This article will use the text of one of those extended explanations to explore the British colonial conception of their moment in African legal history. Other archival and library materials together with fieldwork data are used to show how inappropriate some of those British ideas were to the actualities of the African setting.

The Africa of reality had its own social and legal logic, about which this article offers some new interpretations. Yet, for all the misconceptions that existed, the colonials' effort to insert their model of a court into a complex and little

Editor's note: This chapter is a reprint of Moore, Sally Falk. 1992. "Treating law as knowledge: Telling colonial officers what to say to Africans about running 'their own' native courts." *Law and Society Review* 26 (1): 11–46.

understood African setting was not without enduring results. British colonial ideas of courts and what courts are about have left a substantial legacy that can be seen in many parts of present-day Africa. While I shall not discuss that formal legacy in any detail here, I shall show certain tensions between courts and their social contexts that have persisted. I will, for example, indicate the mechanisms by which the thrust of internal community politics in rural areas affects the courts today even as it did in the colonial period. Local community control of witnesses and testimony and sometimes of local judges is at cross purposes with the central government's putative maintenance of "impartial" courts. That essentially political conflict existed in colonial times and exists now. Thus, what might be called "the colonial legacy" includes the ongoing tension between a centralized national system of courts with a standardized set of principles and rules, and the locally anchored, anti-centralized system of the rural communities. Those communities try to control their own members and do everything to maximize their internal autonomy, allowing their members effective use of the courts only as they see advantage in doing so, bypassing the courts and settling their own affairs internally as they choose. In short, there are features of the localist opposition that have not vanished from postcolonial society. The colonials had to cope with the consequences of this localism but did not understand the nature of local rural communities. Current political officials and magistrates live in both central and local worlds. Yet their knowledge of both has scarcely changed the situation.

What was the colonial vision of law and courts? A remarkably explicit answer to that question appears in the contents of a 1957 legal document from Tanganyika describing the design and purpose of the local courts—the 1957 *Local government memoranda no. 2 (local courts)* (hereafter cited as 1957 *Memoranda*).[1] These local courts were to be run by Africans and would apply African "customary law," but were to do so in a manner consistent with basic British legal principles and the objectives of colonial administration. That this agenda was inherently contradictory was, of course, not explicitly acknowledged, but as we shall see, evidence of considerable practical difficulty is apparent in the text of the 1957 *Memoranda*.

---

1. This document is 120 pages long, including the ordinance, the commentaries, and various forms to be used in the courts. Thus the discussion here is of necessity highly selective in the choice of sections to be analyzed. All otherwise unattributed page and section references are to the 1957 *Memoranda*.

The document is a historical gem. Divided into three parts, it not only contains the ordinance that governed the operation of the courts but also includes two sections of explanatory text, one designed to instruct British administrative officers, the other written for translation into Swahili and specifically edited for the African court "holders." The two commentaries are intended to convey fundamental legal principles, many of them universalized by the author as "principles of natural justice." They were, of course, identifiably British in style and content. Some general remarks summarizing what "was known" about African indigenous law are also included for the colonial officers, so that they will know "what to expect." Operationally, at one and the same time, this legislation involved the delegation of substantial power to African court holders and the reservation of ultimate control by the British. We have, then, a document that encapsulates the colonial conception of itself, its milieu, and its mission.

Such British official pronouncements on the "nature of justice" were phrased with great certainty. They were offered both to legitimize the design of the local courts system and to justify the continuing supervision it would require. Several of these legitimizing ideas deserve to be explored in some detail: ideas about legal evolution and the relative positions of British and Africans in the developmental sequence, about the "nature" of law as necessarily centered on a set of clear rules and durably recorded rulings, and about African legal thought as hopelessly muddled, with no sense of the timely moment to bring a grievance to court, little sense of the importance of evidence and proof, no appreciation of *res judicata,* and no understanding of the need for impartiality. Read today, these statements about the idealized court-as-it-should-be of the British directives and the supposedly unprincipled Africa that badly needed British legal instruction appear as tantalizing artifacts of the colonial imagination.

Hence these memoranda could easily and accurately be characterized as self-serving discourses on power; as justificatory representations of the ideology of control. Actually, in and between the lines, the document is also a statement about the incapacities of colonial government, the difficulties built into its judicial model, and the inappropriate premises on which it was constructed. This contradiction becomes fully manifest when any part of the African side of the equation is put into the picture. For the most detailed part of that essential dimension, draw on ethnographic material from Kilimanjaro, a district in colonial Tanganyika (now Tanzania) occupied by a people known in English as the "Chagga," in whose legal and other affairs I have had a long working interest (e.g., see Moore 1970, 1977a, 1986a, 1991a, 1991b).

The 1957 *Memoranda* describing the British model was put out very late in the colonial period and long after the start of the colonial courts project. However, the document draws many elements of its 120-page text from earlier editions and includes references to experiences in other colonies, accumulated administrative wisdom, and the compilations of anthropologists of the customary law rules of a variety of African peoples, by no means all of them in East Africa.[2] (Reference in the document to the British experience in India is a reminder of the time depth of the British concern with such matters.) Written after more than three decades of experience with these tribunals in Tanganyika, the pamphlet complains about the courts even as it praises them. The complaints and the general administrative unease of the text provide a compressed sketch of what the British thought were their intellectual assets and their practical problems.

The minuscule number of administrators who governed not only hundreds of thousands but millions of Africans could well have had reason to be uneasy. They had to be dominant and decisive, yet the practical "unknowability" of their social surroundings must have been one of the many uncomfortable aspects of the job, given that most of them did not speak any of the many local languages. No wonder that the logic of these officials can often be seen as an effort to keep not just the natives but their own conceptual categories in order. The colonials had to be sure of what they collectively and officially *knew* to tell it to the *others*.

What we see in all of the sections of the 1957 *Memoranda is* a conflation of the requirement that a prescribed organizational order be put in place with the exhortation to accept a particular cultural rationale. The advantages of setting up a central government where there had been none seemed self-evident to the

---

2. Thus, for example, the *Handbook on native courts for the guidance of administrative officers* published by the government of Uganda in 1941 was used in Tanganyika as a model for Part II of the first edition of *Local government memoranda No. 2,* i.e., the section-by-section commentary on the Native Courts Ordinance. It is also instructive to read a footnote in Governor Donald Cameron's 1930 statement on native administration that alludes to the Indian colonial experience and argues that village self-government in India was destroyed by colonial policy and should have been preserved (Tankanyika Territory 1930a: 33.) See also the Foreword to Tanganyika 1953, which says that the memoranda not only are the work of the Local Courts Advisor, Mr. J. P. Moffett, who held the post from 1948 to 1952, but are in a sense a community effort, i.e., based on other earlier sources and documents. The 1957 version analyzed here repeats many parts of the 1953 version verbatim.

colonial officers. With central government they presumed the eventual establishment of standardized laws, courts, and units of administration. The court
official who composed the *Memoranda* (and all those who preceded him whose
ideas he explicitly incorporated) plainly wanted the administrative officers,
through "patient" explanation, to convert "the African mind" into an apparatus
that would "think" the way the British did about legal matters while somehow
retaining a substantive law Africanity. Was the issue one of thought? Or one of
control? Or were the two so closely connected in the administrators' minds that
there was no disentangling them? And is this remarkably anxious text to be read
now as a detailed complaint that, alas, African conformity was not being offered
spontaneously and must somehow be achieved either by enforcement (not desirable and not practical) or by persuasion (not likely to succeed)? The answer to
all of these questions is yes. For the administrative officers the struggle to make
the courts "work" was defined as an almost evangelical effort to insert ideas and
ways of knowing as much as it was a labor of making and keeping an organizational structure in order.

In fact, of course, the British administrators appear to have thought they
knew what they needed to know about Africa to keep working at their local
courts project. (The "details" they were missing about the substantive rules of
African "customary law" could be filled in later.) They envisioned themselves
as involved in laying the foundation for a "modern" local court system to succeed indigenous, precolonial, quasi-judicial institutions. They seem to have envisioned a smooth sequence of replacement without seriously considering the
social-context dependence of legal institutions. Cheerfully unconcerned with
the connections between African community life and their chronic problems
with the courts, the colonials attributed the difficulties they encountered either
to the bad character of particular chiefs to "attitudes" in the "African mind,"
or to unfortunate habits acquired in precolonial legal institutions. There is no
discussion of anything so simple and crude as resistance to colonial rule or, for
that matter, resistance to legal interference in the playing out of community
micropolitics. The 1957 document conceives of African communities as solid
aggregations of kinship groups in harmonious equilibrium, normally peacefully
ruled by their chiefs. The colonials did not picture these villages as they were,
as social arenas seething with internal activity in which social credit was being
accumulated and lost, reputations being made and broken, factions organized
and loyalties mobilized. Had they known what we now know about the internal political life of African neighborhoods and villages, they might have had a

very different understanding of what was going on. But while that might have changed their logic, it might not have altered their plans and policies, which were, after all, hitched to much wider processes.

This article concerns that logic, the premises and conceptions with which the colonials inserted British legal ideas into an African milieu, and the very different rationales certain Africans had for a very different logic. It concerns the way two "legal cultures"—the inside-the-court formal system and the out-side-the-court form of "community justice"—have continued to interpenetrate. And, of course, contrary to what the British expected, the court system has not replaced the community framework.

THE PARADOX OF DIRECTING CHANGE AND PRESERVING "CUSTOM"

The attempted transplantation of British legal ideas to African courts during the colonial period was part of a much larger administrative strategy. The master concept was surely that of indirect rule, the system by which certain local chiefs were designated the official agents of colonial government (Tanganyika Territory 1930a, 1930b; Phillips 1945). In keeping with that broad plan, it was both practical and politic that local courts for Africans be run by "Native Authorities." To be sure, the jurisdiction of these courts was limited under colonial law, and they were to be intermittently checked on by colonial officers. Nevertheless, because Africans ran the courts, and Africans appeared before them, and African "customary" law was applied in them, these courts were thought of by the British as fundamentally African institutions. At the same time they were to be a vehicle for remolding the native system "into lines consonant with modern ideas and higher standards" (Governor Donald Cameron in Tanganyika Territory 1930b, quoted in Tanganyika 1954: 1).

Thus there were two agendas, one for the maintenance of "custom" and one for change and "improvement." The general conception was that Africa was a backward part of the world arrested in an earlier stage of social evolution. Yet, "this is not to say that native judicial institutions cannot change and develop as the people among whom they have evolved advance in prosperity and civilization" (ibid.). In keeping with the idea of evolution as continuous, the link between indigenous judicial institutions and the form of the new local courts was stressed.

Native courts, wrote Cameron,

> are not a new system invented by us, but a continuation of the judicial functions of native authority which have existed in a more or less primitive form ever since the emergence of those units possessing a common language, a single social system, and an established customary law, units which we call tribes. (ibid.)

The official mythology was that once exposed to some of the most fundamental and time-honored British concepts of law and procedure, Africans would see at once how sensible, practical, and moral these ideas were and would reform the native system by adopting them. The "natural" process of legal evolution would thus be accelerated. British knowledge would become part of African knowledge.

> We endeavor to purge the native system of its abuses, to graft our higher civilization upon the soundly rooted native stock. (Cameron in Tanganyika Territory 1930a, quoted in Tanganyika 1954: 1)

> Native customary law is a living system which is constantly going through a process of development and adjustment to new circumstances and new impulses of thought, which in time become crystallized as part of that law. (Cameron in Tanganyika Territory 1930b: 1)

The idea of transplanting legal ideas and institutions is one thing. Doing it is another. Most of the British officials who supervised the native courts in Tanganyika were not lawyers and had no specialized training in the law. There was no assumption that the most fundamental principles of British legal ideology would be part of the culture of laypersons in Britain. That was not an insurmountable problem. As noted earlier, the 1957 *Memoranda* carefully instruct administrative officers in what they need to know. The pamphlet spells out for the administrators both what is to be considered most sacred in the British legal-cultural heritage and what is most commendable about African law. For the administrators' part of the pamphlet, "the African mind," "African traditional procedures," and "African customary law" tend to be mentioned as if there were no need to make distinctions between one people and another. In those few parts of the text where the existence of local "tribal" differences in customary law systems is acknowledged, these differences are taken as largely superficial details. African legal principles and practices are presented to the British officers as being generally rather alike. The tone is that on the whole the Africans are good fellows with a sound legal "tradition," who simply need some guidance to ensure that in the future the courts and the law will evolve as they should.

The pamphlet repeatedly expresses this double-think, this appreciation and critique of African ways. The sermon that Africans and African institutions must be respected is stated again and again. But the disapproval of many African practices is also made manifestly clear. So, for example, in the part of the pamphlet written for African readers, the court-holders and their clerks are told:

> A local court is set up by a warrant signed by the Provincial Commissioner. . . . But the courts are nevertheless not something new created by the Government, they are merely a continuation of the *barazas* which have existed in all tribes for longer than anyone can remember. . . .

> This was a very good system and nearly always justice was done under it. For this reason the British Government decided to allow the people to continue to settle their own disputes in their own way. To assist them, the *barazas* were given a court clerk, courthouses were built and fees were fixed; but the law remained the local customary law and only a few cruel things were forbidden, such as torture, ordeals, cutting off the hands of thieves, selling offenders as slaves and other practices which are not permitted in civilized countries. Apart from these practices the *barazas* were allowed to carry on as before and to settle disputes in the old way. *They were not expected to model themselves on British courts except in so far as their first concern was to dispense justice.* . . . They were not allowed to take very serious cases, such as murder, but all ordinary cases could be heard, and heard in the traditional manner. Because the *baraza* now met in a proper court house and had a clerk, it was not therefore expected to become a kind of "European" court. It was expected to hear cases carefully, however, and to see that justice was done, for that is the main function of a court—to dispense justice—and *this cannot be repeated too often.* (55; emphasis mine)

A skeptical note is audible in the allusion to "civilized countries" and in the phrases about the need to "dispense justice" and in the admonition that "this cannot be repeated too often." An even more critical statement appears in that part of the pamphlet addressed to administrative officers. They are told openly that they must be made "aware of the lines along which it is thought best that . . . [the courts] should develop" (1).

The *Memoranda* are attempts to train the trainer, to outline what the administrative officer must learn and then communicate to the Africans who actually run the local courts. However appreciative of the practicality and popularity of "customary law" the administrator is, he must ensure that only the acceptable portions thereof are actually applied. Thus the Local Courts Ordinance includes a well-known provision common throughout the British colonies and known as "the repugnancy clause." The commentary "clarifies" the meaning of this clause for the young officer by using a strong moral tone and some dramatic illustrations.

The advisory pamphlet says,

> The Ordinance re-introduces the limitation that no customary law shall be administered which is repugnant to natural justice or morality or which, in principle, is in conflict with any law in force in the Territory. It should be noted these limitations apply to the sanctions which local law and custom impose as well as to the substantive body of law itself. It must be most clearly understood that injustice and illegality . . . are "repugnant" in this sense and that only one course is open to an officer in such cases and that is to put them right. (25)

Thus customary law is endorsed provided it is congruent with a British conception of natural justice, morality, or legality. "There are some things which a British Government cannot permit, since they outrage our sense of what is just or right" (ibid.). The illustrations of unacceptable behavior given include the murder of twins and ordeal by poison. However clear these extreme instances seemed to the writer of these guidelines, he also acknowledges that other cases might be occasions for discretionary judgment. A high moral tone was thus coupled with a low level of precision about definitional boundaries.

The document is at pains to say that in any case in which the officer acts to set aside the local law, the government must *explain* the reasons for its decision and must try to elicit consent for its action.

> Whenever this occurs the opportunity should be taken by discussion with chiefs and elders to induce them and their people to consent to the suppression of the objectionable features of the law or custom in question, but care should be exercised that the result is not simply to drive underground what is objectionable. (ibid.)

The idea that verbal argument would change minds and *elicit consent* (innocent prefigurations of Habermas) expresses a British idea of democratic legitimation. It is probably no accident that this consent to directed change in a colonial document is emphasized at the very time that the pressure for the end of the colonial regime had gained substantial force. But it should also be noted that the text nevertheless emphasizes unidirectional explanation. The British explain things to the Africans. There is no suggestion that any effort be made to explore the Africans' rationale for the practices targeted for suppression. What the British prescribe can be "explained." British knowledge of morality and justice can be imparted. It follows that Africans are to be instructed. African practices that conflict with the government's conception of the range of acceptable behavior cannot be "explained." African knowledge on these topics is, by definition, nugatory.

Whenever the British author of the *Memoranda* recognizes that there is a cultural clash, he also sees an evolutionary lag. The "weaknesses" of the native courts as identified by the *Memoranda* are said to arise from "the nature of local customary law" (7). The weaknesses are listed as *(a)* failure to observe the principles of natural justice; *(b)* failure to appreciate the rationale of punishment, with which is bound up failure to appreciate the distinction between civil and criminal liability, *(c)* failure in procedure, and *(d)* corruption (ibid.).

The "failures" and "weaknesses" identified by our administrative guide are given very general labels. They are identified as inherent characteristics, that is, they arise from the "nature" of African ideas and practices. These "weaknesses" seem to be offered as reason why it is difficult to plant the British judicial model in African soil. So much for the many times this is said not to be the colonial objective.

What parts of these official directives were actually put into practice, and what was the nature of the message they communicated to Africans? Obviously the local courts were a colonial institution. The courts were a link in the chain of organization of the colonial state. That tie, to an imposed political system, to a non-African conception of government by definition made those courts something other than purely "local" courts. Nevertheless, in today's postcolonial Africa many Africans themselves have come to think of these colonial local courts and their postcolonial successors as African institutions. For that reason, among others, they are. African governments and African citizens have made these once colonial institutions their own.

The transformative and recombinant potential that resides in all cultural forms and practices is epitomized by this colonial institutional modification and its subsequent African appropriation. The history of the West is replete with examples of such insertion, addition, and cumulation. In the West, there was a time when scholars were the principal people who dwelt on the particular origins of cultural elements and indulged in a kind of cultural etymology (see, e.g., Miner's classic comic piece of 1956 on the foreign origin of American objects and customs). But now, in Europe as elsewhere, with the politicization of ethnic boundaries, the particular origins of cultural items have by no means always lost their political interest (see Herzfeld 1987 on the Greeks and the Turks, for example). Thus it is not surprising that for a certain group of African intellectuals the question what is authentically and originally African seems politically salient today (see Mudimbe 1988). For most other Africans the question whether change means "westernization" is of no great concern provided the standard of living improves.

Present inquiries into the nature of African knowledge seem framed to emphasize the issue of provenance (see Mudimbe 1988; Comaroff 1985). Why ask such a question at this moment? Perhaps to emphasize that the issue cannot simply be treated as a matter of separating out the "traditional." There is much that is now emphatically *African* but that is not a matter of ancient custom at all. Surely "culture" must always be thought of as a cumulative accretion, from many times and sources. In such circumstances, to ask with some historical seriousness how the present African amalgam developed is for theoretical reasons of no small interest. It is possible to attempt such an analysis in the field of local law.

Where the records are full enough and field studies are sufficiently detailed, African legal practices and the ideas that informed them can be followed as they changed over the past century. Even where some legal norms have continuity, the contexts in which they are used have changed (Moore 1986a; Snyder 1981). A larger processual question this raises is whether and to what extent intentionally constructed organizations, inserted institutions, and directed behaviors are recognizably different from culturally inherited ones, and at what point in time this can be said to be the case. At the moment of their inception? After their subsequent "reproduction?"

As we have already observed, in Tanganyika, the introduction of a system of local courts and the transfer of a set of accompanying practices, principles, and ideas was anything but a simple one-time act. The process of structuring this introduction initiated was far from "complete" at the time of independence. Constructing and conveying various legal "packages" was a long-term, ongoing colonial project that the independent government has now inherited and to which

it has made its own amendments and additions. But my work on Kilimanjaro
suggests that not only has much of the British-designed structure of the courts
been inherited, but so have many of the resistances to it and circumventions of
it. That dynamic combination is the African institution today.

THE RULE OF LAW AND LAW AS RULES

One of the central matters on which the 1957 pamphlet instructs the novice officer was what law was to be applied in the courts. The answer displays rhetorical
gymnastics performed in a time-ripened colonial style.

> THE RULE OF LAW
> Fundamental to the British way of life is the concept of the Rule of Law, and
> while there may be many concepts which will not merit transplantation from
> Britain to Africa this is not one of them. In considering the future of the local
> courts it is clearly desirable to bear the Rule in mind and to base their further
> development unequivocally upon its requirements. (13–14)

According to these *Memoranda* the first requirement of the Rule of Law is
"that there should be a known body of law," and the pamphlet argues "that
the development of the courts cannot be guided unless there is certainty as to
what the law is" (ibid.). But, of course, there was no repository to which the
administrative officer could go to discover what the African law was. There
were no written legal archives to consult. The pamphlet wants to redress this
deplorable situation. It identifies the project of recording customary law as a
necessary next step. The fact that customary law systems were themselves dynamic and changing is acknowledged. Such change was, indeed, welcomed as
"most necessary" for a period of fundamental and rapid social transformation.
In this respect, our colonial advisor likens customary law to the common law
of England.

> Customary law as a body of law is comparable in its nature to the common law
> of England, and officers should disabuse their minds of the widely prevailing
> view that the expression "customary law" covers only what remains today of the
> ancient rule for controlling the affairs of any community prior to the advent of

the European; such is not the case. No body of law can remain static; . . . In the last fifty years of European administration in Tanganyika customary law has lost none of its vitality and it follows that it must have developed considerably in that period. (26)

However full of vitality the customary law system might have been, it was time to capture it and set it down. It must be put in writing to fulfill the need for certitude which the Rule of Law demanded. The potential dangers in "codification," the worry that it might lead to "ossification," are considered to be no great risk (14). By recasting African law as a set of rule statements, not only would an authentic African law be accorded its full dignity, but it would be adapted to modern court use.[3]

In this conception, the effort of all parties appearing in court should be to prove that the circumstances of their cases made one or another rule or principle "applicable" as is done in Anglo-American courts. The pivotal notion is that there should be a rule-governed judiciary that dispenses justice uniformly and a rule-minded citizenry that mobilizes that judiciary when it thinks it has a case "under the rules." This ideal of rule standardization goes hand in hand with the requirement of judicial impartiality. Such a model is also predicated on the existence of some kind of authoritative hierarchy that ultimately determines what the rules are and who the judges are—who commands, who obeys, what is obeyed (Hart 1961). A judicial system so conceived is manifestly a close partner of centralized government and bureaucratic administrative structures. Such a design is not practical without a system of writing and record-keeping and without effective techniques of long-distance communication (Anderson 1983). The catch-22 in Africa was that virtually none of the preconditions of the model obtained at the beginning of colonial rule. By the end much still had not been

---

3. The body of rules formally entrusted to the court for enforcement was tripartite: rules from two African sources and from one explicitly colonial one. The African sources were (1) the rules of customary law (which, as the 1957 *Memoranda* note, were not unproblematic), and (2) orders and laws made under the Native Authority Ordinance (i.e., orders and laws made by chiefs and other native authorities in an officially approved manner), and (3) the laws of colonial provenance that specifically conferred jurisdiction on these courts, such as tax laws and the like (25, 87). In the *Memoranda* and other official documents about the colonial courts, the legitimating rhetoric for the court is largely directed toward the "application" of these three types of rules and principles.

successfully instituted (see Chanock 1985: 20; Mann & Roberts 1991: 35–36; Moore 1986a; Snyder 1981).

Was customary law simply a set of rules? There has been a venerable debate on the topic of the complex place of norms in "customary" systems (see Comaroff & Roberts 1977, 1981; Roberts 1979; Gulliver 1969, 1979; Moore 1986a). It is fairly well agreed that in many (most) African settings there was much that operated in the "resolution" of disputes other than a system of norms. But as far as the colonial administration was concerned, that non-rule part of the process was irrelevant to their renovating concerns. The rules should be identified and written down.

Like fat rendered in cooking, the product was to be altered even as it was extracted. The administrators and academics who were enthusiastic about re-corded rules at the time were very much aware of the change embedded in the very act of constructing such a restatement. That was part of the intention, to "modernize" the existing African system by bringing it formally into the courts. The idea was that once converted into a body of stated rules, the law would be only then in a form in which it could be authoritatively interpreted by the judi-ciary. This conception of legal modernization was not confined to Tanganyika: It enjoyed broad administrative and academic support throughout many other parts of Anglophone Africa.

In 1959, a Restatement of African Law Project was formally started at the School of Oriental and African Studies in London. Ten years later Professor A. N. Allott, the project's director, reported on its first decade. He made it plain that restatements were conceived of as a contribution to "nation-building" and "modernization." He explains that there was a large demand "for a convenient and authoritative source of reference on the customary laws. This source had to be cast into a legal form, i.e., its language had to be legal and integrable with the language of the general law" (Allott 1969: 1). Although by no means the first to record customary rules, Allott and his associates performed the task far more technically and professionally than had earlier scholars of African law. As he put it, "Good work was done by anthropologists, but this usually failed to meet the criteria outlined above for a work usable by the courts" (ibid.: 2). The Restate-ment was not primarily conceived as a contribution to social science. It was to be a practical step toward "the reform of local and native court systems, and their partial or total integration in the general judicial system" (ibid.: 1).[4]

---

4.   In the United States a "restatement" approach had been successful in clarifying and summarizing the cumulative gist of court cases on many topics. But the Allott

On the ground that it was necessary to take some measures to ensure that customary rules would not "ossify" but would continue to be alterable, the 1957 *Memoranda* proposed that recorded customary law rules not be given the full status of law. They should not have conclusive and binding authority but be regarded simply as guides (14).[5] Thus in the very same authoritative document, we find statements on customary law that lead in quite contrary directions. The need to produce a written and authoritative set of customary rules was strongly urged to conform to the first principle of the Rule of Law. At the same time it was made clear that once produced, the courts need not be absolutely bound by the customary law rules so written. The latter should serve merely as guides. Thus, the text says repeatedly that Africans are best qualified to know and handle their own business and should do it according to their own rules. The subtext says that the colonial government knows best, and must reserve the power to intervene when Africans fail to deliver "justice." The voice that gives legitimacy to African ways speaks again and takes back that recognition by giving it only conditionally.

The ambivalent situation in which the colonial administrators of this mid-century generation found themselves could not be clearer. They were committed to discovering and respecting the authentic African legal "tradition" and to writing it down in the form of rules. At the same time they recognized that it had already changed a great deal and also acknowledged that they were committed to changing it further. (For recent discussions of the place of African "tradition" in the colonial period see Ranger 1983; Chanock 1985; Moore 1986a.) Thus the double-valenced tone of the 1957 *Memoranda.* The assets of customary law

---

effort, though it carried the same label, was quite different. It was, as is evident from the 1957 *Memoranda*, an academic elaboration on earlier colonial policies. The recording of local customary law had long been one of the tasks suggested to district officers and other administrators. Such documentation was thought useful in carrying out their job of supervising the native courts. Thus it is not unusual to find scattered notes on customary rules in the District Books and in a variety of administrative reports. But Allott was right. These notes were rarely systematic or comprehensive (see, e.g., Griffiths 1930).

5. The author is well acquainted with various anthropological works and refers to a similar "guidelines proposal" Schapera had made many years earlier. In his introduction to the *Handbook of Tswana law and custom* ([1938] 1955) Schapera said in support of it, "Adherence to customary law should neither be blindly rigid nor yet capriciously fluctuating" (ibid.: 27). The fine line was for someone else to draw.

are accorded many nods of appreciation, but its shortcomings are also resolutely and relentlessly noted.[6] This tension is presented in its most general form in the statement: "An understanding of customary law . . . is important not only because proper supervision of the courts cannot be given without it but because it enables one to appreciate what is worthy of retention and *what must be discarded*" (4; emphasis mine).

The commentary goes on to foretell that homogenization and standardization are the "natural" direction in which the evolution of the legal system as a whole will develop. The prediction is that as more and more customary law is recorded, "the general principles of Bantu Law which it is thought are effective throughout the patrilineal area of the territory should begin to emerge and become capable of definition, to the great benefit of all concerned with their practical application" (15). Thus it was anticipated that a kind of uniform Bantu law in the patrilineal area would eventually emerge from the very process of recording the rules. The "local anomalies" and "local dissimilarities" of different customary systems would "be thrown into prominent relief" thus accelerating "the *natural* tendency toward uniformity" (15; emphasis mine). The possibility that legal pluralism might be permanent or at least very durable is not countenanced.

With or without an evolutionary rationale, postcolonial successor governments in Africa have all had to face the uniformity versus pluralism issue. Should there be one set of laws for all citizens or diverse ones that take account of local custom? Clearly these legal issues once faced by colonial governments were not particular to the colonial form but rather are characteristic dilemmas of government centralization in most culturally plural settings (see Hooker 1975).

The report of a Tanganyika government-sponsored conference on Local Courts and Customary Law held in Dar es Salaam in 1963 said: "There was

---

6.   Under the heading "Aspects for retention," the *Memoranda* (4) give this definition of the assets:

> We have seen that customary law is primarily concerned with the restoration of the social equilibrium, with adjustments and reconciliations, with restitution and the award of compensation; that its procedure is informal but effective, designed to bring about an agreed solution, not an imposed judgment; that its sanctions are the fear of offending public opinion, living and dead, and the fear of magical retribution. . . . Customary law is, in addition, local and popular, it is firmly based on the realities of tribal life and thus understandable to all, it is open to all members of the tribe, and finally, it is cheap. These are characteristics which in any system of law would be admirable and worthy of retention.

wide agreement that there was no question of the disappearance of customary law in the foreseeable future as a significant part of African legal systems"
(African Conference on Local Courts 1963: 22). Nevertheless, a later international seminar on African law held at Addis Ababa in 1966 noted the postcolonial pressure on the new nations of Africa to "codify customary law" in order
to "unify" their legal systems (Gluckman 1969: 28). Many countries were said
to consider the unification of laws "a necessary ingredient of nation-building
and mobilization for economic and social development" (ibid.). In Tanzania
(fulfilling the prediction of the *Memoranda* about "natural" tendencies toward
uniformity) the government had already undertaken to produce a formal "restatement" of its own "modified" version of customary law for all of its patrilineal peoples and planned to do the same for the matrilineal peoples, with some
rather unspecific notion that the two sets of rules might be combined at some
eventual time.[7]

What actually ensued in each African country as it contemplated the standardization of its laws is not the present concern. It is rather the very fact that on
gaining independence each African country had to ask itself the same questions.
(See discussion of pluralism in Kuper & Kuper 1965: Introduction; Kuper &
Smith 1969; Hooker 1975. Note also Ofuatey-Kodjoe 1977 on the principle
of self-determination.) To what extent should there be a unitary system, and
to what extent should a multiplicity of local legal systems continue to operate?
Can national centralization of control and some degree of local autonomy in
these matters be reconciled? This, which at first glance seems only a formal legal
dilemma, actually raises the profound political question of African identity at
the national level. The legal uniformity issue is an implicit commentary on the
pluralism of African "knowledge." Which forms of cultural difference are to be
officially *acknowledged?* Which laws are to be standardized and universalized
within the state?

---

7. The system adopted in Tanzania involved locality-by-locality approval and adoption
   of the newly standardized rules. So the District Council Minutes of 15 Oct. 1963
   at Kilimanjaro show that in that session they approved unification with respect
   to *ulinzi, urithi,* and *wosia* (guardianship, inheritance, and wills). However, local
   practices were not changed by this document except for those few cases in which a
   lawsuit was brought by a discontented party. A double system continued inside and
   outside the Courts.

WRITING: LEGAL KNOWLEDGE AND DURABLE RECORDS

The discussion of the Rule of Law and the enthusiasm for the project of recording customary law take for granted the larger, quite general reliance of the "modern" jural institutions on written records. There is a considerable difference between legal systems that are fundamentally oral and legal systems predicated on writing everything down. These differences have been touched on by Goody (1977, 1986) in his work on literacy but deserve more extensive treatment. Used in law, writing is a technique that affects substance.

Despite the declared intention to respect indigenous institutions, the whole conception of what native courts should be and become was founded on the making and keeping of several types of written records. In the beginning these were necessarily minimal and unreliable. In 1930 the *Native courts memoranda no. 2* (Tanganyika Territory 1930b: 7–8) commented on the prevalent illiteracy of chiefs and 'other members of the courts. "Even now it must still be rather the rule than the exception that the clerk is the only literate man among them" (ibid.: 7). It goes on to say that "since they can have no idea what he has recorded," the clerk may misrepresent the record. Administrative officers are admonished to check with chiefs and elders and especially with the litigants themselves to make certain that the record reflects the reality. "No inspection of a native court should be regarded as adequate which goes no further than the written record in the register" (ibid.: 8).

Nevertheless, on Kilimanjaro the supervision of the courts of first instance usually took the form of an inspection of the written case reports. This was so of necessity as the courts were too numerous and too inconveniently located to make ongoing direct observation of hearings a practical option. Even in the late colonial period when the court holder and the clerk were both likely to be literate, there were many ongoing problems. The quality of the records kept still left much to be desired.[8] Thus, after a long statement on this topic, the *Memoranda*

---

8. The 1957 *Memoranda* express the hope that the judiciary and the executive would eventually be separated everywhere, as was already the case for certain districts. The idea was that the local chiefs should continue in an executive role but appoint a judiciary deputy to do the work of the court. It was expected that the judiciary deputy would be more literate and better at making and keeping case records than the chief and his clerk might have been in previous times. "It is to be hoped that" where there is a judiciary deputy, "the court-holder will not only be able to do his own recording but will also be able to supervise more effectively the routine clerical work" (18).

exhort the *new* administrator not to be in too much of a hurry about requiring everything to be in order. Being too exacting might lead to trouble.

In this connection attention may be drawn to the effects of insisting on too high a standard of competence all at once: in some courts, in the past, this has led to the suppression of any evidence thought to be unpalatable to the District Commissioner, to the recording of fictitious pleas of guilty. . . . and to difficult cases not being recorded at all.

> If the colonial control of native courts was to be built on the written record, the misconstruction of records was a way Africans could arrange in their own way what information reached the colonial authorities.

Clearly, the recordkeeping "failures" were not just a matter of an absence of literacy. Having the technical means to carry out the recordkeeping task did not guarantee the administratively desired performance. The example of Kilimanjaro illustrates this point very well. Though there was a high literacy rate in the area, recordkeeping was irregular. As late as 1960, virtually on the eve of independence, the district commissioner wrote a memo to the president of the Wachagga saying that "case files mysteriously disappear from local courts and persons to whom judgment was given find it difficult to establish their rights."[9] The district commissioner recommended that all local court records be kept under lock and key and that the senior court clerk be held personally responsible for them.

The commissioner also complained in some detail to the Chagga Appeal Court about the adequacy of the case records that were *not* missing. He said that all sorts of necessary items were omitted from the local case records, namely, the names of the magistrates and assessors hearing the case, the dates at which the hearings opened and closed, the record of adjournments and the reasons for them. He also objected to Appeal Court judgments that referred to statements and evidence put before that court which were not recorded, and might not have been made in the court of first instance. Moreover, the record was not always clear about whether the parties were present at the reading of the judgment.[10]

---

9.   District Commissioner to President of the Wachagga, Chagga Council File 3/16, Letter 214, dated 13 Dec. 1960.

10. District Commissioner to the Chagga Appeal Court, Chagga Council File 3/16, Letter 208, 10 Dec. 1960.

Thus British recordkeeping efforts were directed not only to the distant goal of writing down the rules of customary law but also to the more immediate one of recording the rulings (and the reasons for them) in particular cases, and toward the maintenance of these records, both to make administrative review possible and to provide an adequate basis for appeals. An implied aim was to make the work of the court durable over time, to make uncontested unappealed decisions permanent, to create in the court an institution whose record of its past was an accessible part of its present.

On each one of these recordmaking and recordkeeping points, it is fairly obvious that the "system" did not work very well. Thus the whole order of courts and of "justice" to be built on the Rule of Law and on thoroughly documented and inviolable records was continuously frustrated by irregularities. Those irregularities were sometimes a matter of inefficiency and sometimes of failure to possess the necessary skills. But they were also used (as the district commissioner's 1960 letters imply) as a means of retaining local power and of putting obstacles in the path of the authorities. A certain degree of studied carelessness could serve local interests by systematically frustrating surveillance. The struggle over recordmaking and recordkeeping may often have been a struggle over the location of control, but since deliberate malice carried uncomfortable political implications, authorities tended to redefine the situation as a matter of incompetence, inefficiency, and ignorance. It may be of some comfort to emphasize superior skill when losing the game.

LEGAL KNOWLEDGE AND THE CONCEPTION OF TIME: PERISHABLE CLAIMS AND IMMORTAL DECISIONS

Two of the matters noted in the 1957 *Memoranda* as difficult for Africans to understand involve legal conceptions of time and timing. Africans are represented as having difficulty grasping the idea that claims can be delayed too long before being brought to court and that cases that have been decided once should not be reopened and reheard. The writer describes a clash between what is in "the African mind" and what should be done—what the colonial administration deems appropriate or even "natural." The officers being instructed are told that Africans think in terms of permanent claims. Africans are said to suppose that unmet obligations give rise to permanent claim rights that may be raised at any time. That is so however much time has passed since the event that gave rise to the grievance. From the administrative view, all this must change. The *Memoranda* instruct the novice: all claims and accusations should be treated as perishable.

> It is quite foreign to traditional African ideas that there should be fixed periods of limitation in the institution of suits, nevertheless it must be explained that a complainant should be reasonably active in filing his claim and that delay may result in its being rejected out of hand. The principle involved is that the delay should not be so great that the defendant is likely to be prejudiced in his defence, e.g., by failure of memory, absence of witnesses, loss or destruction of documents. (9)

> The general principle of *natural* justice is quite clear; he who is aggrieved should, if he desires redress, be reasonably active in filing his claim; if he is indifferent and sleeps upon his rights he forfeits the prerogative of every citizen to ask the State to intervene upon his behalf." (34; emphasis mine)

The courts officer is preoccupied with the question of evidence and its availability. But in many African rural economies, to be worth anything a claim must endure until the obligee has the means to pay it. That may take more than one generation. An indefinite time frame can be a major economic element in the effectiveness of a claim. As the Chagga say, it is no use claiming a cow from a man who does not have one. But if you wait until the original debtor's son or grandson prospers, your claim may be easier to lodge, your case easier to win in the local arena.

The delayed exchange economy has its costs and its quirks. Both debts and assets are heritable, but until there are adequate assets, and the way is socially clear for collection, a debt is not worth very much. For example, there is the question of community sympathy for worthy debtors. Collecting large debts at an "arbitrary" time—without regard to the debtor's ability to pay—can have lasting, severely punitive, and destructive consequences. Local people may not approve of requiring payment, however clear the indebtedness. A debt is not worth very much if there are such obstacles to collection in the micro-political arena. A creditor who presses his claim against a tragically impoverished debtor when the creditor might have waited for a more favorable moment may find himself in trouble. This is likely to be so when the debtor is well liked. There can be other social deterrents to collection. A debtor with a powerful local ally may be impossible to pursue for fear of retribution against the creditor.

The good news for creditors is that the politics of the situation can change. If someone dies or emigrates or other changes of local alignments take place, a claim that was socially impossible to bring forward at one time may suddenly become viable at another. Thus delayed claims have their economic and social rationales. In a sense, one may think of a local community among the Chagga as constantly seething with latent claims which may or may not be brought forward. Timing is crucial. The economic or politic moment may never arise. So, from the Chagga point of view claims can evaporate. They *are* perishable. But the issue of the debtor's assets (at what moment he has any) and the issue of the politic moment are more cogent to the vitality and durability of the claim than the simple passage of time.

The question of producing witnesses or other evidence raises a related point of social technique. For delayed claims to be effective in the absence of the written records, there must be some collective memory of the original transaction. If not, the necessary mobilization of micro-political pressure will not be possible. Thus among the Chagga there is an endless reiteration of new and old obligations. There are many formal and informal, oral, and even ritual ways of commemorating transactions in order to make them public. The memory of some of these bits of knowledge actually fades with time, and some perfectly well-remembered claims "fade" because enthusiasm for particular causes (or persons) becomes increasingly difficult to muster. Even when they do not disappear from local minds, oral "records" leave much room for reinterpretation and negotiation.

The perpetuity of certain claims in many African legal systems is not an indication of a defective concept of time. It is just a different strategic use of time for the purposes of litigation. In a rural settlement in which families live cheek by jowl for several generations and build their expectations on the continuation of those relationships, it is easy to see the logical fit between a heavy involvement in delayed exchange and a practice that tolerates delayed claims. That logic is not the exclusive property of a "traditional" economy. Opportunistic economic or social reasons for harboring and delaying a legal claim often fit just as well into a market-oriented, cash economy. The extension of credit time between sellers and buyers is not unusual in industrial society. Keeping a debtor viable can be a good economic strategy.[11]

---

11. The dichotomy so dramatically sketched by Bourdieu (1977) that clearly distinguishes and contrasts two models of "economy," the gift economy and the

What of the other time-related legal "idea" addressed by the 1957 *Memoranda*, the matter of *res judicata*? Consonant with British conceptions of justice, the *Memoranda* emphasize that full adjudication terminates a legal case once and for all. "It is a salutary principle of law that a matter once decided in a court is final, subject only to interference by a higher tribunal by way of appeal or revisions and that a case," finally determined, "cannot be brought a second time" (35). Subject to these conditions, the case is closed. The *Memoranda* complain, therefore, that from the African perspective, the case may only be closed for the moment.

Most African courts, it goes on to say, have come to understand that in criminal matters a person cannot be tried twice or more for the same offense, "but in civil matters this is by no means so, and cases of a civil nature, which have already been the subject of a decision of a court, are not infrequently resuscitated after many years and retried without question although the courts are aware of the previous proceedings" (ibid.).[12] The *Memoranda* attribute what it calls "the curious behavior" of reopening previously decided cases to "the nature of indigenous judicial procedure" and draws on a rationale attributed to the Kikuyu that had been quoted in the Phillips Report on Native Tribunals (Phillips 1945). The gist of that rationale is that lacking higher appellate courts, a similar function is

---

market economy, divides them into two pure, mutually exclusive types, yet these are actually joined in today's Africa. The concurrence of these two economies is not a new development. Most Africans have long participated in more than one type of exchange, some ritually elaborated and gift labeled, and some nakedly "commercial." All indications are that this economic and conceptual range was in use in many areas long before the colonial period began. This was certainly true of the Chagga. The Chagga have been implicated in a money economy since the late nineteenth century and were involved in long-distance trade at least a half-century before that. Today many Wachagga steadfastly maintain both a "traditional" ethos about certain debts and grievances and also, when necessary or desirable, operate entirely comfortably within the terms set by the "new knowledge" of money, courts, laws and documents. They are involved both in "gift" exchange and "commodity" exchange. No doubt other Tanzanian peoples were and are similarly situated (Iliffe 1979).

12. Allott 1960: 297 noted a similar attitude in Ghana, "Native law and the native courts . . . did not recognize *res judicata* . . . and any claim might be reopened." Lloyd Fallers (1969: 267) quotes Allott and compares the Soga courts after 70 years of British rule, asserting that virtually any complaining party could get a hearing: "Notions related to the Anglo-American *res judicata*, . . . enter into the arguing of a case rather than into its acceptance for argument." Fallers felt that earlier decisions on exactly the same issues would generally be considered decisive in Soga courts but that such previous decisions would never bar a plaintiff from *initiating* a rehearing.

fulfilled for Africans by the possibility "unbarred by time" of going back to the same tribunal of first instance for a replay of the case (ibid.: 36). The reason for this, the text asserts, is that the objective of indigenous judicial proceedings is to create social equilibrium and that if there is a change in the equilibrium, from the African point of view that justifies a change in the judgment. Thus there emerges the possibility of a justified retrial of the same case (ibid.: 2, 36).

The idea that the maintenance of social harmony and equilibrium is the dominant objective of African legal proceedings not only figures in colonial documents like the *Memoranda* but also has been a prominent part of the analytic argument of various anthropologists, including Max Gluckman (1955: 21; 1965a: 279). The idea as expressed in the *Memoranda* is: "The life of the clan (or other unit) proceeded harmoniously only so long as the members discharged their duties and obligations faithfully. If one member defaulted, the equilibrium was upset in greater or lesser degree" (2). This argument is founded on the notion that "[w]hereas amongst Europeans the stress is upon the individual and his rights, amongst the Bantu it was . . . upon the community, upon the family or clan, and its continuing solidarity" (ibid.).

This is an effort to show sympathetic understanding. It belongs to a certain era. Both the colonial officer and the anthropologist of the late colonial period want to argue that African ways of doing things are entirely reasonable given the social premises on which they are based. They also want to argue that African ways rest on a moral foundation rather than on a purely strategic rationale. The image of the moral, rational, and educable African replaces an earlier colonial one of the rebellious, ungovernable indigene. The attitude is: They are reasonable, therefore reason with them. And so with *res judicata,* if African court holders and their elders exhibit consternation when they are told that they cannot rehear and reverse a judicial decision about a piece of clan land made twenty years before, a patient explanation is all that is required. "The courts' consterna-. tion may be in large part dissipated by discussion and explanation and District Commissioners should patiently educate them to a realization of the need for finality in the settlement of disputes" (36). For whom was there such a need and what ends did it serve?

I would argue that the "social equilibrium" presentation of African disputational logic is a mixture of African self-idealization and colonial/anthropological political theory. It is also not without some foundation in fact, but it is a well-edited version of the facts. According to this interpretation of "traditional life," the disputants are obliged to work out mutually agreeable settlements because they are fated to go on living together in the same community. Collective pressures encourage them to achieve a harmonious settlement. That is surely sometimes a part of the story, but it is emphatically the view from the outside. As I have written elsewhere on the question of collective liability, the view from the inside is of a much more competitive, much less harmonious entity. Within these groups there are factions and sub-segments and individual interests (Moore 1972, 1986a). There are superiors and inferiors. There are more and less powerful persons in these communities, and they can mobilize more or fewer individuals in the local political arena. Individuals can not only be discredited, they can be expelled (Moore 1991a). What appears to be equilibrium from the outside is often a temporary moment of agreement in which a dominant segment of the group has prevailed and everyone recognizes that predominance and acquiesces in all public behavior. This is what often gives the appearance of unanimity to collective decision-making (El-Hakim 1978).

This situation is a kind of "equilibrium" if one chooses to call it that, but it is hardly the harmonious justice that the more sentimental version of native life would have us believe. There is ample ethnographic evidence of inner struggles (submerged and explicit) within local groups in anthropological works written both during the colonial and postcolonial periods. Was the situation different in precolonial times? Is there any reason to postulate a harmonious, egalitarian, communitarian past, a Garden of Eden from which colonial intervention caused Africa to fall, a period Chanock (1985) calls "Merrie Africa"? I doubt it.

In my experience on Kilimanjaro, the "disturbance" of "equilibrium" that encourages a Mchagga to reopen a dispute that was previously heard and "settled" in or out of court is a change in the micropolitical situation in the neighborhood that makes the claimant think that a more favorable settlement is possible. The weight of partisan influence can be reshuffled by many events, anything from a sickness, a death, a marriage, a fight, to an enduring absence. Changes in local leadership can produce changes of loyalty. Altered balances in creditor-debtor relations can shift attitudes toward other matters. A witness who was once reluctant to come forward may become willing to speak when the social wind changes. Subtle realignments and redivisions of partisanship may be expected to result from any power shifts within a local group.

How does this change in partisanship outside the courts have impact on what goes on in a contemporary judicial proceeding? Among the Chagga today the answer is obvious enough. The willingness of witnesses to testify, let alone the content of their testimony, is often influenced by intragroup politics. It is not healthy to testify against the wishes of the powerful and their protégés. In circumstances in which agreements are seldom recorded in writing, it is only the testimony of witnesses that makes or breaks a case. Whoever controls the witnesses controls the outcome.

In the 1957 *Memoranda*, *res judicata* is considered simply as having to do with the closure of cases. The principle invoked is that having had one's proper day in court, one cannot start all over again on the same issues with the same evidence in the same tribunal. What is done is done. The closure argument has an internal logic. It puts the matter in terms of closing the dispute between the parties once and for all. But this emphasis on sorting out the disputants' affairs and finalizing some "solution" to their disputation masks the role of *res judicata* in the life of the court itself.

Res judicata is a declaration of the power of the court and is one of the practices that constitutes the bureaucratic-like character of judicial office. Not only does the court thereby rearrange a relationship in a conclusive way, but it simultaneously proclaims the finality of its own authority. What is more, *res judicata* is a statement about the bureaucratic continuity of judicial office. *Res judicata* binds a judge to honor the decisions of his predecessors. The judicial office and its rulings are thus made more durable than the tenure of its incumbents. British law has its own cultural constructions of time.

The *Memoranda* assert that Africans should be taught that a court decision has binding permanence, that claims and grievances must be promptly brought to the court or they will expire. This mission of instruction depends on the attribution of an African counterview: that from the African perspective it is not the decision but the grievance or obligation that has permanence, that a complaint should be able to be made at any time and a case reopened at any time. What submerged assertions are embodied in the difference between the temporal limits on claims and the permanence and finality of decisions? Is this an argument about the difference between African and British constructions of time or is it really about the locus of authority stated in terms of cultural ideas about time? The difference between Chagga and British official attitudes on these matters is undeniable. But as a characterization of the African "mind," the 1957 *Memoranda* misrepresent the central issue. The argument is an argument about the authority of a local institution empowered and endorsed by a central government and about the nature of that institution. It is a question whether what happens in the court is to be defined in terms of the ebb and flow of local micropolitics or in terms of a central government standard, a rule-oriented,

delegating, judicial/bureaucratic model. The judicial/bureaucratic mode is repeatedly presented in the *Memoranda* not as a form of power but as a form of
knowledge.

JUDICIAL KNOWLEDGE, TRUTH FINDING, AND AFRICAN PARTISANSHIP

Deeply permeating the field of Chagga local micro-politics is a syndrome I
call "obligatory partisanship." What this phrase encapsulates is the notion that
certain kinds of social assistance are, at least ideally, supposed to be supplied
on demand in given social relationships. The public demonstration of partisan
support is one of those demand-driven forms of help. Being able to mobilize
such support is a very important social asset and affects various court-related
performances including judging and testifying. This kind of obligation existed
during the colonial period, and it exists in rural communities today.

The 1957 pamphlet tells us early in its pages that there was no indigenous
foundation for the kind of impersonal evidence taking and truth finding that
the British were trying to introduce (2–3).

It should . . . be noted that the attitude towards evidence was quite different from
that which obtains in a modern British court. The elders did not come together
to ascertain the facts, they either knew them already or invoked the aid of the
supernatural to find the truth. They met to decide the penalty. (3)

These assumptions also seem to lie behind the alleged difficulty of persuading
Africans that in a criminal case they ought to presume the innocence of a defendant until guilt is proven. "It is realized that this is a conception which may
come but slowly to African minds, but it is nevertheless a principle which must
be continually kept before them" (41).

The impartiality of judges and the truth telling of witnesses were areas of
court performance that were very difficult for the colonial administration to
manage effectively. The administrators seem to have reserved some of their most
powerful rhetoric for such uncontrollable domains:[13]

13. Our pamphleteer extracted the principles of natural justice from the Phillips Report
on Native Tribunals in Kenya of 1945 (Phillips 1945), which in its turn quoted

Standard of Justice Dispensed.—Now that the courts have been in operation
for over thirty years it is possible to make some assessment of their efficiency,
to indicate their weaknesses and short-comings and to suggest in what respects
guidance is most required. . . . Their weaknesses are largely those which arise
from the nature of local customary law and procedure. . . .

They may be listed as follows:—

(a) Failure to observe the principles of natural justice. . . . Principles of Natural
Justice.—As regards (a), the principles of natural justice have been described as
follows:

(1) A man may not be judge in his own cause; decisions should be on purely judicial grounds and should not be liable to be influenced by motives of self-interest,
political opinions or other extraneous considerations. (7)

Personal interest and corruption are two matters about which administrative
officers are stoutly warned. Yet the problem is pervasive.

A special section has been inserted in the Ordinance to draw attention to one of
the cardinal principles of the Rule of Law, that no one should adjudicate upon
any matter or things in which he has any pecuniary or personal interest. . . . It
is one of the commonest failings of the courts to overlook this principle. (24)

In the Kilimanjaro court records from 1930 to 1980, instances alleging bias
or corruption can easily be found, but so can apparent even-handedness. In
colonial times, in the days when local chiefs or their deputies were the court
holders, there is no doubt that chiefs often used the courts to further their own
interests and those of their close kin and associates. Yet some of the matters that
came before them must have been cases to which they were indifferent, since
each court necessarily handled the accusations and disputes generated by a large
population. As for crude bribery among the chiefs then, and with reference to
the magistrates and the clerks today, there has always been a good deal of gossip, but it is difficult to know how much credence to give it. Certainly there is

---

them from a report of 1932. I have cited only one principle. There are seven in the
document.

great sensitivity on the subject, and accused judges can be very touchy (see, e.g., Marangu, Case 72: 1968; Kilema, Case 78: 1936). In both the cited cases, persons who had been heard to allege that the judge had been bribed were severely punished. In the Kilema case, the judge meting out the punishment was the very chief about whom the allegation had been made (so much for disinterest). In the Marangu case, in the interest of fairness a fellow magistrate was substituted for the one who had been accused, but the two magistrates were friends.

Improper extensions of personal power also took another form, one that the *Memoranda* call "political cases." Thus a chief might use the court to bring a case against an administrative subordinate, a subchief, or other official, find him guilty of some form of insubordination or incompetence, and then dismiss him. The *Memoranda* go on to say: "This is perhaps a very natural error for one who has both executive and judicial functions to discharge, but it should be clear even to a chief that dismissal from office is not one of the forms of punishment which local courts are authorized to impose" (10).

Court holders were not the only people identified as possibly "biased." Witnesses, too, might have less than truth-seeking motives. There were well spelled-out clauses in the Local Courts Ordinance prohibiting the giving of false evidence and outlawing any interference with witnesses (1957 *Memoranda*, secs. 29, 30: 94). But practice was another thing.

In comparative perspective, the "false" or absent witness issue looks less like a question of local Chagga misbehavior and more like a general systemic practice. In many societies the normal expectation is that testimony will regularly be baldly distorted by partisanship, and it is accepted as such. Scholars concerned with such settings have tried to construct explanations making this behavior plausible and understandable to Western readers. The standard rationale is that such evidence giving is more of a testimonial to the character and social place of the person on whose behalf the witness is testifying than it is an account of the "facts" (For a recent version of this explanation applied to Islamic courts in Morocco, see Rosen 1988.) But what is it about a social/cultural milieu that makes the general social standing of the parties primary and the situational facts secondary once they get to a court?

I would argue that the primacy of the persons is a regular product of social settings where obligatory partisanship is a general rule of public behavior. The structural requirement that there be partisanship and that it be given public demonstration necessarily has deep effects on community micro-politics. Collective decision-making and public dispute resolution are common instances of the playing out of such pressures (El Hakim 1978). Lending, borrowing, and collecting debts also have such dimensions. One of the complex preconditions of neighborhood social life among the Chagga today is the frequent requirement of just such a show of partisanship. However, it would be a mistake to think of this as an exotic phenomenon or a rare one. There are often circumstances in many other kinds of society in which people *must* stand up and be counted, in which neutrality is not an option. Circumstances in which an individual must side with one set of persons against another, one ethnic group against another, one political or religious collectivity against another, are all too familiar in the many violent confrontations of our world. The dynamics of obligatory partisanship are also observable in much less extreme circumstances, in the academic department that must make an appointment and divides openly over the candidates, the business meeting that must decide whether to develop a particular product, the political setting in which voting is in public rather than by secret ballot (Bailey 1983; March & Olsen 1976; Simon 1957a; D. C. Moore 1976).

In the courts on Kilimanjaro in the postcolonial period, witnesses often testify (or fail to appear) with the idea of helping to construct a story favorable to the person to whom they owe a partisan account, either because of kin relationship, or for favors done in the past, for favors anticipated, for fear of displeasing, or the like. Sometimes, the effort to produce such witnesses fails. Magistrates tend to "read" that failure as a significant indication of a lack of social respectability. To the extent that the court is dealing with cases arising out of long-term relationships, those relationships are bound to impinge on everything that is said in court (and also what is omitted). There is every reason to believe that this situation is not new. The social standing of individuals in the Chagga village is an ongoing product of the unfolding of myriad intertwined events. Reputation is the product of time. Social position is continuously renegotiated, sometimes to be affirmed, sometimes to be destroyed, sometimes to be rebuilt. As in the collection of debts, time and timing are important elements in the construction of good standing. Allies are always needed, in communications, in exchanges, in acts of cooperation, in the arena of competition, and in the moments of actual conflict. The magistrates today are usually Chagga and live in this milieu even as do the parties who appear before them. They experience daily the contrast between what goes on in the environment in which these social transactions take place and what is considered legitimate in the kind of court conceived by the 1957 *Memoranda* and the later *Primary courts manual* (Tanzania 1964b; see also Tanzania 1963, 1964a).

Do these settings generate two forms of knowledge, one being knowledge of the way to conduct oneself in the shifting sands of ongoing social life outside the job, the other of the way to play one's role as a magistrate, honoring the ideal of impartiality and the rule-governed model of law, and managing a career in a formally organized, bureaucratically designed state institution? Certainly the difference between the designed judicial institution and the "event-evolved" set of neighborhood institutions is very great. In many respects, the court is being directly and continuously stage-managed by the state. The question of the specifics of delegated authority is central to its operation, as is its subordinate position within a hierarchical structure. The other, the neighborhood social field, while shaped and affected by the state, by policy, by the market, by political events, is neither as tightly managed nor as fully planned and designed as the operation of the local court. But that does not make the neighborhood less powerful when it comes to controlling witnesses and the outcome of litigation. The local court escapes its designers in a thousand ways. It did in the colonial period and it does today. What the kinsmen and neighbors "know" may never be declared in court. The magistrate may know the rules in the *Courts manual,* but he may never "know" what actually "happened" in the case before him.

One can only guess what the same multiplicity of domains of "knowledge" and of loyalty must have meant to "court holders" in the colonial period. Certainly, the colonial government regarded its agents, the judges, as highly susceptible to bias, bribery, misjudgment, and error. To ensure against the effects of these failures, the colonial government reserved to itself the ultimate right to undo whatever an African judge might have done. Like Penelope undoing by night what she had woven in the day, the colonial government constructed the courts, defined their work, and insisted on the worth and the permanence of their decisions, but could undo it all.

The law used the performative power of words quite magically. By decree it could make something into nothing. It could nullify proceedings by "quashing" them. For a quashed proceeding, *res judicata* did not apply. It was as if there had been no hearing. When it came to *res judicata* the Africans were supposed to obey the rules as they stood, but the colonial government could declare itself exempt from the norms when necessary through this magical form of erasure.

Thus, as previously noted, the *Memoranda* state: "In criminal cases, it seems to be already appreciated by the courts that a person cannot be tried twice or more for the same offence" (35). But in another section it makes it plain that such double jeopardy could be countenanced if the appropriate colonial officer deemed it necessary. Thus,

> In English law, in a criminal *case* which has resulted in an acquittal, there is no appeal by the complainant against such acquittal. *At the present stage of development* of the local courts it has been considered advisable to make provision for the possibility of an order of acquittal being made on inadequate or incorrect grounds and section 34(1)(b) indicates the procedure to be followed in such cases: the proceedings should be quashed and a re-trial ordered before whichever court is considered appropriate in the circumstances. (47–48; emphasis mine)

However fine a principle, and however well the African courts seemed to understand it, the principle of double jeopardy in criminal cases could be made selectively applicable by the authorities given "the present stage of development of the courts" (ibid.). By thus adopting an evolutionary rationale, the colonial power could legitimately break its own legal rules. It simply established a regular procedure for discretionary exceptions: "The Provincial Commissioner and any Provincial Local Courts Officer or District Commissioner . . . may of his own motion, or upon the application of any interested party . . . quash any proceedings" (95). A subsequent part of section 34(I)(b) reads, "Provided that where proceedings are quashed and an order for rehearing is made as aforesaid, no plea of *res judicata* or *autrefois acquit* or *autrefois convict* shall be deemed to arise out of the proceedings so quashed" (ibid.). In short, when it saw fit, the administration could nullify *res judicata*.

Here again is a complex and convoluted communication. First there is a strong message about the way native courts should operate. They should be like British ones and give full force to *res judicata* and the principle of no double jeopardy. Then comes a statement about the benighted Africans who do not operate that way and who seem to think any case can be reopened at any time. And lastly, in the technical procedural paragraphs of the ordinance we find a carefully crafted exception allowing the British to disregard the very rules they had been trying so hard to impart. The circumstances of governing by indirect rule were leading the British both to empower Africans to run the native courts and also to pull back from some of the implications of that decision. Customary law is both defined as potentially satisfying the requirements of the Rule of Law and then reduced to being a mere "guideline." The local courts are given the powers implied in the principle of *res judicata*, yet a way is provided for the

administration to circumvent those. The colonial government was operating on
two tracks, trusting and mistrusting, delegating and withholding final authority,
creating durable judicial institutions to make lasting decisions, and leaving the
door open to undermine the institutions and do away with the decisions.

CONCLUSIONS

I have here traced a selective course through the 1957 *Memoranda* on local
courts in Tanganyika to look at some of the conceptions the British had of
this judicial project, what they thought about Africa, and about law and the
law courts established there. This could not be a matter of steadily following
a consistent thread of reasoning. For many assertions in the document, there
are twinned, contradictory assertions. And such apparently unambiguous statements as there are often can be shown to have unstated multiple implications.
Thus, for example, the argument that British legal ideas are one of the great
achievements of that civilization is belied by the accompanying argument that
these ideas are actually no more than the embodiment of the universal principles of "natural justice." The idea that social evolution must be generated from
within a society is paired with the idea that in Africa change can be and should
be introduced by the colonial state to accelerate the march toward "civilization."
And the declared courts policy of controlled native empowerment itself incorporates a contradiction because the aims of control and the aims of empowerment are bound to face in opposite directions (see Hailey 1950: 212, 217, 220).
All of these are uneasy statements about the place of the British colonial project
in history, about the location of directed social change both in "real time," that
is, at a particular, dated historical moment, and in some grand, undatable total
trajectory of social evolution.

In that sense, evolution is an idea about the ultimate direction of history, in
which more effective ideas and techniques are eventually bound to drive out less
effective ones, better organizational arrangements to replace worse ones, morality to replace immorality, fairness to replace unfairness, justice, injustice, and
the like. Thus from the evolutionist perspective, social and moral achievement
and technical achievement are all assumed to be driven by the same dynamic
of replacement. The colonial experiment seems to have brought a substantial
amount of evolutionary rhetoric out of its officials, some of it not at all surprisingly implicated in the setting up of systems of courts. In that context, the

British colonial claim to "know" what was best for Africa and most advanced in matters of law and courts in the world was a double statement about time, about the colonial moment in a dated chronological history and the colonial place in an evolutionary trajectory.

But in addition to making explicit statements about legal evolution, the British administrators seemed to harbor less clearly articulated assumptions about how important or unimportant the then African side of things was, given the direction in which and the pace at which history was moving. If indigenous African law was changing rapidly and was, in an evolutionary sense, slated to be first homogenized and then replaced, the implication must surely have been that the details of contemporary indigenous local practice did not matter too much. They were only temporary. But the British also cited the venerated Rule of Law that required that there be a "known" body of law and that there be certainty about it, and argued that customary law should be recorded to meet that requirement. They did not devote much effort to doing so, however.

In Tanganyika, the administrators who dealt with the courts system had an important responsibility and some serious practical problems. They could not supervise the courts very closely. They seldom had the time, the language skills, or the interest to learn much about local "customary" law or the goings-on in local African communities. What they were strongly aware of doing was giving power to some Africans to make judgments about, and impose penalties on, other Africans through their powers as court holders. The technical infrastructure that might have made routine bureaucratic oversight of these courts successful existed neither at the level of recordkeeping, nor at the level of legal certainty, nor at the level of juridical impartiality. By itself, judicial review could not repair these deficiencies and could not function very well unless they were repaired. The colonials needed the cooperation of Africans or their administrative scheme of indirect rule would in practice be controlled by Africans rather than by themselves.

The courts were one of the testing grounds where this tension between central control and local control was manifest. African strategies in response were doubtless variable, different in different places or at different times. In the Kilimanjaro area, it is clear that Africans responded actively to the contradictions in British policy. They had no choice about receiving the framework of imposed institutional arrangements. But as a great deal of the day-to-day management was left in African hands, the practice often could be adapted to local political ends. That semi-autonomy aside, the African chiefs and their deputies and clerks who ran the courts in colonial times were nevertheless repeatedly exposed to the logic of their foreign rulers. After independence many aspects of this logic were formally incorporated into Tanzanian legal rationales, as were colonial administrative forms, but the struggle over local control versus central control continued, and continues.

Outside the courts, African communities have always gone their own way as much as they could, continuing to transact their own business on their own terms and continuing to control their own members through unofficial strategies. That control was and is given its mandatory force by the micro-politics of local social standing. The village capacity to control emanates less from tradition than from the extreme dependence of members on the community to which they belong. Local courts in rural areas are thus in a peculiar relation to two domains. They are the standard creations of national government, but the cases that come to them for decision arise in the ongoing flow of rural life, with its distinctive style. This circumstance raises a question in relation to the colonial instance that has far wider application: Is it possible to know much about a legal system without knowing the character of the case-generating milieu?

Using the Chagga material, it is not at all difficult to show that at the colonial center where the local courts legislation was designed for the whole country (to apply to its many different peoples), the government did not fully understand or accommodate the inner workings of this particular local African society, and that by implication the same was likely true of other local systems. That much is very easily illustrated and probably uncontroversial. To suggest that in that sense the colonial administration "did not know what it was doing" is just the kind of demonstration that pleases in 1992. As the colonial period has been safely over for more than thirty years, showing colonial flaws coupled with colonial arrogance is not only politically risk free, it is a rather conventional version of history for our time (Rabinow in Clifford 1986: 252).

My analytic purpose has been more experimental. Visible beyond the double demonstration that the colonial government, however powerful, was ignorant of many African matters and often impotent in the face of African intentions is a complex set of further questions. As they say in Haiti, "Behind the mountains lie other mountains." The story of the local courts in Tanganyika bears on the cumulative historical production of institutions and on the multiple meanings and sources of legal thought.

How context-dependent are legal principles and procedures? There are at least two quite inconsistent answers provided in the 1957 colonial document.

One assumes that British legal principles are portable and exportable, extractable from their societal context, a piece of knowledge that administrators can keep, cherish, and also give away to Africans at the same time. The counterpiece of colonial logic is that there are basic legal principles that are universal, that there are ideas of "natural justice" to be found in legal thought everywhere, and that the colonial project is simply to further develop those from African root stock. In the first version the colonials were introducing serious reforms on a British model. In the second they were merely building on what they found. In the first version African legal thought was different from the British. In the second the fundamental principles were the same. In our composite document, the British "knew" both to be true.

Much has been written about the nature of Christian missionary activity in Africa. Much less has been said about the secular moralizing, practical admonition, and redefinition of reality that accompanied the legal and administrative apparatus of the colonial period. A glimpse of that secular preaching was presented here, as was the way it was preoccupied with questions of time and timeliness, permanence and evanescence. To the extent that that reasoning had embedded in it a particular idea of African law, it is not difficult to use ethnographic data to show that African legal sociologic was in some particulars built on premises that diverged strongly from those of their colonial rulers. Without fully intending to do so, the colonial administrators forced an active juxtaposition of these two kinds of legal "knowledge" in the court system and had to cope with the consequences. The purpose here has been to examine some of the premises on which these two sets of ideas of "knowledge" were constructed.

Because the concepts used in the colonial system of courts are so familiar, some of their implications are normally invisible: the nature and place of rules of law, of *res judicata*, of case records, of the requirement of judicial impartiality, and a score of others. But some of the submerged implications of these rubrics come to the surface as the colonial government tries to communicate their import. The ongoing struggle between centralized bureaucratic authority and local autonomy is played out in the definition and redefinition of legal ideas and practices. The African side presented here is less familiar, both in content and interpretation. The connection between elements of a delayed-exchange economy and legal ideas about the durability of claims has not been suggested before. And although the proffering of testimony as testimonial has been often been noticed, the connection between the obligatory public demonstration of partisanship outside the courtroom and performances inside the court have not always had adequate attention. Both delayed claims and obligatory partisanship affect what a court *knows* and can *know*.

Thus fundamental thematic issues that concern time, timing, and knowledge implicit and barely noticeable in law in other contexts become unexpectedly visible in this British-African colonial setting. The colonial predicament uncovers some of the premises of our own legal culture. The basic problematic here has been epistemological, the basic framework temporal. Thinking about British ideas in an African setting and about colonial courts in 1992 "displaces" the one and "re-times" the other. The reading of the 1957 *Memoranda* grounds the discussion in a particular text but serves as the occasion to raise questions about history and social context, about time, and about the foundations of legal "knowledge."

CHAPTER SEVEN

Individual Interests and Organizational Structures

Dispute Settlements as "Events of Articulation"

Courts and other institutions of dispute settlement often represent their task as the disinterested enforcement of normative rules, or of general ideas of justice, proper behavior, and the like.[1] This self-description is sometimes taken as literally true and as the whole story. In contrast, when an anthropologist hears a ritual expert describing his purpose in communicating with the spirits, he listens to the statement as a piece of evidence in itself, and is appropriately analytical.

Editor's Note: This chapter is a reprint of Moore, Sally Falk. 1977. "Individual interests and organizational structures: Dispute settlements as 'events of articulation.'" In *Social anthropology and law*, ASA Monograph No. 14, edited by Ian Hamnett, 159–88. London: Academic Press.

1.   The work, both field work and library study, which made the preparation of this manuscript possible, was done in two periods, in 1968-69 under a grant from the Social Science Research Council of New York, and in 1973–74 under a grant from the National Science Foundation, which grants are hereby gratefully acknowledged. A preparatory year spent as a Research Fellow at the African Studies Center at the University of California, Los Angeles (1967–68) and a year as Honorary Research Fellow at the Department of Anthropology, University College, University of London (1973–74) and two periods as a Research Associate of the University of Dar es Salaam (1968–69 and 1973–74) have also been of invaluable assistance, and the author is duly grateful.

It may be useful to treat the statements of agencies of dispute settlement with the same detachment.

One way to do this is to treat proceedings of dispute settlement as ceremonies of situational transformation (Moore 1975b). Looked at this way, the hearing of a case can be seen to have many layers of meaning beyond those most immediately evident. This paper will treat rules as part of the material used in the course of such ceremonies, and organizational aggregates as among the interested parties.

A dispute that arose between two Chagga in 1968 will serve as case material. The dispute was heard twice. Since the underlying circumstances of the quarrel are constant and only the forum changed, it is instructive to notice the differences in rules, interests, and "facts" that were relevant in the two tribunals. The two hearings of this dispute also will be analyzed to show the ways in which a hearing whose declared purpose is the settlement of a *particular* quarrel is simultaneously a *general* event of articulation between levels and kinds of organization. Chagga society has a variety of organizational forms, some quite old and "traditional," others quite new and "planned."

In the 19th century, there were many Chagga chiefdoms on Mount Kilimanjaro. They varied very much in size and power, each having dominion over a separate strip of lush green banana gardens watered by mountain streams. The general organizational structure of these chiefdoms was a three level one: lineage, *mtaa*, and chiefdom. At the bottom were the localized corporate lineages of the various patriclans, each with a discrete territory. A local aggregation of several unrelated lineages formed a *mtaa*, which was a political unit under a headman (*mchili*). A chiefdom consisted of several *mitaa* under the leadership of a chief (*mangi*). The whole was cross-cut by an age-grade organization of military and political importance.

Skipping a hundred years, and innumerable changes on the macro-level of organization, which have had loud echoes on the micro-level, we come to socialist Tanzania in 1974, and the fact that localized lineage branches and the *mitaa* are still significant social units. Officially, on local government charts, they do not exist. What is consequently of organizational interest about the localized lineages is that in some ways they are very much like segmentary units in Durkheim's model of a mechanically solidary society. They also resemble units in an acephalous society, because the lineages are not attached as such to any generalized organization. They are many parallel social bodies, not formally linked into any superordinate administrative system. This Chagga situation suggests the importance of the dimension of *detachment* in complex societies in general. It suggests the utility of looking at a centralized system of political administration as existing on top of a great variety of organized social fields that exist within its geographical domain, but which are normally outside the zones of its strongest direct pull or effectiveness (Moore 1973). On occasion, as when two Chagga lineage-brothers take their case to court, persons in such social fields may plug into the national system. And the reverse, as when TANU (the Tanzanian one-party) set up ten-house cells, the central administration may try to invade the furthest corners of its geographical domain. But in neither case is the lineage, as an organization, attached to the official central system.

In contrast, the Tanzanian national system of courts is a centralized, specialized, hierarchical-bureaucratic organization. It has full-time salaried officials, levels of courts higher and lower, modes of appeal, with rulings of superior courts binding on inferior ones, and the like. It was legislated into existence during the period of British colonial rule, and has been reorganized a number of times, most recently since Independence (see Allott 1970, and Georges 1973). As a consciously constructed, legislated edifice, the national court system is a creature of rules. Conventionally these are classified into two kinds: those having to do with its own *organization* (jurisdiction, powers, relationships internal and external, financing, procedures, and the like) and those having to do with the *grounds on which it makes decisions* in the cases that come before it. In the decision of particular cases, both kinds of rules are always involved, though most of the time most of the rules are not "issues."

Such a system of courts is a bureaucratic animal whose only food is cases. It lives only to process the cases. It prospers and fattens when there are many cases (but not too many). There is no other justification for its existence. It has an internal life as an organization of judiciary officials. But it depends for its cases on an external source of supply. Some events outside the courts must turn into cases, or the courts are out of business. Some individuals, or groups, or agencies (such as the police or administrative agencies) must use the courts as the way to mobilize the power of the state on their behalf or there are no cases.

In contrast to such a specialized and centralized organization are the many separate and varied arenas of action in which disputes actually arise and wrongs occur, but in which people are primarily engaged in activities other than dispute settlement and rule enforcement. The normal activities of an agricultural community would be an example. These social fields also may have internal techniques of rule-making. Frequently they also have their own modes of enforcement quite apart from those offered by the state (Moore 1973). But the handling of all such matters is incidental to other enterprises.

This paper will follow a dispute that arose between two classificatory brothers in a Chagga patrilineage in 1968, from its inception through its "informal" hearing before lineage elders and neighbors, and beyond, through its rehearing and disposition in a Primary Court. All the persons involved in the two hearings were Wachagga. All were using the same fund of Chagga customary law and other common understandings as a general resource for rules and models of proper behavior. However, the organizational implications of the hearings at the two levels were entirely different, and, concomitantly, so were the *place* or rules and interests and the *kinds* of rules and interests that were brought into play. On both levels rules were the only legitimate idiom in which interests could be argued.

The facts of the case are simple. The two lineage brothers have contiguous coffee-banana groves which used to have a common boundary. The line between their properties was marked by a living fence of *masala* (dracaena), a plant traditionally used for such purposes. One brother, Richard, is a bright-eyed, educated, prosperous young clerk who works in the nearby town of Moshi (25 miles away). The other brother, Elifatio, is a tattered, moustachioed, uneducated farmer in his forties.

Along Richard's side of the boundary there is now a fairly wide path. It was cleared and made a public village-way a year or two before the dispute arose by a team of development workers (farmers doing one day a week corvée labor). Formerly the path had meandered through the middle of Richard's coffee grove. He preferred having it on the boundary, and had had something to do with the decision of the TANU leader of the public works team to move it. He may have gained a few inches of land that way, and some privacy. In any case, the path was on Richard's side of the hedge-like line of boundary plants that marked the edge of Elifatio's property.

Elifatio's	x |			|	Richard's
coffee	x |			|	coffee
grove	x |			|	grove
	x |		path	|	
	x |			|	
	x |			|	
	x)			o)	
	x)			o)	
	x)			o)	

x = boundary plants
o = trees

There is a shortage of land on Kilimanjaro, and a population explosion. To try to increase the productivity of his plot, Elifatio uprooted a number of yards of the boundary plants and replaced them with seedlings of a fruit tree, *helimu*. Not only is their fruit delicious, but their leaves make very good goat food. On his side of the path, Richard had made analogous use of the edges. He had planted *asteria*, a low-growing grass-like plant used for animal feed, and it did well.

One fine morning, soon after Elifatio had planted the seedlings of *helimu* trees, Richard came along and pulled them up. He threw them on the path and left. Those were the facts to which everyone agreed (at least for a while). Elifatio soon went to his neighbor, the ten-house leader, head of the lowest unit in the TANU party organization, to complain. He said that he wanted to bring a case against Richard for the damage he had done. The ten-house leader said he would see to it, and a date was fixed for the hearing.

In order to understand the significance of what followed it is necessary to know a little more about the Chagga, past and present. The Chagga people now number about 350,000 and are settled primarily in a wide green belt on the high slopes of Mount Kilimanjaro. Being coffee growers, they have been involved in a cash economy since the 1920s. It was their fate to be energetically missionized from the late nineteenth century (Europeans like the climate) and they are among the most ambitious, educated and prosperous of Tanzania's peoples. Much of their indigenous culture is gone, but some very important elements persist, particularly certain aspects of local and kinship organization and the customs associated with these. Because they irrigated and manured and grew bananas and kept cattle in precolonial times, the socioeconomic base of their society has always been the permanent occupation (over generations) of particular plots of land.

Each household lives in the midst of its permanently cultivated gardens of bananas and coffee, the *kihamba*. In the areas of older settlement, the gardens of patrilineally related men are likely to lie next to each other in localized lineage clusters. Richard and Elifatio are two members of a local cluster of twenty-three patrilineally related households. These local lineage branches are usually small parts of larger patrilineal clans whose member branches are widely scattered around the mountain. The gardens of each local group are interdigitated with neighboring lineages at their boundaries. Also, here and there, are gardens of other, unrelated individuals who settled locally, some as affines, some as borrowers of land, and more recently some as buyers of land. Also, in some places, peppered among the original settlers, are descendants of the local chiefly lineage, since there was a period when chiefs appropriated any unoccupied land they could get their hands on for their myriad children and kinsmen.

Today there is no organization at the clan level at all. But localized lineage clusters are organized internally. The descendants of each great-grandfather form a separate sub-branch. The whole local group recognizes a ranking of all males in order of birth. This is the order in which portions of meat are distributed at collective slaughtering feasts for men and boys. Thus any kinsman of Richard and Elifatio could without a moment's hesitation rattle off a list of the men of the localized lineage in order of birth. Slaughtering feasts including the whole of the localized lineage are few nowadays, since the group is large and cattle are costly. But collective beer drinking is quite frequent. And smaller slaughtering groups, including all the male descendants of one grandfather, or one great-grandfather, continue to assemble several times a year. At the invitation of one of their number, the men and boys get together to kill and divide a goat or two provided by their host. These small groups also always attend the life-crisis rites of all members and their children. Frequently so do most members of the larger lineage group. In short, the local lineage branches feast and drink, celebrate and mourn together, regularly reiterating their collective existence. Members assist each other in work, in times of illness, in times of need. They guard each other's wives, homesteads, and gardens. They take responsibility for the aged and the infirm among them. All land interests are individually held, but are subject to strong contingent claims of kinsmen.

The lineages have lost some of the qualities of corporateness which they once enjoyed. But they continue to be important as firmly consolidated social groups with strong emotional ties, groups that are coherent over time and place, and that control the access of most of their members to land in the lineage area. When there are disputes between lineage brothers, the lineage elders and some of their neighborhood cronies hear the case and decide it. In 1968 and today, in 1974, it is mandatory that they include in such a hearing the neighbor who is head of the ten-house cell concerned. But the cell leader is a contiguous neighbor (and not infrequently a lineage brother himself) chosen by his constituents, he is the sort of person who might well have been included at a neighborhood hearing even before there were TANU cells. He is seldom the most influential man in the neighborhood since one of the requirements of the job is that he be around and available most of the time. That virtually eliminates all the salaried men from candidacy, as well as the shopkeepers. He is normally a farmer without outside employment. One may well ask whether the neighbor's identity as

TANU cell leader is stronger than his identity as long-term neighbor, affine, or whatever else he may be. His prior connection with the local lineage is likely to be strong and of long duration.

It is true that there formerly were more matters that were regarded as entirely private lineage business than there are, perforce, today. But since he is bound by his myriad local ties the presence of an unrelated ten-house leader probably does not greatly alter the outcome of a lineage hearing. Ordinary local hearings at present often consist of an *ad hoc* assemblage of patrikinsmen with a few neighbors present for good measure.

It was just such a group that Elifatio was to face the day of the hearing of his case, on August 16, 1968. The appointed place was a junction of footpaths in the midst of the lineage homeland. First to appear was the ten-house leader, an affine of the two "brothers." He carried a rather bent stick with the Tanzanian flag tied to it on one end—a drooping bit of green cloth. He stuck the stick in the ground and called to a child who was watching to bring chairs. The child duly fetched a few from a nearby house. The chairs were for the principals. Most people sat on the ground. After a while Elifatio arrived, clutching his 271 dead seedlings, dry as a bunch of twigs.

Elifatio was then in his early forties. His clothes were very worn, his trousers patched, his shirt torn. He is the father of three sons and five daughters: many mouths to feed. In 1968, before schools became free, he had many school fees to pay. As indicated earlier, he has had little education himself, can barely read, and makes his living exclusively out of his land. Like all other local Chagga, he grows coffee and bananas, the one for cash, the other for food and beer. He is considered poor by his brothers though he has about three acres of his own, because a three acre plot scarcely takes care of his needs and those of his many dependents. These include two adult members of his extended family in addition to himself, his wife, and their many children.

Richard, the brother whom Elifatio was accusing, has about the same amount of land, three acres, which he will eventually have to divide with his as yet unmarried younger brother, a schoolboy who lives with him. In Richard's household are the young brother, their mother, and Richard's wife and five daughters. Yet he is considered a rich man. That is because in addition to his *kihamba* he has a salaried job in Moshi Town. He is educated, having passed one part of the way through secondary school. He reads and writes Swahili well. And he can type. These accomplishments, together with some contacts, got him a job as a clerk-secretary which he has had for a number of years. Normally, Richard wears the white shirt, dark trousers, and pointy black shoes of an office worker. (A clerk could be defined as a man who wears Sunday clothes every day.)

At the place chosen for the hearing, people arrived little by little. Eventually Richard appeared. Nothing in the neighborhood (nor anywhere else) ever takes place at the time it is nominally scheduled. For one thing, few have watches, and for another, every day holds unexpected encounters as well as routine tasks. Being on time is not urgent. Nothing can start without the principals, hence they can be late with impunity. As for the spectators, they are not really needed, so they can arrive when they please. And so it always is. When Richard finally turned up, there were about eight people waiting, a cluster of kinsmen, the wives of two of them, and myself.

They were ready to begin. The ten-house leader made a little speech about why we were all assembled and then called on Elifatio to make his complaint. He did so, very simply and tersely. "On the 28th day of last month I got up and was working in my *kihamba* and I heard Richard talking to someone and saying that I had interfered with the boundary between our *vihamba*. I had planted these seedlings," he took up his pathetic bunch of dried twigs, holding them rather lovingly and then dropped them to the ground in their dry worthlessness. "Richard was the one who pulled them up. I went to the ten-house leader and complained."

Richard answered, "I deny it. I did not uproot your trees." This answer surprised me, because Richard had not only admitted uprooting the plants in the days previous, but had boasted of having done so. No one else seemed in the least surprised. It seemed to be what was expected. It later developed that Richard's argument was that the boundary was a common boundary, belonging to him as much as it did to Elifatio. Hence, according to local customary rules, nothing could be done to it without mutual approval. Thus Richard could pretend that a mysterious someone whose identity he did not know had interfered with their mutual boundary, and that he, Richard, had rectified the situation by pulling up the seedlings. In fact, the boundary *had* once been a common one. The situation had changed, however, because of the village path, which now lay between Richard's land and the boundary of Elifatio's. If one were to state the central legal issue, it was whether the existence of the path changed the boundary from a common boundary to one that belonged to Elifatio alone.

As Richard seemed to be denying pulling up the seedlings, the ten-house leader asked Elifatio whether he had any witnesses. Elifatio answered that his wife and son both had seen Richard uprooting the seedlings. A discussion following about moving the whole company to the site of the planting, since the wife and son were not at the hearing but at home. Meanwhile, various people appeared on the path, passing by. One man carried a coffee pulping machine. A cheery albino walked through and smiled broadly. No one greeted him. Richard repeated his denial of having uprooted Elifatio's *helimu*.

Elifatio became visibly angry, "Whose trees were the trees that you uprooted?" Richard answered, "I have not interfered with your trees."

At this point one of the senior men said he would like to hear Elifatio's wife and son say that they saw Richard pulling up the plants. The ten-house leader agreed that it would be a good idea, and that as the witnesses lived precisely where the trees had been uprooted, and an inspection of the boundary was necessary, we should all proceed there. Everyone would have a chance to look at the site and hear further evidence. There was some talk about this and then an elder on Elifatio's side shouted at Richard, "Have you ever uprooted trees anywhere, in your *kihamba* or anywhere else?"

Richard answered cagily, "Yes, I have uprooted trees somewhere." His strategy was now plain. He was going to prove that the seedlings were on his own property, hence that he had not disturbed anyone else's.

After more discussion, we all got up and walked to the edge of Elifatio's garden, eventually reaching the path that divided it from Richard's coffee grove. It was a ten-minute walk. As it was toward noon, it was very hot, and everyone was uncomfortable. We all looked at the *masale*, the boundary plant along the edge of Elifatio's property and we saw the gap and loose earth where he had pulled them up to replace them with *haimu*. Evidently he had done something of the sort once before as there were a few well developed coffee trees planted among the *masale* a bit further down the hill. No dispute had arisen at the time of the planting of those coffee trees.

Richard became more voluble, "These *masale* were not planted by Elifatio, but by our grandfather, and this is a new path. The path that was here before went into my *kihamba*." An old man, a neighbor, who was walking by approached, listened a while, and joined in, saying, "Part of this path has been here since the grandfathers of grandfathers. This case could have been settled, but it was not. It is just because of the path, which is the property of the Government. The dispute is not about the *vihamba*. It is about the path."

As if on cue, Richard picked up this direction of argument. "I don't know who planted the trees I uprooted. I uprooted them after I saw that they were planted in the land of the Government."

Another elder, the one of Elifatio's side, said, "Three years ago, the path was
not there. There was another path, a small one, that cut in through Richard's
kihamba. The path was changed at Richard's request and put along the edge of
his land instead of through the heart of his coffee."

Elifatio then began arguing that the land on both sides of the new path was his
in places, and pointed to two trees. "Those trees," he said, "used to be at the edge of
my property, and now they are on the other side of the new path. The path is partly on Richard's land, but it is also partly on mine. Some of mine was taken away."

More people gathered. There were now about fifteen. All were residents of the immediate area, neighbors, patrikinsmen and their wives, except
for two of Richard's white-collar friends. Several newcomers began to put their
views forward in excited voices, "If Richard's father had planted trees along the
masale of Elifatio, would Elifatio have had a valid claim against him? If the road
were closed now, the *masale* planted by our grandfathers would remain where it
is."

A woman pitched in, "The trees Elifatio planted were on Richard's side."
The tide seemed to be turning toward Richard. All speakers became increasingly
vociferous and excited.

A young, educated official of the local cooperative made a long and vehe-
ment speech on Richard's behalf. "All the land on this side (the path side) of
the *masale* is Richard's land." He went on for fifteen minutes looking furious,
gesticulating wildly. He was one of the three white-collar workers there besides
Richard himself. All four men are daily drinking companions and have close
links of friendship that transcend the fact that two of them are not of Richard's
lineage. They are of the same general age-group and of the salaried class.

The ten-house leader thought it was about time for him to say something.
He was plainly no longer in charge of the meeting, and was simply present, not
in control. He said, "The *masale* were removed by Elifatio himself in order to
plant useful things in their place. The boundary was correct because it was set by
the grandfathers. There has never been a dispute about this boundary. There is a
rule about a common boundary that if a tree is on a boundary and its branches
are useful for building, the owners on each side can cut them, one cuts one year,
the other the next." The sense of what he was saying was that Elifatio had lost
his case by analogy, that as it was a common boundary Richard could even have
claimed some rights to his trees.

Richard, who had been very quiet, then showed us where Elifatio had uprooted the *masale* to plant *helimu*. We had all seen it already, but he seemed to

think that walking us all up and down would increase our horror at Elifatio's temerity in disturbing that boundary. At this point the arguments went on in little knots of twos and threes. There was no longer a single proceeding with one person speaking at a time. All participants were arguing vigorously. By now many of the neighbors who were not members of the ten-house cell had come out and joined us.

There ensued a lot of talk about who should pronounce a decision. The ten-house leader tried to defer to the most prestigious of the educated men present. He declined, deferring to the elders and the ten-house leader. There was a great deal of "after you, Alphonse" thereafter, some of which was doubtless caused by my presence and the wish to be correct, lest I report critically to the authorities. The general conclusion was that someone from the ten-house cell had better do it.

Taking advantage of the temporary distraction afforded by this discussion about who should decide, an old man on Richard's side said, "As the *masale* were planted by our grandfathers, Elifatio had no right to touch the boundary. And it was perfectly all right for Richard to uproot the *helimu*."

In despair, Elifatio tried to make a "modern" argument, "I just planted the *helimu* against soil erosion." But it was plain that the *masale* itself would have been effective for this purpose.

An elder on Elifatio's side spoke up, "It was also wrong of Richard to uproot the plants. One must not tear up the plants of others. He should have told Elifatio to uproot them, or he should have gone to the cell leader to complain. He had no business taking matters into his own hands and doing the uprooting himself."

The argument that self-help was wrongful in the circumstances set the co-operative society man off again. "But it was Elifatio who started this dispute because he planted trees between the boundaries of two *vihamba*. Richard did not commit any offence when he uprooted the trees because the trees were in his own *kihamba*. You say Richard committed an offence when he uprooted the trees. I say Elifatio committed an offence when he planted them."

A moderating voice was heard. The senior man of the lineage said, "What remains is to reach some agreement, to make some kind of settlement."

The ten-house leader reprimanded him. "No. We have to say properly who was right and who was wrong. An elder cannot do that. Only the cell leader can. I am following the opinions of the elders for two have said that Elifatio did in fact plant the trees in the land of Richard, and that is what I say. Now, in the future, when you want to plant trees between the boundaries of the *vi-hamba*, those on both sides should come together and make some agreement." The cell leader had spoken. That was it. He had been willing to defer to the prestigious young educated man, but not to the farmer-elders. If the choice were to be between himself and the elders, *he* would pronounce judgment. This acute concern to lead in fact as well as in name was, I was told, enhanced by my presence.

Although everyone had been told that the proceedings were over as far as the cell leader was concerned, the people present went on sitting and arguing as before. An elder on Elifatio's side said, "The path had been here for some time. The path divides the *vihamba*. Each should keep on his side. Richard also committed an offence when he planted *asteria* grass along his side of the path."

The co-operative society man, seeing the anger on Elifatio's face, seemed to want to push him just one step further. He pressed on, "There had better be some reconciliation between these two as they are brothers. It is not good for brothers to fight about such things. There have been no previous quarrels between these two. There is no need to impose a fine. Anyone may have a quarrel. And if Elifatio wants to plant trees now, he can arrange with Richard to do so."

An elder on Richard's side remembered a pertinent rule, "Years ago if a banana plant growing on the edge of a property fell into a neighbor's yard, the bananas became the property of the neighbor. This path should be well maintained and kept wide. People should not plant on the sides of it." He disclosed his own worries, "It should be kept clear, because if someone is sick, perhaps a car might have to come to collect him from his house and take him to the hospital. The paths should be kept open and wide."

The cell leader asked Elifatio if he accepted the decision and if he would shake hands with his brother. Elifatio answered, "If I am defeated, how am I to accept? How am I to shake hands with him?"

Richard shrugged, "If he doesn't want a reconciliation, that doesn't matter. It is up to him."

Elifatio replied, "I am thinking about whether I will appeal. I am not satisfied."

This account is, of course, a selected portion from notes made of several hours of talk. But it suffices to give the sense of what went on. Before going on to describe the retrial of the case in the Primary Court, it may be useful to note some things about this proceeding, first, with regard to the pertinent explicit norms, and second, from the point of view of the interests at work in the hearing. Some of the principal normative arguments could be set up in pairs of opposites as follows:

A new village path can change previous boundaries.	A path through someone's *kihamba*, even if made by the village, may be closed as easily as it was opened. Thus in appropriate cases a village path is just like a private path as far as boundaries are concerned.
It is all right to uproot and replace one's own boundary plants.	It is wrong to disturb a common boundary except with the consent of both parties.
It is wrong to use self-help and to destroy your neighbor's plants. If you think he has planted improperly, you can accuse him and have a hearing.	There is no harm in taking peaceful action when there has been wrongdoing. The inviolability of boundaries must be maintained. One may take action to protect one's own property.

As far as these normative grounds were concerned, a decision either way could have been supported. (There were of course, many other norms in the air and finding them is rather like the children's game of looking at a puzzle picture to see how many faces you can locate in the bushes.) In effect, the ten-house leader's decision was that the new path did *not* change previous property rights. The path, though it passed along the boundary and seemed completely continuous to it was still, by implication, in some sense in Richard's *kihamba*. The path was treated more as a right-of-way than as village property. By ignoring the self-help issue, the ten-house leader implicitly approved Richard's action.

But it would be difficult to argue that the decision had been determined by "the rules," or that generating general rules was the objective of the hearing. Rather the result was sufficiently *associated* with general rules to legitimate it. By "general rules" I not only mean norms applicable beyond the particular case, but also norms not specifically associated with a special organizational setting. TANU rules do not pertain to the boundaries of *vihamba*. The nucleus of white-collar workers does not constitute a rule-making body. The fact that the lineages are unattached as such to any political center means that lineage rules could not play the same connective role that they do in bureaucratic structures. Nor were the lineages closed autonomies which might have made use of special rules to reiterate organizational closure. Instead, the rules mentioned in the hearing came from here and there, were argued by this one and that one, and the decision in Richard's favor was not explicitly attached to any particular rationale emanating from any particular organizational quarter.

The question of interest is, of course, intertwined with the norms of kinship and friendship behavior, as well as with matters of individual gain. This hearing was a situation in which, in the absence of any special factors, it was expected that senior kinsmen would take sides with the protagonists according to their closeness of genealogical relationship. They all did so. The kinship relationship between Elifatio and Richard is that of sixth or seventh cousins. They come from the two major branches of the localized lineage. There is no one who is considered equally related to both. Since this was a case in which there was great uncertainty about the legal question whether or not the boundary was still to be regarded as a common boundary because of the interposition of the path, it was the kind of case in which interest might be expected to operate strongly.

However, it must be emphasized that even though interest deriving from relationship made certain alignments highly probable, the discussion of such cases is always carried on by everyone in normative terms. No one would ever say, "I am on his side. I am his older brother. I know he is right," without offering a normative reason. And, of course, there are many disputes, such as those between "true" brothers, or father and son, in which the matter of closeness of relationship cannot settle the question of interest. Also, it is clear from other cases, as well as being shown by later events between Elifatio and Richard, that especially good relations or especially bad relations with a particular individual can modify the normal alignments of kinship.

Given all these caveats, it is generally evident to the parties when they sit down to a discussion of this kind which persons will certainly come forward and side with them. A *display* of partisanship is mandatory on certain persons, such as very close kinsmen and their wives. Women tend to align themselves with their husbands, since in many respects they are socially dependent persons. There is no expectation of any general display of impartiality. Whoever "chairs" the meeting makes some temporary show of neutrality, but the others are expected to take sides, and to do so early in the discussion. Kinship, then, is one of the interest *factors*. But it is an interest factor itself ordinarily governed by the rules of lineage organization.

Past social relations with the parties is another interest factor. These past social relations can include long-term connections such as Richard's with the three other educated men who were present. Late every afternoon, the men assemble and have a drink of banana beer with their cronies. The men with salaried jobs drink at a different establishment from that patronized by these who are exclusively farmers. There are, in short, nascent ties of class, and these cross-cut lineage loyalties. These too predispose those present at a hearing to certain alignments. Thus the vociferous cooperative society man was sitting with Richard, his friend, his daily drinking companion, his not very distant neighbor. He was more excited than any of the older men, and spoke with a certain arrogance. This was at least in part a matter of individual personality and exuberance. The two other educated men were a decade older and spoke much less, partly, I believe, because in the situation they were aligning themselves with me, as observers, rather than as active participants. We had had other contacts, and they were aware of my work.

Perhaps some of the neighbors who wandered in and out started out without any strong bias in the direction of one or the other of the parties, but that is unlikely where there is such a long common history. It is possible that some of the people who were there were present for the "show" because such events are an interesting distraction in a world of endless numbers of routine tasks. But however neutral their motives for appearing, they were likely to have had some past transactions either with Richard and Elifatio, or with the men who spoke for them.

There is vaguely in the background of all of this a general bias toward men like Richard. There is a feeling that men like him may be a good contact in the future. He is young, personable, educated, and times are changing fast. Perhaps he would be useful if one needed a loan, or a witness, or an introduction, if not for oneself, for one's son. This kind of interest is extremely hard to get at, or be sure of. It is embodied in the remark of one of the educated men who said to me afterwards, "Rich men always win." Yet the same individual had told me before the hearing started that he had no idea how it would turn out.

The elements of interest which have been discussed thus far have all been presented in terms of the individual social relationships of the casehearers with the parties. These have included the genealogical closeness of the kinship relationship, friendship, educational-occupational status, age, sex, or other ground for identification. Also included was the situational factor that is often strategically important in a close group of this kind, indebtedness because of transactions in the past, or the wish to build up credit because of anticipated transactions in the future. It will readily be seen that in particular cases, these determinants may be contradictory. Consequently, to produce choices, some criterion of selection or ranking among determinants must be operative at any particular moment. An analysis of the social characteristics of the persons at this hearing is not difficult to produce. But if their mutual transactional history is also to be taken into account, only a novel could do the case justice. Moreover, one also would have to take into accounts the events during the hearing itself, the force of personality and argument of the various speakers, their efficiency at manipulating symbols and soliciting support, the use of the hearing as a forum for the interplay of individual competition relating to matters quite extraneous to the immediate case, and the like.

However, these causal questions are especially complicated when put in terms of individual choice. If the perspective is changed, and the questions posed are in terms of the organizational implications of the case, much more generalization is possible. A localized lineage is an organization, a traditional one with many cultural elaborations, including norms of solidarity in internal dispute, and norms of ranking in terms of seniority. However, today the lineage exists only unofficially. Its formal competitor on the micropolitical level is the local TANU organization with its ten-house leaders. Its informal competitor, which also does not exist officially, is the tight network of prosperous educated men, each of whom has a business or a job, most of them in government agencies.

This case brings all three of these durable organizational forces on stage together. When the senior elder of the lineage said, "What remains is to reach some kind of agreement," obviously intending to propose the terms of such a settlement as behooves a senior elder, he was at once cut off by the ten-house leader. The TANU man said it was a matter of who was right and who was wrong and that this was for him and him alone to declare. After this power play, it is interesting that he felt it necessary to legitimate his decision by saying, "I am following the opinions of the elders." That is, in fact, what the ten-house leaders generally do. They do not act contrary to the judgment of local senior elders. However, the fact that there was a question about who was to pronounce the decision suggests that there is a latent struggle going on between the lineage and the TANU organization about autonomy at the lowest local level.

However, as indicated earlier, both the ten-house TANU man and the lineage elders are by definition relatively uneducated farmers who are not salaried. Both recognize the social power and public respectability of their educated, employed kinsmen and neighbors, and the greater mobility and outside contacts which they have in the Big World. From the point of view of the Big World these men may be clerks, but on the mountain they are the very epitome of modern city people.

The norms of lineage prescribe that the lineage elders are the ultimate authorities in all matters. The norms of African Socialism proclaim the primacy of its Party functionaries as representatives of The People. The realities of economic and social stratification suggest that as far as the farmers are concerned, the clerks and teachers, and other low-level white-collar workers are the prominent citizens of the neighborhood.

Richard's winning was more congruent with the interest of each sector than his losing. From the point of view of the lineage elders, only those on Elifatio's side of the lineage could be said to be in a position to gain social strength if he had won. But unfortunately for them, the present configuration of the lineage is such that the most senior man of the whole local branch is on Richard's side of the family, and he is a respected man. The second eldest is on Elifatio's side, but he is "a man of quarrels" and is not generally liked. Moreover, the most senior man has two sons who are salaried clerical workers, and one who is a government driver, while the senior man on Elifatio's side has sons who are farmers only. The third ranking elder is again on Richard's side, and again is a respected man with a number of educated sons. In fact, the weight of lineage prestige is altogether on Richard's half on the local lineage. Thus even in terms of internal considerations regarding the relative strength of lineage sub-branches and the traditional deference to seniors, the scales were tipped in Richard's favor.

The ten-house leader is an affine of the lineage. He has many dealings with its members both in his capacity as TANU man and as a private individual. It is in his interest to be on good terms with "everyone," but, if he has to choose among them, it is worth noting that his father's brother's wife was from one of the branches of the lineage on Richard's side, and that the *kihamba* he occupies was inherited from that father's brother, who had himself obtained it from his wife's kinsmen. His stronger connection with Richard's side of the family is thus more than a generation old. If that were not enough to tip the balance, then there is the additional consideration that the salaried men, with their connections outside the local *mtaa* are very useful contacts for him, not only in his private dealings, but in his official ones, for example, when he must collect funds for TANU that are "voluntarily" presented by his constituents toward one campaign or another, a not infrequent circumstance. It is much easier to collect from them as they have more cash, than to squeeze shillings out of their impecunious farmer brothers. The clerks need him to give them a clean bill of health in the Party, but he needs them to maintain his political well-being as well.

As for the local white-collar network, it obtained from the case an essentially symbolic gain, a reinforcement of the ranking system in which they rate higher than their farmer brothers. What they got out of the case was a good laugh. It need not have been a case at all. Richard chose to make it so. He could have left Elifatio's seedlings in place, and simply warned him that if he went an inch further and crossed the boundary line, there would be trouble. But he didn't. He engaged in a show of bravado instead, performing a hostile act of force, and throwing down the gauntlet. It was an act of warning and boastfulness on the part of a young man in relation to an older one. It said, "I am a man to be taken seriously. How dare you cross me?"

Both kinds of questions raised in connection with this case, those having to do with norms and those having to do with organized interests by their very nature emphasize that a disagreement between two individuals can become a public issue, i.e. that its settlement can involve the customs and organized social relations of a particular body public. The lineage, neighbors, friends, and the ten-house leader were drawn in at the request of individuals, Elifatio and Richard. But every such request, every use of these organizational nexus for the settlement of dispute provides an opportunity for certain public collectivities to come into competitive contact, to act authoritatively, to demonstrate and to reaffirm local relationships of superordination and subordination. The persons mobilized are part of the networks of individuals, but they also are aligned in other organized collectivities. Dispute settlements of this kind sort out and give strength to those organizational structures. They give them some of their life by providing occasions for them to act. There are many other occasions, of course, when these neighborhood bodies are mobilized, which range from mutual assistance to common celebration. But very few of these occasions may be compared with dispute settlement in the explicitness with which the exercise of community authority is expressed.

When a case moves from this local neighborhood scene to the Primary Court, the lowest court in the national judicial system of Tanzania, it can also be said to be feeding an organization with the material on which it acts. But since the Court is a specialized agency whose working life depends on a steady flow of cases, the place of the "case" in the life of the Court is very different from its place in the local neighborhood aggregations which serve many other purposes as well.

Cases not only serve the court as its daily business, but in so far as they are appealed or reviewed or decided on the bases of precedents set by superior courts, cases as well as rules serve as one of the links with the higher levels of the national judicial system. The Primary Courts are in the rural areas of Kilimanjaro, one per village. They are the successors of what were formerly Chief's courts. Appeals lie from the Primary Courts to the District Court in Moshi Town (25 miles away) and thence to the High Court of Tanzania. The Magistrates of the Primary Courts are paid out of a national budget for the judiciary, and are, in theory at least, supervised by superior magistrates in Moshi. The Primary Court Magistrates are without formal legal training, though all have had a course of some months at the Local Government Training Centre at Mzumbe.

The law the magistrates were supposed to be applying is partly statutory, partly customary law. No attorneys or other representatives of the parties are allowed in the Primary Courts. Magistrates act as court recorders as well as judges. They write down whatever they think necessary of the testimony and discussion, and the reasons for their decisions, as well as recording the opinions of the two elders (called assessors) who are an official adjunct of the Court. The rules, the bookkeeping, the forms, the scale of fees, the fines and costs, the jurisdiction of the Court and the formal framework in general are laid down in statutes and departmental rules.

In short, in 1968, the Magistrates on the mountain, though all were Chagga, were all members of a national corporate group, responsive to its regulations as well as to local ideas of justice and proper behavior. Since Magistrates were assigned to sit in villages other than their natal ones in order to assure impartiality, whatever biases they might have had (for example in favor of their white-collar brethren) were likely to be of a generalized rather than a personal nature. They did sometimes receive individuals in their private offices, and discussed case business with them. Whether they were thus reached by local networks of influence or not is hard to say. In particular cases, they probably were, but on the whole, the impression one had was that they were quite indifferent to most of the parties who came before them.

It was to such a Court that Elifatio flew when he lost his case against Richard in the neighborhood hearing. On the clerk's advice, he filed a criminal complaint for the malicious destruction of property. What he really wanted was reimbursement for the value of his seedlings, and an opportunity to defeat his "brother" Richard in a public forum. A civil litigation would have cost him a filing fee. A criminal complaint cost nothing. The Magistrates have considerable statutory freedom to give what we think of as civil remedies in criminal cases when they see fit. Elifatio risked nothing and might gain.

Within less than a week after the neighborhood hearing, Elifatio's case actually was heard in court. He thought he was sure to win because Richard had ultimately admitted pulling up the plants in the neighborhood hearing. Everyone had heard him say so. Furthermore, the day before the hearing in Court, the ten-house leader had agreed to come and testify to that effect for Elifatio. There seemed no way in which Richard could wriggle out. He would pay for having used self-help!

But as it turned out, when the day came, the ten-house leader did not appear at all. Elifatio did not ask for a postponement. Whether he did not ask because he did not know he could (unlikely), or whether he did not ask because there was no point in trying to push the ten-house leader (likely) was not made explicit. In any case, Elifatio simply went on to present his grievances without his expected star witness.

In the Primary Court the Magistrate sits up on a raised platform about three feet above the floor at the front of the room. His chair is behind a table on which there are papers and writing materials. He faces the audience. On the platform to one side of him there is a backless bench on which the assessors sit. Below, at floor level stand the complainant and the respondent, one on the left side of the front of the room, one on the right. They stand throughout most of the proceedings, backs to the audience, facing the Magistrate, unless a witness is testifying. The room itself is long, and has a center aisle with benches on either side for anyone who wants to listen. The courtroom has no walls, and is simply a tin-roofed open structure, public in every way. The crowing of roosters provides background noise.

The procedure in the Primary Court is to have the complainant make his statement, and then to allow the respondent to question him. Then the complainant's witnesses testify and may be questioned. Thereafter, the respondent makes his presentation, and brings in his witnesses, all of them subject to questioning by the plaintiff. The Magistrate and the Assessors ask questions and interrupt when they see fit.

Elifatio made his statement and then was asked by Richard, "Why don't you produce any witnesses?" He answered that he thought it unnecessary since Richard had admitted pulling up the plants. Richard then denied doing so. (In the questioning period Richard was not yet under oath, as the oaths are usually sworn just before each party makes his formal statement.) The Magistrate peered at Elifatio rather severely, and asked, "If you saw him pull up the plants, why didn't you make an outcry and rouse the neighbors?" Elifatio made two answers, "I didn't think it was necessary. I was afraid because Richard had a big dog with him."

A number of questions followed from the Magistrate, the gist of which were, "How can you *prove* that Richard pulled up your seedlings?"

Elifatio finally said, "My son saw him pull them up." Elifatio's statement was read back to him, from the beginning, as the Magistrate had taken it down. He was asked whether he agreed to the contents, and was then made to sign it. This routine procedure is cumbersome and slow, since everything is recounted at least twice, and if there are corroborative statements by witnesses, again and again. But it is a procedure that turns a simple conversational account into a formal charge, or response.

Elifatio's son then stood up to testify. He was a thin, sad, and timid looking boy of seventeen, who appeared, as many Chagga adolescents do to American eyes, very much younger. He was tall, and his thin wrists stuck far out of his too-small threadbare cotton jacket. He said that he had seen Richard pull up the seedlings. Richard barely let him finish his statement and said fiercely, "You did not see me. You were told by your father what to say in this court." Richard was using his question period rather irregularly to make statements rather than to ask questions, but this is not uncommon, and the Magistrates only intervene when they want to.

The boy seemed terrified by Richard's outburst. Sternly the Magistrate said to him, "Did you actually see the seedlings in Richard's hand?" "No," he replied. His statements were read back and he signed.

The Magistrate then asked Elifatio if he had any other witnesses, and he said, "Yes, there are the people who heard the case before the ten-house leader."

"No," said the Magistrate, "I will not hear them. I want people who saw Richard uprooting the trees." There were no others.

Richard was then put under oath and asked to make his statement. "I have no statement," he said. Later his lineage brother told me that Richard had said nothing because he did not want to lie under oath.

It was Elifatio's turn to ask questions, but he, poor fellow, was no match for his sharp young kinsman. "What," he asked Richard, "What did you say before the ten-house leader?"

"I denied doing it," said Richard. And that, of course, was true, as Richard had both denied and ultimately admitted it at various stages of the earlier proceedings. Elifatio's questions turned against him. He kept insisting help-lessly that Richard had admitted everything before the ten-house leader. "Then why," asked the Magistrate, "did you fail to win that case?"

One of the assessors put in a word, "If Richard had admitted it, you would not have lost before the ten-house leader. What is the relationship between you?" The Magistrate did not allow the question. He said it was not relevant since no statements had been made about any enmity between the brothers.

Richard offered no witnesses. The case was at an end. The Magistrate acquit-ted Richard forthwith. Was the Magistrate biased in favor of Richard? Possibly he was from the start, inclined to favor another white-collar man. But probably more significant, just before the Court session started, I saw one of the educated men who had been at the neighborhood hearing enter the Magistrate's office with him. It is unlikely that they did not discuss the case.

In any event, Richard had taken what precautions he could to see that he would win. He had approached every single local person who had been at the neighbor-hood hearing the day before his appearance in the Primary Court, and had asked each one not to testify in Elifatio's favor. In fact, I later found out that he had tried to send a message to me to the same effect. While the ten-house leader had told Elifatio he would appear, he had no doubt pledged secretly to Richard that he would not. Thus Elifatio's best witness melted away just when he was needed.

The case in the Primary Court was very different from the same case in the neighborhood. There had been no need for the testimony of the son in the neighborhood hearing because of Richard's admission of guilt. Faced with the Court, Richard lied and won. Moreover, the issues which were central in the neighborhood, and might be said to be central to the case altogether, the ques-tions in whose property the seedlings were planted, and about the path, were questions which simply were not raised nor were they considered in the Court. Yet from the point of view of an outsider, such as an appellate judge or super-visory magistrate (had either had occasion to look at the record, which they didn't) coming to the case with no background, the record would hardly have seemed distorted. Quite the contrary. It seemed entirely justified that the Mag-istrate should have refused to allow the accusations to stand, when the plaintiff's only witness was his minor son, against the denials of an apparently respectable well-to-do brother. Justice was apparently done, whether or not it was really done. The Court upheld the law regarding the presumption of innocence in criminal cases and regarding the plausibility of evidence, though the Magistrate did not state it explicitly in those terms.

When parties come to a Primary Court on Kilimanjaro, from the point of view of the Court, the most important thing is that their situation becomes a case, in other words, that its disposition should fit into one of the general categories from which prescribed consequences flow. A highly personal and idiosyncratic situation from the point of view of the parties is easiest to deal with if it can be classified as an instance of a general category so that it can be dealt with efficiently. Thus a complaint like Elifatio's becomes in the hands of the court clerk a case of malicious destruction of property. The issues for the Magistrate then become: Was property destroyed? Whose property was destroyed? By whom was it destroyed? And, procedurally, he asks for the proof of each of these matters. Once the issues are narrowed in this way, there is no need to inquire into the general situation, the background, the relationship of the parties, the motives, and the like. On the whole, the Primary Court Magistrates show great reluctance to inquire very deeply into motives. Most of the time it is as if they prefer not to know *why* anything has happened, but rather *what* occurred, or even more narrowly, what can be *shown* (persuasively) to have happened. This is all part of their way of de-particularizing a situation, so that it will fit into the rules "everyone knows." One of those rules is that normally no one has the right to destroy the property of another. There is nothing subtle or complex there. All that remains is the proof. If that is lacking, then the disposition is indisputable. If there is proof, the only issue is what must be paid in fines or compensation.

Of the Chagga cases about which I know the "inside" story, a very large percentage appear in Court at least as distorted if not in even more fictitious a form. What one reads in the records and in the decisions of the Magistrates is always fairly plausible. But a knowledge of Chagga life makes one very skeptical about whether the facts as presented have much to do with "what really happened in the particular case." In the Chagga Council Minutes of 22 February 1962, Minute 5, no. 37a Bwana Male said, ". . . when people are sent to court to be charged you cannot know who was wrong and who was right and sometimes justice is and sometimes is not done." If this is so, not in all, but even in a substantial number of law cases, what then is going on in the Court? What function do such hearings have and for whom?

Tribunals such as these are in an important aspect spokesmen for the government. Formal legal institutions contribute to the regular demonstration of the corporate qualities of the state. In their professional acts the Courts give support to the general political-ideological thesis that a government through its laws is the ultimate custodian of the boundaries of public and private morality.

This expository function is fulfilled even if the courts make errors in the decisions of particular cases. What is essential for such representational purposes is that the errors should never be apparent on the face of any decision, and should not be apparent in any other way, even if they occur. Litigants may lie and not be found out. Witnesses may feign illness and fail to appear, or plead faulty memory when they remember perfectly well. If the court gives this credence, then for the purposes of the hearing, what they have or have not said is as effective as if it were true.

If a court is known to be prejudiced or influenced or a trial is rigged, it may still be extremely effective for political purposes. What greater show of power than to contravene all public conceptions of "fairness" in a public ceremonial? Thus public acceptance of judicial decisions may rest on either (or both) of two foundations: the judicial decision as a non-resistible application of state power and/or the judicial decision as an enforcement of local ideas of justice. Even in so minor a tribunal as the Primary Court on Kilimanjaro these twin elements are prominent and intertwined. Those who like a decision perceive it as "just." Those who do not like it perceive it as an exercise of power that must be accepted. The Court's ceremonial proceedings are designed to support both theses, and many symbolic statements are made about power and justice in the course of sorting out disputes and punishing minor violations of law.

Another political purpose that is served by the existence of these Courts is to furnish an avenue by which individuals may appeal to the state to intervene in their affairs. Technically the Primary Courts give every resident direct access to the state, which he can try to mobilize on his behalf. This openness to all depends for its smooth functioning on being used by few. But the political message is for all, and is built into the very existence of the Court.

There is no doubt that rules and interests were both involved in the neighborhood hearing of the case, and were also both involved in the Primary Court. But despite some overlap, there were also some notable differences in the content and significance of the rules and interests in the two tribunals. The rules of procedure in the Court drama have no precise parallel in the neighborhood hearing. The ceremonial performance in the Court is one which is an everyday matter for the Magistrate and an occasional event in the lives of the parties. This familiarity with the organizing rules of the judicial ritual makes the Magistrate more comfortable than the parties and gives him a situational authority. He can and does use that situational authority not only to run the proceedings in an orderly way, but indirectly to make symbolic statements on a small scale that hint at his substantial powers. Most but not all of the substantive rules applicable in the Primary Courts are the rules that "everybody knows," whether customary or statutory. But the parties are always aware that the Magistrate knows more rules than they do and that this esoteric body of knowledge is one source of the power of his office. Most Magistrates take some opportunity during the proceedings to remind their audience of this either through the tone of their questioning, or in their management of what is allowed to be said and what is cut off. In the Court one speaks only with permission of the Magistrate. The non-verbal signs are equally impressive and also are governed by a set of rules. Everyone present is at least subliminally aware of the connection the Court has with the awesome powers of the state, and some of this sense is conveyed by the considerable display of rules and rulings that are pertinent to almost everything that transpires in the courtroom. It is as if it were being said, "There is nothing improvised or accidental about what goes on here. We are keepers of order." Rules have an enormous utility in the Court, both in dramatizing what is taking place, and in linking those events with a larger organizational system, the hierarchy of courts, the government, and in a diffuse way with the whole idea of a social and moral order. Thus in the course of settling particular disputes and enunciating standards of behavior, the Courts are conveying many other connected messages. The use of rules and rulings is an intrinsic part of this complex of activities.

Normative rules about boundaries were very much in the air in the neighborhood hearing, but it could be argued that in this case, at least, they were to a great extent the rationale of partisanship. In the neighborhood hearing the show of partisanship was not merely expected, it was mandatory on certain close relatives and friends. In the Court, by contrast, any show of partisanship or interest in the parties or outcome was a disqualifying circumstance. Elifatio's son was not a credible witness because he was so closely related and was a young person under his father's aegis. His testimony was disregarded. Had the Magistrate been provably an interested party, he too would have been disqualified. In the Court apparent partisan interest was anathema, and the legal rules pertinent to the case were treated as a self-evident set of categories and consequences. In the Court, the statutory category under which a criminal complaint is filed with the Court Clerk preclassifies the case under given rules about wrongdoing. The Court is at liberty to reclassify matters if it chooses, but it is usually far easier to let matters stand, as was done in this case. For the Court, the prime issue was what had happened, that being very narrowly defined by the legal category "malicious damage to property." By contrast, in the neighborhood, what had occurred was settled fairly quickly. Everyone really already knew what had happened before there was any hearing. Interests were also far from concealed. Yet in the neighborhood, the issues of what behavior was proper in the circumstances, and what rules were pertinent, were treated as no simple question, but as a subtle matter, and a complex one. Rules about paths, boundaries and self-help were all stated and discussed and weighed. But the outcome of the hearing was the settlement of two particular issues rather than the development of general rules: 1) that Richard had had the right to uproot the plants, and 2) that the TANU man had the right to pronounce the decision.

There is no doubt that the Court had much more *potential* power than the neighborhood aggregations, and displayed it. But in the end, in this case as in many others, it was the neighborhood social nexus that controlled the result in the Court by withholding testimony. The Court has police power at its beck and call, but the neighborhood social relationships control the witnesses.

What one might call the hidden ruling of the case was that ordinarily in internal matters individuals must submit to the decisions of the lineage neighborhood in which they live out their lives. They challenge it at their peril. For the most part they must accept its organizational structure and the instance by instance consequences of its internal political alliances. They must accept its "interested" decisions. With some elders, the ten-house cell leader and the clerks all against him, Elifatio was finished, even in the external forum that traffics in impersonal rules.

From the point of view of the parties and the society at large, the dispute was "settled." That is, two ceremonies of situational transformation had turned Elifatio's private quarrel into a public ruling he hated but had to accept. He had to recognize that it was useless to go on, that he could not win. That is what the ceremonies meant for him. But in a less particular sense, from an outsider's long-term view, these were events on which various durable organizational interests impinged, and in which they competed for effectiveness. These were events of articulation between levels and types of organization. As such they reflect the extreme localism of social control that still dominates the lives of rural Chagga farmers.

POSTSCRIPT

The dispute was ended but the anger was not. Elifatio and Richard ceased to be on speaking terms. They did not attend beer drinks at each other's houses (for example when celebrating the baptisms of their children) and remained in this state of avoidance and anger for five years. However, through the accident of a death and various surrounding circumstances, Elifatio recently has gained access to some land that Richard wants. Suddenly in 1973, everything changed between the two men. Richard was ready to help Elifatio in all matters. Elifatio was arrested for assault after beating up a woman who had to be hospitalized as a result. Richard bailed him out, and has since succeeded in manipulating the Court calendar in such a way that the case will never come to trial and the charge will soon be dropped. Richard is Elifatio's friend and protector. Thus do temporary individual alliances cross-cut the more durable clusters of "interests" that are currently operative in rural Chagga neighborhoods.

CHAPTER EIGHT

Explaining the Present
Theoretical Dilemmas in Processual Ethnography

If fieldwork is treated as current history, what implications does that have? How does it redefine what the field-worker explores and how does it alter the focus of interpretation? Past history immediately becomes germane. How was the present produced? But the field-worker must also ask, "What is the present producing? What part of the activity being observed will be durable, and what will disappear?" The structural-functional assumption that a society is best studied as if it were a system replicating itself has long been abandoned. The identification of change-in-the-making is one of the present objects of analysis. The normality of continuity is not assumed. Sameness being repeated is seen as the product of effort. Conjectures about the future thus become an implicit part of the understanding of the present.

Assumptions about what lies ahead are visible in current models. So, for example, embedded in arguments about the historical development of the world economic system is an implicit prediction that the world economy will only become more and more tightly linked in the future (Makler, Martinelli, and Smelser 1982; Hopkins and Wallerstein 1982; Knorr-Cetina and Cicourel 1981). A more interdependent, more integrated world village is ahead. Fieldwork informed by

Editor's note: This chapter is a reprint of Moore, Sally Falk. 1987. "Explaining the present: Theoretical dilemmas in processual ethnography." *American Ethnologist* 14 (4): 727–36.

the world system paradigm focuses on activities in the local arena that show attachment to the world economy. These may range from the division of labor to the price of beans. The effort is to find out how far into the vortex a particular community has been drawn. If the spheres of activity that are segregated from fluctuations in the world economy are indeed going to become fewer, the ethnographer's harvest of information on the local state of affairs at the moment of fieldwork is an important datum for comparison with the past and future.

The two-system models, both modernization models and Marxist models, also tend to make assumptions about the direction and character of change. The timing is uncertain, and so are the particular details. But the general trajectory is assumed to be clear. In some quarters in anthropology we are witness to a new form of evolutionism. Nineteenth-century versions of social evolution were often concerned to contrast the crude beginnings of human society in a dim past with a glorious Victorian present. Instead, the implicit evolutionism of our time defines the present as changing in some known direction. But is the direction really known? And are the consequences for any particular people ever certain?

Fieldwork anthropology is generally small scale and short term. Can such an anthropology effectively analyze ongoing local affairs and at the same time connect the local scene with large-scale historical change? Marcus and Fisher, defending the present-oriented style of conventional ethnographic writing say,

> ethnographies that really report present conditions are future historical documents, or primary sources in the making. The challenge, then, is not to do away with the synchronic ethnographic frame, but to exploit fully the historical within it. (1986: 96)

That is good advice, but the question is, how best to do it? Do we record the present and wait for the restudy? Or must the ethnographer try to develop double vision, to see potential long-term implications in the day-to-day stuff? Can that be done in the field, or is it only possible later on, in the analytic writing-up?

More than 20 years ago, Frederik Barth argued that an anthropology focused on the production of culture needed a different theoretical framework from an anthropology focused on social structure (1966). His generative model was a cultural version of economic choice making. He was concerned with values and with the constraints and incentives that canalize choice (ibid.: 1, 11, 12). He said we should study "transactions." That seminal paper has long since been critically assessed and Barth himself has reviewed its perspectives (Barth

1978, 1981; Paine 1974). I have no intention of repeating the exercise here. But I would like to comment on one point that was not remarked upon in the initial discussions. The omission itself reflects a major change that has come about in anthropology. History on the large scale was not explicitly addressed in Barth's model nor in the critiques of it. In fact, the questions of time and scale were left implicit. The impetus for the changes seen in the field of his ethnographic observation invariably originated elsewhere. He made nothing of this. Barth certainly mentioned historical changes. He described alterations in the technology of herring fishing, and in another example, changes in the political economy of the Swat Pathans. But those and other transformations originating outside the field site were treated as the background against which the cumulative effect of local individual choice was examined. Barth has since addressed these issues of scale and time more directly (1978).

It is no wonder that he has done so since anthropological preoccupations with history, micro and macro, have increased a great deal in the past 20 years. Now the study of process over long periods of time is firmly embedded in anthropological theory and practice. In this year's *Annual Review*, Joan Vincent, herself the author of a historical study of Teso District in Uganda (1982), has taken stock of recent works on system and process. She remarks on "the increasing number of monographs that contribute not only to the analysis of processes within systems but of historical transformations" (1986: 114). She is right. There is no doubt that temporal consciousness has become a major element in anthropological thought. That increased consciousness of time and the historical moment raises issues for fieldwork that have only begun to be acknowledged. I want to address some of them here.

In the thick of fieldwork how is the anthropologist to distinguish the transitory from the durable, cultural change from cultural persistence? Local accounts of what is traditional may be quite unreliable. Hobsbawm and Ranger and their contributors to *The invention of tradition* (1983) have made it dramatically clear that what is seen as traditional is often recently invented. The fictitious invocation of traditional origins is often merely a legitimizing strategy. And there are other variations. A genuinely old form can serve to distract attention from new substance. When Africans today invoke the rules of inheritance of their forefathers to explain their present allocations of property, they are choosing to reiterate and emphasize an element of cultural continuity, though they live in a very different economic and political environment from anything their grandfathers ever knew. The traditional used in the present is not the same object it was in the lived-in past. How, indeed, is the field-worker to address the historical process that is unfolding right in front of him or her? How can fieldwork be done as current history? Certainly not by becoming obsessed with classifying everything into what is new and what is old (Comaroff 1984; Moore, in press). That was the style of the "acculturation" studies of yore. The problem with such sortings is that they break up the field of observation into items for a simplified bimodal classification, old and new, and the larger questions of social process are forgotten as the list of old and new cultural items gets longer.

Is it basically a question of re-conception, of constructing a different object of inquiry? Ortner has suggested that "practice" is the key symbol of the anthropology of the eighties (1984: 158). But she also remarks that others would choose "history." She says, echoing Marx, but not alluding to him directly, "History is not simply something that happens to people, but something they make, within, of course, the very powerful constraints of the system within which they are operating. . . . A practice approach attempts to see this making" (ibid.: 159). Ortner tells us that what is being explained by a practice approach is the relationship between "human action" and "the system" (ibid.: 148). In the "practice" paradigm as practiced by Sahlins there is also an emphasis on the cultural and social order as given. Amendments to the received order are made in the practice. We have all marveled at the misadventures of Captain Cook and the mutual misunderstandings of the Hawaiians and Europeans (Sahlins 1981, 1985). Sahlins has said, "An event is not just a happening in the world: it is a relation between a certain happening and a given symbolic system. Meaning is realized . . . only as events of speech and action. Event is the empirical form of system" (1985: 153). But to build a theoretical paradigm on the contrast between structure and practice has the disadvantage of detemporalizing existing structure, removing an abstracted structure from the events that construct it. A paradigm that postulates an existing symbolic system undervalues the continuous renewal needed by any ongoing system. The process of cultural maintenance and the process of cultural change should have comparable theoretical standing. I prefer the term "process" to "practice" precisely because process conveys an analytic emphasis on continuous production and construction without differentiating in that respect between repetition and innovation. A process approach does not proceed from the idea of a received order that is then changed. Process is simply a time-oriented perspective on both continuity and change. There is much more to be said about this but I do not want to dwell any longer on definitions and nomenclature.

The argument I want to make here is that there are methodological consequences for the field-worker in pursuing what I shall continue to call, pace Ortner, a processual perspective. This implies first, some differences in the favored
kinds of field materials to be collected. And second, and more important, there
are differences in the way clues in those data are read and represented. One
could say that in the past twenty-five years there has been a shift in attention
from structure to event. But event today is not simply an instantiation of existing structure in the manner of the Saussurean distinction between *langue* and
parole. An event is not necessarily best understood as the exemplification of an
extant symbolic or social order. Events may equally be evidence of the ongoing
dismantling of structures or of attempts to create new ones. Events may show a
multiplicity of social contestations and the voicing of competing cultural claims.
Events may reveal substantial areas of normative indeterminacy. The linguistic
analogy is an inadequate metaphor. Irangate is better seen as part of a sequential
process of uncertain outcome than as exemplifying a fixed and known grammar
of politics.

Events have long been a basic part of ethnographic data. Rituals, economic
exchanges, public meetings, dispute settlements, you name it, all have figured
prominently in anthropological works. Earlier generations of ethnographers
used these occurrences as reflections of coherent cultural systems. Later observers moved warily in the direction of history. A fight at a funeral alerted
Malinowski to certain normative implications of an accusation of incest (Malinowski [1926] 1951: 77). Fifty years later Geertz saw in a disrupted funeral
in Java all the human strains of cultural and political choice in circumstances
of rapid social change (Geertz 1973). But even in Geertz's more historical interpretation there is a stress on system. He postulates two systems, the peasant
system and the urban system, which he sees incongruously mixed in the lives of
town-dwelling rural immigrants. Geertz speaks of seeing "Redfield's folk culture . . . being continuously converted into his urban culture," but adds that
what is going on in these lower-class neighborhoods is not simply indicative
of what Geertz calls "a loss of cultural consensus, but rather is indicative of a
search, not yet entirely successful, for new, more generalized and flexible patterns of belief and value" (ibid.: 150). Thus when he does not see cultural coherence, Geertz postulates a transitional phase in which there is a search for such a
system of meaning. But one could easily argue that the transitionalism Geertz
observed is the product of his model, the product of his assumption that the
future holds a new and consistent symbolic and explanatory order that is being

"searched for." My view instead is that to the extent that there ever were total-izing coherent systems of the kind anthropology has so often described, they are hard to find in our world. Clusters of related meanings are everywhere, but outside the writings of professional ideologues, political and religious, it is diffi-cult to find in any society universal subscriptions to the overarching ideological totalism that the Geertzian search suggests. To say the obvious, the making of history is taking place in many connected locales at once. Local perspectives and actions necessarily reflect that multiplicity of levels and that heterogeneity of causal forces. The assumption that a plurality of limited systems of meaning are likely to intersect in any ethnographic scene promises a better understanding of the permanently transitional condition around us than any expectation that an encompassing system will one day be worked out.

If one has a special interest in the historical problem, are there certain kinds of events that should be treated as a preferred form of raw data? I would argue that there are. First, of course, events that are in no sense staged for the sake of the anthropologist are to be preferred, together with local commentaries on them. Some of the commentaries are bound to be colored by the presence of an outsider. That cannot be helped. And second, the kind of event that should be privileged is one that reveals ongoing contests and conflicts and competitions and the efforts to prevent, suppress, or repress these. Of course, the field-worker cannot always know in advance what event-contexts will carry this burden of historical meaning. Yet there are certain kinds of incidents, one might call them "diagnostic events," which have a strong likelihood of exposing such informa-tion. Thus, for example, the transfer or acquisition of major items of property can be considered a likely "diagnostic event." So, in a farming area, if land is normally inherited from father to son generation after generation, one is in the presence of some apparent continuity. But if at some point *some* fathers start to sell their son's patrimony to non-kin, some part of the pattern of local rep-lication is being broken. This kind of event is a telling historical sign visible in fieldwork. Quickly, one must try to find out how often it is happening and what people are saying about it. There undoubtedly are many other types of occur-rence that lend themselves to this kind of processual emphasis. What I am sug-gesting is that the identification of appropriate diagnostic events belongs high on the methodological agenda if ethnography is to treat itself as current history.

In 1987 it is difficult not to be dissatisfied with the rigidities of each of the three recent and not-so-recent structuralisms: structural-functional, Lévi-Straussian, and French Marxist. But it is equally difficult not to find use for the insights they have brought. Many of the questions the structuralisms raised remain lively and cogent. Their selective methods, exclusions, and exaggerated claims are another matter. The issue of the day is how to address the fieldwork enterprise in a poststructuralist period, how to understand the fieldwork time as a moment in a sequence, how to understand the place of the small-scale event in the large-scale historical process, how to look at part-structures being built and torn down. Instead of the structuralisms, what is needed is a less prefabricated approach coupled with what Marcus and Fischer call "realist" ethnography (1986). A receptivity to data as it comes along is open to recording uncertainty and disorder on the ethnographic scene. That openness is needed. For a time it may be matched by some uncertainty and disorder in the anthropological enterprise itself, but such a period of redefinition of the fieldwork project may be in order.

Processualism addresses a complex mix of order, anti-order, and non-order. It is often preoccupied with what seem to be and indeed may be contingencies of form. Its observations and interpretations are less neat than those of the structuralisms, but there is a concomitant gain in the detailed depiction of the specific and explosive mixture of the contestable and the unquestioned in current local affairs. There is therefore a tentativeness about processual interpretations of fieldwork that is absent in the structuralisms. That is not because of some paradigmatic failure. It is so because of two significant zones of ignorance. First, the local ethnographic project has usually been carried on without direct study of related large-scale processes. Therefore the character of the larger-scale, the supra-local domain, is not investigated but assumed. The province, the region, the nation, the world are often taken account of as generalized background, a form of knowledge that is not comparable in detail or dynamic to the ethnographer's local knowledge. That zone of ignorance is beginning to be filled in. More attention is being given to the quality of information at those levels and to its significance for the anthropologist's project. There is a second zone of ignorance that also contributes to tentativeness. Ethnography as current history is inevitably and obviously carried on without knowledge of the future. The identification of present processes as historically significant is necessarily provisional. Just as ethnographies are becoming more candid about what cannot be ascertained, so "current history" analyses must be more candid about what cannot be predicted.

I would like now to turn to some instances from my own fieldwork to show how local events and local commentary on them can be linked to a variety of processes unfolding simultaneously on very different scales of time and place, and to note the difference between what might be called the "foreground preoccupation" of the actors or commentators on these events, and the "background conditions" informing their situation that figure much more prominently in the preoccupations of the historically minded ethnographer. I chose these incidents because they all have to do with transfers of land and so fit my proposed instance of a "diagnostic event." On the surface two of the stories are about automobile accidents in Africa, and the third about a court-directed auction of a piece of land. At a deeper level all three incidents concern the meaning of good and evil, the current vicious competition over scarce land, and the ambiguous powers and weaknesses of church and state.

My fieldwork was done among the Kichagga-speaking people of East Africa. They live on Mount Kilimanjaro, a magnificent mountain that provides them with pure water and good soil. In the nineteenth century, the Chagga were banana growers and cattle keepers who were also involved in the long distance trade. As trading caravans made their way to and from the coast to the interior, caravans restocked their provisions and rested in the chiefdoms of the mountain. With the advent of the colonial period in the 1890s, the caravan trade ended and cash-cropping came in. So also did Catholic and Lutheran missions arrive, and a series of colonial masters. The Chagga were first ruled by the Germans (1896–1916), then by the British (1916–61). And since 1961, the year of their independence, they have been not altogether happy participants in Tanzania's experiment with African socialism.

Today Chagga farmers grow coffee as well as subsistence foods in their gardens. Each household lives in the midst of its own banana-coffee grove, often right next door to other patrilineally-related households. The normal way men obtain land is from their fathers. Women do not hold land independently, though as widows they may temporarily succeed to a husband's garden. Of the hundreds of thousands of households on Kilimanjaro, the number of houses that have running water and electricity can be counted on one's fingers. Very few have either. Most houses are constructed of mud bricks, or have wattle and daub walls and tin roofs. The kitchen stove consists of three stones and some firewood. The women fetch the water and grow much of the household's food. But the Chagga are far from cut off from the world. Through their coffee, they are connected with world markets and firmly attached to the Tanzanian national economy. Through Christianity they are connected with world religions, through their schools with non-local knowledge systems, and through their transistor radios, with one or another version of the Nairobi hit parade.

The Chagga population resident on the mountain has grown from about 100,000 in 1900 to more than 500,000 today. The process of population growth links the sexual life of the individual to collective destiny in very obvious ways. Here we have small-scale process with large-scale consequences. The result of this wildfire increase has been a general shortage of land.

The curtain now rises on the first event, which I heard about in 1969. In the course of answering my questions about the genealogy of her family, a young woman, then a teacher in the local elementary school, told me about an automobile accident that had cost the life of a young man from the same village. The accident had occurred only a few weeks earlier. The horror of it was still fresh in everyone's mind. Moreover, the very week of the accident another member of the same family had also died.

What my friend, the teacher, told me was that the accident victim, whose name was Protas, had met his death because of the ill will of certain people in the ex-chief's patriclan. "They were responsible," she said firmly. Protas had been away in Canada for four years receiving advanced technical training at a university. On his return, he was appointed to a high-level position in the national forestry service. Well-off and full of pleasure in himself, he returned to visit the village driving a car. It was expected that he would soon pay off the debts his father had accumulated in the course of a bitter lawsuit over a piece of land. The father's dispute was with a man in the ex-chiefly patrilineage. Though the father lost his initial case, he had angered the chiefly lineage by appealing and persisting in his claims. The Magistrate in the area was a member of the chiefly lineage. My friend Makulata said the Magistrate was the person who had put the death curse on Protas. How did she know? When Protas arrived with his car the Magistrate was heard to say something about how Protas would not be driving very long. I asked, "What exactly did he say?"

"Well," I was told, "the Magistrate made his malevolent intentions known very indirectly." What he said was, "If you have ashes in your palm and you blow them off, where will they go?" Ashes are a metaphor for children in the fire-hearth-womb symbolic discourse of the Chagga. What the statement meant, Makulata said, was, "If you blow a child away from the care of his father, where will he go? Anything might happen to him." As she explained, "There are people hereabouts who have given themselves to the gods of the underworld and their words can destroy a person. Anything could happen."

Needless to say, I was surprised by this account, produced as it was by a well-educated and deeply devout Catholic. The teacher has since become a school principal. She comes of a local elite family. Both of her parents were schoolteachers before her. The incident she described demonstrates the bitterness of the struggles that the land shortage has produced, and the way in which rivalries over property are tangled with ideas about the powers of evil. It was of no small interest that the object of her hatred and suspicion was the most publicly prominent member of the local ex-chiefly lineage, the Magistrate. He was the representative of the old elite and putative author of the death curse. But it is also of no small importance that his supposed victim was a young member of the new elite, the national government bureaucracy.

How is one to reconcile the certainty about the willed cause of Protas' death and the Catholic piety of my friend? It is not difficult to explain. As Michael Taussig (1980) has recently argued, the missionaries not only brought their God with them as they spread the Gospel all over the world, they also brought the Devil. Far from denying the efficacy of witchcraft, the missionaries on Kilimanjaro have often acknowledged its effectiveness. They told their parishioners not that it didn't work but that such acts were morally wrong because they constituted traffic with the forces of Evil. And even the protective amulets and spells provided by the *waganga*, the so-called "witchdoctors," or local healers, were tainted because they, too, drew their powers from the sources of Evil. Only the blessed talismans of the Church were legitimate protection. And only the punishment of God was a legitimate form of harmdoing. Today the churches have been Africanized. Virtually all the priests and pastors on the mountain are Chagga. They continue what the missionaries started. To this day there is preaching in the churches, Catholic and Protestant, against the purchase of objects endowed with occult power. At coffee harvest time, when people have cash, the campaign continues against paying for harm-doing substances or for protective talismans or even for divination. From rituals to amulets, the churches must have a monopoly.

On Mount Kilimanjaro, God can be called on directly to intervene in life. The devout have available a Christian mode of cursing. They can say, "You'll see," or "I leave it to God." Those words can be death threats. God will punish wrongdoers. If someone does another serious harm, it can be expected that God will eventually even things out. The wrongdoer can be reminded that he or she is in mortal danger through the saying of these seemingly innocuous words, *Utaona* ("You will see!"). God is very busy on Kilimanjaro, but, as they say, there is also much evil about.

The second event that I will describe was also a fatal automobile accident. But this time it was not the forces of evil but of good that were said to have caused the accident. One day some years after Independence, the Area Commissioner was being driven around the mountain by his chauffeur. There was a collision. The Area Commissioner was killed, but the chauffeur survived. The chauffeur was prosecuted for criminal negligence. At his trial the driver pleaded not guilty on the grounds that he had been unable to see where he was going because a whole flock of angels flew at the windshield and made it impossible to see ahead. The judge must not have believed him, for the driver was convicted. But the story was told many times around the mountain.

What lay behind it? Not long before, the government, in the person of the Area Commissioner, had confiscated certain lands that belonged to the convent at Huruma. It was a period when the government was trying to reduce the power and property of the churches by taking church estates. The Huruma site had a long history. It was said to have been originally the execution place of the chiefs. Such lands full of ghosts were dangerous and undesirable from the Chagga point of view, so it is no wonder that they did not object to the mission settling there or such was the version of the story told in the 1970s. At first, I was told, the Chagga refused to work the land for the convent for fear of the ghosts, but the priest sprinkled it with holy water and said, "See, nothing has happened to me, and nothing will happen to you." The Chagga then worked the land for the benefit of the convent for many decades and all was well. But when the Area Commissioner confiscated the property the ghosts came back, ghosts of dead nuns and others.

Who knows who believed the driver's story and who did not? There were many people who thought he had made it up to exonerate himself. But that did not mean that it was impossible for angels to fly in front of windshields; only that many people did not believe that it actually had happened in this instance. Then why was the story told all over the mountain with such gusto? Was it hostility to the Area Commissioner, representative of a feared government? Was it a metaphoric way of protesting government interference with the church, a safe means of saying that the government was wrong, that the land should have been left to the convent at Huruma, a way of fantasizing a threat to officials who might interfere in Chagga affairs and confiscate more land? Some Chagga expressed just those sentiments.

The third event I shall describe is an austerely secular one. It was the forced sale of a piece of land. A local man had borrowed a lot of money using his banana grove as collateral. When he failed to pay his debts, he was sued. The court found against him and ordered the land sold. My concern here is not with this unfortunate fellow and his debts, but with what ensued at the auction.

The auction was the occasion of some strenuous political competition between two men of the local village elite. There were three bidders for the auctioned land: the pastor, a local politician, and a "poor man" who was landless. Astonishingly enough, the poor man outbid the other two and acquired the property for a handsome sum. That was a riddle. How was he able to do this? There was a simple explanation. I was told that the poor man who made the big bid was actually the proxy of the local politician who had provided the necessary cash. The poor man would be installed as the nominal landholder, and could live there and grow subsistence crops, but the politician would receive the coffee income from the land. Why have this proxy landholder? In the then new national party philosophy, land was declared to be for the user, for the tiller. Land was not to be held by landlords. One of the first targets of the independent government had been landlordism. Legislation to prevent that form of profit taking was enacted from the start.

The maneuver by the politician was undertaken to forestall any official objections to his increasing his wealth in land. He was a descendant of an ex-chiefly line. There was a hostile faction of locals who were looking for any means they could find to attack him and force him to give up some of his holdings. Some years after independence they threatened to get the government to confiscate some of his land. To avoid this, in 1968 he was "persuaded" to make a substantial gift of land to the village for the construction of a school. However, in subsequent years, having thus shown himself to be a generous socialist, he was not about to stop investing in more land. His secret purchase at the auction was so skillfully arranged that it would have been difficult for his enemies to uncloak him. The puzzle he and various other members of the local elite had to figure out was how to remain a landlord under a socialist regime that intended to do away with all landlords. In this instance he succeeded.

CONCLUSIONS

I have deliberately chosen three chopped-off anecdotes, three tales of events that are not followed over any period of time, because I wanted to show that even the least temporally stretched-out episodes nevertheless can be indicators of process at many levels.

On the local scale, one thread that links all three incidents is the theme of progressively increasing land shortage. It is evident in the bitterness of the feelings that were said to have cost the life of the young bureaucrat from the forestry service, the deep resentment over the confiscation of the convent land, and the lengths to which the politician went to acquire one more coffee grove. All of these events involved unconventional ways of acquiring land, since the normal conveyance is from father to son. If one had focused on that statistically dominant form of conveyance one might have painted a picture of so-called traditional life being perpetuated. But the competitive struggle to acquire and control land evident in the diagnostic events described here also exerts pressures *within* kinship groups and changes the meaning of "traditional" Chagga forms of transfer and inheritance. In the foreground are the local social elaborations of competition between individuals. In the background is the large-scale demographic transformation, the population explosion that does not seem to be abating.

On a still larger scale, too, one of the processes that is offstage in all of these anecdotes is the ongoing formation of the postcolonial state and the evidence of local resistance to it. In the stories of the automobile accidents, we come to understand by indirection that, in the first two decades after independence in Tanzania, to be part of the government bureaucracy was to have access to the largest resource of all, the resources of the state, and that by local standards that was the apogee of success. Even some of the old elite managed to acquire some government treasure as witness the powers of the local Magistrate and the local politician. For the new elite, office in the national bureaucracy, not the local one, was the goal. One of the roads of access was and is education, as shown by the success of the young bureaucrat trained in Canada. More, his brief career also shows that in the first decades after independence the need for technically trained persons was so great that the young could quickly reach high positions. One is led to see this period as a phase in the development of an African bureaucracy, the state not a fixed form but as an entity being produced.

The manifestations of the state in the first two events are effective demonstrations of its power, the affluence of the young bureaucrat, the confiscation of church land. But there are intimations of rumblings against the state. In the third anecdote about the land auction, there is confirmation of the *limits* of state control. The state may make laws, but there remain myriad ways to circumvent them.

Thus, there is even in these three mini-incidents a double understanding to be gleaned about the culture of conformity and resistance. The church and the state are institutions that present authoritative demands and connect these with explicit legitimating ideologies. The demands of both are conformed to and eluded, piecemeal. Their prefabricated totalizing ideologies are both fragmentarily adopted and intermittently resisted.

Hence, in addition to the competition for land and the formation of the state, evidence of a third process is threaded through these stories: the unending competition for moral authority. The curious thing is that even in these brief incidents almost every truth-claim made can be shown to have a kind of self-subversive *anti-statement* attached to it. Thus, in the teacher's commentary on the accident it becomes clear that, while the church claims its truths to be God's truths, it also confirms the existence and effectiveness of the powers of evil. In short, the church itself makes it clear that there are rules other than church-taught rules and powers other than God's powers.

The state has its own rules and moral claims. The state confiscates church lands to show the church to be an exploitative property owner and landlord. But the state's representatives, the young bureaucrat and his ilk, have more money and power than their cultivator cousins. The state moralizes about the exploitativeness of others but it also richly rewards its own.

The politician who secretly broke the law against landlordism by making a poor dependent a proxy landowner had no great respect for the moralizing of the state on this point. He thought it a higher obligation to try to provide well for his sons, and he congratulated himself on giving the landless farmer a place to live and land from which to eat. In participating in the court auction the politician publicly relegitimized the powers of the state, while he diligently subverted them with his proxy bidder.

Thus, within the contents of each of the three events described, there are antithetical messages conveyed. Contradictory interpretations of the world are carried concomitantly, and at the level of action there is evidence of simultaneous conformity and resistance to authority claims.

These anecdotes lead, like a sunburst, in all directions. They could easily be interpreted in terms of the demands of any of the three structuralisms, functionalist, Lévi-Straussian, or Marxist. There are ample hints of interlocked social-organizational frameworks that would have gladdened the heart of any structural functionalist. There are lineages, chiefdoms, missions, parishes, administrative hierarchies, and all their accompanying role sets. But there is a lot more. In the ashes blown from the palm and in the manifestations of evil there are clues to a rich system of symbolic categories. There is, in fact, enough material in Chagga symbolic discourse to satisfy an army of Lévi-Straussian structuralists. And for the Marxists, there are ample indications of the penetration of the market, clear traces of multiple modes of production, perhaps incipient class distinctions, and some indication of the ideological components that accompany these relationships.

But there is no single order of things, no single *episteme* through which the Chagga understand the world (Foucault 1973: xxii). Instead there are many. Nor is there any single mode of knowing that informs the anthropologist. This circumstance is the justification for arguing that certain kinds of events are particularly important forms of diagnostic data. Within their content they display multiple meanings in combination. Immense social effort goes into attaching orderly "official" meanings to action and communication. But as played out in events those official meanings can often be seen to have ambiguous and contradictory counterparts attached to them. The *juxtaposition* in events of competing and contrary ideas, and of actions having contradictory consequences, is the circumstance that requires inspection and analysis. It is through that contiguity of contraries that ongoing struggles to control persons, things, and meanings often can be detected. Those struggles to construct orders and the actions that undo them may be the principal subject matter of ethnography as current history.

At this postcolonial, poststructuralist moment a few things emerge clearly: anthropologists doing fieldwork, instead of conceiving of themselves as looking at whole cultures or whole societies, are now acutely conscious of observing part of the cultural construction of part of a society at a particular time. That being so, local affairs cannot be addressed without serious attention to the larger processual implications of the local moment. Internal evidence of connections with social fields beyond the ethnographic site can lead to some of those historical significations. A new thematic emphasis and a refurbished set of techniques must be put into place if the potential gains to be had from this shift in perspective are to be realized. The new emphasis in fieldwork is on the extent to which the manufacture and control of particular cultural and social constructions is or is not in local hands, and which local hands. The new techniques needed are improvements in the capacity to identify and dissect the types of events that are diagnostic for answering these questions. After all, events are to processes what categories are to structures. And this is the time for processual ethnography.

Figure 1. Map of Tanzania, highlighting Mt. Kilimanjaro

Figure 2. The two peaks of Kilimanjaro, Kibo and Mawenzi, years ago, when they still had snow.

Figure 3. A traditional Chagga grass-haystack house next to a modern cinderblock house, owned by the same family.

Figure 4. A granary. In the background: coffee bushes sheltered by banana plants.

Figures 5 and 6. A large market in Mwika in the 1980s. The bananas will be sold to bar owners for making banana beer.

PART THREE

Excursions into Mythology

In the 1970s, there was a great blooming of theories about myths and symbolic elements in cultures. It was argued that the symbols not only made sense but were systematically ordered. Among other major works, Claude Lévi-Strauss had published La pensée sauvage *(1962, translated as* The savage mind *in 1966) in which he presented striking regularities in "mythological thought." In 1973, Rodney Needham, an Oxford Professor, elaborated on the earlier work of Robert Hertz, publishing* Right and left: Essays on dual symbolic classification. *There were many other books and articles stimulated by the wide interest in these topics. What was evident was that across many cultures having no connection with each other the same symbolic categories and oppositional correspondences were in use: left/right, female/male, night/day, and many more. (This subject matter was an alternative to the Marxist analyses which were also flourishing.)*

Flooded by the enormous literature on mythological regularities, I decided to write about another dimension, the contradictions and official inconsistencies in some myth-systems, particularly involving some sexual matters. The essays in this section are the product of that sideline in my work.

Mythological rationales for actual practices are not difficult to find in the traditions of many societies. Some are quite elaborate. The two articles in this section follow the logic of some of this material. The first essay asks, if the origin myth of a people postulates an original first family, where do the children of the first couple find spouses? The potentially incestuous outcome in some of these tales would presume an act of incest in the sacred original family that is forbidden to their living descendants. A cheerful contradiction!

Elsewhere, hints of an invisible, otherworldly, quasi-incestuous connection between brothers and sisters are found in the beliefs surrounding some kinship systems. Practical links are thought to exist between a particular brother and sister regarding their procreative capacities. The connection can be effected through bridewealth, or through mystical powers over fertility. Such a double set of ideas: stringent incest prohibitions coupled with the actual ties of siblings to each other's marriages and fertility are as tantalizing as they are widespread.

The second of the papers that follow concerns a nineteenth century Chagga ritual myth about the stiching up of the anuses of boys. Young males about to be circumcised and initiated were told ahead of time that their anuses would be permanently stitched up in the course of group initiation in the forest. No such thing actually occurred, of course, but it was a convention of behavior to act publicly thereafter as if it had happened. Men were supposed to hide when they defecated. They were to pretend to women and to younger children that they never had any need to empty their bowels.

In the article describing this peculiar set of ideas and customs, I emphasized the social acceptance of an idea that they all knew to be untrue. It is a rather special instance of the social mandatoriness that mythological systems can achieve. They all were complicit in pretending that something they knew to be false was in fact true. This lie is a rather extreme form of the contradictions that myths can perpetrate.

Was this idea of male anal closure related to circumcision unique to the Chagga? A few years after I read about the old Chagga idea of anal stitching, Nigel Barley described the same complex of ideas and practices he had discovered in a society in Cameroon, the Dowayo (Barley 1984: 74, 75). The whole belief complex of the Chagga about anal closure was long past by the time I visited Kilimanjaro. I only learned of this nineteenth-century Chagga set of ideas, because the missionary, Gutmann, wrote about them, and they were long past even when he was there (Gutmann 1926: 321–38; HRAF trans.: 289–304). But Barley actually saw how the Dowayo behaved to collectively construct and maintain this deception. Since these two peoples, the Chagga and the Dowayo were located geographically far from each other, how did it happen that they produced a similar story of the link between circumcision and sealed anuses?

CHAPTER NINE

Descent and Symbolic Filiation

Kinship networks involve a paradox. On the one hand, marriage links exogamic kin groups. On the other hand, it serves to link them only insofar as the ties of each spouse to his (or her) family of birth are maintained. This continuing connection with the natal groups is often represented by the bond between brother and sister, although it also appears in other forms.[3] As male and female of the same generation, their mutual involvement in their kin group makes them in some respects a counter-pair to husband and wife. Since in many systems this sibling relationship serves structural ends, the brother-sister tie is seldom left simply to spontaneous expressions of devotion which might or might not be forthcoming. Instead, it is reinforced with ritual, social, and economic obligations.

Some cultures also stress rather than minimize the incestuous overtones of the brother-sister relationship. Sometimes, this preoccupation appears in the

---

Editor's Note. This chapter is a reprint of Moore, Sally Falk. 1964. "Descent and symbolic filiation." *American Anthropologist* 66: 1308–20. Reprinted in 1967. *Myth and cosmos*, edited by John Middleton, 63–76. New York: Natural History Press. Also reprinted in 1976. *Selected papers: 1946–70*, American Anthropological Association 75th anniversary commemorative volume, edited by Robert F. Murphy. Washington, D.C.: American Anthropological Association.

1.   While brother and brother, or sister and sister, may effectively symbolize the descent group, same-sex pairs cannot epitomize the bridge *between* kin groups.

form of exaggerated prohibitions and avoidances. In other cases, it is woven through the conception of descent, as opposed to parenthood. It is this tying together of incestuous ideas and descent that is the subject of this paper, particularly with regard to brother and sister.

Common to a variety of descent systems are two means of prolonging the relationship between kin groups established by marriage. Both structural devices have the effect of stressing the bond between brother and sister. One method is to repeat the affinal tie through cross-cousin marriage. This binds brother and sister twice over. The other structural device is to make the children of the marriage to some degree descendants of both kin groups, linking the two groups in their persons. (This may, but need not also involve a prohibition on cousin marriage.) Cognatic and double descent systems immediately come to mind. But unilineal systems may also trace descent in some form through both parents. Full membership in the patrilineage of the father and partial membership in the patrilineage of the mother is one way (Nuer). Or there may be a similar near doubling of membership in the matrilineages of mother and father (Hopi, Plateau Tonga). The tracing of descent through both parents in whatever manner extends the affiliations established by marriage at least another generation in the person of the common descendant. This also has the accompanying result that brother and sister have descent links of some kind with each other's children.

Both sorts of ongoing ties not infrequently place brother and sister together in a highly binding relationship to the progeny of one or both. This relationship is often represented in what might be called "the ideology of descent," as if it were a variety of mystical, sexless parenthood, a form of symbolic filiation.

Radcliffe-Brown thought brother-sister ties particularly associated with extreme matrilineality, while he believed that husband-wife bonds were more emphasized in cases of extreme patrilineality. He felt, however, that most systems fell somewhere in between (1952: 42). I plan to deal elsewhere with a full structural reappraisal of this Radcliffe-Brown thesis, but the present paper will focus on a single aspect of the problem: the representation of brother and sister as a symbolically parental couple in descent ideology. That this occurs in patrilineal and cognatic systems as well as in matrilineal ones will be plain from the materials examined. These include creation myths, on the theory that people model their mythical first family on their own kinship structure, and also include a few well known beliefs and customs relating to fertility and the procreation and well-being of descendants. Most of the

myths collected here show incest explicitly. As would be expected, the kinship beliefs put the matter more delicately and indirectly, but the incestuous
symbolism is unmistakable.

I

Any myth about the creation of man which postulates a single first family is
bound to give rise to some incestuous riddles. There is the first man, or woman,
or couple. They have children. Who marries the children of the first couple?
Adam and Eve had two sons, Cain and Abel. Where did Cain's wife come from?
      Many mythological methods exist to supply respectable mates for the origi-
nal family. Sometimes spouses are simply found when needed. Cain's wife turns
up conveniently in the King James version of the Bible, but Saint Augustine
seems to have had no doubt that the sons and daughters of Adam and Eve
married each other (Saint Augustine 1958: 350). In other myths, many people
emerge from the ground together and there is a kind of simultaneous creation of many ancestors for mankind. However, many peoples cheerfully and
explicitly mate the first family to its own members. A number of such myths are
listed below. These were collected and examined to discover which members of
the family were most often partners in this original incest, and whether there
was any observable correlation between the type of kinship system and the type
of incest described. A few of the myths cited deal with the primary incest of
the gods, a few others with an incest that began a particular lineage, but most
of them tell of an incest from which mankind sprang. All but two are listed
with the associated form of descent. The prevalence of brother-sister incest is
striking, and the correlation of parent-child incest with descent rules quite sug-
gestive. The examples examined have been culled from ethnographies, from the
Human Relations Area Files, from indications in the Stith Thompson Index,
from a picking over of the Handbook of South American Indians and other
general sources likely to include such information. However, the list is a chance
compilation depending upon library accessibility and is in no sense complete.
It is sufficient to suggest the wide appearance of the theme and, perhaps, some
gross correlations.

Table 1. Some Peoples Having Incestuous Creation Legends.

People	Descent	Incest in Myth	References
Greeks	Patrilineal	Brother-Sister	Larousse 1960: 93
Hebrews	Patrilineal	Brother-Sister	Saint Augustine 1958: 350 Graves 1963: 17–18
Murngin	Patrilineal	Father-Daughter Brother-Sister	Warner 1937: 528
Trobriand	Matrilineal	Brother-Sister (implied)	Malinowski 1929: 497
Berber (Kabyle)	Patrilineal	Brother-Sister	Frobenius and Fox 1938: 55
Ngona Horn S. Rhodesia	Patrilineal	Father-Daughter	Frobenius and Fox 1938: 241
Maori	Ambilineal	Father-Daughter	Best 1924: 115–18
Miwok	Patrilineal	Father-Daughter Brother-Sister	Gifford 1916: 143–44
Baiga	Patrilineal	Brother-Sister	Elwin 1939: 313,331
Thonga	Patrilineal	Brother-Sister	Junod 1913: 230
Chibcha	Matrilineal	Mother-Son	Kroeber 1947: 908
Yaruro	Matrilineal	Brother-Sister	Kirchhoff 1943: 462
Hawaii	Ambilineal	Mother-Son	Dixon 1916: 26
Tahiti Celebes Minahassa	Ambilineal	Father-Daughter Mother-Son	Dixon 1916: 26 Dixon 1916: 157
Ifugao	Bilateral	Brother-Sister	Dixon 1916: 170
Kachin	Patrilineal	Brother-Sister	Lévi-Strauss 1949: 307
Mohave	Patrilineal	Brother-Sister	Devereaux 1939: 512
Pawnee	Matrilineal (?)	Brother-Sister	American Folklore Society 1904: 22
Tlingit	Matrilineal	Brother-Sister	Krause 1956: 175,185
Aleut	Patrilineal	Brother-Sister	HRAF citing Veniaminov and Sarytschew

People	Descent	Incest in Myth	References
Alor	Bilateral	Brother-Sister (implied)	Dubois 1944: 105
Yurok	Bilateral	Father-Daughter	Roheim (citing Kroeber) 1950: 273
Island Carib Dominica	Matrilineal	Brother-Sister	Taylor 1945: 310
Veddas	Matrilineal	Brother-Sister	Seligmann 1911: 74
Lakher	Patrilineal	Brother-Sister	Parry 1932: 489
Garo	Matrilineal	Brother-Sister	Playfair 1909: 84
Ba-Kaonde	Matrilineal	Brother-Sister	Melland 1923: 156, 249–59
Cherokee	Matrilineal	Brother-Sister (implied)	Mooney 1902: 240
Dogon	Patrilineal	Brother-Sister	Griaule and Dieterlen 1954: 84–96
Abaluyia	Patrilineal	Brother-Sister	Wagner 1954: 30, 35
Papua of Waropen	Patrilineal	Brother-Sister	Held 1957: 95, 299
Samoa	Ambilineal	Brother-Sister	Mead 1930: 151
Lovedu	Patrilineal	Father-Daughter Brother-Sister Cycle of Kings	Krige and Krige 1943: 5, 10, 12
Tullishi	Double	Brother-Sister	Nadel 1950: 351
Lozi	Ambilineal	Brother-Sister	Gluckman 1950: 177, 178
Andaman Islanders	Bilateral	Brother-Sister	Radcliffe-Brown 1933: 196
Japanese	Bilateral	Brother-Sister	Etter 1949: 29
Ainu	Matrilineal	Brother-Sister	Etter 1949: 20–21
Kei Islands SE Indonesia		Brother-Sister	Dixon 1916: 156
Nambicuara	Bilateral	Brother-Sister	Lévi-Strauss 1948: 369
Egyptians	Patrilineal	Brother-Sister King Osiris	Frazer 1960: 421

Total number of peoples listed 42

Four peoples have more than one type of incest in their origin myth hence the disparity between the total number of peoples and the total instances of incest.

Descent	bro-sis	fa-da	mo-son
Patrilineal	16	4	
Matrilineal	10		1
Ambilineal	2	2	1
Bilateral	5	1	
Double	1		
Unknown	1		1
Totals	34	7	3

Some reservations should be made. For one thing, both myths and social organization change. Even assuming that myth is in some symbolic way a rationalization of a kinship system, it may be more or less durable than the social structure from which it sprang. There is also the related question as to what position the origin myth occupies in the total literature of a people. It may be an old story, part of an obscure heritage, seldom retold, but carried along, or it may have a good deal more vitality than that. This is a nuance which is not always discernible from the ethnographic literature. (For a penetrating discussion of these and related problems concerning the interpretation of myth, see Fischer 1963.)

It should also be said that though the relation of the form of the incestuous myth to the form of the social organization may be posed as a problem in correlations, it is not really suitable to treat it this way. Many, if not most, peoples do not have such a myth, but they have the same types of kinship structure as the peoples who have the myths. The inference to be drawn from this mythological material is that a fictive and symbolic incest is often a significant symbol of ancestry and descent. It may be found in many forms, of which origin myths are but one example. Hence the origin myths alert one to a kind of symbolism that appears in the ideology of some descent systems even in cultures in which this theme is not expressed in the particular form of a creation legend.

Lévi-Strauss has said that "the purpose of myth is to provide a logical model capable of overcoming a contradiction . . ." (1955: 443) and that "mythical thought always works from the awareness of oppositions toward their progressive mediation . . ." (1955: 440). From this point of view these incestuous origin myths refer to a time when there were no people to explain how there came to be many people. They start with one family to show the source of all families. They tell of an ancient incest that sired the human race, yet plainly the descendants are forbidden to emulate their ancestors. Then and now are contrasted in a systematic way.[2]

Inspecting the table, it is clear that brother-sister incest is the one which most often takes place in the myths. This not only violates the incest prohibition; it also necessarily violates exogamic rules in any descent system. Where mythological parent-child incest occurs in unilineal systems, it, too, seems calculated to violate descent rules. The matrilineal Chibcha are descended from a mother-son incest, the patrilineal Murngin, Miwok, Ngona, and the Lovedu rulers from a father-daughter incest. The numbers involved here are too small to constitute a statistical proof, but they suggest a correlation with structure. It is interesting to note parent-child incest in the myths of three out of five ambilineal peoples and one out of six bilateral peoples. Presumably the structural resemblances of ambilineal systems to unilineal ones accounts for this difference, but the numbers are too small to warrant any firm conclusion.

Why should incest in origin myths be a common theme, and why should it tend so strongly to be sibling incest? And why should mythical parent-child incest tend to correlate with descent group exogamy? If one applies psychoanalytic theory, these myths can be regarded as a reiteration of Oedipal fantasies. The beginning of mankind then stands for the early wishes of the individual, and sibling incest is not more than a lightly veiled version of parent-child incest. This interpretation could account for the commonness of the incestuous theme in mythology. It might even superficially seem to account for the prevalence of the brother-sister over the parent-child type. *But it could in no way account for the correlation of mythological parent-child incest with descent.* Whatever element is unaccounted for in the parent-child cases, is logically unaccounted for in the sibling type, for one explanation must apply to all.

Thus even if one accepts psychoanalytic interpretations, they can only explain the general appeal of the theme of incest, not its particular variations or cultural applications. I agree with Murphy that "the stuff of the unconscious tends to be expressed in cultural symbols where it serves some function in terms

---

2. It has been objected that what is involved here and in Lévi-Strauss is not the juxtaposition of opposites, but of negatives. This well-taken point of logic undermines the form but not the substance of Lévi-Strauss' contention.

of social structure . . ." (1959: 97). The explanation of the variations must be sought in the cultural setting in which they are found.

In this matter Lévi-Strauss' approach to mythology (1955, 1962) is very useful. His conception of oppositions ties social structure to myth insofar as myths seek to reconcile what life is with what life is not. There is another string to his bow in *Le totemisme aujourd'hui.* There he deals not with contrasts and negations, but with the replication of social structure in the classification of animals and plants. Hence, mythological symbolism may either repeat or contrast with reality, as the case may be.

The incestuous creation myths do both. In them one finds a literary reconciliation of the incest prohibition and incest itself, both pushed discreetly into the primeval past. Descent postulates common ancestry. Man is of one kind. Thus all mankind has common ancestors. Ancestry is also the basis of the incest prohibition. But if all men are descended from one couple, then every marriage is distantly and vaguely incestuous. In this way, the myth metaphorically and economically states both the unity of man and that marriage is a substitute for incest.

Since the unified descent of mankind is best symbolized in a particular culture not only by incest, but by incest within the descent group, there may be a purely logical reason for the prevalence of the sibling incest theme against the parent-child type. Brother-sister incest conveys concisely for *any* descent system the same triple symbolism that parent-child incest conveys for particular ones, namely the fusion of descent, marriage, and incest. There may be an even simpler explanation. Since primary marriage most often tends to be within the same generation, brother-sister incest may be a closer symbolic replication of marriage than parent-child incest.

Robert Graves, like Frazer before him, interprets mythological sibling incest as an indication of a prior period of matrilineal land inheritance (Frazer 1960: 386; Graves 1963: 4). This seems a curious inference. As the table shows, sibling incest as an origin myth theme is as clearly associated with patrilineality as matrilineality. To treat legends of this type as accounts of early history is a naively literal approach. It is far more likely that these stories are a fictional validation of the present than an embroidered remnant of the past.

There is no better example than the Dogon of the French Sudan who state explicitly that their kinship system is based on their creation myth. So beautifully does their myth illustrate the sibling constellation and its symbolic content in descent ideology that it is worth making an excursion into Dogon cosmology.

A patrilineal people having patrilocal kin groups, the Dogon prefer the marriage of a man with his mother's brother's daughter. Conventionally, he also enjoys sexual relations with his mother's brother's wife. All this according to the Dogon has its precedents in the Beginning of Time.

The Dogon creation myth begins with the egg of the world. (I will spare the reader the rather orgasmic seven vibrations of the universe and some other cosmic upheavals.) The egg of the world is divided into twin placenta, each of which contains a "pair of twin Nommo, direct emanations and sons of God. . . . Like all other creatures these twin beings . . . were each equipped with two spiritual principles of opposite sex; each of them, therefore, was in himself a pair . . ." (Griaule and Dieterlen 1954: 86).

In Dogon belief every human being is the offspring of two pairs of Nommo like those in the original placenta, the father and the father's sister, the mother and the mother's brother. The ideal, but prohibited, marriage is conceived as that between brother and sister. Mystically, opposite sex siblings are conceived as parents of each other's children.

However, in the creation all did not proceed according to plan: "in one placenta . . . the male person emerged prematurely from the egg. Moreover, he tore a fragment from his placenta and with it came down through space outside the egg; this fragment became the earth." Yurugu, for that was the name of this male creature, eventually went back to heaven to get the rest of his placenta and his twin soul. But, unfortunately for him, "Amma (God) had handed over this twin soul to the remaining pair in the other part of the egg. . . . Yurugu could not retrieve her; and from that time on . . . [was] . . . engaged in a perpetual and fruitless search for her. He returned to the dry earth where . . . he procreated in his own placenta . . ." However, this procreation with a symbolic maternal fragment did not produce people, but some sort of incomplete beings. "Seeing this, Amma decided to send to earth the Nommo of the other half of the egg . . ." (Griaule and Dieterlen 1954: 86). Mankind was then produced through the coupling of pairs of male and female twins.

The Dogon regard every male child as Yurugu with respect to his mother. He is her brother, her ideal husband. But since the normal incest prohibitions apply, the wife of the maternal uncle is taken as a sexual partner as a substitute for the mother. The boy is allowed to commit whatever thefts he pleases in his mother's brother's household, as these are regarded as a symbolical search for a wife. This comes to an end when the maternal uncle provides a wife, usually one of his daughters. "Clearly, there is a correspondence here between the maternal uncle's daughter, his wife, and his sister, who is the mother of the nephew. The marriage is thus in some sense a reenactment of the mythical incest. It is also . . . regarded as a caricature and is thus a kind of defiance hurled at Yurugu . . ." (Griaule and Dieterlen 1954: 93).

The Dogon lay out their villages, their fields, and their houses in a pattern that is in keeping with the creation myth. No vestigial tradition, the myth has tremendous vitality and importance. The patriline is thought to follow the original orderly creation of Amma, the uterine group to represent the checkered career of Yurugu. While there is much else that is interesting about Dogon belief, three of its elements are of particular relevance here: first that brother and sister are idealized as a procreative couple; second, the idea that any child is simultaneously produced by two sibling pairs, the father and his sister, the mother and her brother; and third, that structural features, in this case, preferred MA trilateral cross-cousin marriage, can have specific symbolically incestuous meanings.

The basic question that elements in the Dogon myth raise is this: Are the Dogon a special case, or does their myth make explicit certain ideas that are symbolically implied in one form or another in many descent systems? If one reflects on the stereotyped kinship roles often prescribed for parents' siblings of opposite sex in primitive cultures, it is difficult to dismiss the Dogon as unique.

II

Turning from mythology to some beliefs and customs which surround the perpetuation of the descent group, here again examples of the symbolic pairing of brothers and sisters in a quasi-incestuous manner are not far to seek. Brother and sister may together perpetuate the descent group on a symbolic level, while on a practical level marriage produces the actual descendants.

In Africa, the well-known case is that of cattle-linking, in which a man obtains his wife by means of the cattle received for his sister, and she consequently comes to have a special relationship with her brother's children. The striking thing about these African cattle-linked sibling pairs is the extent to which the tie between a particular brother and sister is acknowledged as having a connection with the very existence of the brother's children, giving the father's sister special rights over them. There is a kind of double marriage, the actual one, and the symbolic one of the cattle linking. (See, for instance, Krige and Krige 1943: 142–46 for the Lovedu; Stayt 1931: 174 for the BaVenda; Schapera 1950: 142 for the Tswana; Holleman 1952: 66, 67, 169 for the Shona; and Kuper 1950: 102 for the Swazi.)

In Samoa, the male line of the ambilineal Manuans goes on through the good grace of each man's sister. The father's sister has the ability to make her brother or his male line barren, or can cause them to sicken (Mead 1930: 137). As the keeper of her brother's fertility, a sister becomes in a mystical sense as responsible for a man's procreation as his wife is in a biological sense.

In the Trobriands, one sees the matrilineal counterpart of the African cattle pairing. Trobriand brothers and sisters are paired off for various purposes. Not only does a particular brother supply a particular sister with food, but "This pairing off extends to other things besides *urigubu* [food]. *A sister may ask her brother to make magic designed to get her impregnated by one of the spirits of their sub-clan.* The brother who is responsible for a sister's food is the one who plays the main role of disciplinarian and tutor of her children. The other brothers are secondary in this respect." (Fathauer 1961: 250, emphasis added).

The Trobriand preoccupation with brother-sister incest is clearly threaded throughout the descriptions of Malinowski. The origin of Trobriand love magic is based on brother-sister incest. All clans begin their mythological history with a brother and sister, the sister becoming pregnant without intercourse (Malinowski 1929: 35, 180–82). Trobriand brother-sister pairs are clearly associated with descent and figure as symbolic parents of the sister's children much as the African cattle-linking makes siblings figure as symbolic parents of the brother's children.

Among the Murngin, Warner tells us that "No sister may eat a brother's kill of kangaroo, emu, etc. until the brother's wife has had a child" (1930: 253). It is as if the sister drained her brother's sexual powers by eating his kill. The sister's actions plainly have an effect on her brother's ability to impregnate his wife.

The African, Samoan, Trobriand, and Murngin instances are all cases in which the non-lineal sex has power over the fertility of the lineal sex. But sometimes the position is reversed. The patrilineal Lakher believe that if there is ill-feeling between a woman and her brother or her mother's brother, she will be unable to have children. Patently her relatives retain control over her fertility even after she marries. The ceremony which may be performed to enable her to become pregnant gives her brother or her mother's brother a major role. Either of these men places some fermented rice in the woman's mouth with a hair pin when the moon is waning, and neither of them speaks to her again until a new moon has arisen (Parry 1932: 379–80).[3]

All of these are fairly obvious cases in which brother and sister together are involved with the procreativity of one or the other of them. But the sibling link can be expressed in purely spiritual terms as well. The Mende explain the relationship with the mother's brother this way:

> [S]ince a brother and sister come from the same father they may be considered as one. *Therefore, all that a mother gives her child is given also by her brother, and so her brother's displeasure or pleasure is the same as its mother's.* The physical part of a person, i.e. his bones, flesh, etc. is provided by his father through the semen. . . . The child's spirit—*ngafa*—however, is contributed by his mother. This explains why the blessing of the mother's people is so important to the child and why the father asks them to pray for the child when he takes it away from them. The mother is the child's "keeper" in the same sense as a genie may have control over a human being. (Little 1951: 111, emphasis added)

For the patrilineal Mende, then, brother and sister are triply bound. First, they are one as the bodily (i.e., descent) children of one father; second, they are one as the soul keepers of the sister's children; and third, they are descent antecedents of the brother's children. Husband and wife are actual parents, brother and sister symbolic ones. The Mende attitude is a forceful reminder of the Dogon myth.

---

3.   The Lakher also believe that if a woman's parents are dead, their spirits may be the cause of her infertility. For this last the cure is a sacrifice on the graves of the parents. Thus brothers and sisters are not by any means the *only* custodians of each other's fertility. Among the matrilineal Pende, for instance, a father is said to enable his daughter to bear children, but sometimes the anger of a mother's brother can make a woman sterile (de Sousberghe 1955: 27). Even among the Trobrianders spirit children may be the gift of a woman's mother, mother's brother, or even of her father (Malinowski 1929: 173). Among the patrilineal Nuer, a man's mother or his mother's brother can prevent him from having any male children (Evans-Pritchard 1960: 138). A Nuer son can, by violating certain taboos, render his mother barren (ibid.: 165). The curse of the mother or mother's brother among the Nuer would seem to be the counterpart of the father's sister's curse in Polynesia. Relationships of the spirits obviously can have sexual consequences. The power over fertility is often an expression of multiple structural relationships in terms of sexual symbols. Though this paper is confined to this symbolization as it pertains to brother and sister, it should be borne in mind that it can, as indicated, pertain to other relatives.

The pairing of brothers and sisters as a symbolic couple bears on Lévi-Strauss' interpretation of totemism. Lévi-Strauss (1962) suggests that the reason why animals are suitable symbols of kin groups lies in certain resemblances between the animal world and the human world. The human world and the animal world have in common the subdivisions of their respective kinds. He stresses the fact that totemism involves the use of homologous systems to represent one another. With this general thesis I have no argument.

However, though Lévi-Strauss notes that animal species are endogamous, he does not find it logically troublesome that they are used to represent exogamous groups. Instead, he cites Bergson saying that it is not on the animality but on the duality that totemism puts its emphasis (1962: 111, 135). The material on symbolic incest and descent reviewed here suggests that this part of the Lévi-Strauss argument is superfluous. The endogamy of animal species makes animals not less but more appropriate as emblems of descent groups. This is obviously not because of any actual endogamy in descent groups, but because descent groups are symbolically self-perpetuating. The descent element in unilineal groups is passed on from generation to generation in a self-propelling stream. To be sure, partners from other lineages are required catalysts or vehicles for the production of biological offspring, but the descent element in the offspring comes from within the lineage only. Kind reproduces kind in the animal and human kingdoms.

The beliefs examined here in which brother and sister have custody of each other's fertility, or are mutually involved in the perpetuation of the descent group, or are together connected with the body or soul of each other's children all state formal social ties in a particular symbolic idiom. Firth has said, "Kinship is fundamentally a reinterpretation in social terms of the facts of procreation and regularized sex union" (1961: 577). But if one moves from the realm of structure to the realm of symbolism, the contrary can be true. That is, relationships which are not sexual or filial in reality may be expressed in symbols having a sexual or filial content. Just as fictive kinship may be resorted to in order to bind unrelated persons socially, so fictive incest and fictive parenthood can be part of the idiom of descent.

Symbolic filiation is not at all startling when it does not involve any direct mention of the incest. We are entirely accustomed to it in kinship terminology. When the father's sister is called "female father," the term implies that she partakes in her brother's paternity. Where cousins are classified with brothers and sisters they are linked in a fictitious common filiation. The extension of the incest taboo beyond the elementary family is another of the ways in which symbolic filiation may serve structural ends. Clearly descent and symbolic filiation are frequently interlocked concepts. It is not surprising then, that the brother-sister relationship which has such widespread structural importance, not only often appears as a symbol of descent, but does so in the form of a symbolic parenthood. A full recognition of this pervasive *double entendre* and its many variations can deepen our understanding of descent in kin-based societies.

CHAPTER TEN

The Secret of the Men
A Fiction of Chagga Initiation and its Relation to the Logic of Chagga Symbolism

In the nineteenth century, there were Chagga chiefdoms which initiated their young men into adulthood by putting them through an elaborate series of rituals and ordeals. The first was circumcision. No sooner had the young men fully recovered from their circumcision wounds than they had another trial to undergo. They were sent to the forest for a period of seclusion and instruction. Children and young women were told that during this time in the Kilimanjaro forests the newly circumcised youths were subjected to another operation, this one to plug and stitch closed their anuses (Gutmann 1926: 321–38; Human Relations Area Files [HRAF] 1961: 289–304).

According to this fiction, full-grown men of procreative age did not defecate, but digested their food completely, and this state of being closed was the very essence of manhood. In reality, once secluded in the forest grove, though the initiates were subjected to various ordeals, part of what they were immediately taught was that the tale of the stitching of the anus was a fraud. Nevertheless, they were obliged to take a number of solemn oaths to keep this a secret. They

Editor's note: This chapter is a reprint of Moore, Sally Falk. 1976. "The secret of the men: A myth about Chagga initiation." *Africa* 46 (4): 357–70.

swore to conceal from children and young women the fact that they defecated. No young woman nor any child was ever to see them relieve themselves, nor find their feces. The secret was to be guarded at all costs, and any youth who fell ill was to be cared for by his fellows, not by a young wife. No doubt the closed anus was an open secret as far as many of the women were concerned (Gutmann 1926: 186; HRAF 1961: 164). Male feces were essential to the performance of the female initiation rites (Raum 1940: 350).

This peculiar tale requires explanation. Why was this the men's secret? Why construct this particular lie? What did it mean? It is not a sufficient explanation to remark on the psychoanalytic evidence of common, probably universal fantasies about fecal pregnancies, homosexual intercourse, and the like. These are so ordinary a phenomenon, and the Chagga initiation fiction so rare a one, that the first cannot explain the second. Why did the Chagga elaborate such dreamstuff by making it a part of an official cultural myth? The complete answer to such a question is probably not accessible, given the present state of knowledge about choices of symbols and the impossibility of recovering information on the invention of the myth. What is possible, though, is to show to what other circumstances of Chagga life and thought this particular set of ideas seems logically related. This also will provide an occasion for making some comments on dual symbolic classification, both as it pertains to Chagga symbolic orders, and in general.

The form of Chagga initiation that involved a collective period of seclusion in the forest has not been practiced for a long time. But fortunately, there are detailed accounts in the literature, which, if put together with evidence of other rituals and information culled in the field, enable one to propose an interpretation of the initiation myth that makes it seem far less anomalous. The mysterious notion of anal stitching can be shown to be a logical part of a larger system of related ideas. Current work in anthropology on dual symbolic classification has made it easier to put the pieces together than might have been the case at some earlier period (see particularly Needham 1973). With apologies for the pun, one might say that the idea that men are naturally closed and that women are naturally open lies at the bottom of the matter. Closed and open may thus be added to the many paired symbols already noted in the literature, as well as the contrasting images of females as defecators of feces and menstruators of blood, and males as retainers and containers of blood and feces.

In one layer of Chagga symbolic meaning, open is female, open as the vagina into which the penis goes, the opening or "door" out of which the child comes

(Gutmann 1926: 284; HRAF 1961: 254; Raum 1940: 352). A man has no vagina. He is closed in that place where a woman is open. In this sense, closed is male, open is female. A woman is open when she bears a child, open when she menstruates. She is closed when she is pregnant. Something closes and does not let the blood out, remains closed and does not let the child out until the right time (Gutmann 1932: 39; HRAF 1961: 25). A pregnant "closed" woman is at the height of procreativity and fertility. It is consistent that a man's closedness is also a part of his very masculinity. Chagga women say that the original *ngoso*, the original plug, the primeval masculine power and secret, once belonged to the women, and that it was stolen from them by the men (Gutmann 1926: 365; HRAF 1961: 329). This tale is ritually repeated at the time of female initiation and subsequently at the ritual of the covering of the breasts at the fifth month of pregnancy. Pregnancy, they say, is the female *ngoso*. The theft left women not only without a penis, but without a closed perineum. The plug that remains theirs is the uterine closing off of the flow of menstrual blood that occurs with pregnancy.

A closed woman is a pregnant woman. A closed (i.e., initiated man) is a procreative man. An open woman menstruates. An open man defecates. The symbolic paradigm, or rather one version of it, may be expressed thus:

$$(\text{male-closed-virile}) = (\text{female-closed-pregnant})$$
$$(\text{male-open-defecates}) = (\text{female-open-menstruates})$$

If anyone gets hold of a man's feces or a woman's menstrual blood, the person from whom these substances came can be made sterile. These sources of fertility may affect those who produced them, even after the effluvia have become separated from the body.

The vulnerability to sterility is connected with death. The man or woman who has no offspring dies, and his line dies, and that is the end of him, or her, the complete, absolute end. It is not just the end of life in this world, but the total end. The spirits of more fortunate people live on because of their access to their descendants' offerings. Without them they roam, dissatisfied, rapacious and miserable spirits who ultimately perish, disappear from memory. The capacity to procreate is also the capacity to guarantee oneself a peaceful immortality, a comfortable perpetuity as a link in the unending chain of ancestors and descendants. It is no accident that the Chagga did not inter the corpses of sterile and barren persons in the hut, nor preserve their skulls in the banana grove, but flung their bodies in the wilderness to be eaten by scavenging wild animals and to disappear from sight and memory, lest they and their unsatisfied ancestors disturb and trouble the living (Gutmann 1909: 131 ff.; Dundas 1924: 179). Their sterility might infect the earth.

Hence in Chagga thought openness and closedness are connected with sexuality and thus with life and death. These connections appear in other forms. It is supremely important that a parturient woman remain open, that nothing obstruct the passage of her infant into the world, or she will die or the baby will die. When a hut is constructed, the horizontal stays must never be closed lest this closing interfere with the openness of the birth canal of the child-bearing woman for whom the hut was constructed (Gutmann 1926: 284; HRAF 1961: 254). Openness is necessary for successful delivery. One of the birth anomalies most feared by the Chagga was that an infant be born without bodily openings. Such a birth (though who knows whether it actually occurred) was said to be an omen of disaster for the entire country (Raum 1940: 90). If that which should be open is closed, the meaning is death.

What is the meaning of a man's being closed? As he is already equipped with a closed perineum, why does the initiation myth suggest that his anus should be closed as well? A youth acquires the social right and theoretically the physical capacity to beget children from passing through initiation. What is the association between his begetting children and the fiction of the closed anus? The explicit link is actually quite simple. He must abstain from homosexual intercourse. If he violates this prohibition, a man may die. Once he has passed through initiation a man may be as fertile as any woman. Once he can beget children, he runs the risk of becoming pregnant or of impregnating another man through anal intercourse (Gutmann 1932: 31; HRAF 1961: 19). For a man to become pregnant in this way would mean death because, being closed, he has no birth canal out of which the child can pass (ibid.). The anus of the initiate is not literally plugged and stitched, but is figuratively so. He is *closed* to other men. He must never drink with uninitiated men lest when drunk he yield to anal intercourse and become pregnant. The initiation lesson of the plug is that from that time on the male anus is sealed for sexual purposes. To achieve fatherhood, to beget children, men must copulate with women and abjure other men. That is one of the meanings of the *ngoso*. It is tempting to speculate that an additional level of meaning may be that through the mythical stitching, a fictitious fecal pregnancy becomes a metaphorical part of maleness.

Faeces were used in a number of different ways in the boys' initiation ceremonies. At the very beginning of their period of seclusion in the forest, the initiates cleared a circular area and surrounded it with brambles and thorny bushes so that no one could enter except at a prescribed place. The innermost enclosure was itself surrounded by two further circles of brush. In the central clearing, two pits were dug, one for feces and one for urine. Spatial arrangements thus replicated anatomical preoccupations.

The novices were to use the two pits during their period of training. The fecal pit was deep, and anyone who fell into it was not to be rescued, but to be left to die. There were tales of past novices being pushed in by their comrades to terrify the youngsters (Gutmann 1926: 323; HRAF 1961: 290). The initiates were naked during their whole chilly ordeal, which took place during the cold months of the year. Every morning, they rubbed themselves with urine-wet mud from the shallow urine pit. This muddy coating was their sole clothing during the period of forest seclusion.

The fecal pit was "consecrated" before it was used. The Chief of the Grove was lowered into it on a rope as soon as the digging was completed. The pit was called "the bull." The Chief (head of the initiates' age-set) stretched himself out in the pit four times reciting benedictions to make the age-set procreative, and then ended by cursing anyone who dared to disobey him. Such a miscreant was cursed with sterility. Then the *lodana* was lowered into the pit and tried it out as the Chief had. The *lodana* was an older unmarried man who played the role of supervisor of the proceedings in the grove. In the pit he made the same tests and cast the same spells with some appropriate personal variations. "May the whole age-grade die out if you do not help me to find a wife so that I do not have to die without having procreated. May you rot like feces if you despise me . . ." (Gutmann 1926: 322–23; HRAF 1961: 290).

The urine pit, the fecal pit, and the myth of the plugged and stitched anus were part of the ritual explanation of how boys were transformed into men; *reborn* into men. The urine-mud coating may well have referred to the filth of birth and to the way an infant soils itself. During the first period of the forest ordeal each novice was fed like an infant by his sponsor, an older youth, often an elder brother, and not allowed to feed himself. Later, the young men were permitted to hunt their own food in the style of younger boys. Groups of them roamed the countryside with bows and arrows and hunted birds. They plucked and roasted and ate them. Bows and arrows were weapons used by Chagga men in warfare, and boys commonly used them (New 1874: 388–89). Birds were a food adult men were not allowed to eat (Raum 1940: 275). In addition to shooting birds, the novices participated in many ritual mock "hunts" in which the hunted beast was called a leopard or a lion or some other dangerous wild animal, but in reality the ferocious beasts shot were either plants, or very gentle animals such as gazelles (Raum 1940: 319). In their hunting forays, the youths sometimes passed through populated areas. They made loud noises and sang songs to frighten the women and children into their houses. There were thus at least three false dangers and three mock triumphs in the initiation process, the false stitching of the anus, the false hunting of dangerous animals, and the fake terrorizing of women and children. In one form or another, these are all fictitious representations of the fearlessness and fearsomeness of males and their maleness. Gutmann speculates that the symbolic hunting of initiation may once truly have involved pursuing dangerous animals and making raids on enemies, but one does not know how much weight to give this evolutionary hypothesis (Gutmann 1932: 15–17; HRAF 1961: 8–10).

What other meanings might the ritualized hunt have in the symbolic transformation of boys into men? The Chagga normally hunted very little, did not think much of it, and it had no importance in their economy (Raum 1940: 319). One symbolic key is in the analogy explicitly made by the Chagga between hunting for an animal and making/seeking a child. Throughout the Vunjo area of Kilimanjaro, in a subsequent, third phase of the initiation, the novices were instructed by means of a mnemonic "teaching stick," a notched, decorated, cane-like stick, incised with symbols relating to procreation (Gutmann 1932: 26 ff.; HRAF 1961: 15 seq.). In the ritual lessons explicating the markings on the stick, a fetus was likened to a trapped or arrow-pierced animal struggling to free itself (Gutmann 1932: 30; HRAF 1961: 19). In this imagery, an unborn child is closed in a womb trap. Birth is the struggle of the child to get out. There is also a good deal made of the *rubbing* of the raven on the arrow, of the rubbing of the crested antelope or the red deer in the pit, likely an allusion to intercourse. The hunting phase of the forest ordeal is thus explained. It is of interest that in the girls' initiation instruction there was also a mock hunt in which grasshoppers and tadpoles were caught and alluded to as "leopard" (Raum 1940: 353). These were explicitly designated as symbols of the human fetus. (One wonders whether this may not be part of the explanation of the hunting ritual in the Ndembu Nkula. See Turner 1964: 46.)

In Chagga male initiation, the ritual of the hunt was also connected with the ritual of the fecal pit. A piece of the meat of every animal killed in the hunt was used for a great oath sworn to again and again by the novices. The meat was dipped into the pit of the boys' feces. The youths then had to lick the meat and swear that they would never betray the secrets of initiation. The basic secret was the secret of the plug, the pledge that the defecation of men would not be revealed. The youths had to swear that if any of their age-mates fell ill with diarrhea, they would take care of them so that the secret would not be exposed. A young man who was ill could also turn to an old woman for help (Gutmann 1932: 561; HRAF 1961: 335). The secret had to be maintained to *control* young women and children. (When the German colonial government required the Chagga to install latrines to try to check the spread of various intestinal parasites, the Chagga built the latrines, but the men would not use them. Gutmann 1926: 324; HRAF 1961: 292.) Long after the initiation ceremonies of the grove had been abandoned, it was still not proper for a man to fart, and his wife or a child had to pretend to have done it (Gutmann 1932: 547; HRAF 1961: 326; Raum 1940: 318). A wife who complained of her husband's digestive disorders and said of his noisy innards that it was the "snake of life" speaking was being seriously disrespectful and had to make amends (Gutmann 1926: 186; HRAF 1961: 164). It was a major insult for a wife to say to her husband that he did, indeed, defecate (ibid.). Yet all the women must have known the men's secret or they could hardly have made excuses for them, or invented appropriate insults.

At the close of the procreative period (which formally came to an end the moment a man had a circumcised child) a man could "resume" defecating. It was said that in the old days an old man could perform a ritual which announced to his wife the removal of his "stitching." He and his lineage mates assembled and slaughtered a goat. He then tied pieces of goat meat to his thighs so that the blood would run down over his legs. The meat was removed, the wife of the old man called and told that the husband was bleeding because he had had his *ngoso* removed for the sake of his sons. From then on, her husband would defecate. But she was also told that should her husband fall ill, she should immediately come to his assistance and hide him; otherwise youngsters would deride him (Gutmann 1926: 325; HRAF 1961: 292). Whether this ritual was actually performed or not matters less than that the report of it was made, that Chagga talked about such an "ancient" custom.

On the last day of the initiation seclusion in the forest, the young men took the last of their solemn oaths by the pit of feces, the "bull." Into it they dipped locusts they had caught, licked the besmeared insects and swore never again to eat locust. Locusts were a favorite food of women and children. The young men swore that should they eat locust, the curse of initiation would cut through their connection with the ancestors and would make them sterile. The oath the instructor required of the novices was:

> I swear by the blood pact of all men. I swear by the blood pact of the initiation, never to betray any of its secrets. . . .

The initiation instructor responded saying,

> This is the blood pact of the men! This is your secret. The strokes which you received in this camp prohibit you from eating locusts henceforth. For if you eat the blood pact of man, that is, the locust which you licked, the curse of initiation will cut through your connection with the ancestors, and you will bear no offspring! . . . Liberate these creatures [the feces-dipped locusts] for they are our brothers with whom we made a blood pact. We may not harm them. (Raum 1940: 320, quoting Gutmann 1926: 326; Gutmann 1932: 544; Dundas 1924: 220)

This can be interpreted as a kind of symbolic triple pun. The locusts became the brothers of men. Men swore not to eat themselves, i.e., their own kind. The infantile prohibition on eating feces was extended to a prohibition on eating locust through the ritual doing of the forbidden. Eating was a metaphor for sexual contact, hence "eating locust" and "eating feces" were like the anal intercourse renounced by means of the mythical plugging and stitching.

Half a century after this part of the initiation ceremony had ceased to be performed, adult Chagga men still treated locusts as forbidden food (ibid.). A number of other adult food prohibitions are plainly related to the initiation. Men in the procreative years were not allowed to eat the rectum of animals, though this part might be specifically allocated to an old man past the virile years (Raum 1940: 331). Why were the pieces of meat which represented ferocious animals also dipped in feces and licked like the locusts? Did these, too, become prohibited foods thereafter? Were the Chagga like our biblical forbears, convinced that the only suitable meat for adult men was cattle meat? (See Douglas 1966: 41–57). According to present reports of some old Chagga men, that was the case.

Other foods were also used to distinguish the uninitiated from the initiated. Children and young persons not as yet circumcised could eat raw bananas, and when they ate roasted bananas, these had to be roasted with the skins still on them. Adults never ate raw bananas; and their roasted bananas were always peeled (Gutmann 1926: 181; HRAF 1961: 159). Even in 1974, adult men laughed uproariously when they were offered raw bananas by a European, and refused them. The symbolic referent of raw and cooked, unpeeled and peeled is doubtless circumcision, initiation and adult sexual life. The analogy between eating and sexual activity is a recurrent symbolic theme in Chagga custom and ritual, and it seems analogically related to the association between digestive contents and pregnancy. It is not surprising that some food taboos were symbols of the oaths, secrets and mysteries of initiation.

When the young initiates returned to their lineage areas after the end of the seclusion period, the senior lineage elder greeted them saying:

> Today I am giving you manhood. See to it that you do not betray it. If you sacrifice manhood, you betray the entire age grade, not only yourself. And if the children are allowed to see your "manhood" on the meadow, you bring disgrace upon yourself. Today, I am handing the *ngoso* to you, for I have grown old; you preserve it, you and your older brother. The country is a succession. We leave it to you to seize the *ngoso*, just as we have kept it. Today, I step aside and become like the women. I withdraw the *ngoso* from myself and hand it over to you. If you should see that I fall, you should come to my assistance and help be back on my feet and cover me and bring me safely home. And if you see my manhood do not assume that I still have the *ngoso* for I have given it to you. I am now on a par with a parturient woman. (Gutmann 1926: 336–37; HRAF 1961: 303–4)

There may be one more layer of meaning in the linking of feces with fertility. The Chagga were a people who manured their banana gardens with cow dung, and who themselves defecated in their banana gardens. Their knowledge of manuring predates any direct contact with Europeans in the nineteenth century. It was plainly an old practice, noted in the very earliest travelers' accounts. Chagga cows were kept stalled in the hut, and their dung was carefully collected and spread in the surrounding grove. Feces were thus connected with fertility through technical experience.

However, it would probably be a mistake to assume that in Chagga thought it was precisely a separable chemical property of manure that produced this effect. It was more likely something akin to what we would call a magical property that made manure a fertilizing substance. That is to say, it was an inherent quality of cow manure to cause fertility, just as it was thought that cow dung had a peaceful cooling effect and could be employed in ritual to protect one from angry, hot, dangerous things (Gutmann 1926: 277, 641; HRAF 1961: 248, 576). In traditional Chagga ideology, what was caused by a substance was part of its essence. Thus a poison had death-bringing in it. Manure had peaceful, cooling, fertility-causing, life-bringing in it.

Cattle manure was used in ritual as well as in agriculture to promote fertility. When women brought food gifts to a bride, she saved the woven pads of banana leaves on which they carried their head loads. Eventually, these were thrown on the dung heap in the hut to make the bride fertile. If they were thrown away somewhere else, she would be sterile (Gutmann 1926: 109, 115; HRAF 1961: 93, 99). Fresh cow manure was safely used to extinguish the ritual hearth-fire of marriage that promised children (Gutmann 1926: 343; HRAF 1961: 309). Gentleness was associated with the manure snake, the softness and suppleness of which were compared with the bones of an unborn child (Gutmann 1926: 109, 115; HRAF 1961: 93, 99). Manure was a tranquilizing medium, a pacifying substance with protective qualities, hence in hut-building ritual, the house rods were symbolically tied over the manure-place (Gutmann 1926: 277; HRAF 1961: 248).

Considering the practical and mystical powers of cattle manure, it does not seem illogical that human feces should be mythically represented to have qualities associated with male procreativity. The analogy is imperfect, however, since it was largely the manure of *cows*, that is, of female animals, which was used to fertilize the bananas. This serves as a reminder that these are overlapping symbols and intertwined ideas, not systematically consistent representations. A symbolic representation of the mystery of fertility is not a textbook of simple causes and effects.

The idea of anal plugging and stitching, the false secret that becomes a true closure (homosexual intercourse), the form of the oath not to reveal it (licking feces), and the imposition of the adult food taboos are all aspects of connected messages, all delivered in permutations of a metaphorical code. The ceremonies have to do with the mysteries of procreation, maleness and femaleness, and the puzzling connections among food, sex and life. The basic linking question seems to be, "What makes life?" The symbols and metaphors used to ask the question allude to mysterious connections both direct and analogic, with bodily orifices, with food and excretion, with sexual organs and intercourse, with things put into the body and things put out of the body.

The rituals of both sexes declare that they do not know the answer to the mysteries. Neither sex has the "secret." Somewhere in the fact that the men's secret is a fraud, there is a poignant statement that men do not have the secret, that they do not know the ultimate mystery of the making of life. The women's ritual states that the women once had the secret, but that the men stole it, and that all that is left is pregnancy. Hence the women, too, declare that they do not have the secret. The presence or absence of a penis and the presence or absence of the capacity to be pregnant may be the mutually envied anatomical facts, the two parts of the secret of life. But a statement inherent in the ritual of both sexes is that neither has the *whole* secret. The men claim it and everyone must pretend politely that the men have it, but all men and most women know that they do not. This is, then, not a matter of belief. The ritual message is not a mechanical representation of a believed-in reality (see Needham 1972). It is a matter of some kind of ritual collusion, of collective myth-making, of open secrets, the meaning of which lies as much in the underlying mystery, as in the surface representation.

It is particularly interesting to contrast this ritual view of procreation and its mysteries with a scientific observation made by the Chagga and known to them long before it became a part of European scientific data. The Chagga instructed young men about to marry that they should try to determine experimentally the precise day of the month on which their brides would be fertile. The husband was told to remember on which day of the wife's menstrual cycle they had had the intercourse which resulted in successful conception, and to use that day again the next time he wanted her to conceive (Gutmann 1932: 39; HRAF 1961: 24–25).

One of the interesting questions this initiation myth raises has to do with dual classification. If open is female and closed is male, what is to be understood from the Chagga view that women were closed when pregnant? Were they most like men at that time? Childbirth was formally likened to the ordeal of men at war. Women who had just given birth were hailed as warriors (Raum 1940: 85, 99). Were men perpetually mythically pregnant with feces in the metaphor of the myth? Is the open/closed duality one which minimizes the difference between the sexes, or one which stresses it? It could be argued that symbolically it accomplishes both at the same time. If this is so, what is one to understand from it about Chagga male/female classification, and what possible implications does this have for the analysis of dual classification in general?

Like many other systems of dual classification, in one symbolic order the Chagga associated men with strength and vigor and wellbeing, women with weakness and misfortune, men with the right hand and women with the left. It is a fact of nature that women are weaker than men in muscular strength, and are born and remain incomplete creatures insofar as the model of human completeness includes a penis. They grow up to bleed every month, a reminder to all of their castrated condition. Given a system of causal ideals such as that of the Chagga, in which everything has inherent qualities which may spread beyond itself, may remain in contact after separation, and infuse what it touches with its own qualities, it followed that these menstruating, castrated, weak characteristics of women were frightening and dangerous, and, so to speak, possibly contagious.

But it would be a mistake to stop there, or to go on to list all the other dual pairs that seem to parallel these distinctions between maleness and femaleness, because there is also a counter-pair in Chagga thought. In the counter-pair, it is women who are associated with strength and life-giving since they bear children and give milk, the primal food, and men who are associated with death, since they kill other men in war, and they are the slaughterers of animals. In fact, in pregnancy the menstrual blood itself becomes "the fountain of life" (Gutmann 1932: 40; HRAF 1961: 26). In this pair, women as mother/life-giving and men as killers, the two sexes appear in exchanged positions in relation to fortune and misfortune, to life and death. Yet with respect to right and left, left is always female, right is always male. That is, with regard to a symbol of the attributes of strength and weakness (fortunate virility and strength, and unfortunate castration and weakness) the places of male and female are fixed. However, with respect to their opposition in relation to life and death, male and female may occupy either side of the duality.

It is characteristic of Chagga dual symbolism that this reversibility with respect to life and death exists not only for male and female, but for the life-bringing/death-bringing referents of certain major ritual symbols, such as fire and water. Fire is in some contexts the hearth-fire, the cooking place, the bed of ashes associated with the female genitalia, in others, the fire-brand, the male organ. In both of these cases fire epitomizes life-bringing properties of the two sexes (Raum 1940: 35). In other contexts fire is the great destroyer that burns and consumes and brings death. It is water that can put out the fire that kills, water that can quench death-bringing thirst, water that is benign and cooling, water that together with some magical substances can be used to bless and purify and make all dangerous things peaceful. But water, too, can be violent, turbulent, angry, and it is possible to drown in it. Bad water can bring death. (For evil water, see Gutmann 1926: 633, 659, 669; HRAF 1961: 568, 593, 601; for fire as a killer, see Gutmann 1926: 632, 634; HRAF 1961: 567, 569; for benign water, see Gutmann 1926: 632, 633; HRAF 1961: 567, 568; for hearthfire, see Raum 1940: 352.)

Two other substances, blood and milk, also show similar dualities of aspect. Milk is the flow from the female breasts that feeds children, and from the cow that feeds one and all. Milk is the very source of a baby's life and the sign of a mother's recent childbearing. (There also can be bad mother's milk, the burning kind that makes babies ill. Gutmann 1926: 120; HRAF 1961: 103.) Milk is the gift of the cow and the sign of recent calving. But there is also *male* milk, the milky semen, the milk a man feeds the vaginal mouth to make his child (Gutmann 1932: 40, 431; HRAF 1961: 26, 252). In the making of children, fetuses are considered to be composed of male "milk" and female blood. Hence the milk of procreation is male and the milk of feeding is female. Menstrual blood is female and frightening, the epitome of non-pregnancy, of anti-maleness and castration. Female blood is also the fortunate blood of childbirth and the preparatory blood of female circumcision. But blood is also male. There is the blood of war and wounding, and the blood of cattle slaughtering that men shed and drink, and the blood of male circumcision. Male blood is hence also associated both with death and with procreation.

Blood and milk are both male and female. Blood and milk are both life-bringing and death-bringing. These are sets of dual classifications, but they are double classes, and classes in which the material symbolic elements may occupy opposite positions given appropriate qualifiers of occasion and type. Male and female, life and death, would seem to be the two axes. The two pairs may be in any combination, each pair the possible attribute of one member of the other pair.

Seen in this light, the puzzle of the plugged anus acquires an additional dimension. It is one more reiteration of Chagga ideas about maleness and femaleness and life and death. "May you rot like feces," is a curse of death (Gutmann 1926: 322–23; HRAF 1961: 290). In such an imprecation, feces stand for filth and the decomposition of corpses, feces are the death-stink embodied. But on the other side of the ledger is the ritual use of cow manure to purify, to cool, and to make peaceful the dangerous, hot and violent (Gutmann 1926: 277; HRAF 1961: 248). It is Chagga custom to offer the stomach contents of sacrificial animals to the ancestors, and sometimes the intestinal contents as well. In these contexts, stomach contents and feces are part of the life-maintaining process. I was told that the reason for offering stomach contents was that a beast's stomach is the very essence of its life; it would die without a stomach. Along with other perspectives the Chagga seem to have something of a digestive view of the location of the life force. In the old days women were (and many still are) fattened for three months after their first menstrual periods (now after marriage) and after childbirth. Fat women are "pregnant" with food instead of pregnant with child. The ideal of female beauty is a fat or pregnant young woman. Thus the taking in of food and the contents of the digestive tract are symbolically used to refer to fertility and well-being in some contexts as well as to death and to decomposition in others.

The initiation myth characterizes both the male and the female principles, one directly, the other by implication. The implication of the male closed anus is that defecating is for women, children and old men. Feces are mythologically fully absorbed by virile men, the way menstrual blood is by a pregnant woman. The symbolic equivalence of feces and menstrual blood was noted earlier. An explicit symbolic identification of excreta, menstrual blood, and milk was made in that part of the marriage ceremony in which the wish was expressed that the bride's loin band be soiled with the excrement of babies. At another point, the bride was given a spoonful of porridge called "the child's milk," which "is a covering term both for menstrual discharge and a child's excreta. Their identification is based on the belief that the former is a pledge of offspring for which the latter is the symbol" (Raum 1940: 108).

In their retained form, male feces, like female menstrual blood, are not death but life, not sterility but fertility. Menstrual blood turns from something dangerous into something that makes a child. In one sense, feces are female and a sign of weakness (also child-like and associated with weak old males), but the most positive use of feces is mythically made by virile males. Defecated feces are weak-female, retained feces are male-virile. But the truth which all the young initiates knew, and which, obviously many women also knew, is that men *do* defecate and *do not* carry fecal children, that the complete digestion of food by men is impossible, and that they are, in short, defecators like women.

This double association of femaleness and maleness, each and both with life and death and each and both with blood and milk and feces, helps reveal what seems to be a general circumstance about many Chagga symbolic categories: that they are dual and then doubled again. It may also explain in part why, though female is associated with the left, with misfortune and impurity and like negative categories, she is also associated with the luckiest number of the Chagga, the number four, which is used to announce the birth of a girl (Gutmann 1909: 107, 153; Raum 1940: 96, 97). Three is for males. It also may explain why, despite the negative connotation of femaleness in some dual symbolic categories, the blood wealth payment of the Chagga for a dead woman was said to be eight cattle and eight goats, while the same payment for a man was seven head of cattle and seven goats (Gutmann 1926: 243; HRAF 1961: 216). The answer proposed here is that female has two aspects: inauspicious, dangerous, menstruating, polluting, death-bringing castrated penis-less female, associated with the left when the left has a negative meaning, and the other aspect, pregnant, non-menstruating, child-bearing, maternal, feeding, life-bringing peaceful femaleness associated with the lucky number four. Equally male has two aspects: auspicious maleness associated with purity, cleanliness, strength, virility, completeness (i.e., having a penis), and other life-bringing qualities associated with the right. But maleness is also imbued with violence, the death-pollution of killing in war, animal slaughter, and characterized by male incompleteness in not bearing children and not producing milk-food.

Like any cattle-keeping, meat-eating people intent on breeding their stock, the Chagga kept the cows and slaughtered the steers. A female animal was worth more than a male, for she would produce many calves, while the male could only be slaughtered once. At the same time, a cow also produced milk and manure, food for people and plants. Hence in animal husbandry, females were more valued than males. How much this economic situation entered the mythologizing of the Chagga is hard to assess, but there is clearly a preoccupation with the problem of explaining, comparing and distinguishing male and female roles in procreation and with the comparative value of maleness and femaleness. Certainly there is ample human material for manufacturing sexual fantasies about faeces, milk, blood and pregnancy without depending upon a cattle economy to provide the elements for such ideological constructs. Yet one cannot help but wonder whether the daily use of cow manure and the dietary importance of cow milk, and the preoccupation with cow breeding and steer slaughtering did not provide some stimulus for choosing this set of symbols rather than some other for expressing basic sexual and cosmic riddles.

A few Chagga dual categories, right/left, male/female, life/death, fortune/misfortune, closed/open have been inspected here in the light of the Chagga ritual symbols which have dual or multiple aspects, such as fire, water, blood, milk and faeces. My purpose has been to argue that the male/female, life/death dichotomies are the most basic ones, and that some of the most perplexing psychological riddles are in sorting out the connections between and among these, which are all the more dramatized by attempts to divide them into separate and opposite categories.

Chagga cosmology makes a great deal of systematic sense once it becomes clear that in their system of ideas sexual reproductivity was the model of the most powerful forces of the universe. Some Chagga cursing instruments were decorated with male and female sexual organs, the symbolic agencies of the life and death power (Gutmann 1926: 668; HRAF 1961: 600). The proper combination of male and female created life. Improper sexual combination brought death. Marriage was the life-bringing opposite of incest or other illicit sexual acts which brought death. Hence either life or death could be the result of sexual contact. This paradox, this double meaning of sexuality, is an intimation of the terrible proximity of the life and death forces.

Since the combination of male and female could be either life-bringing or death-bringing, the partial segregation of things male and things female and their social and ritual regulation was a necessary precaution for the Chagga. Combination could take place only under specified conditions. One set of Chagga dual symbolic categories may be interpreted as an effort to stress such separateness and difference. But other simultaneous symbolic orders of the Chagga which have been noted overlap these lists of paired opposites and express in one symbol (which itself has dual or multiple aspects) the components of the dual order. Victor Turner's definitional characterization of dominant ritual symbols as condensing disparate significata applies here (1964). It may be useful to carry the inquiry into disparate referents still further and ask whether the puzzling quality of such multiple meanings does not in itself contain a message. It may be like the sexual "secret" of the Chagga, which neither men nor women "have." If part of the message of these symbols is that there is an underlying riddle that cannot be solved, a riddle about the source and meaning of life, then the fact that all the qualities and elements associated with the Chagga dual categories are not neatly dichotomous, not altogether discrete and exclusive and not consistently systematic is itself part of the meaning of the "system" of symbols. Comprehensible limited surface orders and underlying unfathomable riddles about meaning and relationship may be the very things that are being represented.

It is my argument that the relation of systems of dual symbolic categories to other symbolic classifications may be illumined by inspecting them as attempts to represent just such paradoxical questions *as questions*. Needham has said, "A society need not, after all, employ only a single mode of classification" (1973: xxiii). He goes on to say that "the delineation of a dual classification . . . [does not] . . . imply that this is the only possible order to be found in the facts, or that the people themselves subscribe to no other conventional division of phenomena" (ibid.: xx). A deeper solution is implicit in Needham's remark that, "In the Nyoro case, as usually elsewhere, we have discovered our crucial evidence in the circumstances of birth, the relations between the sexes, and death" (ibid.: 331). In looking at the Chagga material one may ask whether the dichotomies life/death and male/female would not take one more quickly to the heart of their symbolic categories than an investigation that commences with left/right. "These passionate concerns" are what such symbolic orders are all about (ibid.).

The focus on dual categories and their orderliness may have distracted some academic attention from the connected circumstance that these symbolic orders seem invariably to concern the very matters which in a deep sense are least accessible to orderly explanation. Recent scholarly curiosity has often proceeded as Hertz did, from hands to other categorical dualities, rather than from the ways in which symbols, paired or otherwise ordered, embody the universal "passionate concerns" and propose causal explanations (Hertz 1909). Even within a system of dual categories there may be evidence, as there seems to be in the Chagga material, that male/female, life/death are much more fundamental dichotomies than left/right. These may be more fundamental not only as human concerns, but as more dominant cultural categories. The evidence for this in Chagga dual symbolism is necessarily impaired by the fact that there is no way to know at this late date whether lists of symbols gleaned from Gutmann and others are comprehensive. For what it is worth, the evidence from Gutmann and Raum generates a substantially longer list of ritual symbols that have as one of their referents male/female or life/death (fortune/misfortune) than have the connotation left/right. The left/right classification seems to have a more limited transformational range in the dual series, and this may be evidence that it is subsidiary.

Questions about transformational range might profitably be asked on a comparative basis about particular pairs within dual symbolic sets. I have not been able to discover a Chagga cultural context in which the open/closed pair with which this paper began is *directly* linked to a left/right pair, though both pairs of symbols have female/male meanings. There are dangers in arguments based on an absence of available evidence. However, if reasonably substantiated, it may be that breaks in transformational range could tell us something interesting about the analogic relational chains that constitute dual classificatory systems.

PART FOUR

Social Fields and their Politics

In this section, attention focuses on intentional attempts to regulate social fields. Governments do it. So do organizations. And so do myriad other types of action touching on social order. The results are by no means straightforward. To put any new official legal plan into effect in a social field, existing relationships and commitments may have to be modified or replaced or simply ignored. Those existing ties may prove to be durable, or they may engender related or independent alternatives. More subversive reactions to the official attempt to shape a social field can, of course, generate direct counter-tactics. This applies to law as well as to other regulatory attempts. But all is not simple domination and resistance, as some politically attractive but simplified interpretations would have it. For the anthropologist of today, it is the simultaneity of many goings-on, thrusting in many directions, that complicates and enlarges the scope of analysis.

Working in the shifting, kaleidoscopic setting of postcolonial societ, and in the presence of agencies of the Western and global world, anthropological fieldwork today requires multidirectional alertness. It must simultaneously take account of immediate situational features of activities and ideas, yet focus on longer term and larger scale processes to the extent that they can be discerned. Given that there is an element of chance in the actions and expressions observed at a particular moment, there is a question of what elements of the observed practice will be durable, and whether they represent change or momentary variability. Thus there are are least two uncertainties in the processual approach to fieldwork, one is the element of chance in what is observed at a particular time, and the other is the element of subjectivity in interpreting the larger significance of what is happening.

The essays in this section address various forms of organization from three perspectives. The first essay, introduces the concept of the **semi-autonomous social field.** *Instead of thinking of a governed domain as fully under the discipline of its law and its officials, this concept suggests that within many a governed polity there are self-ordering groups and relationships that have a life of their own, and their own rules and practices. If the relationship of law to social organization and action is to be understood, the simultaneous life of these moving sub-fields must be understood in their ongoing activities and sources of authority,*

The second essay takes up the role of mandatory public political meetings as legitimators of a postcolonial "socialist" government in Tanzania. There, in the late-twentieth-century, nationally directed public assemblies of citizens were officially interpreted as popular instances of voluntary participation. Such meetings served the state as **"ratifying bodies public."** *The occasion was wrapped in a mythology that all suggestions for government action supposedly came from "the people" as expressed on these occasions. The themes to be discussed at the meetings were, in fact, enunciated by local Party leaders, no doubt guided by higher Party entities, since the same themes appeared in different localities at the same time. In the written record kept by the local Party branch, the meetings were classified as assemblies of the citizens of a particular area. Few of the citizens of the area actually attended, but that fact was concealed in the nomenclature of locality. No comments were made in any form about the number who came. The meeting was simply recorded as a meeting of the citizens of x. . . . When formally addressed by Party officials, those present were silent and seemed to be paying attention. Listening in that way was taken to signify agreement. This putative simulation of public support was thus achieved and put in the record. This strategy was not unique to postcolonial Tanzania.* **Ratifying bodies public** *have been mounted and used by dictatorships around the world to simulate general popular suppport.*

The third essay describes cases in which third world governments found themselves unable to implement particular plans because more attractive alternatives were available. The instances presented here did not involve the mass mobilization of citizens for anti-government action. They were occasions when the self-interest of individuals made them choose an alternative course of action. The depowering of the government was a side-product of their individual action, not a directed, organized counterplan. The generality of the terms "domination" and "resistance" conceals the dynamic variety that can manifest itself in types of disobedience. An emphasis on the nuances of process brings these differences into analytic focus. A more differentiated understanding emerges of the impossibilities deep within any attempt to exert political control.

CHAPTER ELEVEN

Law and Social Change
The Semi–Autonomous Social Field as an
Appropriate Subject of Study

> *We must have a look at society and culture at large in order to find*
> *the place of law within the total structure.*
> – E. Adamson Hoebel, *The law of primitive man* (1954: 5)

In our highly centralized political system, with its advanced technology and communications apparatus, it is tempting to think that legal innovation can effect social change. Roscoe Pound perceived the law as a tool for social engineering (1965: 247–52).[1] Some version of this idea is the current rationale for most legislation. Underlying the social engineering view is the assumption that social arrangements are susceptible to conscious human control, and that the instrument by means of which this control is to be achieved is the law. In such formulations

Editor's note: This chapter is a reprint of Moore, Sally Falk. 1973. "Law and social change: The semi-autonomous social field as an appropriate subject of study." *Law and Society Review* 7: 719–46.

1. I acknowledge with gratitude a grant from *The Joint Committee on African Studies* and *The Social Science Research Council* given me in 1968 and 1969 which made this fieldwork possible. I also wish to thank Professor Max Gluckman for his helpful comment on this paper.

"the law" is a short term for a very complex aggregation of principles, norms, ideas, rules, practices, and the activities of agencies of legislation, administration, adjudication, and enforcement, backed by political power and legitimacy. The complex "law," thus condensed into one term, is abstracted from the social context in which it exists, and is spoken of as if it were an entity capable of controlling that context. But the contrary can also be persuasively argued, that "it is society that controls law and not the reverse . . ." (Cochrane 1971: 93–94). This semantic morass is partly the result of the multiplicity of referents of the terms "law" and "society." But both ways of describing the state of affairs have the same implication for the sociological study of law. Law and the social context in which it operates must be inspected together. As Selznick has said, there is no longer any need "to argue the general interdependence of law and society" (1959: 115). Yet although everyone acknowledges that the enforceable rules stated and restated in legal institutions, in legislatures, courts and administrative agencies, also have a place in ordinary social life (Bohannan 1965), that normal locus is where they are least studied. (See, for example, the emphasis on the study of official behavior in the recent Chambliss and Seidman 1971, and on dispute settlement in much of the recent anthropological literature, cf. Moore 1969c. A significant exception is the emphasis on "law-in-society" in Friedman and Macaulay 1969.)

Both the study of official behavior and the study of dispute settlement have been very productive. Schapera (1970), in his study of Tswana chiefs, has produced the only anthropological study of tribal legislation and social change, and a very interesting work it is. Thus it is without any critical animus that this paper will suggest that there are other productive approaches as well, that it may be useful for some purposes to return to the broad conceptions of Malinowski (1926: 23) who set out to "analyse all the rules conceived and acted upon as binding obligations, to find out the nature of the binding forces, and to classify the rules according to the manner in which they are made valid." Malinowski looked at ordinary Trobriand behavior to find this material. For reasons I hope to make clear, this breadth of approach applied to a narrow field of observation seems particularly appropriate to the study of law and social change in complex societies.

The approach proposed here is that the small field observable to an anthropologist be chosen and studied in terms of its semi-autonomy—the fact that it can generate rules and customs and symbols internally, but that it is also vulnerable to rules and decisions and other forces emanating from the larger world by which it is surrounded. The semi-autonomous social field has rule-making capacities, and the means to induce or coerce compliance; but it is simultaneously set in a larger social matrix which can, and does, affect and invade it, sometimes at the invitation of persons inside it, sometimes at its own instance. The analytic problem of fields of autonomy exists in tribal society, but it is an even more central analytic issue in the social anthropology of complex societies. All the nation-states of the world, new and old, are complex societies in that sense. The analytic problem is ubiquitous.

Much as we may agree with Professor Hoebel that force, legitimately applied (or the threat of its application), is a useful criterion for distinguishing legal norms from others for certain analytic purposes, an emphasis on the capacity of the modern state to threaten to use physical force should not distract us from the other agencies and modes of inducing compliance (Pospisil 1971: 193–232; Weber 1954: 15). Though the formal legal institutions may enjoy a near monopoly on the legitimate use of force, they cannot be said to have a monopoly of any kind on the other various forms of effective coercion or effective inducement. It is well established that between the body politic and the individual, there are interposed various smaller organized social fields to which the individual "belongs." These social fields have their own customs and rules and the means of coercing or inducing compliance (see Pospisil on "Legal levels and multiplicity of legal systems," 1971: 97–126). They have what Weber called a "legal order." Weber argued that the typical means of statutory coercion applied by "private" organizations against refractory members is exclusion from the corporate body and its tangible or intangible advantages, but that they also frequently exert pressure on outsiders as well as insiders (Weber 1954: 18–19).

Weber also recognized the difficulties of effectuating successful legislative coercion in the economic sphere. He attributed these difficulties partly to the effects of the complex interdependence of individual economic units in the market, partly to the fact that, "the inclination to forego economic opportunity simply in order to act legally is obviously slight, unless circumvention of the formal law is strongly disapproved by a powerful convention . . ." (Weber 1954: 38). He was also very much aware of the chances of getting away with non-compliance, among other things, because:

> It is obvious . . . that those who continuously participate in the market intercourse with their own economic interests have a far greater rational knowledge of the market and interest situation than the legislators and enforcement officers whose interest is only ideal. In an economy based on all-embracing interdependence in the market, the possible and unintended repercussions of a legal measure must to a large extent escape the foresight of the legislator simply because they

depend upon private interested parties. It is those private interested parties who are in a position to distort the intended meaning of a legal norm to the point of turning it into its very opposite, as has often happened in the past. (ibid.)

This paper will argue that an inspection of semi-autonomous social fields strongly suggests that the various processes that make internally generated rules effective are often also the immediate forces that dictate the mode of compliance or noncompliance to state-made legal rules. It will also argue a methodological point: that the semi-autonomous social field is *par excellence* a suitable way of defining areas for social anthropological study in complex societies. It designates a social locale to which anthropological techniques of inquiry and observation can be applied in urban as well as rural settings. By definition it requires attention to the problem of connection with the larger society. It is an area of study to which a number of current techniques could be fruitfully applied in combination: network analysis (Mitchell, et al. 1969), transactional analysis (Barth 1966), the analysis of negotiation (Gulliver 1963, 1969), the politics of corporate groups (Smith 1966), situational analysis and the extended case method (Garbett 1970; Van Velsen 1967; Turner 1957), and the analysis of public explanations made in normative terms (Gluckman 1955, 1965b; Moore 1970).

The semi-autonomous social field is defined and its boundaries identified not by its organization (it may be a corporate group, it may not) but by a processual characteristic, the fact that it can generate rules and coerce or induce compliance to them. Thus an arena in which a number of corporate groups deal with each other may be a semi-autonomous social field. Also the corporate groups themselves may each constitute a semi-autonomous social field. Many such fields may articulate with others in such a way as to form complex chains, rather the way the social networks of individuals, when attached to each other, may be considered as unending chains. The interdependent articulation of many different social fields constitutes one of the basic characteristics of complex societies.

The concept of a semi-autonomous social field puts emphasis on the issues of autonomy and isolation, or rather, the absence of autonomy and isolation, as well as focusing on the capacity to generate rules and induce or coerce conformity. It is the issue of semi-autonomy that principally differentiates this definition of the problem from a purely transactional one. In Barth's model, he has analyzed the ways in which new values and norms can be generated in transactions

(1966). But in each of the cases of change he discusses, the chain of change has been initiated outside the transacting field, whether it is technological change in the case of the herring fishermen, or a road and imposed peace in the case of the Swat Pathans, or a demographic change in Iraq. In Barth's examples, it is after the initial change reaches the social field that transactions generate new norms and values. In Barth's model, rules "evolve." They emerge from many individual transactions and choices which cumulate in new norms and values. There is no doubt that some norms develop in this way and that his model is very useful. But norms are also legislated by governments, or dictated by administrative and judicial decisions, or imposed in other intentional ways by private agencies. These impinge on semi-autonomous social fields which already have rules and customs.

One of the most usual ways in which centralized governments invade the social fields within their boundaries is by means of legislation. But innovative legislation or other attempts to direct change often fail to achieve their intended purposes; and even when they succeed wholly or partially, they frequently carry with them unplanned and unexpected consequences. This is partly because new laws are thrust upon going social arrangements in which there are complexes of binding obligations already in existence. Legislation is often passed with the intention of altering the going social arrangements in specified ways. The social arrangements are often effectively stronger than the new laws. It is not with any optimism about practical consequences that it is suggested that semi-autonomous social fields are of anthropological interest. It is rather because studies in the nature of the autonomy and the quality of their self-regulation may yield valuable information about the processes of social life in complex societies.

To illustrate these points, this paper will sketch the outlines of two quite different social fields—one in the United States, and one in Africa today. The first is a small segment of the dress industry in New York. I have not done fieldwork in the garment industry; the information comes from having spoken with some people involved in it and reading some books. No attempt has been made to deal directly with the issue of change in the dress industry example, since the purpose of the illustration is simply to show how a semiautonomous social field works, some of the internal and external links it has, and how legal, illegal and nonlegal norms all intermesh in the annual round of its activities. The African material was gathered in fieldwork among the Chagga of Mount Kilimanjaro in 1968 and 1969.

MUTUAL OBLIGATION, LEGAL AND NON-LEGAL, IN THE BETTER DRESS LINE

The production of expensive ready-made women's dresses in New York is divided between the *jobber's* establishment, where the designing is done, and in whose showroom garments are displayed to retailers, and the *contractor's* workshop, where the cloth is cut and the dresses are actually made. Some jobbers are themselves designers, some hire a designer. In either case the designing is done at the jobber's end of the arrangement. Sometimes the jobber also maintains a small workshop, an "inside shop" to produce a few garments, but if he is doing well, the inside shop is never large enough to handle all his manufacturing, so he must use outside contractors in addition. The view from the contractor's shop is the one taken here as this was the part of the industry with which my informant was associated.[2]

The garment trade at this level is very volatile, dependent upon the vagaries of fashion, subject to great seasonal changes. At one moment there may be a great glut of work and not nearly enough machines or workers or time to meet some burst of demand for a particular line of garments. At other times business may be very slack, with barely enough work to keep things moving. It is a piecework industry.

The jobber makes a sizable capital investment in the showroom, in the designer, in other skilled personnel, and in the fabric with which a garment is to be made. The jobber supplies the fabric to the contractor. If the jobber does not have the capital to buy the fabric, he may borrow from a *factor* who lends money for this purpose for interest. The jobber may not get his money back on his investment until the next season, and so the factor may have to wait some months for his repayment. Two key people in the establishment of the jobber are his production man, who works out the details of the arrangements concerning the contractors (how much work is to go to each contractor, which style, what the price paid to the contractor is to be for each style, etc.), and his examiner, who looks over the garments after they have been made by the contractor to see that they meet the designer's specifications and the jobber's standards. She sends garments back for reworking if she does not find them up to the standards of the house.

---

2.   The information on which this account is based was obtained from an informant who has had many years of close contact with the dress industry in New York.

On his side, the contractor must have a going establishment, a capital investment in a workshop and machinery, and a group of skilled workers in his employ, the most important of whom is the "floor lady." The "floor lady" not only supervises much of what goes on in the shop, on the workroom floor, but she also is strategically important in negotiations with the jobber's production man, since she and he are the people who bargain out what the price of any garment shall be. She is also the principal trade-union representative in the shop, and represents the workers vis-a-vis the contractor. She leads in deciding what garments they are willing to make and which they are not, since some work is much harder than other work.

There is another figure of importance, on the union side, and that is the union business agent. He is a fulltime employee of the union, and it is his job to see that union rules are obeyed both by the boss-contractor and by the union workers. He also collects dues and has other administrative functions. The basic union contract in which these rules are spelled out is a contract between an association of contractors and jobbers and the International Ladies' Garment Workers' Union. This contract specifies such things as wages and hours. However the exigencies of the business are such that it would be impossible to make a profit unless the precise terms of these contracts were regularly broken. For one thing, when the opportunity arises to do a lot of work, it has to be done quickly or there is nothing to be gained. A design will sell at one particular moment, and not at any time thereafter. Hence, when business is plentiful, workers and contractors must produce dresses in a hurry and put in many more hours than the union contracts permit. On the other hand, when business is slack, workers must be paid even when they are not in fact working. The floor lady, for example, since she is the person in the most favored position in the contractor's shop, may be paid while she cruises around the world on vacation. It is simply understood between the union's business representative and the contractor that he will not enforce the contract to the letter. Presumably any alteration of the labor contract which would make its terms more closely approximate the actual seasonal conditions of the dress business would have undesirable side effects. That part of the bargaining position of the union that depends on overlooking violations would be impaired.

In return for his "reasonableness," the union representative receives many favors from the contractor. He may be given such tokens as whiskey in quantity at Christmas. The contractor may make dresses for his wife (which at the rate of $300 retail value per dress means that three dresses constitute a sizable present). He may present gifts on all the occasions of domestic rites—a child's birth, a child's graduation, marriage, or whatever. The contractor may, over the long term, develop a relationship with the union business agent, in which he visits him in the hospital when he is ill and has a general stance of solicitude and concern for his affairs. Like a concerned kinsman, the contractor may put the union man in touch with a doctor he knows, or try to get occupational advice for the union man's son. The person who is in charge of the gift of dresses to the union man's wife is the floor lady, who will either make them in part herself or supervise their production. She also is a significant figure in the making of "gift" dresses for other persons, most notably for the jobber's production man, whom the contractor must sweeten regularly in order to assure himself that business will come his way. A contractor may develop the same kind of solicitous relationship of giving gifts and performing favors with a few important production men. The examiner is another person who also must be given gifts to insure that everything will go smoothly when she looks over the finished garments produced at the contractor's shop.

All these givings of gifts and doings of favors are done in the form of voluntary acts of friendship, and the occasions when they are given are holidays such as Christmas or other times when this would be in keeping with a relationship of friendship. None of them are legally enforceable obligations. One could not take a man to court who did not produce them. But there is no need for legal sanctions where there are such strong extra-legal sanctions available. The contractor has to maintain these relationships or he is out of business.

The union contract with the association is legally binding, and the activities of the union man and the contractor regularly violate these legally enforceable provisions. They both recognize the business necessity of doing so and engage in repeated exchanges that demonstrate mutual trust. The union man closes his eyes, and the contractor makes dresses for the union man's wife. A satisfactory balance is achieved.

The contractor also depends on his workers to keep mum on this subject, to work the extra hours when these are needed in return for other favors at other times. He also may depend on his workers in other ways. As the garment workers, many of them married women, normally put a substantial part of their earnings into savings banks, they represent a source for loans when the contractor needs capital. The contractor himself may be a convenient source for loans to production men. Production men are salaried in the jobber's establishment, but not infrequently have outside deals in which they want to invest to earn extra dollars. They may appeal to the contractor to help them out. The jobber, too, may depend on the contractor for what are virtual loans. He may count on the contractor not to press for payment of what is owed him for the work done. This amounts to many months' extension of credit, and virtually an interest free loan.

The discussion thus far of the exchanges of favors has not mentioned flattery and sexual attentions, which are also used in the relationships between the contractor and the various women, both in his own establishment and in the jobber's place. Not only gifts, but other attentions may well accompany the more concrete evidence of esteem.

All these extra-legal givings can be called "bribery" if one chooses to emphasize their extra-legal qualities. One could instead use the classical anthropological opposition of moral to legal obligations and call these "moral" obligations, since they are obligations of relationship that are not legally enforceable, but which depend for their enforcement on the values of the relationship itself. They are all gifts or attentions calculated to induce or ease the allocation of scarce resources. The inducements and coercions involved in this system of relationships are founded on wanting to stay in the game, and on wanting to do well in it.

What general principles are suggested by this material on the dress industry? What processes can be identified? For one thing, there would appear to be a pervasive tendency to convert limited instrumental relationships into what are, at least in form and symbol, friendships. It may be that just as fictive kinship is associated with societies in which public organization is ideologically conceived as based on criteria of descent and marriage, so, in societies like our own, in which public organization is ideologically conceived as voluntary, many obligatory, public, strongly instrumental relationships take on the forms and symbols of friendship (see Paine 1969, on friendship and its definition). One might call these "fictive friendships." These fictive friendships are part of the process by which scarce resources are allocated. The flow of prestations, attention, and favors in the direction of persons who have it in their power to allocate labor, capital, or business deals, may be thought of as the "price of allocation." The "price of allocation" is symbolically represented as an unsolicited gift, the fruit of friendship.

Despite the symbolic ambience of choice, there are strong pressures to conform to this system of exchange if one wants to stay in this branch of the garment industry. These pressures are central to the question of autonomy, and the relative place of state-enforceable law as opposed to the binding rules and customs generated in this social field.

This complex, the operation of the social field, is to a significant extent self-regulating, self-enforcing, and self-propelling within a certain legal, political, economic, and social environment. Some of the rules about rights and obligations that govern it emanate from that environment, the government, the marketplace, the relations among the various ethnic groups that work in the industry, and so on. But many other rules are produced within the field of action itself. Some of these rules are produced through the explicit quasi-legislative action of the organized corporate bodies (the Union, the Association) that regulate some aspects of the industry. But others, as has been indicated, are arrived at through the interplay of the jobbers, contractors, factors, retailers, and skilled workers in the course of doing business with each other. They are the regular reciprocities and exchanges of mutually dependent parties. They are the "customs of the trade." (Compare an anthropological account of three garment shops in Manchester, Lupton and Cunnison 1964).

The law is obviously a part of this picture. Surely were it not for the vast amount of pertinent labor law, the union representative would never have come to have the powerful position he occupies. He would not be an allocator of scarce resources. He may not, in fact, enforce the actual terms defining wages and hours in the contract with the union, but it is his legal ability to do so that gives him something to exchange. Were it not for the legal right of the contractor to collect promptly the bills owed him by the jobber, his restraint in not pressing for collection would not be a favor. It is because he has the legal right to collect and does not do so that he has something to give. Thus legal rights can be used as important counters in these relationships. Stewart Macauley has called attention to a number of these issues in his paper on "non-contractual relations in business" (1963).

Many legal rights in this setting can be interpreted as the capacity of persons inside the social field to mobilize the state on their behalf. Just so the capacity to mobilize the union or the association of jobbers and contractors are important counterweights in the business dealings which are carried on in the dress industry. Looked at from the inside, then, the social field is semi-autonomous not only because it can be affected by the direction of outside forces impinging upon it, but because persons inside the social field can mobilize those outside forces, or threaten to do so, in their bargainings with each other.

It would take this discussion far afield to enumerate all the laws that impinge on the individuals in the garment industry, from traffic laws to the rights and obligations of citizenship, but it is useful to emphasize that of the tremendous body of rules that envelop any social field, only some are significant elements in the bargaining, competing, and exchanging processes, while the rest are, so to speak, in the background. Moreover, the moment that one focuses attention on these processes of competition, negotiation, and exchange, one becomes equally aware of the importance of binding rights and obligations that are not legally enforceable. The legal rules are only a small piece of the complex.

The penalty for not playing the game according to the rules—legal, non-legal, and illegal—in the dress industry is: economic loss, loss of reputation, loss of goodwill, ultimate exclusion from the avenues that lead to money-making. Compliance is induced by the desire to stay in the game and prosper. It is not unreasonable to infer that at least some of those legal rules that are obeyed, are obeyed as much (if not more) because of the very same kinds of pressures and inducements that produce compliance to the non-legal mores of the social field rather than because of any direct potentiality of enforcement by the state. In fact, many of the pressures to conform to "the law" probably emanate from the several social *milieux* in which an individual participates. The potentiality of state action is often far less immediate than other pressures and inducements.

THE CHAGGA OF MOUNT KILIMANJARO

The recent history of the Chagga tribe has been repeatedly looked to as a model of successful "development." A hundred years ago, the Chagga were divided into many tiny warring chiefdoms, which raided each other for women, cattle and presumably also for control of the slave and ivory trade routes. Today, the Chagga are the most prosperous and worldly tribe in Tanzania. Symbolic of deeper changes are the visible ones; from a time when they were earringed, spear-carrying Kichagga-speaking warriors, they have become trousered, shirt-wearing, Swahili-speaking farmer-citizens of a socialist state. There is a transistor radio in the village bar. Along with broadcasting government news broadcasts, the radio brings American rock music on the Nairobi hit parade. For eighty years the Chagga have been proselytized by industrious Catholic and Protestant missionaries who enjoyed being posted to the mountain climate. Today most Chagga are Christians, a few are Muslims, and still fewer continue to adhere exclusively to the Chagga religion. Most have been to school and many are literate in some degree. Chagga prosperity comes in a large measure from the production of coffee which has been cultivated on

Kilimanjaro for many decades. Since the 1920s, the Chagga have sold into the world markets the coffee grown in their family gardens. It has been auctioned off through their African-owned cooperative, the Kilimanjaro Native Cooperative Union. Hence they have long been involved in a partially cash economy.

The myriad concomitant changes, societal and legal, which have taken place in Chagga life in this century are too numerous to specify here, but it is useful to have a look at certain aspects of the Independent Government's recent attempts to legislate socialism into existence, and to consider in some detail how these impinge on an ongoing social system with deep roots in the past. Since we live in a period in which the potential effectiveness of central planning and the use of law as the tool of the social engineer are heavily emphasized, it is perhaps worth stressing what is probably obvious, that by no means all, nor even the most important social changes necessarily get their principal impetus from legislated or other legal innovations, even in centrally planned systems. A corollary proposition is probably equally obvious, that the effect of legislative innovations is frequently not what was anticipated, though perhaps with adequate sociological analysis, it might have been predicted.

Legislation consists of conscious attempts at social direction. But, clearly, societies are in the grip of processes of change quite outside this kind of control. On Kilimanjaro two such unplanned processes have been under way for some time: the changes consequent on the introduction of the cash cropping of coffee, and the changes in the availability of land after the explosion of the Chagga population. These have both profoundly affected the context of operation of Chagga law. On the side of intentional social control is much of the recent legislation of the Independent Government intended to promote a socialist egalitarianism. In Chaggaland, some of this legislation can be shown to have had only very limited effects. Traditional Chagga social relationships are proving to have remarkable durability despite the efforts of hardworking social planners in Dar es Salaam to substitute new arrangements for the old.

For example, in 1963, the Independent Government declared that from then henceforth there would no longer be any private freehold ownership in land, since land as the gift of God can belong to no man but only to all men, whose representative was the Government. [The Freehold Title (Conversion and Government Leases) Act (1963). Cf. P. J. Nkambo Mugerwa, "Land tenure in East Africa: Some contrasts," *East African Law Today* (British Institute of International and Comparative Law, Commonwealth Law Series, No. 5, 1966).]

All freehold land was converted into government leaseholds by this act, and improperly used land was to be taken away.

If this Act of 1963 is to be taken as a statement of ideology in an agrarian socialist state, it makes sense. The means of production must not be privately held in such a polity. But as an operationalized piece of legislation in the context of Chagga life, it has had very limited and rather specialized results, since though no one "owns" the land any longer, most people in general have precisely the same rights of occupation and use they had before, to say nothing of contingent rights in the lands of kinsmen, an important element in these days of land shortage. What has been changing drastically over the past few decades in Chaggaland are not the formal legal rules about land rights (these being governed largely by customary law), but the actual ratio of population to land, a change not engineered by any legislation, nor planned by any administrative authorities.

In 1890 land was plentiful on Kilimanjaro. Those were the days when its green slopes were populated by perhaps a hundred thousand Chagga tribesmen who were organized into dozens of small autonomous chiefdoms, each divided from the others by some natural barrier—a deep ravine with a stream, or a wall of high hills. In each chiefdom here and there between the homesteads were some open meadows where fodder could be cut for Chagga cattle and where newcomers could settle. Today there probably are about 400,000 Chagga living on the mountain. The results of this population explosion are being felt at every hand. The shortage of land will soon be severe. More and more huts and houses are built, on ever-shrinking plots. Each house must have a garden around it to support the household. These gardens are crammed with vegetation. At the highest level are the tall banana plants, below them the coffee bushes, and under these the vegetables. The banana is the traditional staple food of the Chagga and the vegetables are also usually for domestic consumption. The coffee is sold for cash.

Each homestead and garden is contiguous to several others. A tangle of such homestead-gardens forms a several-mile-wide band, the banana belt, that rings the mountain. The open lands are all but gone. As in the past, there are no villages. Dwellings and gardens lie one right next to another for miles with narrow winding footpaths between them. A single main road, wide enough for cars, but unpaved and intermittently muddy for many months of the year, cuts through the central banana belt and winds around most of the mountain. A few feeder roads lead down from it and give access to the hot dry lowlands below. Here and there along the main road today one sees a market place, a school, a church, a courthouse, a small collection of tiny stores, a butcher shop, and a beer shop. These clusters constitute Kilimanjaro's civic centers. Otherwise, the banana belt is a continuous string of households and gardens.

The cultivation of coffee has meant that many goods and services purchasable for cash have become available on the mountain. This has opened secondary, non-farming occupations to some men. Land itself, formerly never bought or sold can now be had for cash if the would-be buyer can find someone willing to sell. Long ago, in the days of plenitude of land, a man wishing to settle in an area could have obtained a plot quite easily from a hospitable lineage not unhappy to increase its local male strength, or from a chief wishing to increase the number of his subjects. Now a man must inherit land, be allocated it by his father in his lifetime, or buy it. The government has recently added to these options the possibility of moving away from the mountain to pioneer in unsettled areas of Tanzania in return for a plot of land. Most men do not want to move away.

The opportunities to accumulate the cash to buy land are few. On the whole they are available either to the educated men who have a salary as a source of income, or to the very lucky and enterprising who find ways to launch themselves in small businesses and manage not to fail. What were once open government lands in the immediate area have long since been individually allocated. Thus, for the vast majority of men, the only way to obtain land is to inherit it or to be given it by one's father. The effect of this has been to lighten rather than loosen the attachment of men to their local lineage groups, to stress and strengthen rather than to weaken the importance of that whole body of law and custom pertinent to tile mutual rights and obligations of kinsmen and neighbors. For despite "modernization" in many other matters, many thousands of families still live in localized clusters of kin. The government declaration of 1963 that no one owns the land could conceivably have had considerable significance in a region in which there were vast stretches of unclaimed unoccupied territory. But the situation on Kilimanjaro is just the reverse.

As far as I was able to tell, the government declaration directly affected only three categories of Chagga landholders: tenants of the church, who were given tile land they occupied; persons holding small pieces of unimproved land; and persons holding land that was originally conveyed to their forebears as a loan, not as a total transfer of interest. Technically the buying and selling of rights to land goes on just as before the 1963 Act, though previously sales would have been in the form of rights to own land, while now they are construed as rights to use land. But most people, court personnel as well as ordinary farmers, make no such distinction, i.e., barely acknowledge that any change has taken place, since it so little affects the relative distribution of ordinary rights. What has happened to loaned land, however, is that if it has been held under these conditions for a long time, the occupier now is emboldened to demand that the loaning lineage redeem the land immediately or relinquish all further claims to it. Redeeming involves reimbursement, not for the land, but for the coffee trees and banana plants and buildings. Ordinarily the descendants of the original loaner of land cannot produce the cash on demand and the loan is declared to be at an end. People say, "We do not pay *masiro* any longer. The land belongs to no one." *Masiro* is the customary annual payment of beer or produce from the borrowing lineage to the lending lineage. It amounts to public acknowledgment of the "true ownership," and there has always been an implication in this that should the owner choose to repay the borrower for all improvements, he could at any time reclaim the land for his own. The 1963 Act has meant a marked improvement in the position of borrowers. Now they have the option of demanding payment or relinquishment of interest. In effect, as locally construed, it has put a time limit on the redeemability of their land holdings (the demand of loanee governs the timing) and once and for all ended these loans.

The other effect the 1963 Act might have had is easy to get around. Theoretically it makes it impossible for someone having unoccupied unused land to sell rights in it, since he does not "own" the land. But it is simple enough to build a small building of some sort on the plot and sell that. It is difficult to believe that this highminded declaration of socialist principle was ever intended to have the curious effect it has had on Chagga life. It was directed against the exploitation of tenant-farmers by estate holders. It could scarcely have been intended to single out three limited categories of Chagga farmers for a change in their rights.

Among other things, this illustrates that although universality of application is often used as one of the basic elements in any definition of law, universality is often a myth. Most rules of law, in fact, though theoretically universal in application, affect only a limited category of persons in a limited number of situations. And beyond this fairly elementary proposition, the limited effect of the 1963 declaration on Chaggaland indicates something of greater moment. All legal rights and duties are aspects of social relationships (see Hohfeld 1919). They are not essentially rights in things, though they may pertain to things. They are rights to act in certain ways in relation to the rights of other people. The implication of the Chagga reception of the 1963 declaration is clear. It is only insofar as law changes the relationships of people to each other, actually changes their specific mutual rights and obligations, that law effects social change. It is not in terms of declarations, however ideologically founded, about the title to property. Most Chagga are living where they lived before 1963 *as* they lived before 1963. The semi-autonomous social field that dominates rural Chagga life is the local lineage-neighborhood complex; that complex of social relationships having much to do with land rights continues intact and almost unchanged by the 1963 Act.

The most important component of many farmers' lives is the localized patrilineage or patriclan in which men of the regions of older settlement live. These may be comprised of as many as three or four dozen families residing in contiguous plots, but they are usually smaller. In theory all the clansmen are descended either from a common male ancestor or from a group of brothers or patrilateral cousins, but often the precise genealogical ties are lost beyond four or five generations. Some people would doubtless describe these remains of an earlier form of Chagga lineage organization in terms of the survival of often-expressed values, "Kinsmen should help each other," or "Brothers should support each other" (the term "brothers" being extended to all male kinsmen of the same generation), or "Land should never be sold without the consent of one's brothers." However, these values may also be interpreted as the ideological side of a very considerable modern mutual social and economic interest. They are not *merely* a survival from a traditional past.

At one time there would seem to have been a very firm intra-lineage organization of a corporate nature. Lineages had senior officials who had political, religious and jural functions, both within the lineage and in relation to chiefs and other lineages. All this is gone and has been gone for fifty years. Most lineages do not meet as a body any longer, but small localized groups of lineal kinsmen do meet very regularly, not only at all life-crisis rituals when large groups assemble, but to slaughter animals and eat meat together in small lineage segments. Landholding is individual. However, since each collateral line is the potential heir of any close collaterals who might die without male offspring, the brothers and brotherly lines (and cousinly lines) look on one another jealously. Even today the illness of children not infrequently brings accusations of witchcraft or sorcery by the wife of one brother against the wife of another.

Moreover, brothers are all very much interested in each other's fortunes in the modern setting. Death without male issue is no longer the only way the land of a collateral may become available. Crushing debts may make a man sell land and he is under obligation to offer it to his brothers first. They want it for themselves and for their sons. The situation of land shortage is such, particularly in the socially desirable areas (those in which the kin clusters still live), that kinsmen are not always sad to see their brothers or other neighbors in financial trouble. It follows from this that though there are no longer common lands held by the lineage as a unit, the residuary and contingent interests of kinsmen in one another's property is considerable and gives the more prosperous and enterprising considerable leverage over those less so. This is a profound bond and one with latent organizational implications.

Though there is usually no formal corporate organization of kinsmen today, agnates nevertheless form a bounded unit of individuals closely connected through their contingent interests in one another's property as well as through ties of tradition, neighborly contiguity, and sometimes affection. In this loosely constituted aggregate, certain men are recognized as leaders, others as far less powerful. The basis is seniority, or education—each is usually found in combination with property (or the control by an old man of sons having education or property).

The potential power of seniors to affect the lives of juniors through the allocation of land and through supernatural effects on their lives permeates all contact between them. The flow of prestations and services and deferential gestures toward these men is continuous. The locus of power is acknowledged ceremonially, not only at the moments of allocation of land. Clear rules about seniority are regularly reiterated in the priorities of distribution of meat every time animals are slaughtered, and in the ways in which beer is given out on those occasions to celebrate a baptism, a circumcision or a wedding. Certain of the older men have it in their power to seal the fate of many of the younger ones. The seniors still have much to say about who shall be financed in school, or in an apprenticeship, or who shall get which parcel of land. Their disapproval of a son's choice of spouse may lead to serious troubles. It is Chagga custom in the Vunjo region that a young man is given a plot of land by his father or guardian when he marries. Youngest sons ultimately inherit the plot and house of the father on his death, but older sons are provided for at marriage. These are not legal rights in the sense that a son cannot bring a lawsuit in court to oblige his father to provide such a plot: he cannot. The option lies with the father, to provide or not provide. Woe to the son who displeases his father, or the nephew under an uncle's guardianship who does not accept his uncle's allocation of land with grace. There are more than economic sanctions involved. Kinsmen can have certain magical effects on one another. But even more potent, they can have profound social effects on one another. A man must rely on neighbors and kin for security of his person, his reputation, his property, his wife and his children and for aid in the settlement of any disputes in which he may become involved. Thus the lineage-neighborhood complex is an effective rulemaking and sanction-applying social nexus. While it is not part of the official legislative or administrative system, that system often has occasion to acknowledge its existence and importance.

A direct attempt to change these local social relationships was made when a system of ten-house cells was set up throughout Tanzania. These were grafted on to the local branches of lineage and neighborhood. At the end of 1964, TANU (Tanganyika African National Union), the national party, set up a system of cells to be the base unit of the party. These were to link TANU more effectively with the rank and file, largely to enable the party to collect and distribute information. There had been an army mutiny early in 1964, and no doubt one of the considerations in setting up the cells was the collection of information relating to security. Bienen indicates that the work of the cells was outlined under three main headings, "bringing peoples' problems and grievances to the party and government, coordinating the work of the cells with the development committees, and ensuring the security of the nation" (Bienen 1967: 358). On Kilimanjaro every ten households has a ten-house cell leader, chosen by the member households. I was told that the choice was partially governed by the question whether the man could be in the neighborhood all the time. Chagga with jobs in the town, or salaried jobs in schools and dispensaries on the mountain, or who had shops, were not suitable because they could not be available at all times. Thus there was a systematic selection process which militated against the most educated men, ill favor of their neighbors whose only occupation was farming. The ten-house cell leader, called the *balozi* by the Chagga, is supposed to be informed of all events of importance in his cell: births, deaths, marriages, divorces, crimes, altercations of all kinds, and the like. He must be present at any meeting of importance involving cell members. Periodically, he meets collectively with other ten-house cell leaders, and is given instructions from central party ideologues and planners, which he then conveys to his member households.

Because ten-house cells are units of neighbors, they inevitably involve people who have old attachments to one another, attachments of kinship, affinity and neighborhood. The very non-kinsmen who are in a man's ten-house cell are likely to be of such social closeness that he would normally send them a portion of any slaughter share of meat when he got home from a lineage feast. They are persons who would be called on to help in a house-building or in the cultivation of the *shambas* at the foot of the mountain. They would have been present at any hearing of a law case in the neighborhood that was not strictly an intra-lineage affair, and might even have attended some of those. They would certainly have been at any beer party of any size given in the vicinity. The members of the ten-house cell are, in short, men whose primary identity for one another is as neighbor, affine, or kinsman. Only secondarily are they members of TANU cells. This does not mean that the secondary identity is never important. It sometimes does matter, particularly with respect to the tenhouse cell leader. For example, if there is need of supporting testimony in the Primary Court, it is useful to have the word of the *balozi*. It is sensible not to make an enemy of him, but then it always was wise to have friendly neighbors. The whole ten-house cell apparatus is an addition to pre-existing neighborhood patterns, not a replacement. What has happened is that relationships that were multiplex in the first place have now had a strand added. Not the *balozi*, but the senior man of each minimal lineage branch, the grandfather of the family, or his elder brother, is the person to whom the most important ritual prestations of beer and meat are regularly made. The office of ten-house cell leader does not, after all, carry with it discretion over the allocation of land, nor any mystical powers at all.

The continuing control exercised by the lineage neighborhood nexus over its members is illustrated by every dispute it settles. No man can hope to keep his head above water if he does not have the approval and support of his neighbors and kinsmen. He may drown in debt, and get no helping loan. He may claim lands that should be his by any normative standards, and find that all local witnesses are against him. He may go to court expecting to get redress there, only to find that his witnesses never turn up. Unless the lineage and neighborhood support him through illnesses, through financial crises, through disputes, he is in deep trouble. The ten-house cell system does not change this a whit, or at least had not in 1969. Only the educated who have salaried employment can escape some of these pressures through their affluence and outside connections. Their partial independence has undermined and altered some of the localized control. They "know" people in the town, people in local government, people in the school system. They have salaries in addition to coffee money. Their kinsmen must listen to them. They are, by reason of employment, not tenhouse cell leaders, and also by reason of employment, enjoy a certain higher status than the *balozi*. But they too are farmers, and are inside the lineage neighborhood nexus as well as having connections outside. Their wives and children are in the neighborhood all day, every day. The ties are still strong. Permeable but dominant, the Chagga lineage-neighborhood complex has never fully surrendered to any government—chiefly, colonial, or independent.

Though the lineage-neighborhood nexus has changed again and again over the decades, it has retained considerable autonomy and considerable control over its members throughout. It enforces non-legal arrangements such as the allocations of land by fathers and uncles to sons and nephews, and the attempts by brothers to block the sale of land to non-kinsmen. It conducts illegal hearings on such matters as witchcraft. It also enforces innumerable legal rules from the respecting of garden boundaries to the support of indigent kin. It is both a maker and keeper of rules, its own and those of the state.

Relationships long established in persisting semi-autonomous social fields are difficult to do away with instantly by legislative measures. This is shown in another Tanzanian attempt to legislate egalitarianism as it affected the Chagga: the abolition of chiefship, an institution that was dispensed with by the Independent Government in 1963. This political change was not unwelcome in many quarters of Chaggaland. It completed a process that had been under way since the end of the Second World War. For some years there had been both pressure and legislation in the direction of cutting down the powers of local chiefs. Their self-enriching prerogatives, accumulated in earlier colonial decades, were eroded after 1946 by laws directly cutting down their powers, and also by legislation establishing a few higher executive offices (super-chiefships so to speak) and perhaps most important of all, by enlarging the powers of various representative legislative bodies and councils. What the abolition of chiefship did in 1963 was effectively to give all formal local bureaucratic powers to a new administrative elite, drawn from commoner lineages, and nominated for office according to the length of their membership in and the degree of their commitment to TANU, the governing party. Thus the legislation reorganized and reallocated certain offices, instituting a new criterion of recruitment to office.

However this legislation did not and could not have abolished completely the Informal position of advantage enjoyed by some chiefly families. For one thing, having been better off than many of their subjects for several generations, they were able to afford to pay for the education of more of their children. Their close kinsmen and associates benefitted similarly. Educated men, being few and badly needed in an ever more Africanized administration, occupy many key positions of responsibility, and hence are more powerful than most of their less literate farmer brothers. The ex-chiefs themselves, with a few notable exceptions, are not in these posts; but some of their kinsmen and associates and their children are. Shoulder to shoulder with the new elite are a substantial number of relatives and associates of the old elite who are, so to speak, doubly qualified for office, meeting both traditional and new criteria of recruitment.

An important element in the informal positions of advantage of these men is the network of "connections" that members of chiefly lineages had with persons in positions of power and authority both in businesses and in government. Today such a network is of considerable importance in the chain of relationships that connects rural men to men occupying positions in the cities. Complex links built over many years, ramifying into business, army, church, educational, and other posts tie both the old and elements of the newer elite to each other. The chiefs have become ex-chiefs and many are living quietly in welcome political obscurity. But some, and a few of their erstwhile dependents and hangers-on, long ago acquired the skills and connections to swim in the new seas of opportunity. Thus certain kinds of powerful extended networks in which the chiefs were formerly an important link have persisted longer than the offices that were their original starting point.

This has happened before in Chaggaland, for during the colonial period there was a process of consolidation of smaller chiefdoms into larger ones. The more powerful swallowed the weaker, incorporating them. The chiefs of the smaller entities lost their offices. But it is plain from any detailed study of local officeholding in these areas, that the lineages that lost the chiefship did not entirely lose a generalized position of advantage in the diverse fields of local competition that opened up over the years. Members of such ex-chiefly lineages turn up as small entrepreneurs, such as owners of butcher shops, beer shops, trucks, and as officials of the local Cooperative Society. Often these were the new small capitalists. Though the misfortunes of consolidation had lost these petty chiefs their offices, neither they nor their relatives entirely lost their informal social advantages, and their economic head start.

This Chagga experience of the abolition of chiefships, twice repeated, first in the period of administrative consolidation, and later in the press for equality connected with Independence, has certain very general implications for the study of law and social change. It suggests that those parts of the social system that are most visible to and are considered most accessible to legislative (or other official action) are often the formal parts of the system. Yet the powerful position that comes from the *informal* accretion of economic, educational advantages, and network contacts may be far less immediately accessible to formal legal action, and may have great durability over time. The strategic position of general advantage would also seem to have great adaptability as to sphere of operations, while the office has a specified scope.

The reasoning involved here is pertinent to attempts to legislate basic changes in social relationships in our own society—e.g., to desegregation and to civil rights legislation. Social positions and networks that involve the accumulation of informal, spin-off advantages over time are difficult if not impossible to legislate into instantaneous existence, though it is clear that formal changes can create the conditions under which such advantages may eventually be accumulated. For this reason, newly acquired formal "equality" of opportunity brought into existence by legislation is often not in fact equal to long held social position.

Three examples of externally imposed formal laws and rules affecting existing semi-autonomous social fields have been drawn from the recent Chagga experience: the abolition of private property in land, the establishment of ten-house cells, and the abolition of chiefship. The first two rules were examined insofar as they affected that local, non-corporate social field which I have called "the lineage-neighborhood complex." The third, the abolition of chiefship, was designed to alter a larger scale, higher level corporate social field, the "village." I have suggested that the spin-off products of the old chiefships, the general social position and networks of ex-chiefs and their families and associates, have had a persistence over several generations of time, despite repeated changes in surrounding formal organization and cultural context. Since such networks and chains of transactional relations may generate fairly durable rules regarding the relative status and mutual obligations of their members, it is useful to analyze them as semi-autonomous social fields. The TANU organization has moved from the status of being a non-legal voluntary organization to being part of the official formal *de jure* body politic. The chiefly networks have moved in the other direction, from being attached to legal offices to the status of completely informal connections.

In the Chagga situation as in most others, much that is new co-exists with and modifies the old, rather than replacing it entirely. For the Chagga, there have been some abrupt changes in the legislated rules of the game and many other rule changes that have been generated more gradually. To understand these rules, legal, non-legal or illegal, it is essential to know something of the working social context in which they are found. There is a general utility in looking at legal rules in terms of the semi-autonomous social fields on which they impinge. It tempers any tendency to exaggerate the potential effectiveness of legislation as an instrument of social engineering, while demonstrating when and how and through what processes it actually is effective. It provides a framework within which to examine the way rules that are potentially enforceable by the state fit with rules and patterns that are propelled by other processes and forces.

CONCLUSIONS

The concept of the semi-autonomous social field is a way of defining a research problem. It draws attention to the connection between the internal workings of an observable social field and its points of articulation with a larger setting. Bailey (1960) used a similar set of concepts when dealing with political change. Theoretically, one could postulate a series of possibilities: complete autonomy in a social field, semi-autonomy, or a total absence of autonomy (i.e., complete domination). Obviously, complete autonomy and complete domination are rare, if they exist at all in the world today, and semi-autonomy of various kinds and degrees is an ordinary circumstance. Since the law of sovereign states is hierarchical in form, no social field within a modern polity could be absolutely autonomous from a legal point of view. Absolute domination is also difficult to conceive, for even in armies and prisons and other rule-run institutions, there is usually an under life with some autonomy. The illustrations in this paper suggest that areas of autonomy and modes of self-regulation have importance not only inside the social fields in which they exist, but are useful in showing the way these are connected with the larger social setting.

The law (in the sense of state enforceable law) is only one of a number of factors that affect the decisions people make, the actions they take and the relationships they have. Consequently important aspects of the connection between law and social change emerge only if law is inspected in the context of ordinary social life. There general processes of competition inducement, coercion, and collaboration—are effective regulators of action. The operative "rules of the game" include some laws and some other quite effective norms and practices. Socially significant legislative enactments frequently are attempts to shift the relative bargaining positions of persons in their dealings with one another within these social fields. The subject of the dealing and much else about the composition and character of the social field and the transactions in it are not necessarily tampered with. Thus, much legislation is piecemeal, and only partially invades the ongoing arrangements. Hence the interdependence or independence of elements in the social scene may sometimes be revealed by just such piecemeal legislation.

Examples from two very different settings have been briefly described to illustrate these points. Activities in the garment industry analyzed at one point in time show very clearly what is meant by the concept of a self-regulating social field and the important but limited place of law in it. The key figures in this part of the dress industry are the allocators of scarce resources, whether these resources are capital) labor, or the opportunity to make money. To all of those in a position to allocate these resources there is a flow of prestations, favors, and contacts, producing secondary gains for individuals in key positions. A whole series of binding customary rules surrounds the giving and exchange of these favors. The industry can be analyzed as a densely interconnected social nexus having many interdependent relationships and exchanges, governed by rules, some of them legal rules, and others not. The essential difference between the legal rules and the others is not in their effectiveness. Both sets are effective. The difference lies in the agency through which ultimate sanctions might be applied. Both the legal and the non-legal rules have similar immediately effective sanctions for violation attached. Business failures can be brought about without the intervention of legal institutions. Clearly neither effective sanctions nor the capacity to generate binding rules are the monopoly of the state.

The analysis of this illustration also suggests that many laws are made operative when people inside the affected social field are in a position to threaten to press for enforcement. They must be aware of their rights and sufficiently organized and independent to reach and mobilize the coercive force of government in order to have this effect. A court or legislature can make custom law. A semi-autonomous social field can make law its custom.

The second example, that of certain attempts to legislate social change in Tanzania, shows the same principles in ales, familiar milieu. Here neighborhood and lineage constitute a partially self-regulating social field that, in many matters, has more effective control over its members and over land allocations than the state, or the "law." The limited local effect of legislation abolishing private property in land and establishing a system of ten-house cells demonstrates the persistent importance of this lineage-neighborhood complex. The way in which this legislation has been locally interpreted to require only the most minimal changes suggests something of the strength of local social priorities and relationships. The robustness of the lineage-neighborhood complex, and its resistance to alteration (while nevertheless changing) suggests that one of the tendencies that may be quite general in semi-autonomous social fields is the tendency to fight any encroachment on autonomy previously enjoyed. The advantageous situation enjoyed by some of the kinsmen and associates of ex-chiefs shows that the momentum of such an interlocking set of transactional complexes may not be entirely arrested by legislative alterations of parts of its formal organization.

These examples all involve at least two kinds of rules: rules that were consciously made by legislatures and courts and other formal agencies to produce certain intended effects, and rules that could be said to have evolved "spontaneously" out of social life. Rules of corporate organizations, whether they are the laws of a polity or the rules of an organization within it, frequently involve attempts to fix certain relationships by design. However, the ongoing competitions, collaborations, and exchanges that take place in social life also generate their own regular relationships and rules and effective sanctions, without necessarily involving any such pre-designing. The ways in which state-enforceable law affects these processes are often exaggerated and the way in which law is affected by them is often underestimated. Some semi-autonomous social fields are quite enduring, some exist only briefly. Some are consciously constructed, such as committees, administrative departments, or other groups formed to perform a particular task; while some evolve in the marketplace or the neighborhood or elsewhere out of a history of transactions.

Where there is no state, a wide range of legitimately socially enforceable rules are counted by anthropologists as law. When there is a state, two categories are recognized by lawyers: state-enforceable law and socially enforced binding rules. Pospisil has argued that it should all be called "law," with the qualifier added that it is the law of a particular group. He argues that there are in society a multiplicity of legal levels and a multiplicity of legal systems (1971: Chapter 4). Pospisil is certainly right about the multiplicity and ubiquity of rulemaking and rule-enforcing mechanisms anchored in social groups. In fact he may not even go far enough, since, as this paper suggests, not only corporate groups, but other, looser transactional complexes may have these rule-making and rule-enforcing capacities. But on the point of melting it all together as "law," this is a question of what one is trying to emphasize for analysis. If the bindingness of rules is the issue, then the argument can be made for looking at all binding rules together as products of common processes of coercion and inducement. But there are occasions when, though recognizing the existence of and common character of binding rules at all levels, it may be of importance to distinguish the sources of the rules and the sources of effective inducement and coercion. This is the more so in a period when legislation and other formal measures—judicial, administrative, and executive—are regularly used to try to change social arrangements. The place of state-enforceable law in ongoing social affairs, and its relation to other effective rules needs much more scholarly attention. Looking at complex societies in terms of semi-autonomous social fields provides one practical means of doing so.

CHAPTER TWELVE

Political Meetings and the Simulation of Unanimity
Kilimanjaro 1973

More and more often today, not only religious, but secular collective occasions come within the purview of anthropological observation (see Richards & Kuper 1971). Are the conventional frameworks used in the description and analysis of religious ritual helpful in the study of secular collective occasions? Indeed, are they always adequate to the study of religious ritual itself?

Collective ceremonies are matters to be explained. A staple of every field diary, they are ways into a complex of information (Turner 1968: 2). A ceremony is ethnographic evidence, but of what? The number of meanings, explicit and implied is immense, requiring at the very least what Geertz calls "thick description" to get at the layers of significance (1973: 3). But how far in the direction of a full ethnography does one have to go to provide a sufficient context for interpretation?

That, obviously, depends on one's purpose. This paper presents a selective account of a citizens' political meeting in Tanzania in 1973,[1] emphasizing the ways in which the meeting embodied and elicited apparent consensus. Some allusion

Editor's note: This chapter is a reprint of Moore, Sally Falk. 1977. "Political meetings and the simulation of unanimity: Kilimanjaro 1973." In *Secular ritual*, edited by Sally Moore and Barbara Myerhoff, 151–72. Amsterdam: Royal Van Gorcum.

to the ethnographic background is essential to understanding the inexplicit lo-cal significance of the occasion, but for reasons of space these will be brief. The focus of the present account is on the ritual-like elements in the meeting itself. The meeting is taken as a *type*, as this kind of gathering was a regular occurrence at the time in many Tanzanian communities. No attention will be given to the ways in which the particular occasion was used for the strategic purposes of individuals.

Why call such a meeting a "secular ritual?" Because the analogy to a religious rite draws attention to the general symbolic and doctrinal representations made in the course of business. It keeps the analytic focus from being entirely on the practical purposes listed on the agenda. Traditional religious symbols have the weight of time, repetition, and ideological legitimacy behind them. The ideas, forms, and formalisms of a new socialist government are by definition straight off the planners' typewriters. But these socialist ideas, symbols, and forms of organization have been promulgated with the expectation that they will become permanent. A "tradition" is being initiated, a doctrine represented. The ward meeting on Kilimanjaro can be analyzed partly as a celebration and propagation of these new doctrines, partly as a means of attending to certain local public business. It lies on the boundary between mundane-practical-technical activi-ties and special occasion-ceremonial-representational activities and mixes the two modes throughout.

Connected with both ceremonial and practical aspects is the appearance of unanimous support for the leadership, which the form of the ward meeting elicited. The way in which consensus was achieved made the citizenry into what I call "ratifying body public." In many parts of the world, in societies of varied political type (including our own), there exist corporate organizations in which it is ideologically anathema for the leadership openly to dictate to the follower-ship, and in which the leadership has no right to act independently on behalf of the organization. In these settings, a popular mandate of some sort must be ob-tained, however *pro forma* the manner of its realization. The analytic interest of *ratifying bodies public* is that they constitute a common, garden variety of group political behavior, *not* that they are in any way special to Tanzania. In fact, it is often asserted that unanimous decisions by consensus were once characteristic of pre-industrial societies. Yet it is less often acknowledged that apparent una-nimity can be a matter of style and form, rather than substance. Public unanim-ity regularly achieved may mean either that disagreements have been worked out and bargains struck behind the scenes, or that for some other reason the public occasion is understood not to be the proper forum for the expression of serious stubborn conflict (Bailey 1965: 1–20, 1969: 148). There is no doubt that many of Tanzania's high level ideologues genuinely wish to provide a format for public discussion and popular participation in self-government. But the permissible parameters of political action on the lowest levels of organization are fairly specific, and on the ground, other men are in charge.

The uses of citizens' meetings as a vehicle for the celebration of new political doctrines and their symbols has been noted. But the repetitious elements in the rhetoric and the procedure may serve other purposes as well. Political meetings fall within a type of secular collective occasion common in modern societies: proceedings which are set up specifically to affect situational transformations. Some of these are: judicial procedures, negotiations, elections, as well as the meetings of decision-making bodies. All of these have explicit practical purposes. But all frequently are elaborated with what seem to be digressions, formulae, and formalisms. These appear ancillary to the declared purpose, conventions, or diversions which "surround" it, having no direct cause and effect relation to the stated ends, seeming arbitrarily or indirectly attached to them. Why is the "business at hand," the practical part of the activity, so often interwoven with seemingly gratuitous rhetorical ceremonial and formulaic elaboration?

One can only guess at the meanings imbedded in this. Formal, collective, choice-making institutions publicly acknowledge the control of men over social affairs, and the control of some men over others. These are, in many settings, perilous things to acknowledge. Formalities and formulae are effective ways to organize, mark, and order these events, and in their symbolic content may serve as reminders of the constraints of the larger social/cultural milieu. This being so, much public formality and ceremonial invites interpretation as a dramatization of order.

It makes sociological sense that symbols of social order should be presented and particularly stressed on those very occasions when situational changes actually are being consciously enacted. The elaborate formalities and formulae of some courtrooms and meetings could be described as the magical aspect of a rational activity. Formality in such contexts can convey the message that certain things are socially *unquestionable* (the secular equivalent of the sacred) and by so declaring in such a form, formality helps to make them unquestionable. The public making of choices implies a certain situational uncertainty, a degree of indeterminacy and openness in the social reality (Moore 1975a). Institutionalizing the settings in which choices are made and formalizing them decreases the amount of openness. It "domesticates" the indeterminate elements in the occasion by surrounding them with fixed forms. Some of the orderliness is undoubtedly a practical necessity, a consequence of the fact that if it plans to get anything done, a large group of people getting together needs to be organized in some orderly way. But the formality may go far beyond any organizational requirement. Formality and repetition can help to define and confine an immediate situation, to keep it within bounds. They can limit the range of improvization within a particular staged event.

If that event is a political meeting of citizens that is supposed to propose development projects, in a country ideologically committed to popular participation in government, the ways in which the limits of choice are communicated are as interesting and important as the exhortations to action. A new government, like that of Tanzania, which undertakes to radically remake its society into a socialist state, not only introduces many specific organizational and economic reforms, it also produces synthesizing symbols and explanations of them which it tries to put quickly into circulation. Public meetings are among the principal vehicles that carry the new political faith far into the countryside. On Kilimanjaro, for the Chagga people, these innovations are introduced into an ongoing scene, an established way of life. For the Chagga, in 1973, their own history, customs, and recent experience dominated their particular version of the new socialism. TANU (Tanzania's one political party, the Tanzanian African National Union) and local government meetings are intended to present to the citizens the ideals of socialism, the plans of the leadership, and to provide an opportunity for democratic participation in government. The Party/Government is supposed to be the universal forum in which peasants and workers *learn about* and also *take part in* the building and management of the new society.

Significant for those local people who participate in it, a ward meeting thus is also a part of large scale events. An important element in the background meaning of any particular convocation is the regular holding of similar self-government meetings in all the wards of the nation. The ward meeting exists, among other things, to connect separate domains. Just as religious sacrifice connects the discrete worlds of men and gods, and is an attempt to establish contiguity through the act of sacrifice (Lévi-Strauss 1966: 227) so the Party or ward meeting similarly is an act that establishes contiguity. It puts the village in touch with that unseen and unseeable entity, the state. It does so partly through the presence of leaders who have contact with the next steps up in the Party hierarchy. It also makes connections through the standardized statements that are made, through ideologically prescribed words and categories and concepts used and through the uniform organizational apparatus shared with other political units throughout the country. The local political meeting is in its way (and due in part to its form) more than a local event, and more than a momentary incident. It is one of a long series of parallel occurrences that constitute the base of the national political edifice.

Tanzania, independent since 1961, is a tiny country (population roughly 12,000,000) and is largely rural-agricultural. Her people belong to many dozens of different tribes. The ethnic heterogeneity of the country is compounded by urban-rural differences, and economic, educational, and religious differences. In such a setting "nation-building" is a formidable problem.

There is another difficulty that afflicts Tanzanian politics. There is an inherent contradiction between the idea of a country run from the grass roots by a party of peasants and workers, and a country which has a small educated elite which in fact makes the most important policy decisions (Cliffe 1971–2: 275). In a way, the political meeting of farmers in a rural area embodies this contradiction. It sustains the legitimizing appearance of participation. Meanwhile, it also serves as a platform for publicizing the latest campaigns and directives emanating from central agencies.

On Kilimanjaro, the Chagga population is at least 350,000. In 1973 the Chagga lived, as they had since precolonial times, on permanently cultivated plots of land, normally given to them individually by their fathers. Many Chagga still live in localized patrilineal clusters with strong internal ties. A localized network of lineage-kin and neighbors exchanges labor internally, gives other forms of mutual aid, and celebrates together all the major moments of the life cycle. Nowadays some land rights are bought and sold, and sometimes land has been distributed by the government, but ordinarily land is still acquired through patrilineal kinship. The Chagga long have been half-way into a cash economy, as they grow coffee as well as subsistence foods. Many are literate. Most are Christian. Every sizeable lineage has one or another educated member who has a salaried job, some working nearby, some in the cities.

The Chagga like it very much that Africans are now ruled by Africans. But as might be expected, not all government measures are equally well-received. The government has taken the view that as the Chagga are in a better economic and educational position than many of the other people of Tanzania, they must make way for the development of the more backward peoples, and contribute toward it, rather than continuing to leap further and further ahead themselves. Some Chagga perceive this as a form of discrimination against them, particularly with respect to student places in the secondary school system.

In 1973 independence had touched all rural Chagga, but had reorganized their local social relations very little. To be sure, some individuals such as Chiefs, who were prominent in the pre-independence period, were ousted from office and new offices had come into being. There was a general administrative reorganization. "Chiefdoms" became "villages" and later each village was divided into two "wards." Ten-house cells were organized.[1] But except for the consequence to the office holders themselves, these were not deep changes. Private property in land had been abolished, but traditional individual rights to *use* land continued, so the same people occupied the same coffee gardens as did before independence. The patrilineal clusters and neighborhood ties persisted.

The meeting to be described here was to take place out-of-doors on a large open grassy space in front of a coffee-weighing and storage warehouse that belonged to the coffee cooperative. It was to start at nine and about a thousand people ought to have attended, but nothing began until eleven by which time about fifty-five men had assembled. The warehouse had a veranda on which the paid local party leaders sat on chairs. Everyone else sat on the ground wherever there was a spot of shade, or a wall to lean on. It was a sunny day, and hot.

In theory, at least, all the adults who reside and work in this part of the ward were obligated to come to the meeting, all who were neither ill, nor looking after small children, nor in some indispensable form of work,[2] such as the

---

1. This paper is based on observations made in Tanzania. The author wishes to acknowledge with gratitude a grant from the Social Science Research Council which made field work possible in 1968–69, and a grant from the National Science Foundation No. GI-34953x which funded work done in 1973–74. None of this work would have been possible without two periods as a Research Associate of the University of Dar es Salaam for which the author is duly grateful.

2. The administrative pyramid was as follows:

    Tanu Development Committee
    Ward Development Committee
    Representatives of 10-house leaders
    10-house leaders

    Or rather, this is the administrative pyramid through which proposals for development were to be generated and implemented. Those generated from below could then be presented to the District Development and Planning Committee for approval after having passed the tests of the District Development Team, a technical group which receives proposals, draws up budgets, puts them into technical language and presents them to the District Development and Planning Committee.

    In short, the Ward organization fed proposals into a local center, the District organization. As of 1973, summer, there were 31 wards on Kilimanjaro. There had

manning of the dispensary. It was a meeting for all citizens of the ward which contains at least 1000 households. There are thus at least 2500 adults and at least 100 ten-house leaders in the area. The meeting had been well publicized and it seems probable that everyone was well aware that it was taking place. It was called on a Monday, the day on which everyone is supposed to contribute his full time (unpaid) for public works. On this particular Monday, all labor obligations had been called off to free people to attend the mass meeting. I had first heard the announcement the previous day at a church service attended by about seven hundred people. A "town crier" also went up and down the paths among the farms of the subvillages blowing a *kudu* horn on the day itself announcing the ward meeting. There was no question but that most everyone knew about it.

Not surprisingly, the first men to have turned up were the paid party officials. Later others arrived, and eventually after a two hour wait, some of the leaders began to grumble and urged the Chairman to begin. All local meetings of any kind start late, except for church services, and the nine o'clock time stated as the time of convening the ward meeting was taken as a figure of speech, meaning, "in the late morning." Eventually, some time after the meeting of the original fifty-five men was in session, about thirty more straggled in, one at a

---

been some administrative reorganization in July 1973, and some new procedures laid down, hence there was still some confusion about them during the period of field work. Each ward is a piece of what was formerly a Chiefdom. The pieces, however, are composed of very old political units, the *mitaa*, sometimes called parishes, or sub-villages.

In actual working fact, the old *mitaa*, which were sub-sections of the Chiefdoms, (and in fact long ago, some were themselves tiny chiefdoms) are the underlying political units, though they do not exist officially. These are intricately knitted into the modem structure through manipulations of the representational system. There are a varied number of *mitaa* in each ward. Virtually all local organization of committees and boards involves representation by *mtaa*.

Meetings of the whole citizenry of these local units are called from time to time for various purposes, and meetings of the ten-house leaders of these *mitaa* are held regularly. Such meetings are addressed by a variety of Tanu and Ward Development Committee officials, depending on the occasion.

The meeting described in this paper was a meeting of all the citizens (supposed to be) of four contiguous *mitaa* and held by the Ward Development Committee. Readers need not disentangle all of this, which is offered only to emphasize that the official hierarchy and the local structure have accommodated each other, even though officially the local structure does not exist and is hidden behind official descriptions of what is going on.

It should be noted that the Party men and Ward leaders were and are farmers like the others, though not always of the locality which they lead.

time, bringing the total attendance to about eighty-five. The context of such overwhelming absence from the meeting is as important to interpreting its meaning as what took place.

Looking around at the Chagga farmers sitting on the grass at the meeting it is evident that they are poor by any urban standards, but well off compared with many other tribes. Many of their clothes are the castoffs and stolen clothes of city men that find their way into the country markets. There are also tailors on the mountain who make clothes, and the more dapper, salaried young men are seen in their tailor-made suits on Sundays. Work clothes are worn and patched and muddy and of a marvelous variety of sizes and shapes and colors and styles. One old man wore a huge ancient khaki army overcoat, stained and torn, over his dun-colored ragged cotton shirt and trousers. He carried a cane like any Edwardian British gentleman, and bore himself with the immense dignity of the respected elder he was, his bare feet no incongruity. A prosperous butcher wore a black tail coat with satin lapels, a maroon T-shirt and dark work trousers, and a red fez on his head. In fact, the numbers of kinds of hats one sees at such a gathering is a surprise and a delight. Some, like the butcher, wear the tarboosh; others wear knitted hats with pompoms in wild stripes and patterns. Some old men wear felt hats with brims, oily with age. Leather, plastic, or wool caps with visors are seen on other heads. Still other men wear the embroidered pill-box hats of the Muslims of the Coast, though they are not Muslims, but Christians, most of them. Here and there one sees hats that are relics of discarded uniforms; a stiff-visored officer's cap, darkened with vintage sweat; a battered campaign hat with leather binding, brim up on one side; a navy blue sailor's hat, grosgrain ribbon and all. From what navy, one wonders, did this inland sailor's headgear come? Some of the hats are new and store-bought, some are old and cherished. No one is exactly like any other.

It is not my purpose to ask how these hats came to be on the heads they graced, but to stress the cheery individuality which they represent. Each man has a personal style, in dress, in bearing, in talk, in laughing, in everything. Looking at this colorful variety of personages one reflects on the party message echoed at this meeting and often stated in the press,

> In order to accomplish your sacred mission, your deeds, behavior and
> belief must be in line with those of the Party . . .
> – *Daily News*, East Africa, Feb. 21, 1974. Article Headed, "Youth told:
> Eradicate colonial mentality," quoting Mbeya TANU Regional Secretary.

In Party ideology the political restructuring of the country is not treated solely as a material matter of reorganizing government, reallocating the means of production, and equalizing distribution. It is pictured as a task involving the making of a new kind of man.

> Tanu . . . realises that the building of socialism means the building of a completely new society and a new Man. This new socialist Man must be forged through a new dynamic socialist culture rooted in socialist activity and consciousness.
> – *Daily News,* Tanzania, Feb. 14, 1974. Column headed, "Comment."

In such an ideology, too much individuality may be a sign of "individualism" which is a "bad tendency" and is assumed to be inimical to the goals of cooperation and collective well-being. Chagga farmers have no wish to give up their plots of land to pool them with their neighbors. Yet they cannot conveniently be classified as capitalist exploiters since most of them work their plots themselves. But they nevertheless are suspected by the ideologues of being enemies of socialism. Most Chagga are deeply attached to their land, and fear it may be taken from them. They know that in the capital city they are considered politically wrong-minded. They perceive this as a misunderstanding.

Nyerere has described socialism as "an attitude of mind" to which the actual wealth or poverty of the individual involved has no relevance. It is possible to be a poor capitalist (he would exploit his fellow man if he could) or a rich socialist (he does not believe in exploitation) (Mohiddin 1971–72: 165). Without speculating on what the range of visible signs of a socialist or capitalist attitude of mind might be, it is worth noting the abstract quality of the definition. Socialism in these terms is a form of faith in certain moral principles, a matter of mental attitudes. As a very well-to-do government official on Kilimanjaro once said to me, just before he drove away in his car, "Socialism is not a matter of how much money you have. It is a matter of what is in your heart."

Such abstractness and ambiguity make it possible for local Chagga party leaders on the mountain, the farmers who are simultaneously salaried party men, to reassure themselves and their constituents that they are all good socialists. As one Ward Chairman said to me when I asked him what he thought about a Tanu directive that implied that all Tanzanians should be in *ujamaa* villages by 1976, "The Chagga," he replied, "have no problem with this. *Hakuna shida.* We have always done things in an *ujamaa* (socialist) manner. We share everything with our brothers. We do everything together with our neighbors. You can ask anyone. We already have *ujamaa*."

The men sitting on the grass waiting for the ward meeting to begin often had heard exhortations to become new men, to end all exploitation, to cooperate, to be socialists, to develop their country by working hard, to condemn the colonialists and support the freedom fighters, and the like. These are delivered in an official terminology coined for the purpose in Swahili. The mention of any of the new words evokes the whole set, so often have they been repeated. But most local political meetings, and this one was no exception, while giving voice to these terms, do not dwell on such abstract or distant matters at any length without tying them to the legitimization of specific local projects. The moralizing rhetorical style is generally used to glorify extremely mundane practical matters of local public work and organization.

While the political leaders say, "*Serikali ni sisi*," "The government is ourselves," the farmers at the meeting know that in fact the Ward Development Committee mediates between them and higher levels of government in Moshi. Ideologically, "the people" are the government. But on the ground, there is a clear hierarchy of administrative bodies which runs things. The more centralized administrative levels are closer to the source of government money. In theory, ward plans for local development and requests for funds feed into district offices, and then are forwarded to the regional level and thence to the office of the Prime Minister. National and regional funds and plans flow back in the other direction. Only the level of the ward and those below are of immediate concern in this paper.

In each of the thirty-one wards on Kilimanjaro, once a month a small, core group, the Tanu Development Committee, met to plan the next Ward meeting, to generate plans to be ratified, and to set up the agenda in general. Then, each month, as planned, there followed a Ward Development Committee (WDC) meeting. The WDC includes a much larger group of citizen representatives and local officials than the steering committee. On occasion, the whole citizenry of a locality may be summoned to a WDC meeting. Such was the case at this meeting.

The Chairman started by welcoming me, then read the agenda, and said that anyone who wanted to comment on the items he and the others would be discussing were welcome to do so. They could ask for the floor by raising their hands. BUT THEY WERE NOT TO INTERRUPT. The invitation for popular participation was thus hedged with warnings about orderly procedure.

Since speech-making on these occasions is rather like filibustering, the order not to interrupt is a significant restriction. The agenda included as major items, the obtaining of materials and labor for building additions to a local school, and the locating of a suitable site for a new clinic. The Chairman started reading the minutes of the last meeting when the Tanu Party Secretary interrupted him and said, "Shouldn't we have a short prayer?" Virtually all meetings on Kilimanjaro open with a Christian prayer. Everyone rose, recited a prayer in unison, and then the meeting began in earnest. It continued for more than three and a half hours, so that it must be understood that the description which follows is radically abbreviated.

The minutes of the previous meeting included a denunciation of the sale of beer by unlicensed persons and at illegal hours, both very common practices which had been going on for many years and which had been denounced regularly for just as many. It is not unusual to see politicians drinking along with everyone else at these establishments, or at prohibited hours, which rather undermines the force of their eloquent public condemnation of these illegalities. Another item that had been discussed at the previous meeting was the illegal resale of coffee insecticide that had been distributed free by the government. It was in short supply and a small-scale black market had sprung up. The meeting had been instructed to arrest people selling the insecticide and bring them before the Magistrate. (A check of the records of the courts of several villages for several months thereafter revealed no arrests or accusations on this ground.) These two items of illegal behavior were balanced in the Minutes by discussions about the establishment of a nursery school, the extension of piped water, the repair of a bridge, the state of the local Party treasury, some remarks about the coffee cooperative, a report on the cost of doors and windows for the school, and a discussion regarding school funds.

The general pattern of the previous meeting, the inclusion of a set of items regarding local projects, and a set of items regarding local sinners virtually are standard. The three themes: public works, public funds, and violations of law were the major substantive topics at all the local meetings of various levels that I witnessed, and were threaded through the Minute books I consulted. These dominant themes embody three faces of government: *the state as giver* (of funds and sponsor of public works); *the state as taker* (of funds and local labor); and last, *the state as rule-maker and enforcer.*

Once the minutes had been read and mechanically accepted, the floor was open for the proposal of new business to be added to the agenda. A man in the crowd rose to his feet. The Chairman recognized him and he started to speak about the problem of transportation to the distant *shambas* at the foot of the mountain. It was the time of the year for hoeing the fields on the plain to prepare them for the hoped-for rain. Most people living high on the mountain in the banana belt also have the use of auxiliary fields in the lowland. It is a long walk to the *shambas*. One must get up early in the morning before the sun has come up, to arrive before the worst heat of day. The land must be worked, and then the slow climb back up the mountain is made in the afternoon heat. Sometimes lorries on the roads pick up the cultivators and carry them down or up for a fee, though they are restricted by their licenses to the carrying of goods, not people. The police interfere, chase people out, threaten the arrest of the drivers, and otherwise disrupt this thriving illegal business. The speaker wanted to know what was to be done. Why couldn't the police be told not to interfere? The Chairman said authoritatively that cars and trucks and buses had their own law. There was nothing to do but obey.

He then gave the floor to the next citizen-speaker. This man asked why certain accessible schools had been closed so that people in his area now had to send their children to a school much further away than formerly. One of the Party men answered that there were now fewer children than formerly, hence two schools had been consolidated. In fact, the population is burgeoning, and it is hard to believe that there are fewer children anywhere than formerly, but the statement was made with an authority that suggested that the issue was closed.

Both of these matters, like most of the issues raised by individuals at these meetings are matters decided "higher up" and are things the local, small-time politicians consider it useless to pursue. But they do not admit that they are powerless to do anything about these questions, nor that they choose not to do anything. Rather they suggest that all is for the best. They take the role of *explaining* the state of things, giving rational reasons. This involves no admission of impotence on their part, nor of any failure to represent the needs of their constituents. Instead it associates them with "the powers" and the tone taken, that the farmers are ignorant and need things explained to them, is a statement of the authority of the leadership, and their access to higher councils.

Meanwhile on the road, two women passed, each carrying on her head a few sticks of sugar-cane. They ambled by at a leisurely pace, their full, flowered-cotton skirts swaying left and right as they walked. They were listening to what was going on, but not attentively enough to stop and join. Then a young girl appeared on the road with a basket of coffee on her head. She came to the veranda where the Party leaders sat and went into the coffee weighing room behind them to have her beans weighed. The meeting went on without a ripple.

There were further comments on the question of transportation to the *shambas*. If the government didn't want lorries to do it, couldn't the government arrange to transport people some other way? What about the publicly run bus company, KIDECO, which was operating some routes on the mountain? Couldn't it do this transport work? The Chairman said KIDECO could be asked to run a bus where the private services were inadequate, but it was no use asking them to take people to the *shambas*. Besides, the passengers paid on KIDECO buses just as they paid on any other, at fixed rates by the mile, said the Chairman. The implication was that any bus would be too expensive.

After the airing of these citizen complaints about the closed school and the bus service, the Party leaders had their own complaints to offer. It is a regular pattern of these meetings that the leaders respond to complaints about the government by complaining about the citizenry. What about the repair and maintenance of the roads? Why did people not turn up for the weekly contributed labor? How were the roads to be kept in order if the citizens did not report for work when they were supposed to? Without roads nothing could be done. There could be no development. Ten people could fix a stretch of road, but where are they? The leaders cannot do the work by themselves. People said they did not hear of the work parties, or that notice never reached them. "The roads belong to all of us," said the Chairman, "and we must all take care of them. People must report the names of those who do not come to the public work."

A young man in the audience stood up and said, responding to these exhortations, "Yes, we should make a labor plan for each day until the work is finished." The Chairman agreed and asked the audience, "Did you understand?" There was a weak murmur of assent. I have not seen any counted voting at any of these meetings nor do I know of any Chagga tradition of voting in earlier times. Meetings proceed as if palavering and consensus were the only possible outcome.

Then the Chairman changed the subject and interjected an admonitory tale. Perhaps the connection with the previous discussion was that more effort should be made to catch wrongdoers. A thief had stolen a goat in M— subvillage, and cut its feet (a sacrificial counter-measure against witchcraft). The people in the neighborhood had made a hullabaloo, caught the thief, and eventually he was taken to the police. "I ask you if you see a thief, make an outcry and catch him, so that he may be taken to the police, even if the Ward Leader is not around."

The road work then was discussed again. This time there were many speakers from the platform all reiterating the same general substance. The imagery used in these supporting speeches, and which is conventionally used on Party occasions is that of a great battle, or a great struggle. The fight ahead is always linked to the ones past. The struggle against colonialism and the success in winning independence are cited as if they were precisely parallel to the struggle against everything from bad roads, to inequality, poverty, ignorance, low productivity, and the like. There is a rhetorical matching of the past (bad) to the future (good) as a pair of opposites. The present is represented by allusions to the Party and its activities and organization, and by the occasion of the meeting itself. The present is described as transitional, the past and future as fixed conditions.

Unlike many religious presentations of time which reach back to the beginning of all things and look forward to some sort of ultimate end of time, these secular allusions to time evoke a very shallow past and imply a fairly proximate future. Moreover, their imagery usually is drawn from the social-cultural world of men, not from nature and the cosmos.

The reversibility of the social universe is declared. The poor are to become well-off, the bound to become free, the exploited to be made whole. The weak countries are to become strong, the ignorant to become lettered, the dependent to become independent, and modern things will be everywhere. All this in the future. In one mode of argument, all deplorable conditions are blamed on colonialism, imperialism, exploitation, on the bad outsiders who dominated the past and who plot to undermine the future. The theme of this message is, "Now that we are masters of our own destiny, we can make our world as we want it." It is almost invariably followed by another mode of argument, "All this is possible only if we work for it, only if we give up capitalistic ideas, if we develop a new spirit." It all becomes possible if the directives of the Party are followed and everyone cooperates. Not nearly enough of the people who should come to public work or to mass meetings, or even to official committee meetings actually come. Meetings do not "make." Work parties do not turn up. The double message is almost always there: that what is bad is the fault of others, that what is bad is our own fault.

The Chairman said the ten house leaders were responsible for getting their people out, but that surely no one would come if the ten-house leaders themselves did not come out to work. "We must build the nation," said the Chairman. "We are messengers, we leaders. We must not fail to deliver these orders."

He spoke of the delinquency of the whole ward. By this time two hours had passed.

The Chairman then called on a school master who was on the local education committee (and was seated on the veranda with him) to speak. He stood and said, "It is our great fortune to have obtained the help of the government . . ." What he was reporting was the fact that a plan had been approved to add a class to the existing school. A building had to be built. The government would supply some of the money, for the cement, bricks, plaster, nails, etc. He read a long list including many figures, how many bricks, nails etc. and their prices. But the people of the area would have to supply the labor, and some cash as well. To increase the fund to 5000 shillings every local citizen would have to give five shillings. The necessary supplies would have to be moved by truck and some of the money would go for that. Some of the rest would be used to hire a *fundi*, an expert, in this case a builder, to direct the work and layout the measurements, etc., and another *fundi* to do the plastering, and other such specialized tasks.

Following the schoolmaster's speech, the Chairman made a speech in favor of raising the money, and after him a series of men made similar supporting speeches. After this barrage of eloquence, and each was quite lengthy and full of exhortational rhetoric, an old man, bare-foot and in rags, leaning on a staff made his way to the platform and laid five shilling on the table in front of the Chairman. The Chairman thanked him and there was a small round of applause. Then other people came up one by one to contribute. Each person on the platform contributing a speech as well as his five shillings. Suddenly it occurred to the secretary that he should be making a record of the contributions, and he started to write down the names of those who had paid and that of each new contributor. While this was going on, the Chairman embarked on a new tack: individuals would have to be appointed from each *mtaa*, each sub-village, to be responsible for the collections there. He named someone, to collect in *mtaa* K—. The nominee stood up glumly and accepted the assignment. The crowd laughed. Everyone knows that no one wants such a job. The next man named tried to refuse. The Chairman insisted. A kinsman of the reluctant nominee, a prominent Party man sitting on the platform, made a speech in his defense, saying he was ill sometimes and should be excused. The whole incident provoked much laughter in the crowd. The Chairman backed down, and named someone else.

Then there was a long discussion about who should keep the money and what the accounting procedures should be. Money is a big responsibility. A man who handles it can always say that thieves came in the night and stole some of it while he slept. There are many problems about cash disappearing. Discussions about what to do about money take a long time and involve many intricacies of allocating responsibility. Needless to say, the farmers are not too happy to contribute unless they feel their money will in fact go to the cause specified, and they have some skepticism about it, as there have been some spectacularly bad experiences. Finally after much talk the procedures were settled on. It was clear that the danger of pilfering was on everyone's mind. The ten-house leaders would deliver the money and lists to the Ward Leader.

At last the second item on the agenda was reached: the clinic. The first step to be taken was to choose a suitable site, accessible to two of the sub-villages. A labored discussion ensued about who should choose the site. Again there were many speeches. Eventually the Chairman simply named a committee with two representatives from every *mtaa*. That seemed to satisfy, since the *mtaa* are the traditional political units, and are still very much alive, though they are not part of the official organization.

Three hours had passed. One of the men on the veranda said some of the Committee members were tired. "No matter," said the Chairman, "We must talk about the campaign against short dresses." Such a Party campaign had just been started, nation-wide. The rule was that skirts should reach several inches below the knee, and men's shorts to the knee, though current fashions were much shorter for both sexes. The specifics of this very interesting campaign aside, it is a recognizable part of a general ideological style which identifies the enemies of socialism with sexual depravity. The new-Swahili term used for exploitation, *unyonyaji*, derives from the term for sucking at the breast. It thus evokes not only vague echoes of jealousy of younger siblings, but also the taboo against an adult male sucking at the breast. Imperialism is *ubeberu*, derived from the term for he-goat, a creature whose sexual rapacity is reflected in our own term "an old goat." There is a consistency in the imagery that associates sexual license with capitalism (economic licentiousness) and associates sexual orderliness with socialism (economic morality).

"Short dresses and short shorts dishonor the nation. It is a law of the government and a law of the country," said the Chairman, "We must obey it and see that others obey it." The order was, in fact, a Party rule, but legal niceties of that kind are not given much attention in the countryside. A citizen stood up and was recognized. He was a tailor and dress-maker. He asked exactly how short or how long clothing was supposed to be. "Two inches below the knee for dresses, and . . ." A man got up to show that his shorts were the right length and did it in a clowning way that made everyone laugh. "And pants must be as long as those of brother X . . . here." More speeches were made about decency in dress. No one should be allowed to walk on the road in improper clothing. Nor into a church. Nor into a market. Nor should any tailor be allowed to stay in business. "We will close his business if he dares to make a short dress," the Chairman said. "A committee for enforcing this law must be chosen, to watch for the young girls who break the law." A committee was named to make lists of violators. Each man named stood, and was applauded. Several men who were named to committees were not at the meeting. The basis of the distribution of committee members was again by *mtaa*.

A small boy drove three cows by on the path while this was going on. At last the nominations were finished and the Chairman began to take cognizance of the lateness of the hour. We had by then been in session for three and a half hours. The next items on the agenda were hurried through by comparison with the earlier ones, but each still merited a speech. The first of these items was a call to pay up all membership dues in Tanu and obtain up-to-date memberships cards. The Chairman said, "Not only all men, but all women should belong." But there was some indication that none of this was being taken too seriously as no one could remember who was the head of the UWW, the women's organization of the Ward. This discussion was interrupted by some more clowning about the proper length for men's shorts. A man got up to show his shorts were long enough. He clicked his heels and saluted in an exaggerated military manner. Everyone laughed and applauded, drowning out some of the discussion about membership cards.

When that subsided, the Chairman said that butchers should be on their guard as some clever rogues were traveling the countryside saying that they were veterinary inspectors and collecting samples of meat. They were really thieves. He went on to emphasize that the presence of any stranger in the *mitaa* should be reported at once. Then, like a homing pigeon, he returned to his earlier topic: the collective work. "Some people say to stay at home and not to come out to work. That is wrong. We must all work together." Then he thanked me for attending the meeting, thanked everyone for their contributions to the school fund, and ended by saying "Thanks be to God that we may all build the nation together. The meeting is over." Nearly four hours after it began, everyone got up to leave, presumably eventually to make their way toward the beer shops where a great many worthy Chagga citizens spend their late afternoons.

CONCLUSIONS

An obvious feature of the meeting described here was its double message. For all the explicit verbal commitment to popular initiative, participation, and self-government, to welcoming suggestions from the citizenry, the autocratic and peremptory behavior of the Party officials running the meeting made the opposite quite clear. Only certain very limited proposals made by the rank and file would be welcomed. Also, despite occasional statements to the contrary, the general indifference of the Kilimanjaro citizenry to local Party/Government activities was well-known to all present and evident in the poor attendance. Hence the apparent unanimity achieved by the meeting cannot be taken at face value. What was said in the speeches could be "seen through," and behind it lay unofficial messages and meanings.

This visible underlayer gave the occasion a high degree of what might be called "transparency." The contrived and manufactured quality of the event showed through. The Party rhetoric did not have the "rightness" of long tradition, the legitimacy of custom and habit behind it, nor was behavior consistent with statement. The Ward meeting could be seen as something newly "set up" and arranged, an obligatory and *pro forma* show of support, a required ratification. It is hard to judge how many participants may have experienced that sense of transparency, when all one has to go on are the comments of a few of the men who were there. Some certainly did since they said so. But even if most perceived the contradictions, that does not mean that such meetings lack effect or importance. Among other things Ward meetings serve to support a leadership (both at the local and at higher levels) which depends for its legitimacy on an *apparent* popular mandate, repeatedly given. Meetings make it possible for the citizenry to constitute a "ratifying body public." Thereby, the leadership, from the bottom ranks to the top, can collect universal symbolic tokens of support. The meeting manufactures legitimacy.[3]

---

3.   All Chagga men on the mountain are farmers. A few have craft specialities in addition: tailoring, shopkeeping, carpentering, house building, and such, but the farmers without auxiliary occupations predominate. Not present at ward meetings, unless they occur on the weekend, are the men who reside on the mountain but work in the nearby (twenty-five miles away) town of Moshi in clerical jobs of one sort or another. Nor, of course, do those men attend who work in far-away places, but whose wives and children remain on the land. But these migrants and absentees with skilled jobs are a small percentage of the population.

In order to make social life operable people must behave as if much that is socially constructed is as non-negotiable, as real as something in the natural world. The dramatic format of ceremony is a powerful way to show the existence of a social construct. Collective social rituals can dramatize political postulates. Dramatic styles seem particularly penetrating and "unquestionable" ways to convey social messages (Rappaport 1971). They are, in part, addressed to psychological levels that are not completely conscious. Seeing is believing. Kilimanjaro political meetings served to give life to new offices, new organizations, and to the new ideological language, by presenting them in action as visible, audible, unquestionable entities.

Durkheim said of religious ritual, "the essential thing is that men are assembled, that sentiments are felt in common and are expressed in common acts" (1961: 431). In this tradition some have described ritual as essentially an occasion when believers *express* their beliefs (Wilson 1957: 7; Beattie 1966: 60). The tautological implications of taking such a stance become evident when, in interpreting field material, anthropologists examine rituals to discover the beliefs of the participants. This postulation of a correspondence between acts and thoughts obviously is misleading in many contexts secular as well as religious. Far from "expressing" what was already believed, the TANU Ward meeting was designed to instruct and convert.

But display and communication of what Apter has called "political religion" were by no means the only things that were going on (1965). Borrowing a term from Tambiah and Austin, such political meetings could be described as performatives (Austin 1962; Tambiah 1972: 222). Like performative speech acts, political meetings and rituals do not just communicate information, they *do* something. The performative quality of a ritual is the efficacy attributed to it. A marriage ceremony is not the same as a rehearsal for it, nor is it the same as a marriage depicted in a play. The "real" thing has social/legal effectiveness. In that sense, the performative quality of the Kilimanjaro meeting is of major importance. What took place constituted an official public meeting of the citizens of a ward. To say that it was a dramatization of government is merely to make an analogy. It *was* local government, whether those attending "believed" in African socialism or not, and whether they were permitted to make important decisions or not.

In Tambiah's words, "ritual acts and magical rites are of the 'illocutionary' or 'performative' sort, which simply by virtue of being enacted (under the appropriate conditions) achieve a change of state, or do something effective (e.g.

an installation ceremony undergone by the candidate makes him a 'chief')"
(Tambiah 1972: 221). Tambiah is extending Austin's notion of illocutionary
or performative speech acts to cover complexes of ritual (and/or magical) acts.
The concept can be just as usefully applied to certain secular words and actions.
A signature on a contract or the installation ceremony of a judge are as much
performative acts as are any magical words or object-manipulations. The secular
formalities affect not the spirit world but an equally "made-up" social reality in
which they have meaning and efficacy.

Because performatives have a normatively defined relationship to the effects they are supposed to bring about, they can serve as ethnographic clues to
those larger social/cultural complexes of meaning and "thought" from which
they derive their "efficiency." In the easiest case these are systematic doctrines.
A religion may make the saying of certain words the proper way to contact the
gods. The law may make a document effective only if signed in the presence of
witnesses. Thus a specified set of efficacious symbolic acts may be attached to a
worked-out, connected, body of explicit rules and ideas. I have called this "doctrinal efficacy" in the introduction to this volume.[4] A whole cluster of assumptions about causality (social or cosmological) often lies behind the doctrinal
norms.

A political doctrine may incorporate just such causal ideas about how freedom or equality may be brought about. It may postulate that undertaken in the
right spirit regular open meetings of particular persons (workers or peasants)
will necessarily be democratic, egalitarian and constructive. Such an ideological doctrine lies behind the form of the Kilimanjaro meeting, and the occasion
gains some of its performative efficacy within that frame of explanation.

But there is more to it than that. Doctrinal efficacy of an ideological sort
is not the only source of performative significance. The Kilimanjaro meeting also acquires performative efficacy from its place in an organizational
plan. In Tanzania government is organized into local units of a particular
kind, having prescribed activities. That is, there is a corporate framework in
which the procedural meaning of a political meeting is prescribed. Thus the
Kilimanjaro meeting enjoys a combination of an ideological/doctrinal and an

---

4.   No doubt some Tanzanians who will read this account will be pained by it and
     will say, "What can you do when the leaders at the local level do not understand
     socialism? They need re-education." Be that as it may, it is instructive to consider the
     actual significance of ratifying bodies public in political systems today, even where
     that is not the intended design of government.

organizational/"doctrinal"-procedural base for its performative efficacy. It is performatively legitimated in two systems, ideological and organizational. Within these two frameworks of officially attributed meanings the sheer performance, the regular holding of the meetings in the precribed manner is sufficient to "do something effective" in Tambiah's magical sense (1972: 221).

It is true that the ideology holds that a particular state of mind, a socialist attitude, must genuinely underlie the performance for it to enjoy complete success. But should the attitude be absent, it is also assumed that the right ideas will eventually be produced by the political education provided by the meetings themselves. Yet in practice, as there is no way to insure that the inner attitude will always accompany the outer performance, the performance itself becomes the measure of a presumed attitude. The leadership comes to rely on the performance. The appearance of unanimity is not only necessary, it becomes sufficient.

The Kilimanjaro meeting was a form of political co-ceremoniality staged in such a way as to allow the interpretation that it was an outer sign of political agreement. But to allow this inference, all that was required were the common acts. Attendance, an appearance of polite attention, applause when given the sign, some supporting speeches, and an absence of expressions of serious objection were needed. The leadership could interpret these as a sign of success, as legitimation of its role, and as a carrying forward both of immediate practical tasks and long term political education. What was being actively elicited at the meeting was general non-objecting behavior.

Co-ceremonial behavior produces a multiplier effect. It hints that what is hidden in everyone's mind is as conventionally proper and uniform as what everyone is *seen* to be doing in concert. Each person knows only about himself whether this is so. He may be silent and appear attentive yet not be listening at all. However, he does not know about the others for certain. That is why, on some solemn occasions when two people whisper or laugh, they create a disproportionately serious disturbance. They destroy the illusion of unanimity. They reveal that the conventional prescribed thoughts and sentiments are not entertained by everyone.

Certain collective ceremonies probably are designed to evoke as much as possible the feeling that there should be congruence between outer appearance and inner thoughts, and to produce a sense of guilt where this is not so. The Kilimanjaro meeting seemed to stress that every man attending (as well as those absent) should think of himself as a political sinner, as one who has not done enough, who does not believe enough, who is not committed enough. The exhortations of the leaders communicated quite explicitly to the participants what they ought to be feeling and what their behavior ought to mean. But because the society (or some persons in it) imputed a particular belief to those who perform a particular formal action does not say that the ethnographer has to do the same.

A central quality of conventional, formal, collective procedures is that they are not spontaneous expressions of feeling at all, but involve some, *conventional form of acting, and the acts have an explicit performative significance given in advance.* As such, the ritual aspects of a collective gathering can as often be a means of masking feelings and thoughts as of expressing them. Amending Durkheim, the "essential thing" may be that "men are assembled" and engage in "common acts" *not* that they necessarily feel "sentiments in common" (Durkheim 1961: 431).

The meeting on Kilimanjaro attached fixed conventional meanings to the conventional act of attending such a meeting. In doing so, and in other ways, it communicated the non-negotiability, the unquestionability, the sacredness of certain official interpretations of social life. Such meetings dramatize a political arrangement that is being constructed in part by the drama itself. The repetitive themes in the speeches and format are parts of an attempt to define and teach an official version of social reality while acting it out.

In any social setting, whether traditional or innovative, fixed social forms, rules, symbols, and ideas can be considered elements in the effort to construct a common, durable social reality, to hold it firm, to make it knowable and reliable. Elsewhere I have called all the ubiquitous processes that feed into this attempt "processes of regularization" (1975a). But it is evident when one looks closely at the unfolding details of any particular social situation, that there are counterprocesses continually at work. Individuals (and groups) may reinterpret the constructions others put on social "reality." They may redefine matters or renegotiate them as suits their advantage, or as fits their perception of the circumstances in which they find themselves. They may play openly on such ambiguities, conflicts, inconsistencies, and lacunae in the "system" of rules and symbols and categories as suits their immediate strategic purposes. Or they may do so covertly, even passively, without explicitly seeming to alter anything, simply by not acknowledging the performative efficacy of the acts and interpretations of others.

Because any intentionally engineered social change betrays the degree to which social life is a man-made construct, it intimates an underlying plasticity and indeterminacy in social affairs. The attributes of liminality and states of transition discussed by Victor Turner have echoes here (1969: 95–96). Moments of consciously-designed social change afford a fleeting glimpse of non-order. Radical political reorganization demonstrates the great malleability of social forms. Hence, when a new political regime is decreed into existence, the dangerous alternatives it faces are not only from some other kind of programmatic order, but from any kind of non-order, openness, and indeterminacy. Perhaps the repetitiveness and the ritualized style of many radical reformist governments is at least partly to be understood in this light? Such polities understandably have a preoccupation with orthodoxy.

In the one-party political meetings of Chagga farmers in Tanzania, the twin messages are prominent: 1) that more changes must come and that they must be instituted by "the people" and their organs of government; and, at the same time, 2) that exhortations to institute change and enlist popular participation must not be mistaken for open social choice and ideological indeterminacy. Voluntary involvement, grass roots control, and an un-doctrinaire style are inherent in the Nyerere approach. Yet in many quarters of Tanzania there are others who assume that a politically educated peasantry will ineluctably choose to organize itself and to act in particular, predictable ways, and that if it does not do so, there is no harm in using some pressure to hurry the peasants along on a path that is historically inevitable anyway. The public ward meeting on Kilimanjaro carried both of these communications and a host of others. Its actions and words *appeared* to elicit unanimous support.

The Party leaders were pleased. The matter of the large number of eligible citizens who did not attend, as well as much that is known of the attitudes of local Chagga farmers could be officially ignored. Nevertheless, that unacknowledged social context silently spilled its significance into the meeting. It introduced a potentially unsettling element of indeterminacy into a well-staged production. No matter, the ratifying body public had played its part. The performative efficacy of the meeting was unimpaired.

CHAPTER THIRTEEN

Changing African Land Tenure
Reflections on the Incapacities of the State

Property in land is surely one of the most socially embedded of the elements of a legal order. It is a truism that property is not about things but about relationships between and among persons with regard to things (Hohfeld 1919; Ellickson 1991). In short, to say that someone has a right to land is to summarize in one word a complex and highly conditional state of affairs which depends on the social, political, and economic context. The place, the setting the history, and the moment, all matter.

The title of this study, "Changing African land tenure" has a double reference. Not only are local pressures and struggles continuously changing the terms and conditions of African land tenure, but vigorous efforts to control and direct land entitlements by national authorities and international agencies have also been around for a long time. Periodically a radical reshaping of African land tenure regimes is predicted or advocated. This is the case at present. Current crises are invoked to justify the urgency of such proposals. Depending upon the political commitments of the speakers, the allusion

Editor's note: This chapter is a reprint of 1998. "Changing African land tenure: Reflexions on the incapacities of the state." *European Journal of Development Research*, Special Issue on Development and Rights, 10 (2): 33–49. Also published in 1999. Lund, Christian, ed. *Development and rights: Negotiating justice in changing societies*. London and Portland, OR: Frank Cass.

to trouble focuses on different, negative aspects of the current situation and matching solutions. Commonly alluded to are the deteriorating state of the physical environment, the demographic explosion, the absence of political democracy, the presence of corruption, the need for economic development, the danger of intergroup violence and other serious troubles and inequities. Among the many strategies advocated for a better future, legal changes are often urged, affecting constitutional/political matters, property regimes, and human rights. The implied assumption of the talk about legal change is that laws can both be easily put into place and easily implemented. This paper is a small skeptical commentary on that proposition (see also Low 1996 and Scott 1998).

Having limited space, I will illustrate with a few instances how certain recent programs to create equitable redistributions of property have been frustrated. The method used here is one that uses events as its initial data. The implications embedded in a small diagnostic event are traced outward to infer larger social processes (Moore 1977b; 1986a; 1987; 1993b). First, I will describe a single case history from East Africa, the instance of a well-to-do woman whose present land-holding situation embodies not only the immediate exigencies of a postcolonial world, but is demonstrably connected with at least a century and a half of changing property relations, including the Tanzanian experiment with socialism.

In the second part of this study I want to reflect on current talk about proposed land policies for West Africa. The search for general solutions to West African problems, legal solutions among others, leads to flights of the utopian imagination. Because the states of the region have nationalized land, serious people go so far as to project the possibility of a total redefinition of property interests in the course of denationalization and governance reform. One might have supposed that no such grand change by legislative means would be thought possible, given the variety and importance of local property practices in West Africa and the limited effectiveness of the states involved. What interests me here is a particular aspect of this problem: the way, under various conditions, little people can dismember state policy. Local persons with personal and local concerns often can undo grand plans of reform. The instances I have in mind are not organized movements of collective political resistance. Seemingly trivial actions of individuals can demolish state policy just as effectively.

AN ILLUSTRATION FROM EAST AFRICA

In 1993, Sophia confided to me that she had much to worry about. She was engaged in a complex negotiation over a house she had once owned in one of the principal towns of Tanzania, and things were not going well. She acquired that piece of real estate in an unusual manner. In the last decade of the colonial period, she was the mistress of a British officer and had borne him a son. When the Brits left, the officer, who had a wife and son in England, left with them. However, he was an honorable fellow and wanted to take care of the woman and son he had left behind. At some time before independence, judging correctly that no Chagga patrilineage would give any of its patrimonial lands on Kilimanjaro to the son of an Englishman, he bought Sophia a substantial house and land in a town about fifty miles away from Kilimanjaro. In the colonial period, urban land was outside of the customary law system and was transferrable as freehold (James 1971: 100). But in rural areas, "native law and custom" governed (ibid.: 62–63). Sophia did not live in the town house, but rented it out to some foreign entrepreneurs. Her residence was on rural Kilimanjaro in her widowed mother's very comfortable dwelling. It stood in the midst of a small farm-garden with a banana grove, coffee trees, a cow or two.

When Independence came in 1961, Sophia intended to keep her urban property for her young son and planned to transfer it to him when he came of age. She knew that neither she nor her son would ever inherit her mother's house. It was patrimonial land owned by Sophia's father in his lifetime. When he died his widow, according to Chagga custom, was entitled to continue to live there. But when the widow died, it normally would revert to a male member of the patrilineage chosen by them to succeed.

However, when Sophia's mother died the men of the chiefly lineage did not reappropriate her land, though it was their legal right to do so under "customary law." They let Sophia stay on. Why did they modify the norms of patrilineality in this way? There were two reasons; one was that Sophia had, by that time, already lost the town house, and they wanted to take care of her. But there was a more instrumental reason than solicitude for her well-being. All of the men of the patriline already had plots of land that they occupied on Kilimanjaro. They were afraid that if any of them took another parcel, local members of the ruling party would denounce them and confiscate the property. Government decrees about landholding were interpreted by the party as meaning that one could legitimately occupy only one plot of land. "Surplus" property would be confiscated.

What was the reasoning behind the Tanzanian "one piece of property" policy? When Tanzania became independent of British colonial rule in 1961, there were a few things which President Nyerere thought absolutely inimical to the egalitarian, socialist ideal that he had in mind for the nation. One was the kind of officialized inequality represented by the existence of chiefs. Therefore, chiefship was abolished. The other was the "parasitical" exploitation of tenants implied by the very existence of landlords, who were by definition extracting income without working for it. Every possible measure was to be taken to disempower such an undeserving elite. For Nyerere, landlord-tenancy arrangements were clearly one of the more wicked aspects both of feudalism and capitalism.

To ensure that landlordism would not continue, all titles to land were appropriated by the state in 1963.[1] All that citizens could "own" was the right of occupancy, or beneficial use. And under the new land law, land that one was not occupying and using could not be kept. Thus, it became apparent that Sophia would have to sell the town house that was to have been her son's inheritance. She was especially vulnerable because chiefly families like hers were the targets of particularly vengeful party practice. And, of course, some desirable properties confiscated for "the people" found their way into the hands of Party officials or their relatives.

Sophia solved the two-property landlordism problem as best she could. There was a foreign company doing business in the city where her townhouse was located. For some years she had rented the house to the company for the use of one of its executives. Once the single property rule came in, she changed her arrangements with the company. They would buy the house, so that nominally it was theirs, and the local party ideologues who were confiscating second properties would not then be able to take it away from her. The secret oral condition that accompanied this transfer was that when and if the socialists ever lost power and there were no longer any strictures against multiple tenures, she would be able to buy back the house. The company agreed, but the matter was not put in writing as it was plainly illegal.

Since 1985, the liberalizing pressures from the World Bank have committed Tanzania to a return to privatization, and eased many of the restrictions that the

---

1.   See James 1971 for a review of Tanzanian land law as of the date of publication; and James and Fimbo 1973 and Moore 1986.

socialists had placed on property-holding. Sophia wanted the town house back. Her son was reaching adulthood and she had to worry about his future.

The company did not deny that it had made the agreement to resell the house to her and were willing to do so. The obstacle was the *price*. Sophia insisted that under the original agreement they were to let her buy it back at the price at which she had sold it to them. But that had been more than twenty-five years earlier. Inflation in Tanzania has been horrendous. The company wanted a more realistic price, some approximation of market value. Sophia did not have the necessary money. In a letter to me about a year ago, she said the matter had still not been settled.

The details of Sophia's situation were unique, but her transfer of property to surrogates to conceal continued ownership was not. Scattered all over Kilimanjaro there were relatively well-off individuals (though by no means all as affluent and elite as she) who deposited second properties with nominal surrogates during the more orthodox period of socialist party practice. All of them are now free to try to get them back. This is happening outside the courts, outside of any formal legal system. Since the arrangements were illegal and made because of the government threat of confiscation, there is no tribunal to whom these people can appeal. The state had not deprived them of the property directly, so no rights argument about restitution of property taken without compensation would have been available even if there had been some hearing agency at hand.

What is visible about property law and national policy in this abbreviated case history? Side by side, and, interdigitated in the life experience of Kilimanjaro residents, are a plurality of simultaneous legal, illegal, and nonlegal orders, rules and practices that originated in different historical periods. Individual transactions come in and out of public view, involving different aspects of this complex. The ideologies in play at various times have ranged from all that surrounds the patrilineal bond, to the socialist logic of an inspired leader, to the development rationale of the World Bank. Drawing on different pieces of this experience, people try to combine strategies of self-interest with strategies of self-respect. National development policy and the public welcoming of capitalist strategies by all and sundry, (today, even by Nyerere himself) legitimizes current self-seeking. But it went on even when the official ideology preached sharing, egalitarianism, and brotherhood. Sophia lost on the townhouse deal, but she may succeed with a more recent experiment in landlording, the expansion of her mother's house to accommodate paying guests.

For Sophia and all the others, the law, and the breaking of it or the keeping of it is only one element of many in the management of a life. Myriad such local settings transform the meaning of property and the significance of national legal interventions all over Africa. They are not mobilizations of collective political action, but they can undo the plans of a government as effectively as if they had been.

However, taking such actions into account on a national policy level is a difficult thing to do, especially when it is not clear what is happening or how often. As Herbert Simon (1957b: 199) wrote long ago about "the principle of bounded rationality," decisions are rational in relation to the simplified model we construct of a situation, not necessarily in relation to the real world itself.

RECONFIGURING LAND LAW TO RECONFIGURE A SOCIETY

What I want to do now is to move from the details of the small scale local event to the large scale international palaver. I shall comment on the themes that have appeared in policy-oriented discussions of West African land and which I have heard as a consultant in recent years and have seen in related publications of the OECD, USAID, CILSS and others. Prominently absent from most proposals for the future are allusions to the predictable illegalities and distortions of direction that are likely to occur. The only one that often elicits comment is the abuse of official authority by agents of the state (Thomson and Coulihaly 1994). New versions of this critique of the central state have recently reappeared in connection with the policy of government decentralization sponsored by the international donors. The focus on repairing past problems by changing the form of the postcolonial state seems to have distracted attention from other issues. The way the informal strategies of local people may redirect the implementation of policy have not had sufficient authoritative attention.

Writing in a regional synthesis, commissioned for one of the international meetings on this topic, Gerd Hesseling and Boubacar Ba have no hesitation about saying:

> Thirty years of reform, amendment, adaptation and patching up of the law in the different Sahelian countries have produced some laws of undoubted quality; some are gems of legal technique, others contain original solutions. Nonetheless, since 1980 it has been recognized everywhere that Sahelian land legislation is not readily enforceable at the local level. Almost everywhere land legislation

(in the broadest sense) is seen as an obstacle to fair, balanced, environmentally conscious development. (Hesseling and Ba 1994: 30)

Environmental conservation and economic development loom large in the discourse about land law reform. But other issues figure as prominently. Also addressed are: security of tenure, democratic management, equitable access to land and other resources, and conflict resolution. Each of these terms is a label for a host of implied political meanings. As World Bank conditionalities have shifted so have the significances of these labels.

International policies directed toward a free market economy, privatization, democracy and decentralization of political control, will have major implications for rural land tenure. But what those implications are remains in debate. As political attention shifts from an exclusive preoccupation with the capitals of West Africa to the countryside, and as more and more Africans are drawn into the discussion, there is increasing acknowledgment of the diversity and importance of local social configurations. Land tenure reform is no longer being approached from an entirely unitary, state-centred logic, founded in most of these countries on a history of land nationalisation. But the problem of balance between state and local control has not been worked out (Mamdani 1996).

Policy discussions relating to land law in the Sahel are all skewed by the existence of state nationalization. Thus "security of tenure" for the "peasants" may be read in part as a euphemism for the uncertainties associated with denationalization. For the moment, most states in the Sahel do not seem ready to do much about denationalizing. The state has the "domaine" in the Francophone countries and the "title" in the Anglophone. Sufficient paper gestures have been made in the direction of privatization to keep the flow of international money coming. Thus, for example, not without some urging from the World Bank, a law was passed in Burkina Faso in 1991 to the effect that land in the national Domaine "may be assigned as private property" (Faure 1995). Nevertheless, the principle that in Burkina the state still holds the national "domaine" continues to prevail, and the possibility of private landholding remains a reality only on the books.

One example of changing intellectual conceptions of the situation is described in the work of Professor Etienne Le Roy. At the University of Paris, he has long led a research group on land tenure questions (APREFA).[2]

2. APREFA, Association pour la promotion des recherches et etudes foncieres en Afrique; for Le Roy's view, see Le Roy 1996: 10–12.

Summarizing the shifting attitudes that surrounded its work in recent decades, he says that in the 1970s the theorization of APREFA was Marxist in concept. At that time, he tells us, the basic distinction made was between "traditional" and "modern" systems. Those categories had an evolutionary thrust. The assumption was that private property was the future.

Dissatisfied with that stance in the 1980s, APREFA adopted a different nomenclature, and characterized African land tenure systems as being in a state of "transition." But by 1996 Le Roy says he even finds the theme of "transition" problematic, since it seems to continue to signify an evolutionary direction. He now prefers to say that land in Africa is a form of patrimony that figures in an economy of redistribution. He sets up a series of definitions, labels, and models that he contends follow from such an analysis. This then prepares the way for his critique of a 1995 World Bank document, which prescribes private property as the necessary solution to present problems in African land tenure (Le Roy 1996: 335).

Le Roy is undoubtedly describing accurately the sequence of intellectual attitudes in a particular circle in France, and there are many there and elsewhere who have their doubts about the panacea of individual ownership. But his own generalized redefinition of the *ésprit* of African property in land does not clarify matters. He is proposing a unitary definition of the underlying essence of African land tenure. But is there need for such an essentialist reduction?

To me, any such essentialist analytic path is quite a distance from the multiple, shifting, permutating, recombining practices of rural Africa. As Etienne Le Roy is very much aware, there is a huge diversity of local "systems," and Africans operate simultaneously in multiple legal milieux, as even the outline of Sophia's story indicates. The question is how to address such a complex, and how to understand the way it has been addressed in recent decades by insiders and outsiders.

The outsider view is easier to capture than the multiple insider ones. As I see it the major recent shifts in the international donor discourse relating to land tenure are closely linked to the major political changes that have taken place from the 1980s on. During the cold war, for political reasons, rural economic development was treated as an encapsulated entity, as a technical problem. It was approached as if it had no political dimensions. At that time, rural *governance* was not a topic in the mouths of Western donors. Rural change was conceived in terms of local projects to increase production, and thereby to alleviate poverty.[3] The emphasis was on agronomy and technology. State policies regarding the

---

3.   See Finnemore 1997 on a sequence of World Bank redefinitions of development.

administration of the countryside were not to be questioned. States supported by the Western international community in the interest of the Cold War were not to be criticized openly. The social organization of the countryside as a political issue was untouchable. The alleviation of poverty was the acceptable rhetoric.

Now the whole game has changed. And in many countries the governments have changed, and, at least nominally, their political policies have altered. The political watchwords from the Bank and the donor community (but repeated religiously in official Africa) are democracy, decentralization, and participation. The connection between rural development and political form is no longer taboo. The importance of rural community practice has entered the discussion both in its political and its economic dimensions. In this connection the question becomes critical whether denationalization means individual land tenure or community tenure and community management. But the problematics of rural inequities, and the possibility that rural community management might make social asymmetries worse, not better, and might interfere with land tenure policy, is still not fully integrated into the discussion.

As the case history of Sophia shows, people operating in local social systems often reconfigure the effect of national legislation. That lesson can be repeated many times from the Sahelian evidence. State hatched, or internationally hatched, plans to direct local systems along prescribed paths often have had unexpected outcomes. I shall give two examples of efforts to distribute newly available lands in the Sahel. One concerns the irrigation projects in the valley of the Senegal River (Crousse, Mathieu, and Seck 1991). The other has to do with land made available for human habitation by the eradication of onchocerciasis in the river basins of Burkina Faso (McMillan, Nana, and Savadogo 1990).

The irrigation projects on the banks of the Senegal River were variously set up from about the mid-1970s on. In many localities administrators tried to give equal access to newly irrigated lands along the river. As things developed, about half of the inhabitants of the Senegal River Valley had access to irrigated lands at the perimeters of their villages. At first, in many places, the farmers were organised in community groups to participate in and manage these projects. Everyone in the village who wanted to join was to have equal access and a plot of equal size. The whole was to be managed collectively. In fact, in many groups, the principle of equality was violated from the start, with parcels allocated to the names of dead persons, or absent ones (Mathieu 1990: 73; 1991: 197). These fraudulently registered parcels were in fact controlled by some members of the traditional local elite, and others who were officials or merchants, and counted as *nouveaux riches* (Mathieu 1990; Niasse 1991). Some of these were able to use hired labour and to cultivate at a profit. However, the more impoverished cultivators did badly. They had difficulty maintaining their irrigation channels. They could not recruit the necessary labor from their families, among other things because young men preferred to leave to enter the migrant labor stream. Besides, little by little, from 1985 on, because of international pressure, the state tried to disengage itself from the costs of the inputs (fertilizers, pump maintenance, etc.) and to pass these costs on to the peasantry. The peasants, in turn, borrowed money, mortgaged their parcels, and soon lost their land to the wealthier owners from whom they had received their loans. What is particularly interesting about this example of economic differentiation is that the original economic differences in producer relations were transfers of advantage either from prior social systems, or from new economic and administrative roles. Over time, the profit from the agriculture and the loans intensified the asymmetries, but this was a secondary development. As Mathieu (1991: 213) remarked, the state had a very limited margin of maneuver, caught as it was between the constraints of international finance and local practices.

The second example of foiled large-scale planning that I shall mention was one that took place in Burkina Faso, where eighty per cent of the territory fell within the river basin area of the Onchocerciasis Control Programme (McMillan et al 1990: xvii). It was an area that might have been suitable for irrigated farming, but which was sparsely populated because of disease, lack of drinking water, and various other problems. Spraying was started. It was successful and largely eliminated the parasite. An agency was created to control the anticipated immigration into the area. It was called The Volta Valley Authority (AVV, *Amenagements des Vallees des Volta)*. However, to cut a long story short, their design of model settlements, roads, and services could be applied only in a limited region, because as soon as the word got out that these lands were now habitable, immense waves of migrants from a variety of ethnic groups simply moved in. They did not wait for the special programs that had been designed to be put in place. A dignified distinction was made in the official report on this process between sponsored and "spontaneous" migration. But all did not end well. The report says:

> The continuous stream of immigration, coupled with the extensive cultivation practices used by most migrants is putting stress on area soils. Planners are especially concerned about the steady decline in soil fertility due to decreases in

soil organic matter. More intensive cultivation practices, using manure and the reincorporation of crop residues, have enjoyed limited success. Policymakers believe that because the migrants had insecure land rights, they tended to farm the largest area possible rather than adopt more intensive soil conservation practices. (McMillan 1990: xxii; see also xxxiii and xxxiv)

Land nationalization was only one dimension of insecurity. There also were major questions about the land interests of the indigenous population. The autochthonous residents had allowed the migrants easy access to the lands for cultivation, but these transactions were understood by them to be loans; temporary grants, not permanent, nor heritable ones. Or at least that is what was being said by local people in retrospect. Conflict was on the horizon. Thus, another set of centrally planned interventions was redirected by local events.

But the discourse about how to revise land tenure law does not focus on the implications of such redirections, perhaps because it embraces them. It is evident that the World Bank solution, individual private property and the market, will exacerbate economic and political inequalities, but to the advocates of this position, economic development is the value with the highest priority and inequality is a price worth paying. This clashes with the ideal which others espouse, namely, that land reform should be used as a means of promoting democracy and social justice, of empowering sectors of the population who heretofore have been excluded from political decision-making and economic benefits, and who are now claiming rights they have been denied (Thomson and Coulibaly 1994; Thomson 1994).

The communitarians, such as Thomson and Coulibaly, argue that land tenure reform can and should be used in the service of greater equality, economic and political. Their conception of social justice is clearly based on an ideal model of gender equality and democratic opportunity. But how communal self-governance can be assumed to guarantee such an objective has not been made clear by its proponents. When community management is idealized, what is swept under the rug is the extent to which existing communities in Africa have themselves been the sites of inequalities and the instigators of exclusions.

In a great deal of the discourse about land rights and democracy in the Sahel, the rhetorical preoccupation today is with the excluded, the disenfranchised, the discriminated against. In most areas women do the agricultural work but have no access to a disposable interest in land, and no access to the income from their labors. As the largest group among the deprived, women have become the

turning point of the rhetoric of injustice. But women are not the only excluded
population. Depending upon which local system one is examining, one can find
others equally excluded. The needs of the pastoralists who are denied paths of
access to water and pasture for their beasts clash with the needs of cultivators
whose fields are trampled on. The descendants of slaves or casted persons are
often without civil rights and have no recourse.[4] In many villages, just by reason
of age, young men are without power or property.

And last, but by no means least, are the contentious rights of migrants to
lands granted to them by the autochthonous residents, and which the autoch-
thones now reclaim. Under conditions of land plenty and an absence of land
markets, villagers were often generous. There are many communities in West
Africa where "strangers" who asked to settle locally were offered a plot to cultivate. It is seldom clear under precisely what "legal" conditions these loans or
gifts of land were made. Now all the surrounding circumstances have changed.
There has been a dramatic population increase, the population doubling ap-
proximately every twenty-five years. This demographic change combined with
chronic drought, increasing aridity, and widespread land degradation has generated a great deal of migration. There are even villages where the in-migrants
now heavily outnumber the original population (Laurent and Mathieu 1994).
And in some places the numbers who settle outside their original territories
have been augmented by political, refugee-generating disasters. There is no
longer a plentiful supply of good land.

One often hears it said that in the past the moral precepts of African culture
presupposed that everyone had a *right* to the use of a piece of cultivable land. As
Shipton (1994: 350) summarized the matter, "According to this principle, access
to land should go to those who need and can use it, and no one should starve
for special want of it." Under the same principle, "strangers" or "migrants" who
ask for permission to cultivate should not be refused if there is sufficient land to
share with them. What happens afterwards depends on local contingencies. As
Elias said about African Customary Law:

Of course, the use of land can be transferred temporarily or permanently, as when
immigrant settlers are allowed to settle on family land, at first conditionally upon
proving in the course of time to be satisfactory components of the host commu-

---

4.   See van Dijk (1996: 30) on the exclusion of the descendants of slaves from desirable
land near a new well in Mali.

nity, and later absolutely upon virtual absorption by and complete assimilation with the landowning groups (Elias 1956: 162).

But the question of whether this was a matter of right remains? Was there ever such a *right* in the rule-minded, legal, human rights sense of today? Or are we talking about the frequent practice of generosity in the presence of land plenty, the helping of strangers having been at one time an affordable moral ideal.

In many parts of West Africa today, land shortage and conflict over "rights" to land are major social problems. This is occurring in a geographical area beset by periodic drought, chronic aridity, degradation of the soil, and demographic pressure from a rapidly increasing population. In many parts of the region this has resulted in significant migrations. As migrants move into other people's fallow or into any land that is newly made viable, the potential for conflict increases, whatever the actual circumstances that initially led the migrants to cultivate in other's territory. Governments want to settle the question of who has a right to what. They often think in terms of cadastral surveys and boundary maps, and they are encouraged by the conditionalities of IMF and World Bank interventions, to think of the goal as one of individual private property in land. But who has the greater right, the original inhabitants or the needy migrants? Do both have legitimate claims? Who is to decide that question and who is to enforce the decision?

THE WAY THINGS ARE: RIGHTS, CLAIMS AND, PERHAPS, REMEDIES

There is a striking difference between two of the many currents of talk about rights. One concerns what "should be" and the other concerns "what is." One is located in the theoretical debates that surround the worldwide human rights movement, the other in the reports of anthropologists who describe people who are actually claiming rights in the course of managing their affairs. Transcendant moral, legal, and cultural criteria occupy the theorists. Their question is: what would an abstract and portable international definition of human rights be, one that might serve as a standard anywhere? By contrast, anthropologists are concerned with the actual life situation of particular people at a particular time and place, people who formulate some of their problems in terms of what they see as their rights, their due. The difference I want to emphasize between the grand talk of what "should be" and the particularistic accounts of "what is," is not the distinction between universalism and relativism which is so tirelessly (and often fruitlessly) discussed in the human rights literature. What I want to emphasize is the difference in political subtext between these two perspectives.

The philosophically-minded human rights advocates, social theorists, lawyers, and others set their agenda in an international political arena. They think in terms of international law. They want to transcend all parochialisms to make their case, to mobilize worldwide support for a set of ideals on a transnational basis, hoping that local applications will ensue. It is a top-down perspective. The legalistic definitions that are sought are absolute. One either has a declared right or does not. The rights are entitlements that go with the condition of being human.

This broad international discourse on human rights runs on a track parallel to many other international communications and contacts (see Merry [1992] for a bibliographical overview of the anthropological literature on transnational processes). It intersects with social theory and philosophical thought about the human condition, and it also has links with international organizations and with activist political causes.

The anthropologist may have such connections as well. But the strength of the fieldwork perspective is that anthropology provides a specific description of "what is" happening on the ground at a particular time and place. This includes, to the extent that such is possible, tracing the impact on the social field studied of official interventions, economic upheavals, and the contact with a continuously changing traffic in ideas.

Much is likely to manifest itself indirectly. In that regard, among the most revealing events in the observable scene are likely to be the small-scale contestations over rights that take place between rival claimants. These minor struggles, and the justifications they invoke, expose the dynamics and culture of a wider political arena. Anthropology, to the extent that it considers the future by looking at the present, can give the lofty transnational discourse on moral principles and legal doctrines a distinct whiff of the practical and the possible. Anthropology is positioned to press the question, "How do you get from here to there?"

Thus, precisely because land problems, and the reform of systems of land tenure, engage with all of these complex issues at many levels, and are nothing if they are not practical problems, they are a useful route through which to think about human rights in Africa (An-Na'im and Deng 1990: 218, 245). There is no situation that brings African political incapacities to the surface more clearly.

African states are often confronted with land problems they cannot or will not handle. There are serious questions involved about law, about rights, about the dignity and well-being of human beings.

Human rights, in the strictest, recent, international law sense, began with protections of the rights of individual persons in relation to governments. As an overarching body, the international community of states has collectively committed itself to many such protections, and to doing what it can to see that states honour them (Henkin 1981; 1994). But states often disregard their commitments in this regard, and much of the time the international community does not have the will or the capacity to enforce the commitments that were made. Thus, even to the extent they are clear, the certainties of legal rights are not matched by practical measures for the legal recognition of violations and the enforcement of norms. This has been very extensively remarked on in the African context (Cohen, Hyden and Nagan 1993; An-Na'im and Deng 1990; see also Messer [1993] in an overview of anthropology and human rights).

But whatever the actual complexities and practical limitations on the implementation of human rights as iterated in international law, there is no such limitation on discussing an expanded moral vision of what human entitlements ought to be. "Human rights are among the few utopian ideals left" (Wilson 1998: 1). But, in fact, the possibility of making them operational may be the crucial question.

When one comes to consider land problems in Africa, one is obliged to think not just about what is desirable, but rather about what is possible, where and when. Nor can the blame for every trouble be placed on the state. From the point of view of the victims of events of land deprivation, the ultimate results of very different causes may seem the same. The confiscation of land without compensation by a government, the seizure of land by a powerful individual, or by a rival ethnic group, or a major interference with beneficial use by competitors, or the experience of being driven away by land degradation and drought, all end in deprivation.[5]

The course of capitalist development itself may drive rural people from their land. In West Africa one recent report argued that urban activities are more

---

5. See Faure 1997 on confiscation without compensation in Burkina Faso; and Nowrojee (1993: 19 ff., 49–93) on ethnic violence, land appropriation and government involvement in arming the aggressors in the Rift Valley of Kenya; also note the examples of migration cited earlier here.

"productive" than rural activities, hence that investment should go to urban rather than rural areas. The thesis of the report was that the city is the motor of development. It argued that urban growth stimulates production in the country-side. The general prediction was that the sooner that "unproductive," barely surviving small-holders were pushed off their land by the action of the market, the sooner that economically efficient agro-businesses would be able to take over and make the countryside more productive (Cour 1995). That study implies that the small-holders would then become laborers in the rural areas or join the urban poor in the informal economy. Such development visions of the future can scarcely reassure rural holders. Happily there are critiques that contest some of this analysis (D'Agostino 1995; Dione 1995; Reardon and Staatz 1995).

As far as the logic of a rural agricultural population of smallholders is concerned, if you do not have a piece of productive land you do not have food, and you and your family may die. The right to life in an agrarian society can be conceived as the right to access to land and all the inputs, such as water, necessary to make it minimally productive. Hence for rural agriculturalists, the most urgent issue is not about human rights as a conception, but about survival in the here and now, and to whom to turn for some guarantee of security. It is obvious that there can be more than one claimant for a piece of land, and more than one entity that wants to control the use of land. Who is to judge which claims are legitimate, and what settlements are fair?

Whatever the particular details that precede a loss, there is seldom a neutral forum to which small-holders who anticipate being expropriated or pushed out can present their dilemmas. There is no political arena where they have standing and can communicate their case in advance of loss. However clearly Jurgen Habermas (1996: 122–31) can imagine democratic fora where the moral value of alternatives might be freely and fairly debated, there are usually no such fora for these issues. For example, there is no place where international development agencies and the target populations of particular development programs can have a debate about the issues and policies under conditions of democratic equality.

Besides, moral values, even when agreed upon, may not be sufficient to solve practical problems. Rival populations claiming the same lands, both having good grounds for their claims, may need matters to be resolved by supervised negotiation, or by some other means such as resettlement programs. There may be a need for large scale plans which provide alternative options where accommodating both sets of legitimate claimants is physically impossible. Agencies are needed which can ascertain the legitimacy of claims, and then address them without being confined to a legalistic, adversarial, either/or solution.

Conditions vary. To match them, remedial possibilities must vary. Further, when the direct agency of deprivation is not the state, what follows? Is the state to be held responsible in human rights doctrine for not intervening when there are violations of land rights by one ethnic group against another within its borders? (And when the state is a suspected accomplice of such appropriations as recently in Kenya, what then?) Should state responsibility under human rights doctrines be extended to deprivations due to environmental damage? Should the state (or multi-state regional bodies) be responsible for looking after populations that have been driven out of their territories by aridity or land degradation? Or by the workings of the economy?

Human rights discussions in the abstract, with an emphasis on what is morally desirable, seem quite aimless without a concomitant discussion of the practical conditions under which action could be taken. It seems necessary to ask why there is such a paucity of elective agencies of recognition, debate, and redress. Without a discussion of the political preconditions involved in meeting the human rights agenda, there is little headway to be made.

It is my view that without some attention to practical institutional possibilities from the start, there are no legal rights to discuss, only moral claims and responsive sympathies. Rights without remedies are ephemeral. To ask how to create an appropriate space where legitimate claims could be acknowledged and acted upon is very much to the point. Such practical and pragmatic questions must go in tandem with any discussion of what constitutes a right. Posing the questions may do no more than show that at a particular place and time no morally satisfactory solutions could possibly be realized. It may sometimes be necessary to be willing to acknowledge incapacity.

The practical and operational sides of rights questions should not be ignored. Anthropology is particularly well placed to contribute to that aspect of the discussion. Such practical issues are bound to lead beyond the consolations found in the high-sounding normative statements of international treaties, and beyond the idealistic discourse of a benign philosophical morality. They lead to a knowledge of nasty politics, vicious and violent competitions, and perhaps even to serious reflections on existing economic and political inequities. What would the preconditions be for better possibilities to emerge? That is the question that should be asked more often. If legal and moral human rights talk ultimately leads to such reflections it is a good thing. But by itself, it is not enough.

References

Allott, Antony Nicholas. 1960. *Essays in African law*. London: Butterworth.

———. 1969. "The restatement of African law project of the School of Oriental and African Studies, London: A general report on the period 1959–1969." Mimeograph.

———, ed. 1970. *Judicial and legal systems in Africa*. London: Butterworth.

American Folklore Society. 1904. *Memoirs*. No. 8.

Anderson, Benedict. 1983. *Imagined communities: Reflections on the origin and spread of nationalism*. London: Verso.

An-Na'im, Abdullah Ahmed and Francis Deng, eds. 1990. *Human rights in Africa*. Washington, D.C.: The Brookings Institution.

Apter, David E. 1963. "Political religion in the new nations." In *Old societies and new states: The quest for modernity in Asia and Africa*, edited by Clifford Geertz, 57–104. Glencoe: The Free Press.

Augustine. 1958. *The city of God*. New York: Doubleday and Company.

Austin, J. L. 1962. *How to do things with words*. New York: Oxford University Press.

Bailey, F. G. 1960. *Tribe, caste and nation: A study of political activity and political change in highland Orissa*. Manchester: Manchester University Press.

———. 1965. "Decisions by consensus in councils and committees: With special reference to village and local government in India." In *Political systems and the distribution of power*, edited by Michael Banton, 1–20. A.S.A. Monographs 2. London: Tavistock.

———. 1969. *Stratagems and apoils: A social anthropology of politics*. Oxford: Basil Blackwell.

Barley, Nigel. 1984. *The innocent anthropologist: Notes from a mud hut*. New York: Vanguard Press.

Barth, Fredrik. 1966. *Models of social organization*. Royal Anthropological Institute Occasional Paper No. 23. London: Royal Anthropological Institute.

———. 1981. *Models reconsidered: Process and form in social life*. London: Routledge and Kegan Paul.

———, ed. 1978. *Scale and social organization*. Oslo: Universitetsfort (Bergen: John Grieg).

Best, Elsdon. 1924. *The Maori*: Memoirs of the Polynesian society, volume 5. New Plymouth: Thomas Avery.

Beattie, John. 1966. "Ritual and social change." *Man*. 1 (1): 60–74.

Bienen, Henry. 1967. *Tanzania, party transformation and economic development*. Princeton: Princeton University Press.

Bohannan, Paul. 1965. "The differing realms of the law." *American Anthropologist* (67) 6: 33–42.

Borneman, John. 1997. *Settling accounts: Violence, justice and accountability in postsocialist Europe*. Princeton: Princeton University Press.

Bourdieu, Pierre. 1977. *Outline of a theory of practice*. Cambridge: Cambridge University Press.

———. 1984. *Distinction: A social critique of the judgment of taste*. Translated by Richard Nice. Cambridge: Harvard University Press.

———. 2000. *The weight of the world: Social suffering in contemporary society*. Palo Alto, CA: Stanford University Press.

Bourdieu, Pierre and Jean Claude Passerson. 1977. *Reproduction in education, society and culture*. Beverly Hills: Sage Publications.

Bowen, John and Roger Peterson, eds. 1999. *Critical comparisons in politics and culture*. Cambridge: Cambridge University Press.

Burawoy, Michael. 2000. "Grounding globalization." In *Global Ethnography*, edited by M. Burawoy, J. Blum, et al., 337–50. Berkeley: University of California Press.

Burton, Michael and Douglas R. White. 1987. "Cross cultural surveys today." *Annual Review of Anthropology* 16: 143–60.

Chambliss, William J. and Robert Seidman. 1971. *Law, order and power*. Reading: Addison-Wesley Publishing Company.

Chanock, Martin. 1985. *Law, custom and social order: The colonial experience in Malawi and Zambia*. Cambridge: Cambridge University Press.

Cliffe, Lionel. 1972. "Tanzania – socialist transformation and party development." In *Socialism in Tanzania*, edited by Lionel Cliffe and John Saul, 266–76. Dar es Salaam: East Africa Publishing House.

Cochrane, Glynn. 1971. *Development anthropology*. New York: Oxford University Press.

Cohen, Ronald, Goran Hyden and Winston P. Nagan, eds. 1993. *Human rights and governance in Africa.* Gainesville: University Press of Florida.

Comaroff, John. 1984. "*The closed society and its critics: Historical transformations in African ethnography.*" *American Ethnologist* 2 (3): 571–83.

Comaroff, John and Simon Roberts. 1977. "The invocation of norms in dispute settlement: The Tswana case." *Social anthropology and law,* edited by I. Hamnett, 77–112. ASA Monograph No. 14. London: Academic Press.

———. 1981. *Rules and processes: the cultural logic of dispute in an African context.* Chicago: Chicago University Press.

Cooper, Frederick and Randall Packard, eds. 1997. *International development and the social sciences.* Berkeley: University of California Press.

Cour, Jean-Marie (Director of Study). 1995. *West Africa Long Term Perspective Study* (WALTPS) Carried out by Cinergie Unit of African Development Bank (Abidjan), Secretariat of the Club du Sahel of the OECD (Organisation for Economic Cooperation and Development) (Paris) and CILSS (Permanent Inter-State Committee for Drought Control in the Sahel) (Ouagadougou). Summary Report, SAH/D (94) 439, Paris.

Crousse, Bernard, Paul Mathieu and Sidy M. Seck, eds. 1991. *La vallee du fleuve Senegal.* Paris: Karthala.

Daily News. 1974. Dar es Salaam, Tanzania. February.

D'Agostino, Victoire. 1995. "Notes on the WALTPS (West Africa Long Term Perspective Study): points of agreement and disagreement." Unpublished internal memorandum, Club du Sahel.

De Sousberghe, R. P. L. 1955. *Structure de parente et d'alliance d'apres les formulas Pende.* Brussels: Academie Royale des Sciences Morales et Politiques.

Devereaux, George. 1939. "The social and cultural implications of incest among the Mohave Indians." *The Psychoanalytic Quarterly* 8: 510–33.

Dionne, Josué. 1995. "Comments on the WALTPS (West African Long Term Perspective Study) Results and Implications." FSH Cooperative Agreement. Food Security Briefing Paper. No. 95–02. Michigan State University/INSAH-PRISAS..

Dixon, Roland B. 1916. "Oceanic mythology." In *The mythology of all races,* volume 9, edited by Louis H. Gray. Boston: Marshall Jones Company.

Douglas, Mary. 1966. *Purity and danger.* London: Routledge and Kegan Paul.

Dror, Yehezkel. 1968. "Law and Social Change." In *The Sociology of Law,* edited by Rita James Simon, 663–680. San Francisco: Chandler Publishing Company.

Dubois, Cora. 1944. *The people of Alor.* Minneapolis: University of Minnesota Press.

Dundas, Charles. 1924. *Kilimanjaro and its people.* London: Witherby.

Durkheim, Émile. 1961. *The elementary forms of the religious life*. New York: Collier.

El-Hakim, Sherif. 1978. "The structure and dynamics of consensus decision making." *Man* 13 (1): 55.

Elias, T. Olawale. 1956. *The nature of African customary law*. Manchester: Manchester University Press.

Ellickson, Robert C. 1991. *Order without law*. Cambridge: Harvard University Press.

Elyachar, Julia. 2002. "Empowerment money: The World Bank, NGOs, and the value of culture in Egypt." *Public Culture* 14(3): 493–514.

———. 2003. "Mappings of power: The state, NGOs, and international organizations in the informal economy of Cairo." *Comparative Studies in Society and History* 45 (3): 571–605.

———. 2005. *Markets of dispossession: Empowering the poor in Cairo*. Durham/London: Duke University Press.

Etter, Carl. 1949. *Ainu folklore*. Chicago: Wilcox and Follett.

Evans-Pritchard, E. E. 1960. *Kinship and marriage among the Nuer*. London: Oxford University Press.

Fallers, Lloyd A. 1969. *Law without precedent*. Chicago: University of Chicago Press.

Fathauer, George H. 1961. "Trobriand." In *Matrilineal kinship*, edited by David M. Schneider and Kathleen Gough, 234–69. Berkeley: University of California Press.

Faure, Armelle. 1995. "Private land ownership in rural Burkina Faso." Paper No. 59. London: International Institute for Environment and Development

———. 1997. "Le droit des ruraux en cas de perte du foncier, l'example du Burkina Faso." Paper presented at the Colloque International sur le Foncier au Sahel, Université de Saint Louis, Sénégal.

Finnemore, Martha. 1997. "Redefining development at the World Bank." In *International development and the social sciences: Essays in the politics and history of knowledge*, edited by Frederick Cooper and Randall Packard, 203–27. Berkeley: University of California Press.

Firth, Raymond. 1961. *We, the Tikopia*. London: George Allen and Unwin.

Fischer, J. L. 1963. "The sociopsychological analysis of folktales." *Current Anthropology* 4 (3): 235–95.

Foucault, Michel. 1973. *The order of things*. Random House: Vintage Books.

Frazer, Sir James George. 1960. *The golden bough*. New York: Macmillan.

Friedman, Lawrence M. and Stewart Macaulay, eds. 1969. *Law and the behavioral sciences*. New York: Bobbs-Merrill Company.

Frobenius, Leo and Douglas Fox. 1938. *African genesis*. London: Faber and Faber.

Garbett, G. Kingsley. 1970. "The analysis of social situations." *Man*. 5 (2): 214–27.

Geertz, Clifford. 1972. "Deep play: Notes on the Balinese cockfight." *Daedalus* 101 (1): 1–37.

———. 1973. "Ritual and social change." In *The interpretation of cultures*. New York: Basic Books.

———. 1983. *Local knowledge: Further essays in interpretive anthropology*. New York: Basic Books.

———. 1995. *After the fact*. Cambridge: Harvard University Press.

Georges, Telford. 1973. "The courts in the Tanzania one party state." In *Law and its administration in a one party state*, edited by R.W. James and F.M. Kassam, 9–32. Kampala: East African Literature Bureau.

Gifford, E. W. 1916. "Miwok moieties." *University of California Publications in American Archeology and Ethnology* 12 (4): 139–94.

Gluckman, Max. 1950. "Kinship and marriage among the Lozi." In *African systems of kinship and marriage*, edited by A.R. Radcliffe-Brown and Daryll Forde. London: Oxford University Press.

———. 1955. *The judicial process among the Barotse of Northern Rhodesia*. Manchester: Manchester University Press for the Rhodes Livingston Institute.

———. 1965b. *The ideas in Barotse jurisprudence*. New Haven: Yale University Press.

———. 1965a. *Politics, law, and ritual in tribal cociety*. Oxford: Blackwell

———, ed. 1969. *Ideas and procedures in African customary law*. Oxford: Oxford University Press for the International African Institute

Goodale, Mark. 2009. *Human rights: An anthropology reader*. West Sussex: Wiley-Blackwell.

Goody, Jack. 1977. *The domestication of the savage mind*. Cambridge: Cambridge University Press.

———. 1986. *The logic of writing and the organization of society*. Cambridge: Cambridge University Press.

Griaule, Marcel and Germaine Dieterlen. 1954. "The Dogon." In *African worlds: Studies in the cosmological ideas and social values of African peoples*, edited by Daryll Forde, 83–110. London: Oxford University Press

Graves, Robert and Raphael Patai. 1963. "Some Hebrew myths and legends." *Encounter* 114: 12–18.

Griffiths, A. W. M. 1930. "Land tenure, Moshi District." Manuscript Collections of Africana. Rhodes House Library. Oxford. Unpublished source. MSS Afr. S. 1001, 63, 88.

Gulliver, Phillip H. 1963. *Social control in an African society*. London: Routledge and Kegan Paul.

———. 1969. "Dispute settlement without courts: the Ndendeuli Southern Tanzania." In *Law in culture and society*, edited by Laura Nader, 24–68. Chicago: Aldine Publishing Company.

———. 1979. *Disputes and negotiations: A cross-cultural perspective.* New York: Academic Press.

Gupta, Akhil and James Ferguson, eds. 1997. *Anthropological locations.* Berkeley: University of California Press.

Gustafson B. D. 2001. "Native languages and hybrid states: a political ethnography of Guarani engagement with bilingual education reform in Bolivia, 1989–1999." PhD dissertation. Cambridge: Harvard University.

———. 2002. "The paradoxes of liberal indigenism: indigenous movements, state processes and intercultural reforms in Bolivia." In *The politics of ethnicity: indigenous peoples in Latin American states*, edited by David Maybury-Lewis, 267–306. Cambridge: Harvard University Press.

Gutmann, Bruno. 1909. *Dichten und denken der dschagganeger.* Leipzig: Evangelist Lutheran Mission.

———. 1926. *Das recht der dschagga. Arbeiten zur entwicklungspsychologie*, volume 7, edited by Felix Krueger, Munchen: C. H. Beck. English translation 1961 (slightly cut) by A. M. Nagler, *Human Relations Area Files,* New Haven: Yale University

———. 1932. *Der stammeslebren der dschagga,* volume 12. Edited by Felix Krueger. Arbeiten zur Entwicklungspsychologie. Munchen: C. H. Beck

Habermas, Jürgen. 1987. "Lifeworld and system: A critique of functionalist reason." In *The theory of communicative action*, volume 2. Translated by Thomas McCarthy. Boston: Beacon Press.

———. 1996. *Between facts and norms: Contributions to a discourse theory of law and democracy.* Translated by William Rehg. Cambridge: M.I.T. Press.

Hailey, Lord. *An African survey.* 1938. Oxford: Oxford University Press.

———. 1950. *Native administration in the British African territories.* Part I. London: HMSO.

Hann, Chris, ed. 2003. *The postsocialist agrarian question.* New Jersey: Transaction Publishers, Rutgers University.

———. ed. 2005. *Property relations* (Report on the focus group, 2000–2005). Halle/Saale: Max Planck Institute for Social Anthropology.

Hart, H. L. A. 1961. *The concept of law.* Oxford: Clarendon Press.

Held, G. J. 1957. *The Papuas of Waropen.* Koninklijk Instituut voor Taal-, Land- en Volkenkunde, Translation Series 2. The Hague: Martinus Nijhoff.

Henkin, Louis, ed. 1981. *The international bill of rights*. New York: Columbia University Press.

―――. 1994. *Human rights: An agenda for the next century*. Washington, D.C.: American Society of International Law.

Hertz, Robert. 1909. "La preeminence de la main droite: etude sur la polarite religieuse." *Revue Philosophique*. Translated and republished by Rodney Needham. In *Right and left: Essays on dual symbolic classification*, edited by Rodney Needham, 3–31. Chicago: University of Chicago Press.

Herzfeld, Michael. 1987. *Anthropology through the looking glass*. Cambridge: Cambridge University Press.

―――. 2001. "Performing comparisons." *Journal of Anthropological Research* 37 (3): 259–76.

Hesseling, Gerti and Boubakar Moussa Ba, with the collaboration of: Paul Mathieu, Mark S. Freudenberger, Samba Soumare. 1994. *Land tenure and natural resource management in the Sahel*. CILSS (Permanent Inter-State Committee for Drought Control in the Sahel), OECD (Organisation for Economic Cooperation and Development), Club du Sahel.

Hobart, M. 1987. "Summer's days and salad days: The coming of age of anthropology." In *Comparative anthropology*, edited by Ladislav Holy, 22–51 Oxford: Basil Blackwell.

Hobsbawn, Eric and Terrence Ranger. 1983. *The invention of tradition*. London: Cambridge University Press.

Hoebel, E. Adamson. 1954. *The law of primitive man*. Cambridge: Harvard University Press.

Hohfeld, Wesley N. 1964. *Fundamental legal conceptions as applied in judicial reasoning*. New Haven: Yale University Press.

Holleman, J. F. 1952. *Shona customary law*. London: Oxford University Press.

Holy, Ladislav, ed. 1987. *Comparative anthropology*. Oxford: Basil Blackwell.

Hooker, M. B. 1975. *Legal pluralism*. Oxford: Clarendon Press.

Hopkins, Terence K. and Immanuel Wallerstein. 1982. *World system analysis*. Beverly Hills: Sage.

Hoshour C. A. 2000. "Relocating development in Indonesia: A look at the logic and contradictions of state directed resettlement." PhD dissertation. Cambridge: Harvard University.

Hyden, Goran. 1980. *Beyond ujamana in Tanzania*. Berkeley: University of California Press.

Iliffe, John. *A modern history of Tanganyika*. 1979. Cambridge: Cambridge University Press.

James, R. W. 1971. *Land tenure and policy in Tanzania.* Nairobi/Dar es Salaam/Kampala: East African Literature Bureau.

James, R. W. and G. M. Fimbo. 1973. *Customary land law of Tanzania.* Nairobi/Kampala/Dar es Salaam: East African Literature Bureau.

Johnston, H. H. 1886. *The Kilimanjaro expedition.* London: Kegan, Paul, and Trench.

Junod, Henri A. 1913. *The life of a South African tribe.* Neuchatel: Atlinger Freres.

Kirchhoff, Paul. 1948. "Food gathering tribes of the Venezuelan Illanos." In *Handbook of South American Indians,* edited by Julian Steward, 445–68. Washington, D.C.: Government Printing Office.

Knorr-Cetina, K. and A. V. Cicourel. 1981. *Advances in social theory and methodology.* London: Routledge and Kegan Paul.

Kraus, Auriel. 1956. *The Tlingit Indians.* Seattle: University of Washington Press.

Krige, E. G. and J. D. Krige. 1943. *The realm of a rain queen.* London: Oxford University Press.

Kroeber, Alfred. 1947. "The Chibcha." In *Handbook of South American Indians,* edited by Julian Steward, 886–909. Washington, D.C.: Government Printing Office.

Kuper, Hilda. 1950. "Kinship among the Swazi." In *African systems of kinship and marriage,* edited by A. R. Radcliffe-Brown and Daryll Forde, 86–110. London: Oxford University Press.

Kuper, Hilda and Leo Kuper, eds. 1965. *African law, adaptation and development.* Berkeley: University of California Press.

Kuper Leo and M. G. Smith. 1969. *Pluralism in Africa.* Berkeley: University of California Press.

Guirand, Felix, ed. 1960. *Larousse encyclopedia of mythology.* London: Batchworth Press.

Laurent, Pierre Joseph and Paul Mathieu. 1994. "Authority and Conflict in the Management of Natural Resources." In *Improved resource management: The role of the state versus that of the local community,* edited by Henrik Secher Marcussened. Occasional Paper No. 12. International Development Studies. Roskilde: Roskilde University.

Leach, Edmund R. 1961. *Rethinking anthropology.* London: The Athlone Press.

Le Roy, Etienne, Alain Karsenty and Alain Bertrand, eds. 1995. *La securisation fociere en Afrique.* Paris: Karthala

Lévi-Strauss, Claude. 1948. "The Nambicuara." In *Handbook of South American Indians,* edited by Julian Steward, 361–69. Washington, D.C.: Government Printing Office.

———. 1949. *Les structures elementaires de la parente.* Paris: Presses Universalitaires de France.

———. 1955. "The structural study of myth." *Journal of American Folklore* 68: 428–44.

———. 1962. *The savage mind.* Chicago: University of Chicago Press.

————. 1962. *Le totemisme aujourd'hui*. Paris: Presses Universitaires de France.

Likosky, Michael. 2005. *The silicon empire: Law, culture and commerce*. Aldershot: Ashgate.

Little, K. L. 1951. *The mende of Sierra Leone*. London: Routledge and Kegan Paul.

Litwak, Eugene and Henry J. Meyer. 1966. "A balance theory of coordination between bureaucratic organizations and community primary groups." *Administrative Sciences Quarterly* 11: 3–58.

Llewellyn, Karl N. and E. Adamson Hoebel. 1953. *The Cheyenne way: Conflict and case law in primitive jurisprudence*. Norman: University of Oklahoma Press.

Lowenthal, Max. 1950. *The Federal Bureau of Investigation*. New York: Sloane.

Lukes, Steven, ed. 1986. *Power*. New York: New York University Press.

Lupton, Tom and Sheila Cunnison. 1964. "Workshop behavior." In *Closed systems and open minds*, edited by Max Gluckman, 103–28. Chicago: Aldine.

Macaulay, Stewart. 1963. "Non-contractual relations in business: A preliminary study." *American Sociological Review* 28: 1–19

Maelezo ya Mahakama za Mwanzo. 1964. Dar es Salaam: Government Printer.

Makler, Harry, Alberto Martinelli and Neil Smelser, eds. 1982. *The new international economy*. Beverly Hills: Sage.

Malinowski, Bronislaw. (1926) 1951. *Crime and custom in savage society*. New York: Humanities.

————. 1929. *The sexual life of savages in north-western Melanesia*. London: Routledge and Sons.

Mamdani, Mahmood. 1996. *Citizen and subject: Contemporary Africa and the legacy of late colonialism*. Princeton: Princeton University Press.

Mann, Kristin and Richard Roberts, eds. 1991. *Law in colonial Africa*. Portsmouth: Heinemann Educational Books.

March, James G. and Johan P. Olsen. 1976. *Ambiguity and choice in organizations*. Bergen: Universitesforlaget.

Marcus, George E. and Michael M. J. Fisher. 1986. *Anthropology as cultural critique*. Chicago: University of Chicago Press.

Marealle, Petro Itosi. 1947. *Maisha ya Mchagga hapa Duniani na Ahera*. Nairobi: The English Press.

Mathieu, Paul. 1990. "Usages de la loi et pratiques foncieres dans les amenagements irrigues." *Politique Africaine* 40: 72–81.

————. 1991. "Irrigation, transformation economique et enjeux fonciers." In *La Vallee du Fleuve Senegal*, edited by Bernard Crousse, Paul Mathieu and Sidy M. Seck, 197–214. Paris: Karthala.

Maurer, Bill. 2002. "Anthropological and accounting knowledge in Islamic banking and finance: Rethinking critical accounts." *Journal of the Royal Anthropological Institute* 8 (4): 644–67.

McMillan, Della, Jean-Baptiste Nana and Kimseyinga Savadogo. 1990. Country case study, Burkina Faso: Land settlement review: Settlement experiences and development strategies in the Onchocerciasis Control Programme areas of West Africa. Binghamton: Institute for Development Anthropology.

Mead, Margaret. 1930. "Social organizations of Manua." Bernice P. Bishop Museum Bulletin, volume 76. Honolulu, Hawaii.

Melland, Frank H. 1923. *In witch-bound Africa*. London: Seeley Services & Co Limited.

Merry, Sally. 1992. "Anthropology, law and transnational processes." *Annual Review of Anthropology* 21: 357–79.

Messer, Ellen. 1993. "Anthropology and human rights." *Annual Review of Anthropology* 22: 221–49.

Middleton, John and David Tait, eds. 1958. *Tribes without rulers*. London: Routledge and Kegan Paul.

Miner, Horace. 1956. "Body ritual among the Nacirema." *American Anthropologist* 58 (3): 503–7.

Mitchell, J. Clyde. 1969. *Social networks in urban situations*. Manchester: Manchester University Press.

Mohiddin, A. 1972. *Ujamaa na kujitegemea."* In *Socialism in Tanzania*, edited by Lionel Cliffe and John Saul, 266–76. Dar es Salaam: East Africa Publishing House.

Mooney, James. 1902. *Myths of the Cherokee*. Washington: Government Printing Office.

Moore, D. C. 1976. *The politics of deference: A study of the mid-nineteenth century English political system*. Hassocks, Sussex: Harvester Press.

Moore, Sally Falk. 1955. "The Department of Anthropology." In *A history of the Faculty of Political Science, Columbia University*, 147–60. New York: Columbia University Press.

——. 1958. *Power and property in Inca Peru*. New York: Columbia University Press.

——. 1963. "Asymmetrical cross-cousin marriage and Crow-Omaha terminology." *American Anthropologist* 65 (2): 296–311.

——. 1964. "Descent and symbolic filiation." *American Anthropologist* 66 (6): 1308–20.

——. 1969a. "Descent and legal position." In *Law in culture and society*, edited by Laura Nader. 337–348. Chicago: Aldine

——. 1969b. "Introduction: Papers on theory and method." In *Law in culture and society*, edited by Laura Nader, 374–400. Chicago: Aldine.

——. 1969c. "Law and anthropology." In *Biennial review of anthropology*, edited by Bernard J. Siegel, 252–300. Stanford: Stanford University Press.

———. 1970. "Politics, procedures and norms in changing Chagga law." *Africa* 35 (4): 321–44.

———. 1972. "Legal liability and evolutionary interpretation: Some aspects of strict liability, self-help and collective responsibility." In *The allocation of responsibility*, edited by Max Gluckman, 41–107. Manchester: Manchester University Press.

———. 1973. "Law and social change: The semi-autonomous social field as an appropriate subject of study." *Law and Society Review* 7 (4): 719–46.

———. 1974. "Civil cases and social contexts: Kilimanjaro 1974 and its judicial past." *East African Journal of Law* 7 (2): 189–204.

———. 1975a. "Epilogue: Uncertainties in situations, indeterminacies in culture." In *Symbol and politics in communal ideology: Cases and questions,* edited by Sally Falk Moore and Barbara Myerhoff, 210–39. Ithaca: Cornell University Press.

———. 1975b. "Selection for failure in a small social field: Ritual concord and fraternal strife among the Chagga, Kilimanjaro, 1968–69." In *Symbols and politics in communal ideology,* edited by Sally Falk Moore and Barbara Myerhoff, 109–43. Ithaca: Cornell University Press.

———. 1976. "The secret of the men: A fiction of Chagga initiation and its relation to the logic of Chagga symbolism." *Africa* 46 (4): 357–70.

———. 1977a. "Individual interests and organizational structures: Dispute settlements as 'events of articulation'." In *Social anthropology and law,* edited by Ian Hammett. ASA Monograph No. 14, 159–88. London: Academic Press.

———. 1977b. "Political meetings and the simulation of unanimity: Kilimanjaro, 1973". In *Secular ritual,* edited by Sally Falk Moore and Barbara Myerhoff, 151–72. Assen/Amsterdam: Royal Van Gorcum.

———. 1978a. *Law as process: Essays on law and anthropology.* London: Routledge & Kegan Paul.

———. 1978b. "Old age in a life-term social arena: Some Chagga of Kilimanjaro in 1974." In *Life's career: Aging,* edited by Barbara Myerhoff and A. Simic, 23–78. Los Angeles: Sage Publications.

———. 1985. "Dividing the pot of gold." *Negotiation Journal* 1 (1): 29–43.

———. 1986a. *Social facts and fabrications: "Customary" law on Kilimanjaro, 1880–1980.* Cambridge: Cambridge University Press.

———. 1986b. "Legal systems of the world: An introductory guide to classifications, typological interpretation and bibliographical resources." In *Law and the social sciences,* edited by Leon Lipson and Stanley Wheeler, 11–62. New York: Russell Sage Foundation for the Social Science Research Council.

————. 1987 "Explaining the present: Theoretical dilemmas in processual ethnography." *American Ethnologist* 14 (4): 727–36.

————. 1988. "Legitimation as a process: The expansion of government and party in Tanzania." In *State formation and political legitimacy*, edited by Ronald Cohen and Judith D. Toland, 137–54. New Brunswick: Transaction Books.

————. 1989. "The production of cultural pluralism as a process." *Public Culture* 1 (2): 26–48.

————. 1991a. "From giving and lending to selling: Property transactions reflecting historical changes on Kilimanjaro." In *Law in Colonial Africa*, edited by Kristin Mann and Richard Roberts, 108–27. Portsmouth: Heinemann and Currey.

————. 1991b. "Inflicting harm righteously: Turning a relative into a stranger: An African case." In *Fremde der gesellschaft: Historische und sozialwissenschaftliche untersuchungen zur differenzierung von normalität undfFremdheit*, edited by M. T. Fogen. Frankfurt am Main: Vittorio Klostermann.

————. 1992. "Treating law as knowledge: Telling colonial officers what to say to Africans about running 'their own' native courts." *Law & Society Review* 26 (1): 11–44.

————. 1993a. "Introduction: Moralizing states and the ethnography of the present." In *Moralizing states and the ethnography of the present*, edited by Sally Falk Moore. American Ethnological Society Monograph, volume 5, 1–16. Arlington: American Anthropological Society.

————. 1993b. "The ethnography of the present and the analysis of process." In *Assessing cultural anthropology*, edited by Robert Borofsky, 362–76. New York: McGraw Hill.

————. 1994. *Anthropology and Africa: Changing perspectives on a changing scene*. Charlottesville: The University of Virginia Press

————. 1995. "Imperfect communications." In *Understanding disputes: The politics of argument*, edited by Pat Caplan. London: Berg Publishers.

————. 1996. "Post-socialist micro-politics: Kilimanjaro, 1993." *Africa* 66 (4): 587–606.

————. 1998. "Systematic judicial and extra-judicial injustice: preparations for future accountability." In *Memory and the postcolony: African anthropology and the critique of power*, edited by Richard Werbner, 126–51. London: Zed Books.

————. 1999. "From lawyer's law into the academic zoo." *Political and Legal Anthropology Review* 22 (1): 101–5.

————. 2001a. "Certainties undone: Fifty turbulent years of legal anthropology, 1949–1999." Huxley Memorial Lecture, *Journal of the Royal Anthropological Institute* 7: 95–116.

————. 2001b. "The international production of authoritative knowledge: The case of drought-stricken West Africa." *Ethnography* 2 (2): 161–89.

————. 2002. "An international legal regime and the context of conditionality." In *Transnational legal processes: Globalisation and power disparities*, edited by M. Likosky, 333–52. London: Butterworths.

————. 2005. "Comparisons: Possible and impossible." *Annual Review of Anthropology* 34: 1–11.

————, ed. 1993. *Moralizing states and the ethnography of the present*. American Ethnological Society Monograph Series, volume 5, 1–16. Arlington: American Anthropological Society.

————, ed. 2004. *Law and anthropology: A reader*. Oxford: Blackwell Publishers.

Moore, Sally Falk, and Barbara G. Myerhoff. 1977. "Introduction." In *Secular ritual*, edited by Sally Falk Moore and Barbara G. Myerhoff, 3–24. Assen/Amsterdam: Van Gorcum.

————, eds. 1975. *Symbol and politics in communal ideology*. Ithaca: Cornell University Press.

————, eds. 1977. *Secular ritual*. Assen/Amsterdam: Van Gorcum.

Mudimbe, V. Y. 1988. *The invention of Africa*. Bloomington: Indiana University Press.

Murphy, Robert F. 1959. "Social structure and sex antagonism." *Southwestern Journal of Anthropology* 15: 89–98.

Nadel, S. F. 1950. "Dual descent in the Nuba hills." In *African systems of kinship and marriage*, edited by A. R. Radcliffe-Brown and Daryll Forde, 333–59. London: Oxford University Press.

Needham, Rodney. 1972. *Belief, language and experience*. Chicago: University of Chicago Press.

————. 1973. *Right and left: Essays on dual symbolic classification*. Chicago: University of Chicago Press.

New, Charles. 1874. *Life, wanderings and labours in Eastern Africa*. Cass Library of African Studies, Issue 16. Missionary researches and travels. London: Frank Cass.

Niasse, Madodio. 1991. "Les perimetres irrigues villageois vieillissent mal." In *La vallee du fleuve Senegal*, edited by B. Crousse, P. Mathieu, S. M. Seck, 97–115. Paris: Karthala.

Nowrojee, Binaifer. 1993. *Divide and rule, state sponsored ethnic violence in Kenya*. New York and London: Human Rights Watch.

Ofuatey-Kodjoe, W. 1977. *The principle of self-determination in international law*. New York: Nellen Publishing Company.

Ortner, Sherry B. 1984. "Theory in anthropology since the sixties." *Comparative Studies in Society and History* 26: 126–66.

Paine, Robert. 1969. "In search of friendship: An exploratory analysis in 'middle-class' culture." *Man* 4 (4): 505–24.

———. 1974. *Second thoughts about Barth's models.* Occasional Paper No. 32. London: Royal Anthropological Institute.

Parry, N. E. 1932. *The Lakhers.* London: Macmillan and Company.

Phillips, Arthur. 1945. *Crown counsel, colony and protectorate of Kenya.* Report on Native Tribunals. Nairobi: Government Printers.

Playfair, Alan. 1909. *The Garos.* London: D. Nutt.

Plucknett, Theodore F. T. 1956. *A concise history of the common law.* Boston: Little Brown and Company.

Pospisil, Leopold. 1971. *Anthropology of law: A comparative theory.* New York: Harper and Row.

Pound, Roscoe. 1965. "Contemporary juristic theory." In *Introduction to Jurisprudence*, edtied by Dennis Lloyd, 247–52. London: Stevens and Sons.

Rabinow, Paul. 1986. "Representations are social facts: Modernity and post-modernity in anthropology." In *Writing culture: The poetics and politics of ethnography*, edited by James Clifford and George Marcus, 234–61. Berkeley: University of California Press.

Radcliffe-Brown, A. R. 1933. *The Andaman Islanders.* London: Cambridge University Press.

———. (1952) 1965. *Structure and function in primitive society.* Glencoe: The Free Press.

Ranger, Terence. 1983. "The invention of tradition in colonial Africa." In *The invention of tradition*, edited by Eric Hobsbawm and Terence Ranger, 211–62. Cambridge: Cambridge University Press.

Rappaport, Roy A. 1971. "Ritual sanctity and cybernetics." *American Anthropologist* 73 (1): 59–76.

Raum, O. F. 1940. *Chagga childhood.* London: Oxford University Press for the International African Institute.

Reardon, Thomas and John M. Staatz. 1995. "Reflections on WALTPS (West African Long Term Perspective Study) results and recommendations: Implications for food security in West Africa" Food Security Briefing Paper, No. 95–02. Bamako: PRISAS, Institut du Sahel.

Richards, Audrey, and Adam Kuper, eds. 1971. *Councils in action.* Cambridge: Cambridge University Press.

Rifle, John. 1979. *A modern history of Tanganyika.* Cambridge: Cambridge University Press.

Roberts, Simon. 1979. *Order and dispute: An introduction to legal anthropology.* Harmondsworth: Penguin.

Robinson S. 2000. *Fish for the future: An examination of efforts to rebuild and conserve fish populations*. Paper presented at Annual Meeting of the American Anthropological Association, San Francisco, USA.

Rogers, Susan Geiger. 1972. "The search for political focus on Kilimanjaro." Ph.D. dissertation. Dar es Salaam: University of Dar es Salaam.

Roheim, Geza. 1950. *Psychoanalysis and anthropology*. New York: International Universities Press.

Rosen, Lawrence. 1989. *The anthropology of justice: Law as culture in Islamic society*. Cambridge: Cambridge University Press.

Sahlins, Marshall. 1981. *Historical metaphors and mythical realities*. Ann Arbor: University of Michigan Press.

———. 1985. *Islands of history*. Chicago: University of Chicago Press.

Sawyer, Akilagpa. 1977. "Judicial manipulation of customary family law in Tanzania." In *Law and the family in Africa*, edited by S. A. Roberts, 115–28. The Hague: Mouton.

Schapera, Isaac. (1938) 1955. *A handbook of Tswana law and custom*. London: Oxford University Press for the International African Institute.

———. 1950. "Kinship and marriage among the Tswana." In *African systems of kinship and marriage*, edited by A. R. Radcliffe-Brown and Daryll Forde. London: Oxford University Press.

———. 1970. *Tribal innovators: Tswana chiefs and social change 1795–1940*. London: The Athlone Press.

Scott, James. 1998. *Seeing like a state*. New Haven: Yale University Press.

Seligmann, C. G. and B. Z. 1911. *The Veddas*. London: Cambridge University Press.

Selznick, Philip. 1959. "The sociology of law." In *Sociology today*, edited by H.K. Merton and L.S. Cotterrell, 115–27. New York: Basic Books.

Shann, G. N. 1956. "The early development of education among the Chagga." *Tanganyika Notes and Records* 45: 21–32.

Shipton, Parker. 1994. "Land culture in tropical Africa." *Annual Review of Anthropology* 23: 347–77.

Shore, C. and S. Wright, eds. 1997. *Anthropology of policy: Critical perspectives on governance and power*. London/New York: Routledge

Simon, Herbert. 1957a. *Models of man*. New York: John Wiley and Sons.

———. 1957b. "Rationality and administrative decision making." In *Models of man*, 196–206. London and New York: John Wiley and Sons.

Smith, Michael Garfield. 1966. "A structural approach to comparative politics." In *Varieties of political theory*, edited by David Easton, 113–29. Englewood Hills: Prentice Hall.

Snyder, Francis. 1981. *Capitalism and legal change: An African transformation*. New York: Academic Press.

Stahl, Kathleen. 1964. *The history of the Chagga people of Kilimanjaro*. The Hague: Mouton.

Stayt, Hugh A. 1931. *The Ba Venda*. London: Oxford University Press.

Steward, Julian, ed. 1946–1950. *Handbook of South American Indians*, Bulletin 143, 6 volumes. Washington: Bureau of American Ethnology

Tambiah, S. J. 1972. "Form and meaning of magical acts: A point of view." In *Modes of thought, edited by* Robin Horton and Rught Finnegan, 199–229. London: Faber and Faber.

Taussig, Michael. 1980. *The devil and commodity fetishism in South America*. Chapel Hill: University of North Carolina Press.

Taylor, Douglas. 1945. "Carib folk-beliefs and customs from Dominica, B.W.I." *Southwestern Journal of Anthropology* 1: 507–30.

Thomson, James T. 1994. "The role of the state versus the community in governance and management of renewable natural resources." In *Improved natural resource management: The role of the state versus that of the local community*, edited by Henrik Secher Marcussen, Occasional Paper No. 12. International Development Studies. Roskilde: Roskilde University.

Thomson, Jamie and Cheibane Coulibaly. 1994. "Decentralisation in the Sahel: Regional Synthesis." SAH/D (94) 427. Paris: Club du Sahel.

Thompson, Stith. 1961. *Motif-index of folk-literature*. Bloomington: Indiana University Press.

Tylor, Edward B. (1871) 1958. *The origins of culture, part I: Primitive culture*. New York: Harper and Brothers.

Turner, Victor W. 1957. *Schism and continuity in an African society*. Manchester: Manchester University Press.

———. 1964. "Symbols in Ndembu ritual." In *Closed systems and open minds*, edited by Max Gluckman, 20–51. Chicago: Aldine.

———. 1968. "Mukanda: The politics of a non-political ritual." In *Local level politics*, edited by M. Swartz, 135–50. Chicago: Aldine.

———. 1969. *The ritual process: Structure and anti-structure*. Chicago: Aldine.

van Dijk, Han 1996 "Land tenure, territoriality and ecological instability." In *The role of law in natural resource management*, edited by Joep Spiertz and Melanie G. Wiber, 17–45. The Hague: VUGA.

Van Velsen, J. 1967. "The extended case method and situational analysis." In *The craft of social anthropology*, edited by A. L. Epstein, 129–52. London: Tavistock Publications.

Verrier, Elwin. 1939. *The Baiga*. London: John Murray.

Vincent, Joan. 1982. *Teso in transformation*. Berkeley: University of California Press.

———. 1986. "System and process, 1974–1985." *Annual Review of Anthropology* 15: 99–119.

Wagner, Gunter. 1954. "The Abaluyia of Kavirondo." In *African worlds: Studies in the cosmological ideas and social values of African peoples*, edited by Daryll Forde, 25–54. Oxford: Oxford University Press.

Warner, W. L. 1930. "Morphology and function of the Murngin kinship system." *American Anthropologist* 32: 207–56.

———. 1937. *A black civilization*. New York: Harper Brothers.

Weber, Max. 1954. *On law in economy and society*. Edited by Max Rheinstein. Translated by Max Rheinstein and Edward Shils. New York: Simon and Schuster.

———. (1954) 1978. *Economy and society*. Berkeley: University of California Press.

Wedel, J. R., and G. Feldman. 2005. "Why an anthropology of public policy?" *Anthropology Today* 21 (1): 1–2

Willis, Paul. (1977) 1981. *Learning to labour: How working class kids get Working class jobs*. New York: Columbia University Press.

Wilson, Monica. 1957. *Rituals of kinship among the Nyakyusa*. Oxford: Oxford University Press.

Wilson, Richard A. 2001. *The politics of truth and reconciliation: Legitimizing the post-apartheid state*. Cambridge: Cambridge University Press.

———, ed. 1997. *Human rights, culture and context*. London/Chicago: Pluto Press.

World Bank, Africa Region. 1990. "The population, agriculture and environment nexus in Sub-Saharan Africa." Unpublished draft document for discussion.

PUBLIC DOCUMENTS

1978 Population Census, Vol. IV. A summary of selected statistics. Bureau of Statistics, Ministry of Planning and Economic Affairs. Dar es Salaam, Tanzania.

African Conference on Local Courts and Customary Law. 1963. Report of the Proceedings of the Conference held in Dar es Salaam, Tanganyika. 8–18 September 1963. Under the Chairmanship of the Ministry of Justice of Tanganyika, Sheikh Amri Abedi. Geneva: H. Studer S.A.

Case reports from courts of Mwika, Mamba, Marangu, Kilema, Keni-Mriti Mengwe, and Moshi Town, 1927–1961. Once located in local courthouse buildings on Kilimanjaro, later in the faculty library of the Law School of the University of Dar es Salaam. All case records are handwritten in Swahili.

Tanganyika Territory. 1930a. *Native Administration Memoranda No. 1. Principles of Native Administration and Their Application.* Dar es Salaam: Government Printer.

———. 1930b. *Native Administration Memoranda No. 2.* Native Courts. Dar es Salaam: Government Printer.

Tanganyika. 1954. "African Local Government in Tanganyika." *Local Government Memoranda No. 1.* Part 1. Dar es Salaam: Government Printer.

———. (1953) 1957. *Local Government Memoranda No. 2. (Local Courts).* Dar es Salaam: Government Printer.

———. 1963. *Sheria ya Mokakama za Mahakama.* Dar es Salaam: Government Printer.

———. 1964a. *Maelezo ya Mahakama za Movanzo.* Dar es Salaam: Government Printer.

———. 1964b. *Primary Courts Manual.* Dar es Salaam: Government Printer.

The Agricultural Policy of Tanzania. 1983. Dar es Salaam. March 31.

Uganda. 1941. *Handbook on Native Courts for the Guidance of Administrative Officers.* Kampala: Government of Uganda.

Index

A

Abarbanel, Jay, 14
Abolition of chiefships, 271
Absent witness, 157
Accountability, 26, 33, 36, 38-40
Alleviation of poverty, 309
Allocations of land, 37, 84, 86, 101,
    103, 108, 113, 117, 122, 125, 126, 197,
    267-270, 274
Allott, Antony Nicholas, 142-143, 151,
    169
Anderson, Benedict, 141
An-Na'im, Abdullah Ahmed, 314, 315
Anus, 19, 229, 230, 232-234, 241, 242
APREFA, 307, 308
Apter, David E., 295
Augustine, Saint, 217, 218
Austin, J.L., 295-296

B

Ba, Boubakar Moussa, 219, 306, 307
Bailey, F. G., 158, 273, 279
Barley, Nigel, 214
Barth, Fredrik, 31, 196, 197, 254, 255
Beattie, John, 295

Believers, 295
Bergson, Henri, 227
Best, Elsdon, 218
Bienen, Henry, 268
Bohannan, Paul, 15, 16, 252
Bolivia, 39
Borneman, John, xv, 32, 33, 45, 73
Bounded rationality, 306
Bourdieu, Pierre, xix, xxiii, xxxix, 116,
    150
Bowen, John, 31
Brother and sister, 214-216, 223-227;
    Incest of, 213-214, 215-228
Bryce, Roy, 14
Burawoy, Michael, 35, 40
Burkina Faso, 27, 307, 309, 310, 315
Burton, Michael, 31

C

Cameron, Governor Donald, 132,
    134, 135
Caravans, 23, 82, 83, 202
Cash, xxxv, 23, 49, 62, 80-86, 90, 97-
    102, 106, 108, 112, 114, 119, 123-126,
    150, 171, 173, 184, 202, 204, 206,
    262-265, 281, 291, 292;

Fictive kinship and fictive par-
enthood, 227, 259
Male terminology and, 12, 215, 227;
Patrilineal kinship, 17, 48, 62, 79,
80, 81, 83, 85, 93, 94, 95, 97, 108,
117, 118, 121, 122, 144, 145, 170,
171, 202, 203, 216, 218-226, 266,
281, 282, 303, 305;
Patrilineally related households,
83, 171;
Transactions and, xxv, 26, 81, 82,
94, 95, 101
[See also: Comparison; Incest;
Lineage; Mythology]
Kirchhoff, Paul, 218
Knorr-Cetina, K., 195
Krige, E. G., 219, 225
Krige, J. D., 219, 225
Kroeber, Alfred, xxxviii, 9, 10, 218, 219
Kuper, Adam, 277
Kuper, Hilda, 13, 14, 19, 145, 225
Kuper, Leo, 14, 20, 145
Kuria, Gibson Kamau, 24

L

Land, xiii, xvi, xx, xxiv, xxvi, 17, 20,
23-25, 27, 32, 36-39, 42, 47, 49, 59-
66, 68, 69, 73, 77-86, 88-91, 93-103,
106-115, 119-127, 152, 170-177, 193,
200, 202-208, 222, 262-267, 269,
270, 272, 274, 281, 282, 285, 288, 294,
301-304, 306-317;
Nationalization and, 302, 309, 311;
Rights in, 24, 36, 38, 47, 64, 92, 95,
98, 101, 122-127, 179, 263-267,
281, 282, 305, 311-317;
Selling and buying of, 79-103, 125,
126;
Shortage and, 25, 63, 64, 68, 73,
77, 80, 81, 84, 85, 95, 97, 99, 102,
108, 111, 114, 122, 125, 171, 203,
204, 207, 263, 267, 313;

Tenure, xiii, 27, 61, 63, 98, 121, 154,
262, 301, 307-309, 311, 314
Landlordism, 52, 206, 208, 304
Large-scale systems and processes,
xxiv, xxviii, 32, 35, 36, 82, 107, 114,
115, 127, 196, 201, 203, 207, 310
Laurent, Pierre Joseph, 312
Leach, Edmund R., 11
Le Roy, Etienne, 307, 308
Lévi-Strauss, Claude, xxi, 7, 19, 213,
218-222, 227, 280
Likosky, Michael, 31, 38, 42
Lineage, xxiv, xxx, 20, 48, 62, 64-68,
80, 89, 93-95, 97, 101, 109-113, 122,
123, 168-173, 176, 177, 179-184, 187,
192, 203, 204, 217, 227, 235, 237, 264-
270, 272, 274, 275, 281, 303;
Neighborhood nexus and, 269-
270;
[See also: Kinship]
Little, K. L., 226
Llewellyn, Karl, 3, 6
Lowenthal, Max, 5, 14
Lukes, Steven, 115
Lupton, Tom, 260

M

Macauley, Stewart, 260
Maeda, Justin, 21, 22, 50
Makler, Harry, 195
Malaysia, 38, 42
Malinowski, Bronislaw, 59, 199, 218,
225, 226, 252
Mamdani, Mahmood, 307
Mann, Kristin, xii, 79, 142
Maps, xxxv, 9, 62, 313
March, James G., 114, 158, 161
Marcus, George E., xx, 196, 201
Marealle, Petro Itosi, 48, 49, 59, 72
Martinelli, Alberto, 195
Mathieu, Paul, 309, 310, 312
Maurer, Bill, 36

HAU Books is committed to publishing the most distinguished texts in classic and advanced anthropological theory. The titles aim to situate ethnography as the prime heuristic of anthropology, and return it to the forefront of conceptual developments in the discipline. HAU Books is sponsored by some of the world's most distinguished anthropology departments and research institutions, and releases its titles in both print editions and open-access formats.

www.haubooks.com

Supported by

Hau-N. E. T.
Network of Ethnographic Theory

University of Aarhus – EPICENTER (DK)
University of Amsterdam (NL)
University of Bergen (NO)
Brown University (US)
California Institute of Integral Studies (US)
University of Campinas (BR)
University of Canterbury (NZ)
University of Chicago (US)
University College London (UK)
University of Colorado Boulder Libraries (US)
CNRS – Centre d'Études Himalayennes (FR)
Cornell University (US)
University of Edinburgh (UK)
The Graduate Institute, Geneva Library (CH)
University of Helsinki (FL)
Indiana University Library (US)
Johns Hopkins University (US)
University of Kent (UK)
Lafayette College Library (US)
London School of Economics and Political Science (UK)
Institute of Social Sciences of the University of Lisbon (PL)
University of Manchester (UK)
The University of Manchester Library (UK)
Max-Planck Institute for the Study of Religious and Ethnic
Diversity at Göttingen (DE)
Musée de Quai Branly (FR)
Museu Nacional – UFRJ (BR)
Norwegian Museum of Cultural History (NO)
University of Oslo (NO)
University of Oslo Library (NO)
Pontificia Universidad Católica de Chile (CL)
Princeton University (US)
University of Queensland (AU)
University of Rochester (US)
Universidad Autónoma de San Luis Potosi (MX)
SOAS, University of London (UK)
University of Sydney (AU)
University of Toronto Libraries (CA)

www.haujournal.org/haunet